Praise for *Management Consultancy: The Role of the Change Agent*

'This textbook brings together management consultancy and change management theory and practice and internal and external approaches to change agency. It does so in an accessible way, breaking up text and including practitioner accounts and regular 'consultancy in action' sections. The authors provide a wealth of teaching and consulting practice to address the contemporary challenge of achieving change through participation and learning.'

– Andrew Sturdy, *Professor of Management, University of Bristol, UK.*

'Speaking as a former internal consultant, and partner in my own consultancy practice, and as Chair in Strategic Management researching consultancy and change, this book provides detailed, rigorous, and very readable coverage of the field.'

– Bill Cooke, *Professor of Strategic Management, University of York, UK.*

'This book offers a comprehensive perspective on change agents and their role in facilitating change. Based on academic research and extensive change management practice, the book offers students and practitioners key insights into the practice of change agents and provides valuable tips how to develop your skills to facilitate change. As change is now ubiquitous, these are crucial skills for the future of work. The book is a valuable resource for students interested in consulting, change management and leadership.'

– Natalia Nikolova, *Director UTS Advanced MBA, UTS Business School, University of Technology Sydney, Australia.*

'Written by a mixture of practitioners and academics, this book provides valuable insights into both the theoretical and practical skills of being a change agent. There are clear learning objectives at the beginning of each chapter which set the overall context and ample 'stop and reflect' points which give structured opportunities to stop and consider the wider context of change and culture. Good vignettes help to conceptualise and bring concepts to life

Excellent for those wanting to guide and influence change as an internal change agent or considering a career within the wider management consultancy field. This book helps you to understand the skills and knowledge required to fulfil these roles. A well-written and wide ranging, comprehensive account of the role of the change agent.'

– Julian Bond, *Senior Fellow and Director Nye Bevan Programme, Alliance Manchester Business School, University of Manchester, UK.*

'As a leading Data Governance Consultancy, we found the theories from this book to be well structured with a number of useful tips that our management consultants can use in their day-to-day work. The combination of theoretical and practical examples helps to realise the key factors for the successful implementation of any change programme.'

– Melanie Jenner, *Director, DTSQUARED.*

MANAGEMENT CONSULTANCY

The Role of the Change Agent

Julian Randall, Bernard Burnes
and Allan J. Sim

macmillan international
HIGHER EDUCATION

RED GLOBE PRESS

© Julian Randall, Bernard Burnes and Allan J. Sim, under exclusive licence to Springer Nature Limited, part of Springer Nature 2019.

All rights reserved. No reproduction, copy or transmission of this publication may be made without written permission.

No portion of this publication may be reproduced, copied or transmitted save with written permission or in accordance with the provisions of the Copyright, Designs and Patents Act 1988, or under the terms of any licence permitting limited copying issued by the Copyright Licensing Agency, Saffron House, 6–10 Kirby Street, London EC1N 8TS.

Any person who does any unauthorized act in relation to this publication may be liable to criminal prosecution and civil claims for damages.

The authors have asserted their rights to be identified as the authors of this work in accordance with the Copyright, Designs and Patents Act 1988.

First published 2019 by
RED GLOBE PRESS

Red Globe Press in the UK is an imprint of Springer Nature Limited, registered in England, company number 785998, of 4 Crinan Street, London N1 9XW.

Red Globe Press® is a registered trademark in the United States, the United Kingdom, Europe and other countries.

ISBN 978–1–137–60521–4 paperback

This book is printed on paper suitable for recycling and made from fully managed and sustained forest sources. Logging, pulping and manufacturing processes are expected to conform to the environmental regulations of the country of origin.

A catalogue record for this book is available from the British Library.

A catalog record for this book is available from the Library of Congress.

Contents

List of Figures and Table — x
Biographies — xi
Preface — xiii

1 In the Beginning There Was Change — 1

- INTRODUCTION — 1
- ORGANIZATIONAL CHANGE AND CHANGE MANAGEMENT — 2
- THE UNDERPINNING THEORIES THAT UNDERWRITE CHANGE INITIATIVES — 2
- LEWIN'S LEARNING APPROACH TO CHANGE — 3
- THE DRIVERS OF CHANGE — 5
- THINKING ABOUT CHANGE — 6
- THE TRADITIONAL ORGANIZATIONAL HIERARCHY — 7
- WHAT MANAGERS DO — 8
- THINKING ABOUT THE WORKERS — 9
- A DIFFERENT ORGANIZATIONAL PARADIGM — 9
- PERSPECTIVES ON CHANGE MANAGEMENT: OUTSIDE-IN OR INSIDE-OUT — 11
- SOME QUESTIONS FOR YOU TO DISCUSS — 12
- WHAT MANAGERS KNOW — 15
- N-STEP APPROACHES — 16
- LEARNING AND PARTICIPATION — 19
- SO, WHAT IS IT THAT WE WANT TO DISCOVER? — 20
- GUIDELINES FOR FACILITATING EMPLOYEE PARTICIPATION — 21
- CHAPTER SUMMARY — 22
- REFERENCES — 23

2 Consultants and Change Agents — 25

- INTRODUCTION — 25
- THE WORK OF CONSULTANCY — 28
- IS THE CONSULTANT A MANAGER OR LEADER? — 29
- THE CONTEXT OF CHANGE — 30
- CONSULTANT AND CLIENT RELATIONS — 32
- COPING STRATEGIES CONSULTANTS USE — 34
- POSITIVE RESPONSES — 35
- POLITICS AND CHANGE — 37
- EXPLORING THE ROLE OF INTERNAL CHANGE AGENTS — 39
- PARTICIPATIVE CHANGE AND THE CHANGE AGENT — 40
- MANAGING THE TRANSITION — 41
- SHAPE THE POLITICAL DYNAMICS — 41
- A USEFUL CHECKLIST — 42
- THE ROLE OF THE INTERNAL CHANGE AGENT — 45

	TYING IN CHANGE WITH FUTURE SUCCESS	46
	CHAPTER SUMMARY	47
	REFERENCES	47
3	**Consultancy Skills: Agreeing/Negotiating a Contract**	**50**
	INTRODUCTION	50
	CULTURE	51
	THE 13 CLASSIC CLOSES	57
	FINDING OUT MORE ABOUT YOUR CLIENTS	58
	CHAPTER SUMMARY	65
	REFERENCES	66
4	**Culture and Identity: Exploring a Company's Culture**	**67**
	INTRODUCTION	67
	QUALITATIVE INTERVIEW WORK	69
	SURFACING BASIC ASSUMPTIONS	69
	AMBIGUITY AND AMBIVALENCE	69
	DRAWING UP A QUESTIONNAIRE	70
	TRANSCRIBING YOUR DATA	70
	IDENTITY AND IDENTITY WORK	71
	THE ROLE OF THE CHANGE AGENT	72
	THE QUALITIES OF AN EFFECTIVE FACILITATOR	72
	PLANNING THE CHANGE TEAM	73
	INTERNAL CHANGE AGENTS	74
	SIGNIFICANT FACTORS FOR PARTICIPATIVE CHANGE	75
	DEMONSTRATING THE CONSULTANCY QUALITIES	77
	CONSULTANCY IN ACTION	78
	FINDING OUT MORE ABOUT PEOPLE AND THEIR ASSUMPTIONS ABOUT THEIR WORK, MANAGERS, AND THEIR COMPANY	78
	THE INTERNAL CHANGE AGENT AND DEVELOPMENT	81
	OBSERVING ORGANIZATIONAL CULTURE	82
	THE LINK BETWEEN TRANSFORMATIONAL LEADER AND INTERNAL CHANGE AGENT	82
	THE CHANGING ROLE OF THE INTERNAL CHANGE AGENT	83
	CHAPTER SUMMARY	84
	REFERENCES	85
5	**Changing the Culture: What is Feasible?**	**87**
	INTRODUCTION	87
	SO, CULTURE CAN BE…	87
	SCHEMAS AND SCRIPTS	88
	PERCEPTIONS AND ATTITUDES	89
	ACCESSING BASIC ASSUMPTIONS	89
	CHANGING BASIC ASSUMPTIONS	90
	EMERGENT CHANGE AND SIGNIFICANT AREAS	91
	GAINING AND MAKING ALLIANCES	92
	OPEN MEETINGS WITH THE STAFF	92
	ACTIVITY	93
	ACTIVITY 2 CHANGING CULTURES OVER THE YEARS	99

	CONSULTANCY IN ACTION	101
	CHAPTER SUMMARY	108
	REFERENCES	109

6 Identifying the Role of Training in Achieving Strategic Outcomes — 111

	INTRODUCTION	111
	LINKS BETWEEN STRATEGIC OBJECTIVES AND INDIVIDUAL KEY TASKS	112
	IMPLICATIONS FOR CHANGE	113
	COMMUNICATING A VISION	114
	SOURCES OF INFORMATION ABOUT COMPANY PRACTICE	114
	STANDARDS AND TARGETS	116
	BEHAVIOURAL TERMS	116
	CONDITIONS	117
	STANDARD	118
	TRAINING AND DEVELOPMENT	119
	ANALYSING A TRAINING NEED	119
	DESIGN THE TRAINING	120
	VALIDATION	120
	EVALUATION	121
	SUMMARY	122
	CONSULTANCY IN ACTION	124
	TO RUN AN EVENT OR NOT TO RUN AN EVENT?	125
	DESIGN, PROCESS AND FLOW	126
	FACILITATION STYLE AND ENGAGING PARTICIPANTS	128
	LAST BUT NOT LEAST THE VENUE!	129
	CONCLUSIONS	129
	CHAPTER SUMMARY	130
	REFERENCES	130

7 Negotiating Successfully Through Change — 132

	INTRODUCTION	132
	THE CONTEXT OF NEGOTIATION	133
	FEATURES	133
	ADVANTAGES	134
	BENEFITS	134
	PRESENTATION	135
	HANDLING CONCERNS AND OBJECTIONS	135
	THE CONTENT OF NEGOTIATION	135
	NEGOTIATION TASK FOR TWO GROUPS	143
	CHAPTER SUMMARY	145
	REFERENCES	146

8 Internal Change Agents and Participative Change — 147

	INTRODUCTION	147
	THE RISE OF THE INTERNAL CHANGE AGENT	149
	STARTING AT THE BEGINNING	149
	EXPLORING THE CHANGE ENVIRONMENT	149

	ADVANTAGES OF EXTERNAL AND INTERNAL CHANGE AGENTS WORKING TOGETHER	150
	NEED TO MOTIVATE CHANGE	151
	MANAGING THE TRANSITION	151
	GUIDELINES FOR FACILITATING PARTICIPATIVE CHANGE	152
	SKILLS WHICH CAN ENHANCE AND DEVELOP DIALOGUE	152
	IMPORTANT CHANGE INTERVENTIONS	152
	DIFFERENT ROLES FOR CHANGE AGENTS	153
	CHANGE AGENTS	154
	CRUCIAL ROLES FOR CHANGE AGENTS	154
	DEVELOPING SKILLS AND COMPETENCIES IN INTERNAL CHANGE AGENTS	155
	SPECIALIST SKILL	156
	ISSUES THAT NEED IMMEDIATE ACTION	156
	CREDIBLE LEADERSHIP	157
	CONSULTANCY IN ACTION	157
	WHAT IS A CHANGE AGENT?	158
	AM I A CHANGE AGENT OR AM I NOT?	158
	THE CHANGE AGENT AS CATALYST	158
	THE CHANGE AGENT AS SOLUTION GIVER	159
	THE CHANGE AGENT AS PROCESS HELPER	159
	THE CHANGE AGENT AS RESOURCE-LINKER	160
	CHANGE AGENTS ARE EVERYWHERE	160
	CONCLUSIONS	161
	CHAPTER SUMMARY	162
	REFERENCES	162
9	**Consultants, Ethics and the Law**	**165**
	INTRODUCTION	165
	WHAT IS ETHICS?	166
	HOW CAN WE BE ETHICAL?	166
	WHY BOTHER?	168
	THE STAKEHOLDER PROBLEM	169
	DISCUSSION	170
	GUIDANCE	171
	CONSULTANCY IN ACTION	173
	CLIENT ENVIRONMENT, REGULATORY CONTEXT	173
	YOUR RELATIONSHIP WITH YOUR CLIENT	174
	ASSISTING YOUR CLIENT IN RELATIONSHIPS WITH OTHERS	175
	WHY SOME PROJECTS MAY FAIL	176
	FORESEEING THE CHALLENGES	177
	EVALUATING THE STRATEGY	177
	HANDLING PEOPLE PROBLEMS	178
	CHAPTER SUMMARY	179
	REFERENCES	179
	ONLINE RESOURCES	180

10	**Organization Development and Future Challenges**	**181**
	INTRODUCTION	181
	THE NATURE OF CHANGE	181
	N-STEP APPROACHES TO CHANGE	183
	PROBING EFFECTIVE CHANGE AGENCY	183
	TRADITIONAL VIEWS ABOUT THE WORK OF CHANGE AGENTS	184
	BOUNDARY SPANNERS	185
	FUTURE CHALLENGES	186
	CONTINUING TREND OF INTERNAL CHANGE AGENTS	186
	TENSIONS APPARENT FOR OD PRACTITIONERS	186
	CONSULTANCY AND CHANGE: THE FUTURE	187
	REFERENCES	187

Index   190

List of Figures and Table

Figures

1.1	Traditional organization levels	7
1.2	Fayol's management steps	8
1.3	The Shamrock organization	9
1.4	Inside-out and outside-in approaches	11
1.5	Nadler's approach to change	17
1.6	Schein's cultural layers model	19
3.1	The sales cycle	51
3.2	Outline of the four-phase model	62
3.3	Kotter's eight-step change model	63
5.1	A consulting reflection framework	102
5.2	Turnover by year	104
6.1	Systematic training cycle	119
7.1	Styles of negotiation	141

Table

7.1	Adversarial/Assertive	142

Biographies

Bernard Burnes has been Professor of Organizational Change at Stirling Management School, University of Stirling, UK, since 2013. Before that, he was Professor of Organizational Change at the Manchester Business School at the University of Manchester, UK. He is one of the leading international authorities on organizational change. He trained as an engineer, holds a BA (Hons) in Economic and Social History and a PhD in Organisational Psychology. He has published widely in academic and professional journals and is the author of over 60 academic journal articles, some 30 books and around 60 book chapters. He is the author of *Managing Change* (7th edn), the bestselling European textbook in the field. He is also the editor of the Routledge book series *Understanding Organisational Change*, joint editor of the *Routledge Companion to Organizational Change*, and associate editor of the *Journal of Change Management*. His research covers organizational change in its broadest sense; in particular, he is concerned with the way in which different approaches to change promote or undermine ethical behaviour in organizations.

Supannee Keawchaum is a Lecturer at the Innovation and Management College, Songkhla Rajabhat University, Thailand. She has ten years' experience working in HR gained from her career at Asian Honda Motor Co., Ltd and Toshiba Thailand Co., Ltd. She completed her MBA and PhD in Management Studies at the University of Aberdeen, UK. She currently teaches Human Resources Management in Industries. Today, she is interested in leadership, psychological contract and organizational learning.

Elaine Mottram began her working life as a physiotherapist working for Grampian Health Authority, UK. She moved into working as a trainer and internal change agent before setting up her own consultancy, Pensando. Her work includes developing self-awareness in the context of emergent change at work.

Julian Randall ran his own management consultancy, Randall Consultancy, for 17 years working with HM Customs & Excise, The Crown Agents, the Water Industry and the retail sector. He obtained his PhD at the University of St. Andrews, UK, and is currently Senior Lecturer in the management of change at the University of Aberdeen. His research interests include the perceptions of individuals affected by imposed change and its influence on their evaluation of their job, work, career and the organization. He has published on these and related topics in *Organization Studies*; *Organization*; *The Journal of Organizational Change Management*; and the *Journal of Qualitative Research in Organizations and Management*, and is on the editorial board of the *Journal of Change Management*. He is programme leader of the MSc in Management Consultancy and Change and the MBA (HRM) at the University of Aberdeen.

David Sherrit has worked in learning and organization development for over 30 years. He has worked in the oil and gas sector since 1992, working for Elf, Baker Hughes INTEQ and currently Chevron Upstream Europe in a range of management and OD roles, and prior to 1992 worked in the retail sector and the National Health Service (NHS). He is a graduate of the Roffey Park MSc in People and Organization Development and is currently embarked on a Post Graduate Certificate in Executive Coaching. Areas of interest and research include relationships at work; culture and change management; leadership coaching; and resilience.

Norrie W. Silvestro is a highly experienced occupational psychologist. He has extensive experience of assessing and developing leaders and their teams. He completed his PhD in Occupational Psychology at the Department of Occupational Psychology at Birkbeck College (University of London), UK. As an independent psychologist, he has also consulted to and advised across a wide range of public, private and family business organizations in the UK and in the Middle East. Dr Norrie W. Silvestro began his career as a Training Manager with a large public sector government organization. From there, he moved on to become the Head of Organization Development and Training within the National Health Service (NHS) (UK). He subsequently set up his own business as an independent Chartered Occupational Psychologist. Later, he spent 18 months in Saudi Arabia as the Head of Talent Management within an international family business. Recently, he has returned to his role as an independent Chartered Occupational Psychologist specializing in talent management, leadership and team assessment. He has delivered in-depth assessments for senior level Civil Service appointments. He is also a qualified executive coach; and works as an Associate for a number of specialist organizations. He holds qualifications in the application of a wide range of psychometric tools for assessment and development purposes. Norrie is also an Associate Fellow of the British Psychological Society and an Honorary Research Fellow at the Business School of the University of Aberdeen. He has published his experience in applying occupational psychology in OD, family business, talent management and coaching contexts.

Allan J. Sim previously worked as a consultant for a wide variety of organizations and is currently a Senior Lecturer in Management Studies at the University of Aberdeen, UK, and the Retention Officer for the University of Aberdeen Business School. His particular areas of interest are in business ethics, corporate responsibility, globalization, culture, consultancy and change, as well as in areas of teaching and learning. His writing interests lie in those areas but with a current focus on ethics, consultancy, and teaching and learning.

Sarah Smith is currently the Talent Manager at Aberdeen Asset Management plc. Her career journey of over 17 years began as a Customer Services Advisor at Aberdeen Asset before she moved through various areas of the business including Compliance, Operations, Business Systems and Learning and Development. During this time, Aberdeen Asset have made numerous acquisitions so she has been fortunate to be part of a fast-growing organization which is ever-changing and growing. She is a qualified Coach and NLP Practitioner and able to regularly practise; and holds an Honorary Research Fellowship from the University of Aberdeen, UK. She is also a part-time lecturer on postgraduate courses in change and human resource management (HRM). Her research and writing interests are based on organizational change and internal change agents, psychological contracting, behavioural competence and coaching for performance. She is also a trustee for a third-sector organization and a business mentor.

Thom D. Young graduated in law from the University of Edinburgh, UK, before completing his MA in Peace Studies at Bradford University, UK. After the publication of his dissertation, he lectured in law at Preston Polytechnic and then at the University of Dundee, UK. He qualified as a Solicitor in 1980 and practised for 33 years, specializing in employment law and mainly advising SMEs including subsidiaries of multinationals, and gained a reputation for going well beyond the legal issues and giving practical, common-sense advice. He has been an Employment Consultant since 2013 with a particular interest in organizational culture. His research and writing interests include underlying assumptions about people at work and their effect on perceptions of others; HR policies as artefacts of organizational culture; the impact of employment law on perceptions of HR performance; and the convergence of psychological contracts with actual terms and conditions and development of relationship-focused employment contracts.

Preface

Management consultancy has always attracted widely different opinions from different groups. Managers are often sceptical about their impact on organizations but seem to spend time and money on their services, particularly where their own competences are found wanting in the face of organizational challenge. Journalists are ambivalent about their benefit to the sectors they serve and seize on the data suggesting that 70% of change programmes fail. Academics have tended towards the view that consultants make many claims for the efficacy of their work but there is little evidence to support this. And yet Management Consultancy as a business sector continues to flourish and large sums of money are commanded by those who can convince others that without their services there can be little or no chance of success in critical business enterprises involving innovation or change.

For those who have been involved in change initiatives and sought to facilitate transitions at work, the questions about our worth are always asked – and rightly so. And for academics, the search for validation and evaluation of consultants' claims are a worthwhile and necessary endeavour if we are ever to learn from what we do and identify what is successful and what is unlikely to succeed. But for those seeking to make their way into this working environment the questions have an added relevance: Is this a worthwhile occupation for me?

Given that management consultancies continue to recruit graduates in significant numbers of students each year, increasing numbers of universities have sought to set up programmes that are aimed specifically at this topic. The MBA degree which has been regarded as the gold standard among recruiters to the industry has always seemed to have a generalist approach and is not designed to address the specific areas of knowledge and skill which consultants need to be successful. So, in our own programmes we have sought to address those in more detail, aware that while the underpinning theories of academic knowledge are important to identify, the skills on which the consultant depends for success should be addressed too.

In Chapter 1, we have included an overview of the context of change and the work of organizational development (OD), which has been an enduring feature of change interventions and can be summarized as market-led and resource-led approaches that are sometimes combined to address both efficiency and effectiveness factors as change outcomes.

In Chapter 2, we look at the role of the consultant tasked with managing change but also, whether we like it or not, looked to as an exemplar of change; a supporter of change; a prophet identifying a different vision which the company wants to realize. There are within the role different functions which need to be clarified early on and this leads into the skill needed from the outset in qualifying the aspirations which the proposers of change want to embark on.

Our own approach has been to encourage participative change initiatives. We have always believed that resistance to change is normal – not an aberration. However, imposed change rarely considers the views and ideas of those who will need to live out the change in their personal and professional lives. In Chapter 3 through to Chapter 8 we will look at different aspects of how this exploration can be initiated. We also include accounts from different practitioners of their own experience of supporting change in their careers as change agents.

In Chapter 9 we consider the legal and ethical considerations which run through all change interventions and include the views of a legal practitioner who has devoted his consultancy to advising clients on how to stay out of the courts and employment tribunals rather than waiting until they fail before helping them.

In the final chapter, Chapter 10, we look ahead to some of the challenges that will continue to face people working in organizations and the implications of continuous change for both individual development and organizational outcomes. We will also include the benefits to be derived from engaging internal change agents and their role as boundary spanners not just during change programmes but also in supporting the sometimes neglected work of evaluating the outcomes of what has been achieved.

We have included exercises that you can use either as an individual reader or in tutorial groups. There are accounts and examples of work that successful change agents have used that you can use in interactive work developing the skills which make the work of the change agent both fulfilling and successful.

We hope you enjoy reading this book.

1 In the Beginning There Was Change

Julian Randall and Bernard Burnes

> **Learning Objectives**
> After studying the chapter, you should be able to:
> - Appreciate the reasons for change
> - Understand the role of the change agent
> - Link the outcomes of change to strategic objectives
> - Distinguish outside-in from inside-out approaches to change
> - Identify levels of culture and their role in organizational change
> - Appreciate the benefits of Lewin's learning approach to change

INTRODUCTION

The basic message from this chapter and indeed the book as whole is that change should be a learning process for organizations. As such, consultants should see themselves as educators whose role is not just to bring about change but also to inculcate the skills, knowledge and understanding necessary to make change work after they have left the organization.

The learning process begins with an understanding of the nature of change. It is now usual for most of those writing about the topic to assert that 'we live in a world of rapid and unprecedented change', but how true is this? Are there ways in which we could gain evidence to support this assertion? It seems that each generation has had to grapple with 'unprecedented' change – often to survive as a group or tribe in the face of unexpected challenge from the environment, or from others seeking to take over what they see as their rightful position. The arms race, for example, seems always to have been with us as human beings. Those developing better weaponry can face their less well-equipped opponents with greater confidence; hunt for food more effectively; and assure themselves of security and a peaceful life, for example. So, technology has always been with us as a driver for change.

It might be worth stopping for a moment and examining some of the assumptions which are commonly held about change and exploring how well founded they are. Consider the following questions and how you might answer them.

> **STOP AND REFLECT**
> - What does 'organizational change' mean to you?
> - What did it mean to your grandparents?
> - Has the pace of change at work and in society changed?
> - Why is organizational change important?
> - How can we manage organizational change?

You may have reflected that change is not always welcome. Even technological change which offers the easier management and enjoyment of our daily lives can take some mastering. Try reading the instruction manuals that come with new computerized equipment: how easy are they to understand and implement? It probably helps to have someone more experienced to show you how to operate it in the first place.

Also, what evidence is there that past generations experienced change at a more leisurely rate than ourselves? The Industrial Revolution is still the prime example of rapid, discontinuous and fundamental economic and social transformation. In the space of a few decades, the UK was transformed from an agricultural society, where most people lived in the countryside and worked on the land, to an industrial nation where more people lived in towns and worked in factories (Burnes, 2017). Nothing since has come anywhere near matching the Industrial Revolution for the speed and impact of change. However, not everyone was affected or perceived it in the same way. The advent of the textile factory destroyed the livelihood of handloom weavers, something which they did their best to resist. On the other hand, for the sheep farmers who supplied the new factories with wool or the consumers who could purchase a wider range of clothing at reduced prices, the factory was a welcome development. The same applies today. When Amazon started selling books online, book retailers, big and small, saw it as threat to their businesses. Consumers, though, welcomed the wider range of books, the ease and speed of purchase and, often, the reduced prices. Though we might not always like change and often resist it, for most people and many organizations, the only alternatives are adapt or die.

Therefore, in general, organizational change is crucial and cannot be avoided. Our challenge is to respond early enough to find ways to live with it and develop our expertise sufficiently quickly to embrace new ways of doing things.

Change is usually a response to external challenges, often unexpected and unwelcome challenges. It requires the adoption of different ways of doing things. We tend to find this easiest when there are others around who can help us understand and respond to change positively. This is where consultancy comes in. Consultants advise, guide and support. At their best, they can offer us ways of adapting to change and exploring the options that may be available to us to face up to challenges. They can help us interpret and implement the guide books that govern change events.

ORGANIZATIONAL CHANGE AND CHANGE MANAGEMENT

So, what is organizational change, and can it be managed? In the first place, we might agree that organizational change is a move from one state (where you start from) to an end point (where you want to be) with a period of adjustment or transition between them. There is usually a time scale during which this will take place thus allowing for planning and preparation time. But it often seems that the assumption behind change lies in problem-solving based on changing or adapting procedures to respond to challenges. Dawson (2003: 11) describes this as 'new ways or organizing and working'. He refers to such changes as processual change – change to policy, procedures and practices which once mastered would become the newly dominant 'way we do things round here' (Deal and Kennedy, 1982). This approach sometimes asserts that changing what we do also leads to changes in the way we think about what we do – behavioural change leading to attitudinal change (Champy, 1995).

This raises the question of how we manage the change. What is it that people need to know to enable them to change what they do? What new skills will they need to learn? How will that change the way they think about what they do? Most importantly, who will be able to put together and run a programme of change which will enable people to make the transition successfully?

THE UNDERPINNING THEORIES THAT UNDERWRITE CHANGE INITIATIVES

There are many strands of knowledge which have been developed and drawn on in the attempt to understand the change process (Stickland, 1998). Some theories may derive from psychology – how people motivate; how people learn; how people assimilate knowledge, learn new skills and adapt their attitudes to change. Others are based on sociology, which studies how human beings work together in teams; what the practice of management is; whether good leaders are born or trained; and how groups find a working consensus, common practices and consistent behaviours. Finally, there is the influence of social anthropology in which early studies of tribes and their myths, sagas and stories suggested a culture of a shared understanding about the world around them; how they interpret events and derive meaning; and how they ascribe values to the world around them. Such terminology lent itself easily to those interpreting cultural change in organizations. Consultancies often have their own favoured approaches to the management of change and their starting point may well be assumptions drawn from the findings of such studies, sometimes based on cognitive, psychomotor and affective tests which are sometimes used to indicate who will be successful in adapting to change initiatives (Toplis et al., 1987).

Different change approaches all make claims for their own effectiveness. It is a sobering thought, then, that some 70% of change initiatives are alleged to fail (Hughes, 2015). There are a range of reasons why this may be the case. In some cases, the objectives of change are over optimistic; in others, the solution suggested may be unrealistic. In some instances, the approach chosen might be unsuitable or those seeking to utilize it may lack the skills or motivation to see it through. Whatever the reason, the evidence is that change carries a high risk that it may fail to satisfy the expectations of the clients or other stakeholders involved in the change. Hence, there is a widespread scepticism about the upbeat claims that change consultants sometimes make.

LEWIN'S LEARNING APPROACH TO CHANGE

How can change agents avoid the pitfalls of change and fulfil the expectations of their clients? In seeking to answer this question, we draw on the work of the founding father of organization development (OD), Kurt Lewin. Few students of management are unaware of his contribution to the field of change (Burnes, 2004). Lewin's Planned approach to change comprises four elements: field theory, group dynamics, action research and the three-step approach to change. Lewin believed that the key to achieving lasting change was to facilitate group learning through democratic participation and so enable individuals to understand and restructure their perceptions of the world around them (Burnes, 2004). After his death in 1947, Lewin's work continued to be developed by influential scholar-practitioners, especially Chris Argyris, Edgar Schein and Douglas McGregor, all of whom stressed the learning aspect of change.

The learning approach to change can be seen clearly in Lewin's three-step model, which is familiar to most practitioners and students. Its apparent simplicity hides a complexity that is based on both sound theory and extensive practical tools and techniques developed by those who followed on from Lewin (Burnes and Cooke, 2013). Lewin's three steps are as follows:

- Unfreezing the present level
- Moving to a new level
- Refreezing to the new level

To achieve the first step, **unfreezing**, Lewin advocated full, willing and open participation of all those who would be affected by change. He believed that unfreezing was a challenging process of learning and unlearning. Those involved had to learn about their changed context and understand that what was suitable in the past might be unsuitable in the future. What they had learnt in the past had to be unlearnt. As Schein (1996: 28) maintains, the key to unfreezing:

> was to see that human change, whether at the individual or group level, was a profound psychological dynamic process that involved painful unlearning without loss of ego identity and difficult relearning as one cognitively attempted to restructure one's thoughts, perceptions, feelings, and attitudes.

As Schein (1996: 32) also notes, unfreezing is not an end in itself; it 'creates motivation to learn but does not necessarily control or predict the direction of learning'. But it does lead to the second step, moving.

Moving involves gathering and analysing information regarding the current situation and future alternatives. For Lewin, those involved need to consider all the forces at work and identify and evaluate, on a trial and error basis, all the available options, before selecting and implementing the one deemed most appropriate (Burnes, 2017). Moving is an iterative and not a linear process. As Lewin argued, any attempt to predict or identify a specific outcome from Planned change is very difficult because of the complexity of the forces concerned. Therefore, those involved need to evaluate continuously where they are going and why. They need to be prepared to backtrack and amend their plans as they develop, which, of course, is the essence of a learning approach to change.

The purpose of Lewin's third step, **refreezing**, is to stabilize the changed behaviour to prevent those concerned from regressing to their old behaviour. Lewin referred to this as creating a new 'quasi-stationary equilibrium' because he understood that while behaviour would continue to change, albeit slowly, the important issue was not to regress to the old unsuitable behaviour. For Lewin and his successors, one of the most effective means of preventing regression was to ensure that those concerned had been involved in developing and choosing the new arrangements, because involvement in decision-making greatly enhances commitment to change (Burnes and Cooke, 2013).

The importance of Lewin's learning approach can also be seen in his concept of field theory, which is now often referred to as force field analysis (Burnes and Cooke, 2013). This sees current behaviour as being supported by two opposing sets of forces:

- Forces supporting change
- Forces opposed to the change

When these forces are in balance, behaviour remains stable. To change behaviour, therefore, the change agent needs to work with those involved to identify the two sets of forces and determine which force needs to be either increased or decreased for the desired movement to take place. Part of Lewin's intention in helping people to understand their feelings on a proposed change was to help them identify, understand and analyse the relevant forces involved in changing what they do.

Though many have attacked Lewin's three-step model as simplistic, its defenders point out that its insights into human behaviour are based on rigorous theory and relevant practice (Burnes, 2004). For example, Elrod and Tippett (2002: 273) found that:

Models of the change process, as perceived by diverse and seemingly unrelated disciplines [such as bereavement theory, personal transition theory, creative processes, cultural revolutions and scientific revolutions] ... follow Lewin's ... three-phase model of change.

Also, as Hendry (1996: 624) commented:

Scratch any account of creating and managing change and the idea that change is a three-stage process which necessarily begins with a process of unfreezing will not be far below the surface.

One of the main criticisms of Lewin's model comes from Kanter and colleagues (1992: 383) who state that 'organisations are never frozen, much less refrozen', but are fluid entities with many 'personalities'. Yet if we look at Kanter's 'Ten Commandments for Executing Change', we find that the tenth commandment is 'Reinforce and institutionalise change', which sounds rather similar to Lewin's refreezing. In any case, as mentioned above, Lewin referred to refreezing as creating a 'quasi-stationary equilibrium', one where the forces driving behavioural change and those resisting it were in balance.

This is, of course, the normal state for most of our behaviours, which is why we find it so difficult to change them.

Having looked at Lewin's learning approach to change, it is now worth considering how it can be used to reveal the answers to the critical questions about the prospects for change in an organization.

> **STOP AND REFLECT**
>
> - How does change link with strategic management?
> - How does change link with operations management?
> - How critical are workers to the success of change?
> - How can change agents avoid resistance?

As a consultant, the first step in the learning process is understanding the links between your role and the organization's objectives, which is critical to gaining buy-in to the need for change. Similarly, understanding the departmental goals which individuals share will be important to discussing the need for change in operations to support the strategic objectives. The knowledge gained should then help prepare the ground for the final two questions: workers who see the links between what the company needs to achieve and what they do will be more likely to appreciate the need for change and be less resistant to change from the outset. In a sense, there is nothing new here; Drucker (1954) identified these elements and called this alignment of organizational objectives, departmental goals and individual tasks Management by Objectives. Drucker argued that understanding and linking these three levels is crucial to organizational success.

THE DRIVERS OF CHANGE

Before we continue our discussion of approaches to change, we should first look at the underlying drivers that govern most change initiatives:

1. **Efficiency:** The question that drives most change in organizations is, 'How best can we organize the activities of employees to provide the desired goods or services at the right time, in the required quantities, to the agreed quality and at a cost that satisfies the needs of all parties?' We might note that though these efficiency factors should reinforce each other, they do not always do so – marrying cost with quantity or quality with time can be difficult to achieve, as many transport operating companies worldwide have found out.
2. **Effectiveness:** To an extent this is something that is ultimately judged by customers when comparing an organization with its competitors. Customers usually have a choice of who to do business with. In comparing many companies and their products or service, they will usually choose the one that appears to meet their needs most effectively.
3. **Profit (or value for money):** This will always loom large in an organization's thinking. Creating a large enough surplus to satisfy shareholders and the organization's investment needs is vital. In an era when potential investors find easier ways of gaining quick returns on their money than investing in business ventures, businesses are finding it more difficult to raise external funding, especially since the 2008 financial crash. Therefore, keeping and satisfying shareholders is a top priority for most businesses.
4. **Staffing costs:** Finally, there is the pressure to reduce the wage bill. Automation has achieved this in the manufacturing sector. However, for service industries the costs of staff can be as much as 75% of

the overheads of running the business. To reduce staffing costs, more and more businesses appear to be moving towards low-cost, low-benefit forms of flexible working, such as zero-hours or interim contracts. However, while these can bring short-term savings, they may have a longer-term adverse impact on service/product quality, customer satisfaction, workforce stability and the overall image of the organization, as Sports Direct and Uber discovered. Therefore, changes that affect staffing costs need to be viewed through both short-term and long-term lenses.

THINKING ABOUT CHANGE

Approaches to change have been various and depend on the starting point of those who want to initiate change. Dawson (2003: 12), for example, identifies three likely areas which are involved in change initiatives:

- Technical organization of work – strategy and structure
- Cultural dimensions of work – workplace beliefs and values
- Political aspects of work – political processes and power relations

But our starting point may also raise questions about our assumptions concerning change and how it takes place. Take each one separately and consider how far change agents can address each of these factors.

Ostensibly, what can be most easily observed can be readily addressed by the change agent. If change management is as easy as changing processes of production, then there should only be the question of training the workforce to adapt to new methods and cope with the new processes.

But what of the cultural dimensions of the work (the way we think about and value what we do)? Are these as easy to access, and if they are, how likely are they to yield easily to imposed change?

Then finally, how do we find out about the political aspects of the work? Will such approaches as T-groups or focus groups reveal constraints due to personal animosity or historical factors affecting change?

EXAMPLE

Recent action on the railways indicates that unions are unhappy about train drivers operating the train doors, which have traditionally been operated by the guard. As we know, guards are also ticket inspectors, so you might think that they would be glad to have this extra duty taken off them by the driver. Interestingly, the public debate has been cast as union obduracy in the face of an obvious updating of terms and conditions to take account of new technology.

What the debate has not included is the role that the guard is trained to undertake should the train break down between signals. At this point the driver is tasked with contacting the signaller while the guard walks back behind the train and places detonators at strategic points on the line so that following trains will be alerted to an obstruction ahead and thereby avoid a rear-end collision. For travellers, the thought of a long journey with 500 other passengers and no supervision apart from a driver is not always reassuring. So, is this about unions resisting change or about essential Health and Safety being put at risk in the hope of achieving easy economies, increased profit and fewer union members?

Learning about the sector and its customs and practices is an essential part in alerting the change agents to likely blocks to agreement for change. These blocks are not always self-evident to those who do not know the history of the working practices of an industry and their historical derivation.

Key messages

- Change affects all aspects of our lives – work and home
- Change presents opportunities and threats
- People need to be able to accept the challenge of change
- The way change is implemented is critical to success

Exploding myths

- Change is optional
- Change happens quickly
- Change requires perfect plans and solutions
- Resistance to change is to be deplored

THE TRADITIONAL ORGANIZATIONAL HIERARCHY

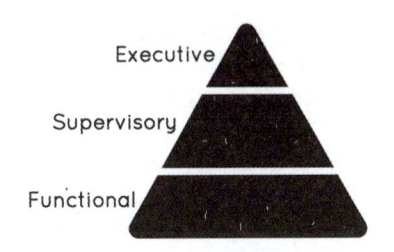

Figure 1.1 Traditional organization levels

The structural approach and bureaucracy

Max Weber, academic, economist and sociologist, identified three forms of legitimate authority:

1. Rational-legal
2. Traditional
3. Charismatic

And five concepts for rational-legal authority:

1. Specialization of activities and duties
2. Hierarchy of control and supervision
3. Rules and procedures for decisions and actions
4. Separation between office (post) and office-holder (person)
5. Appointed officials with technical qualifications

Controlling large numbers of people requires a hierarchy and that hierarchy was often organized with a span of control of 1:8. Consequently, as more people were employed in an organization, more levels of management were required to control them.

There were appropriate levels of responsibility from the executive, who were there to plan and make decisions; the supervisory, who would implement the plans and make sure that the workers did what the company needed to achieve its designated results; and then the staff at the functional end of the business who were trained to carry out their duties efficiently and effectively.

We most often see these arrangements in total organizations, sometimes designated by rank, sometimes in uniform, and always taking orders from the top down with little by way of upward communication, which was much less often sought (yours is not to reason why, yours is but to do and die). After all, a business is not a democracy and few armies would survive for long if they had to take a vote on whether to fight a war or not or decide by consensus the best way of going about it.

OD began to emerge in an era where most large private sector and public sector organizations were structured along bureaucratic lines. As it developed its democratic-participative approach, OD came to be perceived as both a challenge to bureaucracy and a means of overcoming some of its main shortcomings. OD consultants were like architects – redesigning the structure of the organization and bringing together the disparate elements to create a flatter, more flexible, participative system that was more in tune with the needs of the modern world.

WHAT MANAGERS DO

Complementing the structural approach to running organizations, we should also recognize that there is also a structured approach to what managers do. This was first put forward by Henri Fayol (1949) who identified the aspects or steps of the manager's job as shown in Figure 1.2.

Once again, for the consultant, tracking whether these steps are in place may be difficult to do, but both observation and time logs can be a useful start for accessing what managers do and how they act from moment to moment.

The bureaucratic approach to structuring organizations and Fayol's approach to defining managerial work came together most clearly in Scientific Management, as prompted by Frederick Taylor and epitomized by Henry Ford's production techniques. Ford created a moving assembly line that controlled the pace of work by bringing the car to the worker and not the worker to the car. He used Scientific Management principles to study work and break it down into small, low-skilled components that could be either easily and cheaply performed or mechanized. The result was that instead of human beings controlling the machinery of production, Ford's moving production line made people part of the machine and they were controlled by the machine. The result was that production doubled and the number of workers required to build each car halved. Thus was born the world's first mass-produced car – the Model T Ford. Less well known is that Ford also had to increase wages significantly to attract and retain those who would work at the frenetic pace required and that eventually mass-production was superseded by more flexible systems that addressed different customer needs. So, Ford's statement that you could have any colour as long as it was black lasted only until the competition offered the customer a choice of different-coloured vehicles.

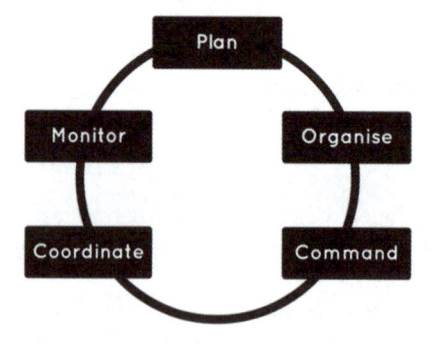

Figure 1.2 Fayol's management steps

THINKING ABOUT THE WORKERS

Ironically, the trend to systematically dehumanize work, which scientific managerialism seemed to engender, coincided with the beginnings of a movement to acknowledge human involvement in work. In 1919 the Institute of Personnel Management was established to promote the better management of employees. The standing of this and similar organizations was reinforced in the 1920s and 1930s through the findings of the Hawthorne experiments, which suggested that by meeting workers' social needs, as well as their economic needs, managers could achieve higher levels of productivity and greater worker commitment to the job (something that those advocating zero-hours contracts seem to be less certain about). This led to the founding of the Human Relations movement in the USA, which shared some overlapping ideas and personnel with the OD movement (Burnes, 2017). The 1950s saw the establishment of the Tavistock Institute in the UK and its development of the socio-technical systems approach to change (Burnes and Cooke, 2013). This OD-type approach to change sought to align the human and technical sides of the organization through a participative change process. The 1950s also saw the emergence of Reg Revans' Action Learning approach to management development. Revans viewed decision-making as a collective learning process. The birth of Action Learning, allied to the growth in OD's participative approach to management, created the conditions for upward as well as downward decision-making and communication in organizations. This meant that it was possible for those affected by change to contribute their knowledge to the decision-making process and have a say in what change took place and how it could best be implemented.

A DIFFERENT ORGANIZATIONAL PARADIGM

Though bureaucracy was an effective way of managing large organizations, the increasing size and diversity of markets and the broadening out of customer tastes and requirements meant that organizations in the 1960s began to search for more flexible ways of managing their workforces (Bennis, 1966), especially in terms of:

- Time – for how long do you need people at work?
- Full-time vs. part-time workers – could part-timers be a better way of managing the peaks and troughs of customer demand?
- Costs – do people doing similar jobs need to be given the same pay and conditions?
- Functional flexibility – can one person be trained to do more than one job, thereby eroding the inflexibility of union demands for distinctive work functions?

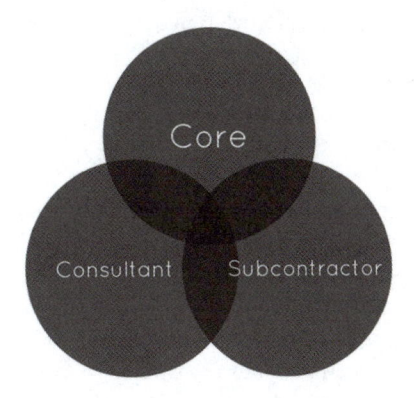

Figure 1.3 The Shamrock organization

Charles Handy's Shamrock model suggested that the old triangle of the traditional hierarchy was already beginning to break down (1989). He argued that core workers would be engaged from the age of 27–45 and that thereafter they would have a choice of moving into subcontract work (low-tech; no-tech) or consultancy (high-tech; professional). His later work (Handy, 1994) suggested that the top age for core workers was more likely to be 35 – meaning that workers would have to move more quickly to establish a portfolio career in which their knowledge, skill and experience would be regularly placed back on the employment market as jobs became more flexible and companies less enduring. Perhaps here we see the trend of the human resources (HR) consultant, or interim manager – and more recently the internal change agent, whose employment would last as long as the project on which they were working but after which they would be required to move on.

So, what we see is a move from the traditional (modernist) organization to something less rigid (postmodernist).

Modern

- Rigid bureaucracy
- Mass markets
- Technological determinism
- Differentiated, demarcated, deskilled jobs
- Centralized, standardized employment

Postmodern

- Flexible networks
- Niche markets
- Technological choice
- Multiskilled jobs
- Complex, fragmented employment

(Clegg, 1989; Burnes, 2000)

STOP AND REFLECT

- How can the change agent bring about awareness of the need for change?
- Will managers always know what is the need for change?
- How can the change agent influence what managers believe about change?
- Is the change agent a doctor (diagnosing problems and prescribing treatment)?
- Is the change agent a sounding board (listening and reflecting)?
- Is the change agent just an implementer?

We can assume that the change agent has been invited into the organization with a consultancy role in mind. Our first two questions suggest that although the invitation appears to come from an accepted need for change, whether the reasons given are accurate or not remains to be discovered. It is often found that the Board commissioning the change are not themselves agreed on what the problem is and some of them may even be adamant that a consultant's services are not needed (as managers are fond of remarking to consultants, 'you borrow our watch to tell us the time').

Certainly, some awareness of the sector we are invited into is an advantage. Working with other organizations in a sector may well provide an insight into trends and tendencies that are affecting everyone, not just the company who has invited us. But then again, every company has its own history and culture, so the assumption that everyone in a sector will exhibit the same response to change is something that cannot be taken for granted.

If we accept the consultant's role as similar to the medical practitioner, then we assume that doctors are medically trained to conduct a preliminary investigation; use their knowledge to assess what the problem is; and come up with a treatment that will be effective. As we will see, many of the leading consultants tend to take more of an educational role, which seeks to explore what people' perceptions in the company are and how that links with the problems they face. This might suggest that the sounding board may be closer to the style of consultancy which works best in companies the consultant is less familiar with.

Finally, there may be situations in which the consultant has an expertise which requires them to implement an agreed programme of change – this may be the case, for example, with the implementation of IT or HR systems.

PERSPECTIVES ON CHANGE MANAGEMENT: OUTSIDE-IN OR INSIDE-OUT

One way of looking at change initiatives is to consider what it is that organizations are attempting to achieve. De Wit and Meyer (2004) 3rd edition suggest that there are two approaches: inside-out and outside-in. These can be illustrated as shown in Figure 1.4.

Some different approaches:

- Total Quality Management (TQM) (focusing on inside-out strategy)
- Business Process Re-engineering (BPR) (focusing on outside-in strategy)
- Technological Change (changing the way we do things)
- Culture Change (changing the way we think about what we do)

Total Quality Management

TQM is, as its name suggests, focused on the internal and procedural aspects of production, or **inside-out**. It seeks to support and reinforce a consistency that will alleviate error and wastage, for example. Its progenitor, W. Edwards Deming, identified the wastage that occurs in many manufacturing processes and suggested a 14-point approach to put in place a system that includes:

Constancy, philosophy, evidence, beyond price, detect problems, training, supervision, eradicate fear, break barriers, educate and retrain, management structure.

Outside In
- Market led
- Customers
- Competition
- Effectiveness

Content

Inside Out
- Resource led
- Efficiency factors
- Time
- Quantity
- Quality
- Cost

Figure 1.4 Inside-out and outside-in approaches

Deming laid out six principles on which his philosophy was based:

1. Quality is defined by the customer (effectiveness)
2. Understanding and reducing variation is essential (error and wastage rate)
3. Top management commitment and understanding is vital (Oakland (1987) suggested 85% of quality depends on their involvement)
4. Continuous change and improvement for all people – internal and external (this is where misunderstandings can occur)
5. Ongoing education and training for all to achieve constant improvement (see Wilson, 1992)
6. Performance ratings used sensitively

If we look at Wilson's (1992) list of the TQM cycle we can see how the links between the steps are structured:

1. Define customer need
2. Improve organizational processes to achieve that need
3. Reduce costs
4. Productivity increases with quality
5. Gain increased market share
6. Growth of business

Firstly, defining customer need might seem to be self-evident. But how easy is it to do that accurately? The market abounds with examples of good ideas which were thought to be ideal for answering customer needs but failed to attract the support their sponsors hoped for.

If the market research has been done successfully, we now move on to the second stage: improving organizational quality to address that need. Again, that might seem obvious, but what are the challenges here? Radical change is not cost-free, and it could be very costly to implement the change, particularly if deadlines are pressing.

Then there is stage three: reduce costs. What costs are referred to here? It could be that this refers to error or wastage rates incurred by the old way of doing things. However, if this loss accounted for 5% interference cost overall, then there is only 5% that we can eliminate. Once we have achieved those cost savings there are no more cost reductions to be achieved.

Does productivity increase with quality? It depends how we calculate productivity, of course. But again, it could be that quality comes at a cost, or takes more time. So, more investment, say in training, may be required to support more demanding standards.

Our fifth and sixth stages assume that what we are producing will be adopted readily by the market. But that could take time or may not come at all. So, growing the business is not guaranteed by increasing efficiency.

Finally, we are back to defining customer need. The diagram suggests that this is a cycle which will be automatic and lead to yet more change. But as is sometimes pointed out, if we have gone for an ISO standard then we may find that a predetermined set of procedures cannot easily adapt to achieve the new customer needs in the future.

SOME QUESTIONS FOR YOU TO DISCUSS

TQM is a system of organizing production which was intended to encourage job sharing; functional flexibility within the working team; and autonomy in deciding work quotas and targets. Quality assurance is wider in its scope than just a production system. Traditional quality checks would have satisfied the needs of quality assurance. But the supporters of quality management agreed that senior management is responsible for 85% of problems which arise from poor quality at work (Oakland, 1989). However, senior

> **STOP AND REFLECT**
>
> - Is TQM always necessary for quality assurance?
> - Is leadership commitment always necessary?
> - Is TQM appropriate for all organizations?
> - What is the problem with a predefined quality standard?
> - What did the first Lexus car (produced as a perfect vehicle by Toyota but which no one wanted to buy) tell us about quality standards?

managers are not always convinced that this is the case, so the consultant needs to tread carefully while explaining why this can be the case.

TQM was born in manufacturing and attempts to use it in service industries have been less successful than its proponents had hope for. Customer care, for example, is a good example of how often organizations get this wrong – not because they don't have a system but because the system does not allow for varied responses or sometimes any knowledgeable human voice to speak to at all.

Predetermined standards are always superseded by the next step which means that standards are not absolute but must always be changing to meet increasing customer expectancies. Similarly, what satisfies one customer may not satisfy another – so quality is subjective and sometimes quite arbitrary, as those working in the hospitality industry will know very well.

> **FINALLY, WHAT IS MEANT BY...?**
>
> - Intangible benefit
> - Sectional interests
> - Customer as judge
> - Sponge phenomenon
> - Different rigidity
> - Delivers customer satisfaction

Intangible benefits are those which cannot be directly experienced. Not all that is designed into products or services is appreciated by the customers. They may not even be aware that such aspects have been addressed on their behalf. They assume that planes are safe to fly in but are often unaware of the manufacturing and servicing systems which support their safety in the air or what they cost.

Sectional benefits mean that within companies there will be different perceptions about the relative benefits of quality. What is regarded as essential to engineers in the production area may seem irrelevant to salespeople who are looking for demonstrable benefits which satisfy customers' immediate needs.

Customer is judge, of course. But on what basis do customers judge what is a benefit or advantage to them? Different customers value different benefits and knowing what the customer wants done, while being the gauge of success here, is not always possible to know during the design and production stages of development.

Sponge phenomenon is the process by which the achievement of perfect quality can soak up significant amounts of investment, thus making the pursuit of perfect quality prohibitively expensive to achieve. Therefore, some measure of variance is usually accepted. (Legislation governing how much milk there is in the container allows a variance of +/−2.5%, for example.)

Standards strictly imposed can mean **rigidity**. Invariable systems can sometimes be experienced as a constraint imposed on the end-user (speed-limiters can be an example of this).

Finally, where is the evidence that standards deliver **customer satisfaction**? For example, there have been cases where the implementation of the performance-quality standard Charter Mark, awarded by the UK government based on recognized working methods, resulted in poorer service even though the businesses met the required standards. In one example, the quality standard was based on all incoming calls to a civil service department being answered within five rings. Management put pressure on staff to achieve the 'five-rings' target, which they did. However, often the person who picked up the call could not answer the caller's questions and had to pass the call on to others (leaving the customer to tell the same story to several different people before getting a satisfactory answer). The efficiency standard was met – at the expense of effectiveness for the end-user.

In summary, TQM is alive and well in many sectors of industry. Sometimes it appears under different headings, such as Six Sigma or is linked to Just-in-time approaches to change. This suggests that the focus of inside-out approaches continues to be relevant in many industries, and consultants may well be asked to implement such a change strategy.

Business process re-engineering

If we look at the alternative approach to change, BRP, or **outside-in**, then we will note that it is market-led rather than resource-led. This suggests that the focus of TQM on improving the efficiency and consistency of what people do is complemented by looking at what competitors are achieving or customers demanding and seeks to make that central to answering the market need. As we will see, it may then seem easier to bring in people from outside who can deliver what is needed more quickly.

One of BPR's proponents (Champy, 1995) offered the following definition:

> **Reengineering** is the fundamental rethinking and redesign of business processes to achieve dramatic improvements in critical, contemporary measures of performance, such as cost, quality, service and speed.

Ostensibly that sounds similar to the objectives of TQM. However, it offers a more radical approach to implementing these improvements. Basically, BPR looks at bringing in those who will be able to deliver to the new standards. Older workers may be thought to take longer to adapt or be unable to master new technology fast enough. So, bring in operators who can.

BPR is sometimes complemented by the concept of empowerment – giving workers the discretion to make decisions about the business and customer service without waiting for management approval. This concept often included:

- Training to perform a variety of roles within a process, thereby improving functional flexibility
- Areas of responsibility to make decisions on behalf of organization without seeking management approval
- Authority to fulfil responsibilities in a learning and supportive environment

EXAMPLE

Shortly after taking over the west coast main line in the UK Richard Branson empowered platform supervisors to authorize a taxi for any passenger who had missed a connection due to the late running of a connecting train service. One such passenger asked for assistance and the supervisor duly authorised a taxi home for her. Her journey came to £639.00.

The following day the press headlines decried this simplistic approach to business that had misfired so badly. Richard Branson's response was that a small ad in the national press would have cost him far more than the taxi fare – and as it was he got free headlines in every newspaper.

Central to the implementation of BPR are the following questions:

- **Purpose:** What are we doing here anyway?
- **Culture:** How do we generate a better environment?
- **Process:** How do we get the kind of processes we want?
- **People:** Who do we want to work with?

Initial meetings with staff groups can be an opportunity to generate a discussion on these questions to explore the thoughts and feelings of those involved in radical change.

The management credo included the following statements:

- Leave behind perfectionist thinking
- Embrace the creed: get it right and make it better and better and better
- Hold fast to our faith in human beings
- Give up ex officio authority; move to existential authority
- Overthrow the tyranny of numerical accounting
- See people as being multiskilled
- Learned willingness/individual accountability
- Only way to gain control is to give it up

It also contained some warnings about what happened to those who failed to respond to radical change quickly:

- Don't live too long with people who refuse to change their behaviour; this applies to managers as well as workers
- Don't expect people to change their behaviour unless you change what they do
- Don't expect cultural change to happen immediately
- Don't articulate new values and then delay re-engineering management processes to make it happen

(Champy, 1995: 109)

It may be that such radical approaches to change account for the high proportion of change initiatives which fail to fulfil their initial promise (Burnes, 2017).

So, in summary what we can say about BPR could be listed as follows:

- It is an **outside-in** strategy (De Wit and Meyer, 2004)
- It is **market-led**, not resource-led
- It takes **effectiveness** as the governing factor
- It then seeks out the people who will deliver that goal even if they are complete outsiders to the business
- It can diminish customer confidence/contacts
- It is radical in its approach to recruitment (President Reagan and his sacking of striking air-traffic controllers)
- It is unsentimental about long-serving and faithful employees who don't fit the new profile (ease them out)
- It rarely works in business success terms (too radical and disliked by long-standing customers who can lose their well-liked regular contacts)

WHAT MANAGERS KNOW

Managers will often have acquired knowledge about trends and theories from popular writers. Threshold knowledge is important in any learning situation and, for the consultant, what managers believe can be significant to success or failure. Some writers call these initiatives fads and fashions. They may include such topics as:

- One Minute Management
- Management by Objectives
- Matrix Management
- Team Based Management
- Process Re-engineering
- Knowledge management

- Total Quality Management
- Learning organizations
- Knowledge management
- Excellence literature
- Emotional intelligence
- Chaos theory

It might be worthwhile stopping and considering each of these initiatives and how well established they are in management practice.

> **STOP AND REFLECT**
>
> - How well grounded in academic theory are guru writers' claims and assertions?
> - How well supported are their conclusions by empirical evidence?
> - How generalizable are their findings between organizations?
> - How far are their recommendations implementable by a change agent?

Some of the most popular writers, such as Tom Peters, are distinctly vague and inconsistent about the underpinning theories that their ideas depend on, still less on the empirical evidence which supports the assertions made about their likely effectiveness (Burnes, 2017). Generalizability is an increasingly important factor to ensure that what works in one company has a reasonable chance of succeeding in another. Without that, consultants are operating at the risk of generalizing from a narrow base of expertise which may not be applicable elsewhere. Indeed, one of the objections to imposed change is precisely that is assumed to be valid and reliable elsewhere. The question is, how do we know?

N-STEP APPROACHES

Following on from Lewin's three-step model of change, many guru-managers and celebrity academics have developed their own n-step approaches to change. One such example is Kanter and colleagues' (1992: 382–3) ten commandments for executing change, which are as follows:

1. Analyse the organization and its need for change
2. Create a shared vision and a common direction
3. Separate from the past
4. Create a sense of urgency
5. Support strong leader role
6. Line up political sponsorship
7. Craft an implementation plan
8. Develop enabling structures
9. Communicate, involve people and be honest
10. Reinforce and institutionalize change

You might like to stop and consider how useful such to-do lists may be to the consultant.

> **STOP AND REFLECT**
>
> - Is this step approach logically sequenced?
> - Which are general principles, and which are specific actions?
> - What does 'separate from the past' mean?
> - How do you create a 'sense of urgency' as a change agent?
> - Define 'strong leader'.
> - What is political sponsorship?
> - Should being honest be the first principle in the list?
> - Could a change agent use this list as a blueprint for implementing a programme of change?

The fact is that such general change steps are difficult for other consultants to implement. They are stated in general terms and not always arranged in a logical sequence. While they probably sound good when delivered to a management audience, their practical utility for other consultants is difficult to establish.

However, not all n-step approaches are just a to-do list couched in general terms. Some have been thought out more carefully and are derived from underpinning theories about how change works. One such is Nadler's (1993) 12-step approach in which the author examines the three main reasons why people resist change and then arranges his programme to address these directly. His steps both look more structured and follow a logically sequenced pattern (Figure 1.5).

These are just two of the many n-step approaches on offer. Some, like Kanter and colleagues', seem very general and difficult to implement; others, like Nadler's, seem more specific in their suggestions for an implementable change programme.

Before we leave n-step approaches, we will touch on the work of Bullock and Batten (1985). This is perhaps the most comprehensive attempt to elaborate on Lewin's work. It is an integrated, four-phase model of change and is based on a review and synthesis of over 30 models of change derived from Lewin's original work. Bullock and Batten's model describes Planned change in terms of two major dimensions: change phases, which are distinct states an organization moves through as it undertakes Planned change; and change processes, which are the methods used to move an organization from one state to another.

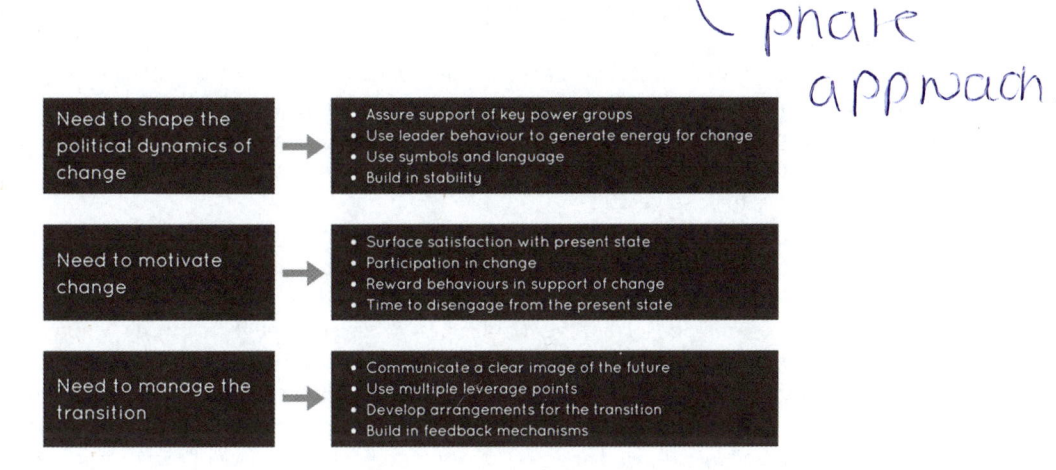

— phase approach

Need to shape the political dynamics of change	→	• Assure support of key power groups • Use leader behaviour to generate energy for change • Use symbols and language • Build in stability
Need to motivate change	→	• Surface satisfaction with present state • Participation in change • Reward behaviours in support of change • Time to disengage from the present state
Need to manage the transition	→	• Communicate a clear image of the future • Use multiple leverage points • Develop arrangements for the transition • Build in feedback mechanisms

Figure 1.5 *Nadler's approach to change*

Key to these phases and processes is the issue of learning – organizations learning about themselves and learning about change.

The first phase is **Exploration**. This phase comprises investigating if there is a need for change and searching for and contracting with outside assistance, i.e. a consultant. This equates to Lewin's 'unfreezing' step.

The second phase is **Planning**. Building on the information gained in the first phase, this phase seeks to diagnose the problem, establish change goals, design the intervention and gain the support of key decision-makers.

The third phase is **Action**. This phase involves implementing the change plan, evaluating its impact and taking any corrective action necessary. The second and third phases equate to Lewin's 'moving' step.

The final phase is **Integration**. This involves consolidating and stabilizing the changes so that they become part of the organization's normal, everyday operations. This relates to Lewin's 'refreezing' step.

Interestingly, when reviewing the various change models, Bullock and Batten found that the phase most often omitted from the process of change was exploration. This would seem to suggest that most organizations and indeed consultants are happy to proceed with change without exploring too deeply what is the case for change and, if so, what needs to be done. They also found that once a change plan had been implemented, phase 3, the evaluation was not always undertaken. This seems to imply that change agents quit the company before the evidence of effective change is available.

Before we move on from this elaboration of Lewin's Planned approach to change, it is useful to consider the following questions:

> **STOP AND REFLECT**
>
> - Are there situations where imposed change might be the only option for the change agent?
> - How would that change be introduced to those who will experience it?
> - What consequences might change imposed in this way have in the longer term on the organization?

In terms of the first question, as Burnes (2014) notes, no approach to change is suitable for all situations and all cases. Planned change was specifically developed for situations where behaviour change was necessary. Initially, this focused on change at group level, but overtime OD practitioners have developed more organization-wide variants. However, in cases where organizations need to take immediate action to address a financial crisis, the slow, participative nature of Planned change is unlikely to be appropriate. Having said that, even in wartime, army commanders usually seek advice about feasible options; a good account of such leaders and their approaches to such decisions can be found in Adair (1974) where he gives examples of accounts of successful managers of change in wartime.

In answer to the second and third questions, we should note that Planned change lies at the heart of OD and it provides a host of tools, techniques and advice that can make a change programmer more effective and support change agents in achieving success (see Cummings and Worley, 2015). In addition, the Planned approach reminds the change agent that change is an iterative learning process that requires widespread participation if it is to be successful.

Before moving on to examine learning and participation in more detail, we should briefly touch on the issue of emergent change. The emergent approach to change was developed as a rejection of Lewin's work (Burnes, 2004). For its adherents, emergent change is based on the view that change is not a linear or rational process or a one-off isolated event but is best achieved through an interwoven pattern of (mainly) small- to medium-scale continuous changes and that it concerns key change decisions which evolve over time and are the outcome of political and cultural processes in organizations (Huczynski and Buchanan, 2013). However, while it attracted a great deal of attention and support as an analytical tool with which to study change, its tendency to see change as a political process and its lack of practical advice on how change should be managed have meant that it has had little impact on the actual practice of change (Burnes, 2017).

LEARNING AND PARTICIPATION

Lewin saw change as a learning process – for change to be successful, all those concerned learn about themselves, their situation and how to bring about change. Lewin developed participative management to ensure that workers could be fully involved in change and so enabled to express their opinions, contribute and develop their knowledge and understand the reasons for and objective of the change. Lewin also recognized that involvement leads to commitment and commitment is essential for success (Burnes, 2007 and 2017; Oreg et al., 2011). In any case, it makes eminent good sense that those who wish to initiate change should seek the views of those who will be affected by it. Despite what they might think, senior managers do not know everything about their organizations. Similarly, even consultants who have long experience in an industrial sector still need to realize that what holds true for the sector as whole may not hold true for a particular organization or group. Assuming that everyone views or experiences the world as we do is a classic mistake that is made all too often by change agents and managers. This is why the first element in Lewin's Planned approach to change is force field analysis – learning about the forces that are shaping current behaviour and which ones need to change.

The only people who may be uncertain of a participative approach to change are those who are paying for it. After all, the bigger the company, the more groups and people will need to be involved and the longer the planning process will take. However, as a study of Japanese, Chinese and American companies found, those companies that spent the most time planning change and who involved the most people had the shortest implementation periods and fewer implementation problems. The reverse was also found, a short planning period with very few people involved led to slower implementation, more problems and less chance of success (Martinsons and Davison, 1999).

One of the main factors that shape the behaviour of individuals and groups in an organization is its culture. Therefore, when a consultant first goes into an organization, they need to learn about that culture. However, those in the organization also have to understand their culture and how it may facilitate or constrain change. They need to recognize that what they see as normal or common-sense behaviour is shaped by a multitude of forces, many of which they may not even be aware of. Deal and Kennedy (1982) suggested that culture in a company is 'the way we do things round here'. That makes perfect sense to anyone who has had to start a new job, but that is only the surface or visible manifestation of culture. It is what underlies 'the way we do things' that consultants need to learn about.

Schein (1985) suggests three levels of culture, as shown in Figure 1.6.
On first entering a new workplace, it is the **visible artefacts** that usually present themselves. They comprise:

- The actual physical layout of the workplace
- What people seem to be doing
- Comings and goings of people
- Processes and procedures between people
- Language
- Symbols
- Uniforms

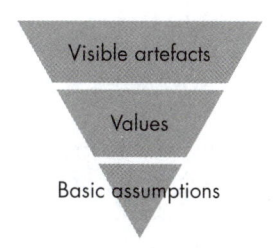

Figure 1.6 Schein's cultural layers model

What may be less apparent will be the **values**:

- What is it that people believe about their work?
- What do they value about what they do?
- What are the priorities they think are important?
- What are things they do not value/think are a waste of time?

Values are inherent in any group a consultant will be dealing with. So, gaining the group's trust is essential in identifying these values and in understanding how they influence its behaviour. Not all peer groups are willing to share their views immediately, particularly if they are suspicious about newcomers and their motives.

More challenging is identifying an organization or group's **basic assumptions**. These cannot be asked about directly and can only emerge in conversations – often away from the workplace. Informal social contact outside work may be a more likely occasion to hear more about the company and its past. Schein acknowledges that basic assumptions are often unexpressed and indeed only become expressed when they are threatened by outside events. Unsurprisingly, such a threat will often be the prospect of change, but again, the consultant is unlikely to hear these expressed until confrontation occurs, wittingly or unwittingly.

Given the complex role played by culture in any organization, the need to learn about it is essential to the change agent's effectiveness. Senior managers will often state that they are fully conversant with the company, its people and its culture, but will then confess that they have little or no contact with staff at the operational level, where the majority of employees work. Often, when asked to describe the company's culture, they will struggle to offer anything other than vague generalities, such as 'we are one big family' or 'we are customer focused'. This is why it is not only essential that the consultants learn about the culture for themselves, but that they help the members of the organization to do so as well. All of this suggests that Lewin's T-groups and Bullock and Batten's Exploration phase are an important investment to a change programme.

There are a number of techniques for beginning to explore an organization's culture. These include observing working practices, chatting informally with as many people as you can and convening interdisciplinary groups to discuss why certain behaviours and actions seem to occur, and what they mean for the effectiveness of the company.

SO, WHAT IS IT THAT WE WANT TO DISCOVER?

A good place to start is by seeking to understand the organization's current behaviour. The congruence model of organizational behaviour is useful in this respect. This maintains that an organization's success is related to the degree of alignment it achieves with its environment. To understand the degree of alignment and how it influences behaviour, it is useful to explore how well staff understand the following issues:

- Environment (outside-in/market-led approach). How in touch is the organization with what is going on in the marketplace?
- Resources (inside-out/resource-led approach). What is the training and development approach of the company to its people?
- History of the organization (where have they come from). How many long servers are there in the organization and what critical events have shaped the organization's current behaviour?
- Strategy (where do they want to go?). Do people know where the organization is aiming to be in the next five years and what they need to do to get there?

- Thinking holistically. How many people have seen the connection between trends and tendency in the wider world and the impact this is having on their present situation?
- Cause and effect. What are the links between strategic objectives and day-to-day operations? Do people recognize these links readily or is it all 'up to management'?

The information gained should be discussed with staff to develop a shared understanding of the organization's current behaviour, the challenges it faces and the sort of changes it might need to make. This is Lewin's unfreezing stage where staff learn that what worked in the past may not work in the future. This then prepares the organization for Lewin's next step, the moving phase. In approaching this, it is useful to explore the following questions with staff:

- **What is the motivation for change?** (Put yourself in their shoes – how would you feel?)
- **How should the transition be managed?** (Start from where they are and consider the journey they will need to make to be successful)
- **What are the political dynamics?** (Be aware of the fault lines on the Board and within the organization – and work to bridge them)

On the last point, this is one reason for having interdisciplinary groups for initial meetings. Although we talk about culture as if it were a corporate entity it needs to be acknowledged that there are subcultures which sometimes coincide with the departments within the organization. Production people rarely see things in the way that salespeople do. One group is interested in processes for achieving success in assembly and quality, adhering to the time lines and cost constraints. The other is predominantly interested in what makes customers want to buy their product against the competitors' offerings. Similarly, sales and marketing rarely see eye to eye either. Marketing can generate leads which sales people find unrealistic and sales people want immediate orders not just long-term prospects. There is a tendency for other departments to be suspicious of Finance and HR as being management monitoring systems. Often such fissures between groups will become apparent during initial meetings on the questions above.

The **facilitator** of such sessions should be armed with a pen and flip chart and write down the ideas that come from the group without comments. As a change agent, you will need to:

- Surface dissatisfaction with the present state
- Gain participation in change
- Reward behaviours supporting change
- Find time and opportunity to disengage from the present state
- Disengage at the right time

Arguably, you have now embarked on the first step and may even have gained some insights into the second. The other three steps will come later – though some hints may have emerged about what would be acceptable or unacceptable to the group.

GUIDELINES FOR FACILITATING EMPLOYEE PARTICIPATION

- Be open in your questioning (Tell me about… What do you think about…?)
- Show you listen and understand (use nodding dog; eye contact and write down all ideas)
- Don't make any judgements yourself (no evaluations – 'that's not a good idea…')
- Only intervene to restore order
- Use sharp-angle closing (Why do you say that?)

- Seek examples of general complaint (Is there a story/example that illustrates the point?)
- Summarize (what we have achieved/what we haven't achieved)
- **Remember: no badges of rank and no visitors allowed in without prior agreement**

This last can be difficult for uniformed organizations. But if you don't do it you may find that junior ranks only speak when more senior ranks have spoken – which means that if seniors don't speak, no one does.

Such initial meetings are crucial to the learning process, especially for the facilitator. However, it is essential that the staff involved are also helped to learn about themselves, their group and their organization by offering their own views and considering what others say. Sometimes the old principle applies: 'How do I know what I think, till I hear what I say?' Afterwards you may hear people say, 'I never knew that X thought that.' This is learning for everyone and is always informative.

There is one other opportunity which the facilitator has during these sessions: identifying potential change agents. If change is to be successful long term then it must have within itself the ability to recruit internal change agents. Once the external change agents have gone, who else will be there to continue to promote the change?

So, remember:

- Everyone is a potential change agent (even the militant at the back)
- Opportunities are presented for individuals to self-select themselves into change agency roles (encourage and support volunteers)
- Change agency requires no special consideration for selection (just learning and listening – the rest you can train)

(Doyle, 2002)

Basic assumptions of a good facilitator:

- Assume individuals are rational animals
- Assume that individuals will want what managers want
- Assume that training and development will close that gap
- Assume no casualties of the change process
- Take account of long-term custom and practice
- Assume that all individuals have ability and potential
- Assume that commitment can be won by patience, negotiation and reassurance

CHAPTER SUMMARY

Though there have been many challenges to Lewin's Planned change model, it remains the most developed and best supported approach to change (Burnes and Cooke, 2013). Through the efforts of the OD community, Planned change is supported by an extensive array of practical and tried and tested tools and techniques which have proved extremely beneficial to change consultants (Cummings and Worley, 2015). It is not perfect, but in the hands of an experienced change agent, it has much to offer in opening up the issues affecting change. Above all else, it provides a process through which change agents and organizations do not just achieve a one-off change but develop the knowledge and skills to continue to bring about change in the future.

For video content relating to this chapter please visit the companion website at www.macmillanihe.com/Randall-Management-Consultancy.

REFERENCES

Adair, J. (1974). *The Skills of Leadership*. Aldershot: Wildwood House.

Bennis, W. (1966). *Changing Organizations*. New York: McGraw-Hill.

Bullock, R.J. and Batten, D. (1985). It's just a phase we're going through: A review and synthesis of OD phase analysis. *Group and Organisation Studies*, 10(December), 383–412.

Burnes, B. (2000). *Managing Change: A Strategic Approach to Organisational Dynamics*. New York: Financial Times and Prentice Hall.

Burnes, B. (2004). Kurt Lewin and the planned approach to change: A re-appraisal. *Journal of Management Studies*, 41(6), 977–1002.

Burnes, B. (2007). Kurt Lewin and the Harwood studies: The foundations of OD. *Journal of Applied Behavioral Science*, 43(2), 213–231.

Burnes, B. (2014). *Managing Change*. Harlow: Pearson.

Burnes, B. and Cooke, B. (2013). Kurt Lewin's field theory: A review and re-evaluation. *International Journal of Management Reviews*, 15, 408–425.

Champy, J. (1995). *Reengineering Management*. New York: Harper.

Clegg, S. (1989). *Frameworks of Power*. London: Sage.

Cummings, T.G. and Worley, C.G. (2015). *Organization Development and Change*. South Western: Cengage Learning.

Dawson, P. (2003). *Understanding Organisational Change: The Contemporary Experience of People at Work*. London: Sage.

Deal, T.E. and Kennedy, A.A. (1982). *Corporate Cultures: The Rites and Rituals of Corporate Life*. Reading, MA: Addison Wesley.

De Wit, R. and Meyer, R. (2004). *Strategy: Process, Content, Context: An International Perspective*. London: Thomson.

Doyle, M. (2002). Selecting managers for transformational change. *Human Resource Management Journal*, 12(1), 3–16.

Drucker, P.F. (1954). *The Practice of Management*. New York: Harper Row.

Elrod, D.P. and Tippet, D.D. (2002). The 'death-valley' of change. *Journal of Organisational Change Management*, 15(3), 273–291.

Fayol, H. (1949). *General and Industrial Management*, trans. P. Straw. London: Pitman.

Handy, C. (1989). *The Age of Unreason*. Boston, MA: Harvard Business School Press.

Handy, C. (1994) *The Empty Raincoat: New thinking for a new world*. London: Hutchinson.

Hendry, C. (1996). Understanding and creating whole organisational change through learning theory. *Human Relations*, 49(5), 621–641.

Huczynski, A.A. and Buchanan, D.A. (2013). *Organisational Behaviour*. Harlow: Financial Times and Prentice Hall.

Hughes, M. (2015). *The Leadership of Organisational Change*. London: Routledge.

Kanter, R.M. (1991). Transcending business boundaries. *Harvard Business Review*, 69(3), 151.

Kanter, R.M., Stein, B.A. and Jick, T.D. (1992). *The Challenge of Organisational Change*. New York: Free Press.

Martinsons, M., Davison, R. and Tse, D. (1999). The balanced scorecard: A foundation for the strategic management of information systems, *Decision Support Systems*, 25(1), 71–88.

Nadler, D.A. (1993). Concepts for the management of strategic choice. In C. Mabey and B. Mayon-White (eds), *Managing Change*. London: Open University and Paul Chapman Publishing.

Oakland, J.S. (1989). *Total Quality Management*. Oxford: Butterworth-Heinemann.

Oreg, S., Vakola, M. and Armenakis, A. (2011). Change recipients' reactions to organizational change: A 60-year review of quantitative studies. *The Journal of Applied Behavioral Science*, 47(4), 461–524.

Revans, R.W. (1980). *Action Learning: New Techniques for Management*. London: Blond & Briggs.

Schein, E.H. (1985). *Organisational Culture and Leadership*. San Francisco CA: Jossey Bass.

Schein, E.H. (1996). Kurt Lewin's change theory in the field and in the classroom: Notes towards a model of management learning. *Systems Practice*, 9(1), 27–47.

Stickland, F. (1998). *The Dynamics of Change: Insights into Organisational Transition from the Natural World*. London: Routledge.

Toplis, J., Dulewicz, V. and Fletcher, C. (1987). *Psychological Testing: A Manager's Guide*. London: CIPD.

Weber, M. (1946/1958). Essays in sociology. In M. Weber, H. Gerth, and C. Mills (trans. and eds), *From Max Weber*. New York: Oxford University Press.

Wilson, D.C. (1992). *A Strategy of Change*. London: Routledge.

2 Consultants and Change Agents

Julian Randall and Bernard Burnes

> **Learning Objectives**
>
> After studying the chapter, you should be able to:
> - Define the term 'consultant'
> - List the main forms of consultancy/consultant
> - Define the role of the consultant
> - Appreciate the role of the change agent and how this can differ from the role of the consultant
> - Explain the consultant–client relationship
> - Discuss how organizational politics impact on the consultant's role
> - State the key questions that a consultant needs to ask before committing to a change event

INTRODUCTION

In this chapter, we will look at some of the definitions that surround consultancy. What is management consultancy, anyway? Are all those claiming to be consultants doing the same sort of work? And how are they perceived by others who see them at work or come into their orbit through programmes of change?

It should be said at the outset that consultancy as an industry has grown over the last century. Just over a hundred years ago Frederick Winslow Taylor was advising Henry Ford on standardized working patterns for workers in car production and the search for efficiency improvement, consistent standards of production and technological advance has not slackened since then. Some people have claimed that Taylor advised Ford, but the evidence to support this is unclear. Indeed, Ford claimed that his system was different from Taylor's – it wasn't, but that's what he said. The fear of being left behind by the competition is a potent driver in all business sectors and managers working in an industry are often less confident that they know what the future patterns of work need to be to ensure that they stay at the forefront of the competition. When it comes to IT, for example, 'you don't know what you don't know' (Bloomfield and Danielli, 1995). So, it can help to bring in those who do know to show you how to implement new systems and demonstrate the benefits for your business.

Learning what other organizations have done and how they did it can give rise to fads and fashions (Collins, 2000). Managers don't want to be left behind and listening to what others say and reading upbeat accounts of change often stimulate the demand for direct help from an outside agency. Heusinkveld and Benders (2005) refer to this as 'commodification'. Consultants sell packages or products – examples would be Total Quality Management or Business Process Re-engineering. Sometimes those who are successful selling such ideas then become consultants in their own right, spreading the word and writing the books which influence managers to enquire about securing their help. So, for example, *In Search of Excellence* sold more copies worldwide than any previous management book and it projected one of its authors, Tom Peters, into the role of a worldwide speaker and management guru (Burnes, 2014).

But what role do consultants play in the organizations they work with? Though most consultants claim that they have their own systematic, tried and tested approaches to change, the reality is that they often have to depart from the *'script'* in order to get their job done. Leading consultants use terms such as *'grace'*, *'magic'* and *'miracles'* to describe these moments of creativity and inspiration (Lichtenstein, 1997). Hislop (2002: 658) reflects this in listing some of the metaphors used to describe consultants:

> *witchdoctors (Clark and Salaman, 1996a; Micklethwait and Woolridge, 1996); story tellers (Clark and Salaman, 1996b); performers (Clark, 1995; Clark and Salaman, 1995); magicians (Schuyt and Schuijt, 1998); seducers (Sturdy, 1998); religious leaders* (Huczynski, 1993)

None of these titles is particularly flattering and may suggest that there is a hidden agenda to consultancy which Fincham (1999) describes as 'an insidious power, unaccountable and unseen'. However, not all writers see it quite so bleakly. Kitay and Wright (2007) suggest that there are a wide range of consultants at work – many of them small consultancies or even sole proprietors. Their work can be wide-ranging and often embraces different roles. These can include, they suggest:

- Professional (in the sense of knowledge, skill and experience required by the project)
- Prophet (a visionary who can see the future needs which an industry may face)
- Partner (tailoring their services to the needs of the client)
- Business person (can manage themselves and the project both efficiently and effectively)
- Service worker (the client's needs change so the consultant needs to adapt and respond to such changes as they arise)

STOP AND REFLECT

- Where do you see consultancy fitting into these different definitions?
- Are your ideas based on previous experience of consultants?
- Describe your experiences
- Why do you think that researchers are sceptical about consultants' claims about their work?

Experience governs much of how we see our lives. How we evaluate events depends on our own assumptions of what is right and wrong, or good and bad. Also, we might add that the consultant's work usually takes place in the context of change – something that few people welcome and many actively resist. So, in a sense, it would be difficult for a consultant to come out of any change programme with totally positive approval ratings from all those involved.

If you have had an involvement with consultants during a programme of change then you will probably have had a chance of seeing them at work more closely. Again, this personal contact may have impressed you as either competent and committed or not. You may have reflected that much of the consultant's work is involved with top-down or imposed change, which can make it difficult to see them in a more thoughtful or discussive role. On the other hand, you may have come to appreciate the consultant's skills and expertise of a professional implementer or organizer, who had the ability to build bridges between individuals and groups and cope patiently and honestly with a sometimes hostile environment of doubt and suspicion.

Why researchers seem to have a sceptical view of consultants may be because they often research the sponsors of change programmes, 70% of which, it is sometimes suggested (Grint, 2005), fail to meet their objectives, rather than the providers, whose view may be that they had to embark on 'mission impossible'. Or perhaps it is, as Sturdy and colleagues (2009: 641) says, 'we still don't have a clear idea of what consultants and clients do jointly'.

We have decided in this book to complement the term 'consultant' with the term 'change agent' which we think more fairly expresses what change programmes require. Caldwell (2003) identifies four models of change agent:

- Leadership models, where change agents are senior managers
- Management models, where change agents are middle-level managers/functional specialists
- Consultancy models, where change agents are external or internal consultants who can be called on to operate at any level
- Team models, where change agents work in teams that operate at various levels in an organization

As can be seen, from Caldwell's perspective, there is a wider variety of internal change agents than external ones. This may be why there is a growing interest in the role of internal change agents, particularly in terms of the role that HR can play in the change process (Ruona and Gibson, 2004). Wright, for example, in his article 'Reinventing HRM: Business partners, internal consultants and the limits to professionalization' (2008), refers to the HR role as increasingly focused on a more strategic aspect required in most businesses. According to this account, the HR manager becomes a business partner whose role can include strategic partner, improving efficiency, ensuring employee engagement, and change advocate and agent. He suggests that HR 'need(s) to challenge accepted wisdom and raise taboos' (p. 1073) and promote 'boundary spanning activities/gaining senior management patronage' (p. 1074). He acknowledges that HR 'contains a disparate group of skills and experience' and asks whether these activities have made any difference to HR's professional status (p. 1076). More recent work reinforces the point that there is an increasing flow of consultants who take up management roles in internal change agent roles as well as appointments from within the organization (Sturdy et al., 2016). We will also offer in subsequent chapters the accounts of those who have undertaken this internal change agency work, several of whom, as Sturdy suggests, have had previous experience as external change agents prior to undertaking their internal change role. However, though the importance, range and number of internal change agents is growing, this appears to be on an ad hoc and fragmented basis. In most organizations, their recruitment, development and placement are often left to the individual functions and managers, with no attempt to co-ordinate the process. From the perspective of change effectiveness, development and learning, clearly this makes tracking what they do difficult. So, as the role and significance of change agents are increasingly becoming recognized, HR will need to take responsibility for co-ordinating their activities.

As discussed in Chapter 1, the most developed and applied approach to change is the OD model (Burnes, 2004, 2007, 2014). Certainly, there is strong evidence that the approach of Lewin and the OD community has been highly influential, even where the writers do not always use the term OD or acknowledge the source of their tools and techniques (Burnes and Cooke, 2012). In examining the origins and development of HRM, HRD and OD, Ruona and Gibson (2004) found that there are many similarities and overlaps. Indeed, many of the developmental tools used by HRM and HRD, such as employee surveys, team building, coaching and leadership development, can all be found in OD. In terms of current HR and OD concerns, both now focus on strategic issues linked to core competences; system design and transformation; organizational learning and culture; and radical innovation. This is why Ruona and Gibson (2004: 61) argue that:

Organisations are facing unprecedented challenges. They are increasingly forced to limit their costs, maximise their returns, and act strategically in an extremely complex, global society. Organisations need integrated and innovative solutions. The potential impact of HR is maximised by a more formally integrated HRM, HRD, and OD.

THE WORK OF CONSULTANCY

We can probably agree that consultation is concerned with advice (giving and receiving). This suggests that those seeking it want to find out more about their business and its underlying disciplines, and those giving it are thought to know more than those who seek that advice. O'Mahony and Markham (2013: 11) suggest that there are three different aspects to the consultant's work:

1. Identifying the problem – for example, company X's costs are too high
2. Researching and recommending a solution – for example, proposing the use of software Y instead of Z
3. Helping implement that solution – for example, building an IT system to automate the payroll function

The first aspect is sometimes referred to as diagnosis – the doctor's first task on being presented with a new patient. The second aspect is prescription. And finally, there is implementation. The authors suggest that consultants may be involved in any one or all of these aspects during a programme of change.

This offers a range of activities which may be strategic, giving advice at Board level, or a functional implementation of, say, an IT system.

So, what sort of consultancy might be involved in the following examples?

- Advising a company on which products it should launch in a new market
- Giving a friend advice on their start-up business
- Running an outsourced IT support function

Certainly, in the first example we might agree that a strategic level of advice is appropriate in this case. It would involve both diagnosis and prescription. It might also suggest that advice is being sought from an agency with experience in the new market involving ongoing work in making new contacts or supporting the business in the new field.

The second example is less clearly expressed but does suggest that the first aspect will be required – diagnosis. How far the advisor can go with prescription will depend on the relevance of their experience and expertise.

The third project at first suggests a functional job already decided by the customer, though most designers will usually want to discover a little more about the reasons the company want the database and what functions they need it to include. They might also want to hear what sort of budget the Bank has in mind to pay for this database.

STOP AND REFLECT

- Why do some firms seek to use internal rather than external consultants?
- Why are there international variations in the use of consultants?
- Why has the use of consultants increased over the years?
- Why are consultants more popular in some sectors, markets or countries than others?
- What role do history, culture and psychology play in the selection of consultants?

The first question could support several answers: the firms appreciate someone who understands and is part of the company culture; they are cheaper to employ than using outside consultants; they are easier to control as they part of the core staff or are on a consultancy contract controlled internally; only an insider would understand and appreciate the company's activities; or there is a need for security/official secrets are involved.

Local cultures have their own view of the value of using outsiders to solve problems or implement programmes of change. Consultancy goes down well in some societies where outside expertise is welcomed. The gauge of effective consultancy practice is networking and in some societies that network is part of the local culture.

Technology is a great driver of change in all organizations. The onset of social media and its impact on marketing and purchasing patterns would be a good example of these changes. So, for example, nearly 50% of Christmas shoppers buy their presents online. That is not to say that people don't browse in shops, but it does suggest that an effective, user-friendly website is essential for a retail business to create and sustain customer loyalty and sales. Consultancy is usually essential to remain in the forefront of such a technology-led initiative.

Organizations that are used to outside expertise need to have developed the skills of managing and negotiating contracts and monitoring their outcomes effectively. It is always clear when managers do not have these skills – the costs spiral and the goals are not met by the deadline.

There is a popular saying among salespeople that 'people buy from people they like'. This suggests that shared culture, shared expertise and previous experience – usually good – play an important part in how consultants are chosen.

IS THE CONSULTANT A MANAGER OR LEADER?

There is an ongoing debate which has endured as long as these two words have been current in the management dictionary. Peter Drucker used to make the distinction that the leader does the right thing, and the manager does things right. The distinction itself deserves further discussion.

Certainly, we would need to clarify the definition of each of the terms, before going further. For instance, are we talking about the ultimate leader (CEO) or anyone who exercises a leadership role in the organization? Similarly, is the definition of management the same as Mary Parker Follett's (1940), that management is getting things done through other people?

One question you may reflect on: Have you ever had a manager from whom you expected no leadership? Similarly, have you ever had a leader who could not manage? The answer to the first question is usually no. To the second question, if those leaders were unable to manage themselves and their business, they would rapidly lose the respect of those who work for them.

So, the short answer to the question is probably that the roles of manager and leader do overlap – regardless of the individual's job title. Management of others does require leadership (on occasion) and leadership requires someone who can demonstrate that they can manage – certainly themselves and then the company, through its people.

Now look at the role of the consultant and ask the same question: Is the consultant a manager or a leader? Here are some questions that may help you to decide:

STOP AND REFLECT

- Is the consultant a manager?
- Can the consultant give orders to the company's staff?
- What is the consultant's relationship with the staff?
- What is the consultant's relationship with senior managers?
- What status do consultants have in the company they are working with?
- How should the consultant exercise leadership?

Clearly, if by manager we mean someone who exercises management responsibility for others then in that sense the answer would be no. If, however, we have been delegated to conduct, say, training sessions, then at that point the management engaging us would reasonably expect us to exercise the care and responsibility that a reasonable manager would be expected to do.

There will be occasions when our instructions are reasonable and need to be observed by staff we are working with. So, for example, if you are on your own with a group and the fire alarm sounds, you will be expected to evacuate the staff as any responsible manager would be expected to do.

The third question is a difficult one and is negotiated almost moment to moment as we get to know people and work with them more closely on a change programme. Then our relationship will change and develop over time as trust hopefully develops between us.

With senior managers, we are respectful and aware that they are commissioning us to conduct a change programme on their behalf. But there is a balance to be struck between being friendly and the danger of indulging in informal feedback (which is sometimes sought), reflecting on things we have been told by other staff. Discretion is needed to strike this difficult balance effectively.

Leadership is expected of the consultant where a group or individual requires support or clarification on matters pertaining to the change programme we are responsible for. Added to which, the change agent is expected to be a role model and in that sense a leader of the change at all times.

THE CONTEXT OF CHANGE

As we mentioned in Chapter 1, change is rarely a welcome prospect and individuals will have their own reasons for experiencing doubt that all will turn out well for them at the end of the change programme. The fact that strangers are brought in to conduct the change is itself a message that managers are entrusting decisions about the future to outsiders and that those outsiders are unlikely to know of the previous efforts individuals have made for the company during their working careers. Particularly during mergers there will be fears that the dominant company will be seeking to make savings and those savings will mean cuts – probably to jobs. So, fears about change are reasonable to hold by those subjected to change.

What we observe, then, is not just uncertainty about the process of change, but uncertainty about the psychological contract. This concept included a distinction between two elements:

Transactional:

- Money
- Time
- Terms and conditions

Relational:

- Loyalty
- Trust

(Macneil, 1985)

Change programmes can often involve redundancy, job loss and career termination and the impact will affect both elements for those affected. What was also noted in the job insecurity literature is that this will affect those who stay even though they still have a job themselves. After all, if they can do this to my friends and colleagues, they can do it to me. So, for those remaining, there can still be a loss of loyalty and trust and also a sense that fellow workers, who should have stayed, were chosen to go in an arbitrary or unfair way (Hallier and Lyon, 1996).

Consultants and Change Agents   31

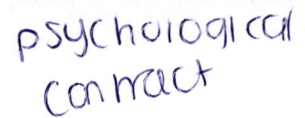

During change programmes, there can be a feeling that all is not what was expected by individuals or groups when they joined or started work at the company and this can give rise to ambiguity: I can see why change has to happen, perhaps, but I am still uncomfortable about it and how it is implemented, and I may need to make some decisions about my own future career. Ambiguity arises when what was expected is now overturned by events and this can lead to ambivalence.

Piderit (2000) suggests that ambivalence can involve what she describes as three levels:

- Cognitional – I don't think I understand this need for change
- Emotional – I don't feel comfortable with this change
- Intentional – I would certainly be inclined to … (leave, move…)

Change can be rationalized at the cognitive level (this change could have been predicted), but that does not mean to say that it is acceptable at a personal level. My feelings about the change may conflict with my theoretical acceptance of the need for change (I didn't like the way things were done).

Added to this there can be a measure of surprise at the way change was handled (Louis, 1980). I never expected that to happen; I am surprised that a professional company would do something like that … Louis refers to this as either confirmed or disconfirmed basic assumptions. Such assumptions can be deeply held beliefs or norms which are part of the company culture. But their violation leads to surprise and requires sense-making (Weick, 1995).

So, the challenge of change can give rise to internal conflict and to surprise, say, that managers have decided to take the action of calling in consultants rather than conducting the change themselves – perhaps they want to avoid the criticism that they have had to reduce the workforce by deflecting the blame onto outsiders. If it gives rise to disconfirmed basic assumptions that may evoke feelings of shame or blame towards managers (Tracy and Robins, 2006).

Faced by external threat individuals are then faced with two questions:

- What is the threat that I face?
- What can I do about it?

(Lazarus and Folkman, 1984)

Surprise at the unexpected can trigger sense-making, in which individuals seek to explain to themselves and others what is happening around them. Weick suggests that:

- People create plausible explanations – what seems reasonable to them
- People interpret what they experience and ascribe meanings and derive values
- These explanations enable them to explain the significance of what is happening to them

(Weick, 1995)

Already before the consultants have appeared and spoken to them, previous experience of poorly handled change may be the background for misunderstanding, confusion and scepticism about the claims that consultants make about themselves and their work.

For all workers, the challenge of change can give rise to reservations about what I may be asked to do. Will it fit in with my professional role as I have known it and experienced it to date, or am I going to be asked to do things differently in the future? This is referred to as Identity, which it is suggested is the answer to two questions:

- Who am I?
- Who ought I to be?

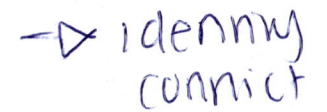

(Corley and Gioia, 2004)

As a professional I expect to do things in a certain way – the way we have been trained and the way we expect to be treated at work. Is this going to be changed now to something different which will affect my professional status? So, for example, customs officers who were used to conducting inspection visits to businesses to check on their tax claims found themselves asked to conduct 'educational visits' instead. For older officers, such a change was resisted and led to avoidance and reinterpreting the management directive (Randall and Procter, 2008).

We mention these aspects as the context of change so that it is clear that even before their arrival, consultants can expect audiences that are less than reassured by their arrival; uncertain of the future; and suspicious of those brought in to implement the change.

CONSULTANT AND CLIENT RELATIONS

Before going into a client meeting what should the consultant prepare? Discuss how you would clarify your position.

> **STOP AND REFLECT**
>
> - Whose side is the consultant on?
> - How should the consultant sympathize with those affected by change?
> - How should the consultant deal with concerns and objections?
> - Should the consultant give their own accounts of change experience?
> - Should the consultant promise positive outcomes for the change?

The easy answer would be to say that you are neutral. Unfortunately, you may not be perceived that way. It is likely that you will be considered, in the first instance at least, as a tool of senior management – after all they did ask you to come in, presumably. And they are paying you more money on your day rate than most staff receive in their salaries. Certainly, you are likely to be treated with some reserve and there will be a period of testing during which staff will seek to find out what your views are about issues that they are concerned about.

This brings us to the second question. How should you sympathize with others affected by change? Well, calling on your own experience would be a useful place to start. Most people have experienced job insecurity of one kind of another. So, you will understand what that feels like. Then there is communication. People like to know what is going to happen and how soon. So, work out with your sponsor what can be revealed and ensure that as far as possible no confusion occurs through unnecessary delay. Vacuums in communication simply lead to rumours, uncertainty and speculation.

The standard approach to concerns and objections is to accept them. Acknowledge them openly and discuss their implications where possible. As with all questions there are three possible ways of dealing with them:

- Honesty (say, if you don't know something)
- Deferral (use realistic deadline and dates: 'we should know that by...')
- Avoidance (to be used when confronted in a way that puts your integrity at risk)

Telling your own stories is a difficult dilemma. Most people do not want to hear what others have been through, still less listen to improving stories with allegedly happy endings. Your own experiences should only be divulged where they are directly relevant to the question you have been asked to address and can be supported by evidence.

The final question follows on from the previous one. No, if we cannot offer the guarantees that staff are often looking for then suggesting that there would be a positive outcome would probably be unwise and counterproductive.

But what of the responses of your clients? One regularly quoted stage model of transition includes the steps:

- **Denial** – carrying on as if nothing is wrong
- **Anger** – frustration and resentment
- **Bargaining** – acknowledging the situation, attempting to gain more time
- **Depression** – mourning for things lost and lost prospects
- **Acceptance** – preparing to move forward

It should be said that this model was developed by a doctor, Kubler-Ross (1969), based on her work with those dying of conditions with little or no chance of healing or remission. The author accepted that there were many other outcomes and that the journey to acceptance was not always as obvious as the model might suggest. However, what it does do is alert us to the possible change to emotional states, which those undergoing change can experience. However, we should note that acceptance may not be the ultimate outcome.

What does merit more attention is the bargaining or negotiation which is mentioned. Here there is an option which consultants must be ready to act on when opportunity arises. It may be that deadlines can be changed and that the way the programme is structured can be varied to suit the needs of those undergoing it. Such positive suggestions would be worth encouraging and working to resolve and even lead to trust developing between consultant and clients. It is part of Bullock and Batten's Exploration phase (Bullock and Batten, 1985; see also Chapter 1).

There are some positive interventions that may offer opportunities to build on goodwill. These include:

- Reassuring employees that it is normal to experience emotional responses during change
- Allowing the display of emotion (absorb, accept, and reflect)
- Exploring the basis of bargaining/negotiation
- Encouraging people to move on into the future
- Assessing and reinforcing the benefits of change
- Accepting that different people may take different times to adjust to change
- Encouraging managers to accept the role of support for staff

It is worth remembering that there are three aspects of what we put across to others:

- **Features** (details often factual which relate to the programme)
- **Advantages** (notice this may be the opinion of the promotors of the change – others may remain to be convinced)
- **Benefits** (what it really offers those who are to experience the change programme)

The last point is important and it is worth engaging senior staff to be present at all crucial meetings of staff – especially at the launch of the change programme. It is then that questions are often asked about the future – and staff need clear answers from members of senior management rather than this being left to an external consultant to answer.

So, how would you deal with the following challenges?

- Promises that have not been kept by managers/consultants in the past
- Aggression or anger from staff
- Being ignored by staff
- Being rejected by staff

The first situation is difficult, but it is likely to come the way of most consultants at some point. Remaining loyal to the managers will be important, if the consultancy is to be effective. So, while not rushing to judgement, it should be possible to check out any such claims and then decide how to respond once the facts are clear. This may sometimes happen if constraints on the budget mean that promised or expected resources have not been provided when promised.

All decisions are uncertain in their outcomes – especially about job security. So, make sure that people are made aware of the likely outcomes before embarking on any change activities. Deferred announcements about closing down branches or altering job descriptions need to be addressed clearly and honestly.

The consultant can accept, listen and be supportive but should beware of offering to be a messenger to senior management. Encouraging those involved to make a direct approach themselves is a more prudent plan – though advice on putting together a diplomatic intervention will usually be appreciated.

The final three challenges are always possible in a consultancy situation. If they happen, remember that people are free to speak or not, as they wish. The consultant is mature, assertive and accepting of dissent or disapproval. Staff have a right not to engage with the consultant socially if they don't want to. It is their choice.

COPING STRATEGIES CONSULTANTS USE

How far might the following coping strategies be useful in dealing with confrontation?

- Emotional distancing – avoiding compassion/expressing other feelings
- Telling oneself that harsh outcomes are normal in the context of change events
- Denying that injury can be caused to those affected by change
- Physically distancing oneself
- Dealing with redundancies in a business-like fashion with minimal interaction with those affected

It is sometimes suggested that medical professionals use the first strategy to ensure their mind is always on the job, which they must concentrate on without distraction. In that case, it is self-evident that such detachment is vital for the progress of the patient. Apart from such instances, however, distancing would not seem to be a useful strategy if the consultant is to win goodwill.

As long as telling oneself that disruption is inevitable does not lead to becoming careless or thoughtless about the impact of change, then that may be a way of rationalizing the inevitable. However, it should not lead to any apparent lack of empathy when dealing with those affected.

Denial is always a negative strategy and is best avoided.

It is always a good strategy to work for loyalty and trust with others, whoever they are.

Physical distancing or avoiding others is not a good idea: ours is an interactive role with people and we need their co-operation to be successful.

Being factual is important. However, appreciation of impact on those who have to come to terms with those facts should encourage supportiveness and care.

So, finally, as a consultant can you undertake the following tasks?

- Make announcements on behalf of managers about changes in terms and conditions?
- Express your own views about the justice of what is being proposed during the change?
- Agree to act as a spokesperson to managers on behalf of the staff?
- Act as a go-between for aggrieved parties?
- Suggest outcomes to company problems?

Certainly, this would not be advisable on any account. This is a matter that must come from the company's representative – as must issues of pay or any changes to the employment contract. This is yet another reason for senior managers to be involved in meetings early on.

You will be asked early on in open staff groups whether this is likely. Deferral is a reasonable response: 'that is not a matter that I can comment on. It is the company's right to discuss such matters with you.'

If you are asked whether you agree with something the company has decided, be careful before you make a comment. You might be better off using an avoidance strategy: 'what I think is less important than what you believe. This is your company and your culture, and it is important that such matters are resolved here.'

The answer is no (politely). That is not your role. Encourage complainants to go directly to their manager or HR with such messages.

This is not usually wise. Do not broker one-to-one meetings between those with personal issues. If there is a need for advice then a steer towards HR would be advisable.

You could say that that is what you are there for. But any decisions you come to should be included only in your final presentation and report.

In short, the role of the consultant is to make it easy for other people to succeed during a change programme. There is a word for this: **Facilitator**.

So, remember the following hints in trying to achieve that:

- The change agent is there to make it easy for people to succeed
- So show you listen and understand
- Explore positive prospects for the future after change
- Gain commitment for the work of change
- Inspire confidence in the benefits of change

Do all these things and you will be successful; later in the book we will discuss techniques to achieve this and hear from those who have had to do this in their working lives as change agents.

POSITIVE RESPONSES

What can the consultant/change agent do to encourage positive responses? Here are some suggestions:

- Reassure those who experience emotional reaction to change
- Absorb, accept and reflect on concerns and objections
- Encourage and support negotiation
- Reinforce the benefits of change
- Accept that people take their own time to adapt to change events
- Encourage managers to support their staff during change

The above suggestions would favour an open approach to the responses received from groups when the change agent first encounters them. Advice for dealing with concerns and objections always states:

Accept the concern and objection (at very least the thoughts and feelings are genuine and should be respected for that reason alone).

The third point is subtler and alerts us to the prospect that even disagreements can indicate some room for negotiation and manoeuvre, which may be useful to refer to and work on later as the change plan unfolds.

Most managers who have conducted any interviews with staff know that exploring future prospects are always more positive than focusing on the past. Though, in the face of change, the past can sometimes look secure in comparison with an immediately uncertain future.

Adjustment times for people will obviously vary but taking them into account at the outset will usually indicate to your audience that you are reasonable and supportive.

This final point is vital to you as a change agent, so:

- Never allow managers to escape the responsibility they have to step forward and be part of the programme.
- Always be suspicious of senior managers who want to pay you to run a programme of change while staying away themselves. This always gives the worst of all messages (this is nothing to do with us) as it allows them to hide behind the excuse that any redundancies were the decision of the change agents alone.

So, change agents must be ready to accept that not all interventions will be positive. For many organizations, change has been a constant in people's lives. This can give rise to a weariness which makes engagement in a positive way more difficult to achieve. One typical example would be:

I've worked for this company for more than 10 years and I've seen it all. I can't say it makes me feel motivated or interested in what's going on in the company. You know, there is always something new that has to be done and something old that should be thrown out. But most of it is just boring talk and I don't have much interest in that kind of talk any longer. I have heard it all before. How do I feel about it? Nothing, really – just fatigue. (Qtd. in Frost and Robinson, 1999: 120)

How would you deal with such an intervention?

It is difficult without asking the person to expand on the details – and that could take some time; and if the intervention takes place in a group it could seriously detract you from achieving your objectives within the time available. But if you feel that this can be usefully probed and that someone is talking on behalf of the group, then you might find it worthwhile to be encouraging. This will also avoid any accusations that you ignored the comment, thus appearing unsympathetic.

The lessons of Emotional Intelligence suggest that we should:

- Accurately perceive emotion
- Use emotion to facilitate effective thinking
- Understand emotion in oneself and others
- Cope positively with emotions in oneself and others

Think for a moment of how you might achieve each of these objectives.

Referring to emotion can sometimes be a way of releasing tension in a group. So acknowledging in your own words what it is you are hearing and asking whether that is a fair summary of what has just been offered to you is one way of doing this ('You sound aggrieved about that. Would that be a fair comment?').

The second point could be explored by asking a follow up question to probe the basis of the feeling ('Why do you think that is?').

Putting yourself in the other person's position is always a good strategy. It demonstrates empathy and should encourage patience.

This is a difficult verb to use as 'cope' suggests that we proactively do something to intervene in another's emotions. But one way might be to defer the meeting while emotions calm.

All of the above suggests that the facilitator should get used to using the following skills:

- **P** – probe
- **L** – listen
- **O** – observe
- **D** – decide
- Make it easy for people to succeed

Rosemary Stewart (1985, 1991), after many years of researching what makes managers effective, came to the conclusion that 75% of what managers do is intuitive. By that I think she meant not that managers guess what the right thing to do is but that they use their intuition to assess what is going on in the people around them before making a judgement about what is the appropriate action to take in response to what they hear and see going on around them.

POLITICS AND CHANGE

This brings us to the contentious question of how far politics should be engaged in as a management strategy.

First, what is management politics? Here are two definitions:

- Organizational politics exploits unofficial networks and contacts to achieve personal gain
- Organizational politicking involves engaging in activities to acquire, develop, retain and use power, in order to obtain your preferred outcomes in a situation where there is uncertainty or disagreement

Which of these can I use as a consultant?

Of the first definition we might agree that 'personal gain' is not something that the consultant or change agent should be guilty of. Ours is not a popularity-seeking role and seeking political influence with or over others would put us in a poor light as neither honest nor trustworthy.

But what of the second? We will be responsible for the success of the change programme once it starts. So, can we use behind-the-scenes influence to gain advantage over those who seek, say, to obstruct us? Perhaps we should alter the word 'power' here to 'influence', based on negotiation and reason. The problem with behind the scenes interventions is that they rarely remain under wraps for very long and then political manoeuvring will be revealed with equivalent loss of face to the consultant's image as an honest operator.

There are those who will point out that there can be benefits to political manoeuvring:

- Accelerates change – though proponents of this theory do not say why
- Stimulates debate – certainly – but is that always beneficial?
- Critical source of dynamic energy – but is it positive energy?
- Keeps conversation about change 'in play' – it certainly does that but not always in a beneficial way
- Recognition and achievement for the change agent – again this may not always put us in a good light
- Increases involvement of political players – which might have been avoided, had they not been tempted to become involved.

And the downside to politics:

- It absorbs energy that could be better used elsewhere
- Power brokers advance their own cause, while others lose out
- It creates a climate of mistrust and suspicion – and this can rebound on the change agent

- It distracts from organizational goals
- It is an unproductive use of resources
- It excludes people unable to play politics

Change agents might be better employed applying themselves to the job in hand – which is promoting the change programme openly and honestly, and ensuring that misunderstandings, so often triggered by politics, are avoided.

So, remaining positive becomes the focus of the change agent's role:

Increasing commitment

1. Communication: tell people what is going on
2. Participation and involvement: get people involved in the change process from the outset
3. Education and support: help staff see it from the organization's viewpoint
4. Negotiation and agreement: similar to step 2
5. Problem finding (often co-operation)
6. Role modelling (be the change you want to promote)
7. Changing reward structures (often overlooked – but what is in it for those who take part?)
8. Manipulation and co-optation (getting the reluctant to get involved)
9. Explicit and implicit coercion (ensuring that obstructiveness is dealt with before it corrodes goodwill)

Getting agreement

The effective change agent then calls on the positive intervention skills of the diplomat. Rackham and Morgan (1978) offer the choice of several positive interventions:

- Proposer (moving on stalled debates positively)
- Building (responding to and referring to others' ideas)
- Suggesting (tentative offers of ways for moving on)
- Objective/neutral bystander
- Summarizer (reminding groups where they are and moving the debate forward)

Supportive learning environment

- Make it safe to be open about one's views, ask questions and own up to mistakes
- Value different viewpoints (accept concerns and objections before modifying them)
- Be open to new ideas (write them up to show you accept them)
- Take time for reflection (no rush: sleep on it)

Concrete learning processes

- Set up formal, systematic and clear processes for generation, collection, interpretation and dissemination of information
- Encourage experimentation with new products and services
- Get people involved with intelligence gathering
- Identify and solve problems
- Focus on future education and training

So, how can the change agent offer leadership behaviour that reinforces learning? Consider the following suggestions and explore how you might implement these:

- They actively question and listen to others, prompting dialogue and debate
- They show they value different viewpoints and time spent on identifying and solving problems
- They inspire others by their own positive behaviour and beliefs
- They are prophetic and visionary about the future

So, the first meeting with staff groups needs to be facilitated with care. Use open questions. A useful one is:

What are the five challenges that the organization faces over the next two years?

Write up all answers offered from the floor. If you use a flip chart you can keep the sheets for future reference and evaluation at the end of the change programme. This should also demonstrate to the group that you are addressing the second point of valuing different viewpoints and spending time on identifying problems.

The second task to follow up with is:

Put the five challenges in order of priority.

As we have seen, this should cause some discussion and even dissent within the group.

The point of this session is both to inspire the group with the openness of the facilitator and to provide them with an opportunity to explore their own aspirations.

Finally, the prophetic and visionary aspect should be encouraged. The change agent can hopefully draw on their own experience of successful change and how it can change the way people think about what they are going to do in the future.

All of this should enable the change agent to begin to pin down action points for the future. In summary:

- Review the past
- Explore the present
- Create future scenarios
- Identify common ground between all parties
- Create action plans

All of this addresses the first of Bullock and Batten's phases in successful change:

Exploration.

EXPLORING THE ROLE OF INTERNAL CHANGE AGENTS

As we said at the beginning of this chapter, there is more emphasis being paid to the role of the internal change agents in promoting and supporting change in organizations. This is in part because more consultants are apparently joining core staff in companies and being used for their previous experience and skills. But there is less attention paid to the role that the internal agent can play working with external change agents and, indeed, how important their role is in continuing to keep the momentum of change going once the external change agents have left at the end of the formal change programme (Sturdy et al., 2016).

In this book, many of the chapters have been contributed by authors who have been internal change agents or have exercised both internal and external change agent roles during their careers as change agents. Their accounts touch on the work that they have been involved with and they reflect on the issues that they have had to try and address in their change agency roles. The rest of this chapter will seek to explore some of the approaches the change agent needs to adopt to achieve change and the skills and knowledge required to be successful.

PARTICIPATIVE CHANGE AND THE CHANGE AGENT

We have already mentioned our own preference for emergent or bottom-up change, rather than imposed or top-down change. As Bullock and Batten (1985) demonstrate, the Exploration phase before a change programme is embarked upon and the implementation phase at the end of the formal programme are often neglected and this can lead to higher levels of dissatisfaction than are acknowledged in the change management literature.

We have also seen that a realistic attempt to analyse why change often triggers resistance can be seen in Nadler's work. Nadler (1993) suggests that the fears that traditionally surround the prospect of change can be proactively addressed by structuring the change programme into three different steps:

- **Motivate change**
- **Manage the transition**
- **Shape the political dynamics**

Taking each step at a time, we can break them down into subsections. So, for **motivating change**, ask yourself, as an external change agent, how you might approach each of these factors:

- Surface dissatisfaction with the present state
- Gain participation in change
- Reward behaviours supporting change
- Disengage at the right time

From the outset, it should be simple to achieve the first, given that most people have a ready ability to say what they do not like. However, in the change management context perhaps that is not always as easy as it appears. Certainly, where people feel they can speak frankly, such openness may be feasible. But with a meeting run by a consultant paid for by the management that might be considered by staff as a career-limiting intervention to make.

This leads us to the second point: if we are to gain participation then we need to be careful how we brief the group about our objectives. For that reason, change agents may find it easier to speak in general terms about the threats to the sector; the challenges faced in the future; and the responses needed to counter those challenges.

The initial meeting may reveal that there are some who are confident and informed in their views and unafraid to speak out frankly. This may be the first time that potential internal change agents come to the attention of the external change agent. As we know, having ideas accepted is itself a reward – so this is yet another reason for writing up ideas offered and building on them – always referring back to the person who made the original contribution to check their acceptance.

Pitching a discussion into the future is itself a way of concentrating on the positive features of a situation and avoiding the tendency to indulge in nostalgia about the past. Similarly, opportunities to talk informally are also a good investment. Time spent in reconnaissance is seldom wasted and individuals may be more inclined to speak frankly at their workstation both about their job and the future prospects of the organization.

How much time to spend on these activities of what Lewin referred to as the unfreezing stage will be a matter of judgement, which only experience can bring, taking into account the constraints of time and budget for exploratory meetings.

MANAGING THE TRANSITION

How would you deal with the suggested steps here?

- Develop and communicate a clear image of the future
- Use multiple and consistent leverage points
- Develop organizational arrangements to support the transition
- Build in feedback mechanisms

The first point could be a difficult one to be frank about without relevant experience and honesty. This is where internal change agents may have an advantage. Most groups are suspicious of outsiders coming in to manage a change programme. A group of doctors, for example, will usually ask, 'Are you a doctor?' Most consultants cannot offer the credibility of direct and current experience and the outsider's credibility in front of such a specialist audience will therefore be reduced. So, finding among the group those who have previous experience of change and are confident to speak about it positively could be a useful investment later on in running the change programme.

Leverage points are usually associated with rewards which are available for those whom you want to engage successfully in change. Most people, for example, are interested in continuing professional development. So, involvement in the change programme may enhance their experience and develop the portfolio of skills and knowledge that they can offer in the future. Being trained to conduct training or development activities can similarly be seen as a benefit, which can be used to enhance career prospects following the change programme.

Finding the best way to embark on change will be important in its implementation. One way may be visits to sites where such programmes of change have been implemented successfully in the past. People are more likely to believe what fellow workers say than listening to the words of a consultant, however experienced they may be.

Involving willing staff as internal change agents can also mean that there is a built-in feedback mechanism independent of the traditional management hierarchy. This will come into its own once the final phase of the change is embarked upon – **implementation**. We need to ensure that when the external change agents have left there will be others in the change team who will be staying to ensure that the change is supported and evaluated over the long term.

SHAPE THE POLITICAL DYNAMICS

Finally, how would you address the following items?

- Ensure the support of key power groups
- Use leadership behaviour to support the change
- Use symbols and language to create energy
- Build in stability

We have already mentioned the importance of involving the management team, especially the CEO. It may be that there are unions or professional associations involved in the workforce, too, and thought should be given to ensuring that they are fully aware of what is planned during the change programme. Trying to manage a programme of change without important influencers onside is a recipe for misunderstanding which is best avoided.

Two things are important: making sure that the opening and closing sessions of the change programme include a prominent role for the CEO or change promotor. Questions about the company's policy particularly on employment and possible redundancy will usually come up and they should be answered by the senior person in the organization – not a consultant.

Secondly, symbols of change can be important in organizations that want to change a culture (the way we do things round here). So, for example, the arrangements for named car parking slots and separate dining rooms and canteens for different status of staff were immediately addressed by Japanese companies who recruited staff from traditionally run companies. It brought home to workers that there were now different attitudes to status and reward in the new company, demonstrably different from the old way of doing things (Wickens, 1987).

Finally, stability here does not mean lack of change. It does mean adhering to the programme of change; committing to promised outcomes; and assuring people that notice of change will always be given before it is implemented.

A USEFUL CHECKLIST

What people know about their own company's situation is always enlightening for the change agent running exploratory events within interdisciplinary groups to discover. We can divide this knowledge between inner and outer contexts of change:

Inner context:

- History of the organization
- Structure
- Culture
- Politics

Outer context:

- Competition
- Customer demand
- Technology
- Innovation

(Pettigrew, 1987)

STOP AND REFLECT

- What sort of questions could you ask that might reveal what is known about each of the topics?

The history of the organization will depend on how long the company has been in existence and how many long-serving people there are in your audience. In some instances, individuals may be more interested in their own discipline than they are in the organization and for that reason they tend to move on when career opportunities occur (doctors and academics are professions that come to mind here). On the other hand, those who see the organization as a calling as well as a career may be very knowledgeable and also proud of the historical achievements of the past.

Structural change might be a useful way into this topic. Some organizations are very rank conscious (Civil Service and Police come to mind). So, how often have such changes been visited on the organization (and were outside change agents involved in this)? Change has been a regular occurrence in most industries, and it would be unusual for individuals and groups to have no views on their experience.

Culture is more difficult to broach directly, in the main because popular definitions of the term are diverse and there can be as many views as there are people. In interdisciplinary groups, it is also more difficult to receive a single message and for different disciplines there will be different ways of 'the way we do things round here'. It may be better to learn initially by walking about, informal visits and speaking to people in the workplace.

Politics is another difficult subject to raise, largely for the reasons that we mentioned in the previous topic, culture. If we are talking about politics as the behind-the-scenes manipulation of other people, then it will definitely not be possible to raise it directly. A question about how the company deals with problems may, however, be useful to start from. People have strong views about whether issues are addressed directly or alternatively overlooked or avoided by members of management.

As to the outer context, this is more significant in some ways, because it indicates how far people in the organization see themselves in comparison with others. Most people have strong views about the competition, and salespeople in particular will be knowledgeable about the detail of what is offered by them and sometimes dismissive of the company's own ability to compete effectively. In contrast production are usually convinced that what they produce is the best and that there are other reasons why products may not be selling as well as people had hoped (such as that their salespeople aren't highlighting the appropriate features of the product or service).

Customer demand might well start with how many people actually use the company's product or services. It is always interesting to discover how much people know of the views outsiders have of them and that may well be a question worth raising.

Technology and innovation often go hand-in-hand. So, you can raise them together, particularly if you are asking the question about the challenges the company faces over the next two years. It is the future that determines how far a business will survive and flourish and effectiveness is gauged by how far the end-user is satisfied with what is available to them. How many in your audience are aware of this as the driver for their survival in their marketplace?

Quinn (1980: 51) has a useful list of factors that he thinks are important in being responsive to groups and individuals throughout the life of the change programmes:

- Sensing needs (I get the sense that you disagree with that...)
- Amplify understanding (Tell me more about that...)
- Building awareness (From what you say it would seem that you feel strongly about that – do you want to expand on that?)
- Creating credibility (I think most people in your position would feel that, too)
- Legitimizing viewpoints (What you say makes perfect sense. However, ...)
- Generating potential solutions (Suppose we were to...)
- Broadening support (How many of you would agree with this?)
- Identifying indifference and opposition (You don't seem very impressed by what's been said so far. Why is that?)

Most change agents would probably agree that the interactive parts of their role are among the most demanding but also the most satisfying part of their job. Dealing with live audiences is always exciting and challenges all the talents that the change agent can call on – including humour. Finding a level with an audience requires maximum concentration. Presentation skills are a small part of this. However, it is the interactive question and answer sessions that follow which are the gauge of skill, experience and attitude.

So how would you deal with the following needs?

- Change perceived risks
- Structure necessary flexibility
- Put forward trial concepts
- Create pockets of commitment
- Eliminate undesirable options
- Crystalize consensus
- Manage coalitions

It may help to refer to the list of interventions that lead to positive outcomes:

- Proposing
- Building
- Suggesting
- Objective/neutral bystander
- Summarizing

Modifying what people feel about risk must be one of the most difficult tasks for the change agent. Most companies want their staff to become more involved in the customer side of the business and there are those who find that uncomfortable and would rather be involved with routine, functional tasks. Training will be important but so also will support and reward. Change rarely endures unless there is a long-term strategy that supports it. It may be that internal change agents who have had experience and are enthusiastic may be the best proposers of this kind of change.

We do well to recap on the four types of **flexibility**:

- Time
- Number
- Cost
- Functional

Any changes here could involve amending the employment contract. This could have important consequences to individuals not just in their work but also in their domestic arrangements as well. The more radical such changes are, the more likely it is that there will be some people who are unwilling or unable to embark on such change confidently or at all. We need to think carefully about dealing with the likely options before raising such issues.

Putting forward trial concepts might well be a good place to begin. And it is better to offer more than one option as different opinions arise from discussion – which is a good way to discover who is willing and able to undertake change and who is not.

Creating pockets of commitment will mean building. It may also suggest syndicate or working in sub-groups who would probably work together on something they had expressed an interest in. This is the beginning of evidence of aptitude or ability which can be built upon. And, as we said, positive, responsive individuals may make good internal change agents once trained and working with the external change agents.

Getting people working with groups with whom they share interests may also help answer the last three questions. They become themselves pockets of commitment; they help eliminate negative opinion; they crystalize consensus; and they help you manage coalitions (in other words they may manage themselves – useful after the external change agents have left).

THE ROLE OF THE INTERNAL CHANGE AGENT

The importance of this role cannot be overestimated if external change agents want the programme to succeed after they have gone. It is also important if a serious attempt is to be made at evaluation.

Be clear about the distinction between validation and evaluation:

Validation tests whether individuals can do what they are now required to do in their changed role.

Evaluation seeks to establish what difference this has made to the end-user and the business that serves them.

So, choosing internal change agents is important for the success of any change programme. Here are some of the qualities which it is suggested you look for in likely candidates:

- Sensitivity
- Clarity
- Flexibility
- Team building
- Networking
- Tolerance of ambiguity
- Communication skills
- Interpersonal skills
- Personal enthusiasm
- Motivation and commitment
- Selling
- Negotiation
- Practical awareness
- Influencing skills
- Helicopter perspective

(Buchanan and Boddy, 1992)

Take each quality and assess how far the personnel profile of knowledge, skill, experience and attitude apply to each quality (you may choose more than one).

There is a well-known saying among professional trainers that you cannot change attitudes by training. So, remember that training can increase knowledge; it can develop skills; it can enhance experience; but there are some factors in the above list which individuals either have or they do not (and training might make very little difference to their performance).

Finally, we can minimize resistance by remembering the following guidelines:

- Participants feel the project is their own (not imposed from without, therefore emergent change)
- Project has wholehearted support from the top (CEO attends opening and closing sessions with staff)
- Participants see change as reducing their present burdens (what's in it for them...)
- Projects accord with values/ideas of participants
- Project offers new experience which interests participants
- Participants feel their autonomy and security are not threatened
- Proponents are able to empathize with opponents
- Provision is made for feedback during the project
- Participants experience acceptance, support, trust and confidence between each other
- Project remains open to revision and accommodation to amendment

(Watson, 1966)

TYING IN CHANGE WITH FUTURE SUCCESS

Changing a culture is often cited as the reason for embarking on change programmes. Those who have attempted to achieve that know just how difficult this can be to achieve in practice. So, integrating change into the daily HR development of the organization will need to be addressed so that we are focused on achieving the change realistically. Here is a list of the interventions that all individuals working for organizations experience:

- Recruitment and selection
- Induction training
- Supervision
- Management/review
- Appraisal and reward
- Development
- Organizational structure
- **Communication**

Take each topic and ask what sort of change might be required by the company to achieve successful cultural change in the long-term.

The **selection criteria** used to advertise for recruits to the organization need to be carefully considered along with the standards which you expect people to meet in their daily performance. During the interview the questions asked and the evidence of previous performance sought need to mirror the chosen criteria closely.

Induction training is essential in all organizations. But just how formulaic is it? How far does it address the important behaviours that the organization now depends on? What happens to those who fail to meet up to the standards required?

Are **supervisors** trained to develop others coming up through the organization? Will they be confident to mentor or coach those in need of extra support to achieve the new standards? Are they good at giving feedback and sympathetic to those who struggle to learn new skills?

Management/review. How often do line managers review work lives and career development? What sort of records are kept of ongoing performance? Who holds and reviews those records?

How thorough are **appraisals** in the organization? What action is taken on suggestions for improvement and positive requests for training and support? How far does HR review the performance of appraisers and the performance of their departments on such matters as intermittent absence; staff turnover; low productivity? (Does HR conduct exit interviews on those who have left us?)

Who monitors **wage levels** in the organization? Are outside agencies involved? Is it dealt with during the appraisal or at a separate time?

Development. How seriously does the organization take **continuing professional development**? Is time off/financial support available for those who want to improve their skills outside of the work time? Do we encourage staff to keep a personal development plan?

Does the **organizational structure** facilitate upward communication; ideas sharing; brain storming; away days; suggestions schemes?

All of the above interventions are part of overall communication between the staff and the company. After change programmes, internal change agents will be important in monitoring how far these interventions have changed the company for the better. This is an important part of **evaluation** and after the external change agents have left it is unlikely to continue without internal change agents to carry it through.

So, for credible leadership as a change agent (internal or external) it is suggested that we work to achieve the following objectives:

- Know their business
- Share their values
- Be symbolic

- Be inspirational/aspirational
- Be a prophetic voice
- Have you been there?
- Are you a good listener?
- Prepare to succeed

CHAPTER SUMMARY

An effective consultant will require a range of knowledge and skills consolidated by relevant experience to answer client need within the change programme. There may be a few very specific programmes which can be managed by one consultant, but generally a team of consultants and associates will often be working together. So, the skills required by consultants will include personal and business-related abilities and aptitude to work well with a diverse range of people whose life and work may initially be unfamiliar. Underpinning this range of expertise will be the attitudinal aspects that distinguish most good teachers and facilitators. These include sympathy, supportiveness, patience and personable empathy with others. There has recently been an interest in the work of boundary spanners: managers who work abroad and are capable of building bridges across geographical and cultural divides to achieve common organizational objectives among disparate groups of people. It seems to the present authors that this profile of skills also fits the work of the consultant and in subsequent chapters we have featured accounts of individuals whose work we have shared and who we believe illustrate the thoughtfulness and reflectiveness occasioned by working with others through change programmes. We share a common belief that participative change programmes are more likely to succeed in exploring critical issues; looking at different options for implementation; and evaluating the effectiveness of change in the longer term. Given the changing and fragmenting working environment that a global business environment seems to require, we believe that the call for gifted and effective change agents is unlikely to diminish.

For video content relating to this chapter please visit the companion website at **www.macmillanihe.com/Randall-Management-Consultancy.**

REFERENCES

Bloomfield, B.P. and Danielli, A. (1995). The role of management consultants in the development of information technology: The indissoluble nature of socio-political and technical skills. *Journal of Management Studies*, 32(1), 22–46.

Buchanan, D. and Boddy, D. (1992). *The Expertise of the Change Manager: Public Performance and Backstage Activity*. New York: Prentice Hall.

Bullock, R.J. and Batten, D. (1985). It's just a phase we're going through: A review and synthesis of OD phase analysis. *Group and Organisation Studies*, 10(4), 383–412.

Burnes, B. (2004). Kurt Lewin and the planned approach to change: A re-appraisal. *Journal of Management Studies*, 41(6), 977–1002.

Burnes, B. (2007). Kurt Lewin and the Harwood studies: The foundations of OD. *Journal of Applied Behavioral Science*, 43(2), 213–231.

Burnes, B. (2014). *Managing Change* (6th edn). Harlow: Pearson.

Burnes, B. and Cooke, B. (2012). The past, present and future of organisation development: Taking the long view. *Human Relations*, 65(11), 1395–1429.

Caldwell, R. (2003). Models of change: A four-fold classification. *British Journal of Management*, 14(2), 131–142.

Clark, T. (1995). *Managing Consultants*. Milton Keynes: Open University Press.

Clark, T. and Salaman, G. (1995). Understanding consultancy as performance: The dramaturgical metaphor. In I. Glover and M. Hughes (eds), *Professions at Bay*. Aldershot: Gower.

Clark, T. and Salaman, G. (1996a). The management guru as organisational witchdoctor. *Organisation*, 3(1), 85–107.

Clark, T. and Salaman, G. (1996b). Telling tales: Management consultancy as the art of story telling. In D. Grant and C. Oswick (eds), *Metaphor and Organisations*. London: Sage.

Collins, D. (2000). *Management Fads and Buzzwords*. London: Routledge.

Corley, K.G. and Gioia, D.A. (2004). Identity ambiguity and change in the wake of a corporate spin-off. *Administrative Science Quarterly*, 49(2), 173–208.

Davenport, T. (1993). *Process Innovation: Reengineering Work Through IT*. Boston, MA: Harvard Business School.

Fincham, R. (1999). The consultant–client relationship: Critical perspectives on the management of organisational change. *Journal of Management Studies*, 36(3), 335–351.

Follett, M.P. (1940). *Dynamic Administration: The Collected Papers of Mary Parker Follett*, ed. E.M. Fox and L. Urwick. London: Pitman Publishing.

Frost, P.J. and Robinson, S.L. (1999). The toxic handler: Organisational hero and casualty. *Harvard Business Review*, 77(4) 96–106.

Grint, K. (2005). *Leadership: Limits and Possibilities (Management, Work and Organisations)*. Basingstoke: Palgrave Macmillan.

Hallier, J. and Lyon, P. (1996). Job insecurity and employee commitment: Manager's reactions to the threat and outcomes of redundancy selection. *British Journal of Management*, 7, 107–123.

Heusinkveld, S. and Benders, J. (2005). Contested commodification: Consultancies and their struggle with new concept development. *Human Relations*, 58(3), 283–310.

Hislop, D. (2002). The client role in consultancy arrangements during the appropriation of technological innovations. *Research Policy*, 31, 657–671.

Huczynski, A. (1993). Explaining the succession of management fads. *International Journal of Human Resource Management*, 4(2), 443–463.

Kitay, J. and Wright, C. (1997). From prophets to profits: The occupational rhetoric of management consultants. *Human Relations*, 60(11), 1630–1640.

Kitay, J. and Wright, C. (2007). From prophets to profits: The occupational rhetoric of management consultants. *Human Relations*, 60(11), 1613–40.

Kubler-Ross, E. (1969). *On Death and Dying*. New York: Macmillan.

Lazarus, R.S. and Folkman, S. (1984). *Stress, Appraisal, and Coping*. New York: Springer.

Lichtenstein, B.M. (1997). Grace, magic and miracles: A 'chaotic logic' of organisational transformation. *Journal of Organisational Change Management*, 10(5), 393–411.

Louis, M.R. (1980). Surprise and sensemaking: What newcomers experience on entering unfamiliar organizational settings. *Administrative Science Quarterly*, 25(2), 226–251.

Macneil, I.R. (1985). Relational contract: What we know and do not know. *Wisconsin Law Review*, 4, 483–525.

Micklethwait, J. and Woolridge, A. (1996). *The Witchdoctors: Making Sense of Management Gurus*. London: Mandarin Books.

Nadler, D.A. (1993). Concepts for the management of strategic choice. In C. Mabey and B. Mayon-White (eds), *Managing Change*. London: Open University and Paul Chapman Publishing.

O'Mahony, J. and Markham, C. (2013). *Management Consultancy*. Oxford: Oxford University Press.

Pettigrew, A.M. (1987). Context and action in the transformation of the firm. *Journal of Management Studies*, 24(6), 649–670.

Piderit, S. (2000). Rethinking resistance and recognising ambivalence. *Academy of Management Review*, 25, 783–794.

Quinn, J.B. (1980). *Strategies for Change: Logical Instrumentalism*. Homewood, IL: Richard D. Irwin.

Rackham, N. and Morgan, T. (1978). *Behaviour Analysis in Training*. New York: McGraw-Hill.

Randall, J.A. and Procter, S.J. (2008). Ambiguity and ambivalence: Senior managers' accounts of organisational change in a restructured government department. *Journal of Organisational Change Management*, 21(6), 686–700.

Ruona, W.E.A. and Gibson, S.K. (2004). The making of twenty-first century HR: An analysis of the convergence of HRM, HRD and OD. *Human Resource Management*, 43(1), 49–66.

Schuyt, T. and Schuijt, J. (1998). Rituals and rules: About magic in consultancy. *Journal of Change Management*, 11(5), 399–406.

Stewart, R. (1985). *The Reality of Management*. Basingstoke: Palgrave Macmillan.

Stewart, R. (1991). *Managing Today and Tomorrow*. Basingstoke: Macmillan.

Sturdy, A. (1998). Strategic seduction? Information technology consultancy in UK financial services. In J. Alvarez (ed.), *The Diffusion and Consumption of Business Knowledge*. Basingstoke: Macmillan.

Sturdy, A., Clark, T., Fincham, R. and Handley, K. (2009). Between innovation and legitimation: Boundaries and knowledge flows in management consultancy. *Organization*, 16(5), 627–653.

Sturdy, A., Wright, C. and Wylie, N. (2016). Managers as consultants: The hybridity and tensions of neo-bureaucratic management. *Organization*, 23(2), 184–205.

Tracy, J.L. and Robins, R.W. (2006). Appraisal agency of shame and guilt: Support for a theoretical model. *Personality and Social Psychology Bulletin*, 32(10), October, 1339–1351.

Watson, G. (1966). *Resistance to Change*. Washington, DC: National Training Laboratories.

Weick, K.E. (1995). *Sensemaking in Organizations*. Thousand Oaks, CA: Sage.

Wickens, P. (1987). *The Road to Nissan*. Basingstoke: Macmillan.

3 Consultancy Skills: Agreeing/Negotiating a Contract

Julian Randall and Sarah Smith

> **Learning Objectives**
>
> After studying the chapter, you should be able to:
> - Understand the consultancy sales cycle
> - Know how to prepare for the first meeting with a client
> - Understand how to build a rapport with the client
> - Pilot yourself through the negotiating process
> - Be familiar with the 13 classic approaches to closing a sale
> - Identify potential problems and issues
> - Define what is required of you by the client

INTRODUCTION

In this chapter, we will look at the first approach that the change agent makes to the potential client. We will suggest that is a time to ask questions and listen, rather than to proceed into an impressive PowerPoint presentation of what you can do for them. So, we will be looking first at the areas which you will want to explore in detail and the messages that you will pick up from the client as you do so.

Meeting clients for the first time presents the consultant with an opportunity to find out about those who have called for assistance in implementing a change programme – they are sometimes referred to as the advocates of change. What is the purpose of the initial interview and how should the consultancy team prepare for it?

It is true that company websites can be visited; research into the sector can be conducted; and previous experience in the sector may also be useful. But these sources are to some extent historical and may lack detail of the current situation that has triggered the call for change. There is, over and above that, the impact that a first visit always makes on visitors and the learning to be derived for a reasonable decision to be made about whether this is a worthwhile opportunity for the change agent to engage with or not.

We say this because while business is always welcome and a call to compete often flattering, the purpose of the qualifying interview should be to gain constructive and worthwhile work which will please the client and lead to a positive evaluation of the consultancy business at the end of the agreed contract. To put this in context we can review what is sometimes referred to by sales organizations as the sales cycle (Figure 3.1).

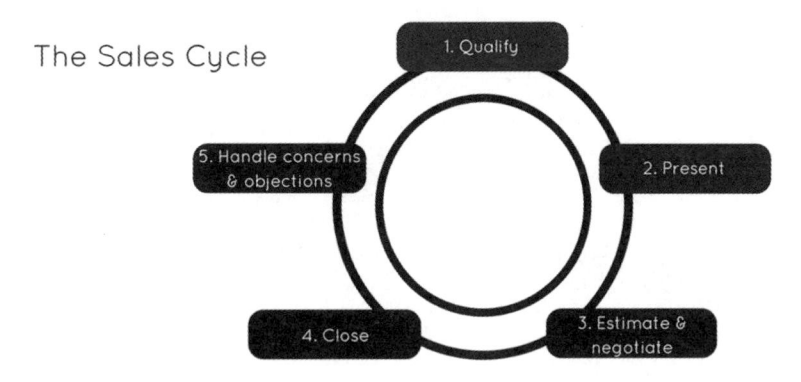

```
                        1. Qualify
The Sales Cycle
5. Handle concerns                    2. Present
& objections

         4. Close         3. Estimate &
                            negotiate
```

Figure 3.1 *The sales cycle*

Most business dealings involve the steps of this cycle beginning with qualifying the prospect. In this chapter, we want to look at three areas which require different skills and which will present different challenges to the consultancy team. These are:

- Qualifying your prospective client
- Negotiating your contract
- Closing for commitment

We will look at each of these steps in turn and consider what should be addressed and how to address it. But before we do that we can look first at the context in which consultants operate.

CULTURE

Walking into an organization can itself be an enlightening experience. Those who work regularly in an organization eventually take for granted the sights and sounds that accompany the environment they work in. For the visitor, this is the first sign of what Schein (1985) referred to as **visible artefacts**. They may also be the first indicator of Deal and Kennedy's (1982) definition of culture as 'the way we do things round here.'

But beneath this superficial level of behaviour lie other factors that Schein lists: **values** and **basic assumptions** – these are attitudinal and therefore much more difficult to assess for the first-time visitor. What people think about the work they do is not often divulged to occasional or passing visitors and basic assumptions, as Schein acknowledges, are often unconscious and only surfaced in their holders by external threats.

This raises the questions: how should the first interview be conducted with a potential client? What are we trying to achieve? In answer to this we might say that we want to let them know about ourselves; who we are; our track record with change events; and why we are different from other consultancies whose help they may be seeking. But it is also the opportunity to find out more about them, and whether we would be able to work with them. So, there is a certain amount of preparation to do.

Preparation is key and some guidelines for making sure you are in the best position to succeed are worth considering here:

Timely arrival

- Arrive in reception 15 minutes before the time of the interview (this will give you time to observe how others are received by the organization)

- Be agreeable to all in reception (receptionists and secretaries are often asked by their managers how visitors conducted themselves)
- Refuse all refreshments (the last thing you need is balancing cups, shaking hands and greeting others)
- Make sure you are prepared (note taking and checklist of what you need to find out)

Introductions

- Greet all those present (according to the accepted convention)
- Offer both your names (Good morning, I am Jo Robertson)
- Wait until you see which name is used in response to your greeting (use the convention they adopt whether formal or informal)
- Wait to be invited to sit down
- Do not put anything on their furniture
- Do not cross your legs (apart from at the ankles and then place under your chair)
- Sit up and look interested (eye contact)

Body language

Be aware of your own body language:

- Lean forward slightly. Do not lean back in your chair
- Engage eye contact especially when the other person is speaking
- Break eye contact when you are speaking (to avoid dominance)
- If speaking to a panel look at everyone when you speak – not just the person who has asked you a question
- Be aware of signals from your colleague(s) – so have a signalling system (e.g. take your glasses off if you wish to indicate you have a question)
- Beware of leakage (drumming fingers, tapping feet, etc.)

Interviews are sometimes described in different ways. How would you describe the process of a business interview?

- A controlled conversation
- A two-way discussion
- A hidden agenda
- Exploring objectives

We might begin by asking who has control? Two-way interactions between the respondents have about them unknown and often unexpected aspects.

And the second point: how often does an interview offer the chance of a two-way discussion? The hidden agenda which participants have about the content prepared and the outcomes required does not always allow time for exploration and listening opportunities. And yet, ideally, that is what we want to achieve: exploring objectives which each side has and finding some common ground on which agreement can be reached.

So, here are some suggestions for inclusion in the first, qualifying interview:

Step by step through the qualifying interview

1. **Check the title** (to see if you have got it correct)

    - Now probe to find out what the job entails
    - Be especially careful of the title Company Secretary (they can cover many different functions in an organization)
    - Similarly, Assistants/Deputies
    - Don't assume that a long job title means more responsibility
    - In academia, for example, Directors rarely direct in the traditional sense of strategic decision-making (you would need to speak to the Dean or Vice Principal)

2. **The budget**

    - Who are the budget holders for the change programme (is it the person in front of you or has it to go to the full Board)?
    - What range of budget are they looking at (what is the basis of the funding for this)?
    - What are their time scales (when do they want to start and how long have they allowed for implementation of the programme)?
    - What is their billing convention? (Some large companies, for example, pay 90 days after the work is completed)

3. **Have they had experience of change programmes before?**

    - Ask about it: ('Tell me about it...' is a good opener)
    - Probe to establish: when; what; where; how long; who; why; outcomes? (Such closed questions are sometimes referred to as testing questions)
    - Probe any signals (vague statements that sound interesting): 'It was a difficult time for us...', 'What was difficult about it?'

4. **What did they like about it?**

    - Who; what; when; where; how; why?
    - Probe any signals
    - Remember the answer is what they will be looking to replicate next time. So, take a careful note of what they say

Expectancy theory (Vroom, 1964) alerts us to the background of most human interactions: what people expect to happen affects their evaluation of the outcome. So, knowing what people expect from previous experience of change is valuable information to acquire – in this way we are alerted to what we need to achieve if we are to implement a change programme successfully.

5. **What did they dislike about it?**

    - Who; what; where; why; how?
    - Probe any signals
    - Remember you will be trying to avoid repeating this experience

The obverse side of the previous question lies here and is again crucial to establish. A look through TripAdvisor on all the main sites will indicate that many comments state what was not liked by the client. Again, it shows what we would need to avoid if we want to work with the clients we are interviewing.

6. **What are they looking for ideally this time around?**
    - Again, who; what; where; when; why; how?
    - Probe any signals
    - This is the blueprint for you to work on when you come to make your presentation to the Board

Most people have a clear idea of what they want to achieve in the future though they may not have formulated it too clearly. This question will encourage clarity about the expected outcomes of a future change programme.

7. **Read back your summary of points 3–6**
    - Then at the end ask: Is there anything that we have missed here that you think we should know about?

Repeating by reading from the notes you just made in an interview enables the change agent to establish that she was listening and has reflected accurately on what she has heard.

Qualifying interview follow-through

- You now need to explore any issues that you derived from your research – be careful how you phrase them (they may be about lost markets or missed business opportunities)
- You may also be asked questions about your own work at this point (be clear about what you want to reveal here)
- Speak in general terms about what you have done in the past; your philosophy; approach (participative change; learning experience)
- Speak about sectors you have worked in but beware of getting too specific about it (there can be a risk of inadvertently revealing information about other organizations)

The option of a presentation

If you are pressed to do a presentation on the spot:

- Mention the benefits they raised separately and give an example of the features that you have that can support the benefit they are looking for
- Then mention the advantage that this can have for them (working towards your unique selling proposition, USP)
- Finally leave them with the one question that they should ask other potential consultants coming after you
- Close for commitment (the next meeting; any follow-up by you)

Handling concerns and objections

- Accept the objection (I can understand your point)
- Now state the compensating benefit (let me go back to something you said when you spoke about…)
- Repeat the feature(s) that support the benefit which you know you can deliver
- Reinforce the USP that you can offer
- Check (Have I answered your question? Is there anything else that I can tell you?)

Some basic questions to ask

- What do you want to achieve (from a change programme)?
- What will that do for you and the company?
- What will it be like when you have achieved it/How will you know when you have achieved it?
- What outside resources do you need?
- Who can help you?

- What will this goal confirm about you and the company?
- What other benefits might there be for you?
- What is the first step to getting what you want to achieve?

You will notice that there is more about the client and their expectations than there is about what you and your consultancy have done in the past. The advice given is that no presentation should be made until you are quite sure of the basis on which you are making it.

Express your own thinking

- Here is what I think (as a consultant, and this is why I say that...)
- I have come to this conclusion because...
- If we were to do this, you would see something like this...
- How does this sound to you so far?
- What flaws suggest themselves to you?
- Do you have any concerns about this?
- Have I missed out anything?
- What else should we consider at this point?
- So, if we can..., then would you...?

Sounding reasonable and open to suggestions and ideas is often a key distinguishing feature which will mark you out as distinctly different from competitors. Many consultants will have gone through a PowerPoint presentation, which they aim to impress the client with. In contrast, the open approach confirms that you are different in the way that you deal with potential clients and open to new ideas about their needs and aspirations for calling for a change event. One client fed back at the end of the interview: *'The last company talked at me for three hours. You have listened to me throughout.'*

Signals

During your interviews, you may receive signals from your prospective client. They may be witting or unwitting but should always be probed to establish what is meant.

How would you respond to the following signals?

- We never negotiate on price
- Do you give the 10% local authority discount?
- How long would we have wait for the programme to start?
- We always insist on the best quality
- We can't answer that now
- I will have to ask about that

One of the classic closes that we will come back to is what is referred to by professional negotiators as **sharp-angle closing**. It simply means asking a question to clarify the question that has just been put to you.

So, to the first comment, we might ask: 'What do you negotiate on?'

A straight probe might be best to the second comment, particularly if you are uncertain what they are referring to. 'So, what is the Local Authority discount?'

Again, you want to know what they expect. So, you might ask: 'When do you want it to start?'

The next comment: 'How do you define "the best quality"?'

Probe the next comment: 'When can you come back to us?'

A similar response might be: 'When will you have a chance to do that?'

Probe the penultimate signal: 'So, who could answer that?'

Probe the final signal: 'Why is that?'

Links to negotiation

Negotiation simply means doing business. But it may help to see it in the stages which we offered above in the sales cycle. Most negotiations do not proceed smoothly around the cycle and clients can sometimes surprise by intervening in ways that we had not expected or could not have prepared for. This means that sometimes we have to go back to the beginning to check out what we are hearing before proceeding through the cycle again and linking up with what has already been agreed. Concerns and objections are always likely to surface. But it is better to deal with them on the way through than face a block at the end when trying to finalize agreement. So, use open approaches to negotiation:

- Use constructive discussion approaches
- Establish a degree of rapport and build on it
- Offer an agenda for the meeting and/or a summary of what it is about
- Ask for contributions to the agenda
- Search for and disclose to others what is needed
- Ask and answer questions and then check for understanding
- Summarize regularly
- Signal your willingness to consider movement if reciprocated
- Respond to their signals in a positive manner

Move from the problem to the implications

- What are you satisfied with in your present situation?
- What disadvantages do you find from using external trainers?
- Are there any reliability problems with the system you use?
- So, what is the unreliability costing you in emergency outsourcing when the equipment goes down?
- How much is absenteeism costing you in extra overtime working and hiring temporary staff?

Negotiation is about probing, listening and responding to what you are hearing from your interviewee. As we do that we can choose whether to extend the discussion by asking open questions or close it down

---

QUESTION TECHNIQUES

Open questions (getting more information and discussion):

- Tell me about
- What do you think about...?
- What do you feel about...?
- Do you have a story that illustrates that point?
- What else is there that would explain that?
- Do you have examples of this?

Closed questions (gaining detail and checking understanding):

- Who?
- What?
- When?
- Where?
- How?
- Why?

by asking for specific answers. There is a balance to be struck between developing ideas and closing for commitment and moving on.

We mentioned earlier the need for clarifying issues specifically and gaining commitment from our clients to move on. Salespeople have a series of strategies that they use to achieve these objectives. They are sometimes referred to as the 13 classic closes. We will outline them briefly and consider them in turn.

THE 13 CLASSIC CLOSES

Opening

1. Order-book close (take notes and notice how this can later link up with summary closing)
2. Sharp-angle closing (clarify a question by asking another question, as we have seen in the example exercises above)
3. Alternate closing (either... or..., which do you prefer? Useful for gaining commitment for follow-up: would you prefer Monday or Tuesday? 2pm or 3pm?)
4. Under/over technique (avoid giving away unless you get something back. Example: 'Do you give the 10% local authority discount?' Answer: 'Yes, if you pay X% up front')

During the negotiation

5. Puppy-dog close (offer a pilot scheme, for example. If they like it they will want to keep it)
6. Handle concerns and objections (these can come at any time so always be ready for them and probe: for example, 'Why do you say that?')
7. Dutch auction close (go up to the market price, come down to your own day rate – a useful technique when price is raised with you)
8. T-square close (write down all the things that are a benefit then get the client to list the disbenefits. Now you know what you need to answer to conclude the business successfully)

Closing stages

9. Summary close (use your notes to read off what has been agreed then ask if there is anything else you need to consider before proceeding to close)
10. Closing on an objection (Is this the only thing that stands between us? If we can reach agreement on this, are you happy to go ahead?)
11. Major and minor close (first choice and then second straight after. 'It seems that we need to decide whether to do X or Y. Which would you prefer?')
12. Ultimatum close (used by life insurance salespeople. Bottom line statement: 'So, what happens if none of these strategies work?')
13. Silent close (exactly what it says. The first to break the silence loses the initiative. So, ask a summary question and then wait for the answer – resist the temptation to speak first)

It should be said that most negotiators use only those closes which they are comfortable with and which seem appropriate at the time. Much is based on responding to clients in a positive way and only withdrawing if it becomes apparent that there is no common ground on which agreement can be reached or that the client is not someone that you feel you could work with successfully. The purpose of closing is to gain commitment from the client not to force them to do what we want.

The wrong signals

These will be personal to each consultant. But there are some which may indicate that the style of management exhibited by your host is not one you could comfortably work with.

> A famous economist went to see the President of the United States of America. He went into the office and proceeded to outline what he saw as the solutions to world economic problems at the time. The phone rang frequently, and the President always answered it immediately, interrupting his guest's presentation. Eventually the economist left the office during yet another call. The President noticed that he had left but at that moment the phone rang, and he took the call. It was the economist.
>
> **President**: I thought you were meant to be in here presenting your ideas to me.
> **Economist**: I realized, Mr President, that I could only keep your full attention by ringing you.

So apart from personal style issues, what else might indicate to you that there are potential blocks to change at this early stage in your relations with your potential client? Here are a few that we can consider:

Potential problem areas:

- Unspecific or vague objectives (in the near future; as soon as possible)
- The way in which roles were defined (focused on control rather than ideas and collaboration)
- Time pressure to achieve targets (Many senior executives want change overnight, so probe to seek realistic time extension if you need to)
- Human issues outside comfort zone of your respondent ('We don't have time for that')
- Perceived intractability of people problems (others have tried that here before and it has never worked)
- No contingency plans (no allowance for time or cost overruns)

So, what are the indicators that the client has an openness to participative change? Well, here are some of the indicators which may suggest a rapport between client and change agent:

- Participants feel the project is their own (not imposed from without therefore a good prospect for participative change)
- Project has wholehearted support from the top (CEO is happy to get involved at critical stages of the change programme)
- Participants see change as reducing the present burdens for everyone (What's in it for staff not just managers...)
- Projects support positive values/incorporates the ideas of participants
- Project offers new work experience to interest participants
- Staff feel their autonomy and job security are not threatened
- Proponents of change empathize with objections
- Provision is made for group and individual feedback during the project
- Staff experience acceptance, support, trust and confidence in each other
- Project remains open to revision as the programme unfolds

FINDING OUT MORE ABOUT YOUR CLIENTS

Edgar Schein (1978) developed an approach to change which he called **process consultation**. He viewed change as dependent on getting the client involved with their own challenges at work. The benefits of such an approach can include:

- Enabling the client to develop his/her own diagnosis of the situation and develop skills to act upon it
- Uncovering organization and group cultural assumptions
- Taking for granted that if the client can begin to solve his/her problem, he/she will have learned something about the process of how to solve problems (participative change assumes this approach)

All we need do as change agents is facilitate this process. One way of approaching this might be to conduct some qualitative interviews with key people in the organization, and here we conclude by reviewing what this might involve.

Qualitative interview work

- The qualitative interview sounds very like the qualifying interview. The two should not be confused, though the exploration may be similar
- The purpose of the qualitative interview is to uncover the perceptions that key individuals may have about their job; work; career; manager; and organization

It has a particular purpose:

- We seek to uncover the basic assumptions which individuals hold about the important aspects surrounding their work
- We can explore our empirical evidence to identify assumptions made about their commitment to their work, say, or the demands they perceive reorganization may put on them in the future

We have already mentioned Schein's three levels of culture and noted that while visible artefacts may be easier for outsiders to access, probing the deepest level of basic assumptions becomes much more difficult to address directly. So, it is as well to remind ourselves about some important aspects of **basic assumptions**:

- Some deep beliefs and norms come from a cultural background often absorbed prior to employment
- Some experiences make people less able to cope with uncertainty during change (previous failure, for example)
- Long-serving staff know what they like and they like what they know (so change is a disturbance to them. Constant change can alienate or make people who appreciate stability in their working lives resistant to change)
- Some people prefer working on their own (pilots; surgeons; salespeople) so they resent being brought in for extra meetings – especially meetings during which they are asked why they do what they do. To them what they do is self-evident and not something they want to share with others
- Fewer people are **initiators**: these individuals love change – the more the better. They make good launch teams for change programmes but may need to keep moving on in their lives.

Finding out the basic assumptions a key group may have in common and those about which they differ is important to uncover before embarking on a change programme. It is a significant part of understanding resistance when it arises.

Surfacing basic assumptions

As we mentioned earlier, we cannot ask for basic assumptions directly without risking that we will be given an acceptable account which may not address critical factors. Louis (1980) suggested that there were a number of questions which interviewers can ask which might probing more deeply into deeply held, and sometimes unconscious, beliefs. This is based on a literature on surprise and sense-making (Weick, 1995) which suggested that during change which violates basic assumptions, surprise is likely to be surfaced. Louis's questions were couched around past change experience:

- What happened that surprised you?
- What happened that didn't surprise you?

- What didn't happen that surprised you?
- What didn't happen that didn't surprise you?

Louis suggested that where there is surprise it is likely that basic assumptions have been disconfirmed and that similarly where there is no surprise, basic assumptions are likely to have been confirmed. So, when constructing a questionnaire suitable for exploring crucial issues with key people these questions can be worth including.

Ambiguity and ambivalence

Surprise can also indicate ambiguity as far as individual perceptions are concerned. This has sometimes been referred to as cognitive dissonance (Festinger, 1957). It means that factors presented to an individual appear to conflict. Ambiguity can lead to ambivalence for the individual where this conflict evokes two deferring responses. Piderit (2000) suggests that there are three levels to consider here:

1. Cognitive level:

I can't see why we should have to do this/I can understand why we have to do this

2. Emotional level:

I felt we needed to change/I felt uncertain about the change

3. Intentional level:

So, what ought to happen, then?/suppose they find they are unable to influence change? 'I am going to leave'/'I will stay on and fight'

Drawing up a questionnaire

Here are some suggestions for building up a questionnaire which has about it a logical sequence as far as the interviewee is concerned. It can also reveal levels of ambivalence, surprise, sense-making and therefore, basic assumptions. Usually 12 questions are enough. You may find it useful to split them into three sections.

Establish past experience

1. Tell me about how you started in the organization
2. What sort of training did you receive?
3. How have you progressed through the organization?
4. What does your current job involve at the moment?

Now look at the current state of things

5. Describe your past experience(s) of change
6. What surprised you about it?
7. What didn't surprise you?
8. What lessons have you learned from this?

Now move into the future

9. Where do you see yourself in (five) years' time?
10. What changes do you see happening in that time?
11. What support would you find most helpful during change?
12. How would you implement change given a choice?

Finally, assumptions that facilitate change

- Individuals are rational animals
- Individuals and managers want the good of the company
- Training and development can close the gap between where we are and where we need to be
- There need be no casualties during the change process (including any who need to leave)
- Take account of long-term custom and practice
- Individuals have ability and potential to respond to the challenge of change
- Commitment can be won by patience, negotiation and reassurance

Your role as the change agent:

- Know their business
- Share their values
- Be symbolic (inspirational)
- Be aspirational (think about advantages for them)
- Be a prophetic voice (where will the industry be in five years' time)
- Been there? – draw on that experience
- Listen and be responsive
- Be realistic about what can be achieved

CONSULTANCY IN ACTION

Sarah Smith, Talent Manager at Aberdeen Asset Management

Change Agents, external or internal are tasked with managing a phase of transition. Commonly, agents are involved in development, improvement and efficiency change management. This part of the chapter refers mainly to internal change agents.

Many authors have designed phase models as tools for managing change: Davis and colleagues' (1967) Problem-Solving Model; Beckhard's (1969) Need Satisfaction Model; Donleavy and Pugh's (1977) Growth Model; Lewin's (1958) Ice Model; and Beckhard and Harris's (1987) Transition Model; to name only a few. They describe phases which can be identified throughout the change process.

Perhaps Bullock and Batten's (1985) four-phase model describes the phases in a way that simplifies the process and could embrace most change approaches. The themes of Exploration, Planning, Action and Integration offer a logical sequence and Exploration allows the Planning phase to take account of the impact change will have and how it can be measured. Phases also offer an opportunity to evaluate the impact of the change rather than leaving it to the end of the process. With an increasing focus on organizations being able to react quickly to change it can be worthwhile to build in monitoring during the life cycle of the project (Figure 3.2).

Popular change approaches like Kotter's eight-step model (1996), updated in 2014, and Lewin's model recognize that as the environment changes the steps need to be repeated. The phase approach embodies this continuous review as learning emerges from the interventions undertaken. In practical terms as an internal change agent, selecting a model may not be essential but a preset procedure can be useful to demonstrate the stages to those taking part.

Strong personal relationships can provide a compass for internal change agents as they embark on a change approach and previous knowledge and established relationships with the stakeholders can be a benefit. Having knowledge of a previous change project in an organization, and understanding what the success and developmental factors are, can provide a considerable advantage. Not only is there an awareness of the values and vision of the company, but of who the enablers are and what direct impact the change has had on them and the organization in the past.

Outline of the Four-Phase Model

Change Phases	Change Processes
1. Exploration	a. Need awareness b. Search c. Contracting
2. Planning	a. Stabilisation b. Diffusion c. Renewal
3. Action	a. Implementation b. Evaluation
4. Integration	a. Diagnosis b. Design c. Decision

Figure 3.2 Outline of the four-phase model

Referring to the four-phase model (Figure 3.2), the Exploration phase may be less formal than it would be for an external consultant. Exploratory conversations can be more open and honest and concerns can be addressed early. The Planning phase can also benefit from having knowledge on barriers to success, budget constraints and what has worked (or not) in the past. Being an internal change agent can also provide access to the appropriate decision makers and so avoid engaging with those who may not have discretion to make decisions but can slow down the process by keeping themselves involved.

The pressure to deliver change can be less demanding than it would be for an external agent. In an environment where individuals are drafted into projects and initiatives and away from the 'business as usual' (BAU) tasks, contracting and rule setting do not always take place formally, or at all. With less structure and process to follow, the internal agent has to work harder to build buy-in momentum around a change. Of course, there is a danger that past change that has not been successful can be associated with the person who tried to promote it, especially in a blame culture. So, constant reassessment is required in order to survive commercially, and while traditional models may be useful, detailed adaption may be necessary.

Kotter's eight-step change model describes three overarching phases: creating a climate for change; engaging and enabling the whole organization; and implementing and sustaining change. This can usefully illustrate the steps for practically applied change programmes (Figure 3.3).

The most challenging steps are the first step, creating urgency, and the last, making it stick. Kotter (1990) refers to people at all levels needing to be convinced of change. In the absence of urgency, imposed change efforts can be slowed and are easier to defer. He adds that clarifying how the future will look in comparison to the past and convincing your audience that you can make the changes stick will assist in creating a realistic and convincing vision. So, being able to create a vision and describe the consequences of not carrying out the change is an important step that is often given less time and attention while getting involved in the pragmatic tasks of arranging change events. We need to build a team that can help reinforce a sense of urgency upwards as well as laterally in the organization. These team members will become the ambassadors needed to encourage engagement, provide information and help prevent loss of momentum. The change team should internalize the vision and be able to identify the steps ahead and inspire others to follow. It is not to say that this team will help create the vision, however. The communication to the team assisting with steps 1–3 must fully understand the vision, plan, timelines, stakeholders and consequences of failing to enable change. In smaller organizations the person working with you on the communication may also be interviewing staff members. This provides the advantage of consistency and will assist

Kotter's 8-Step Change Model

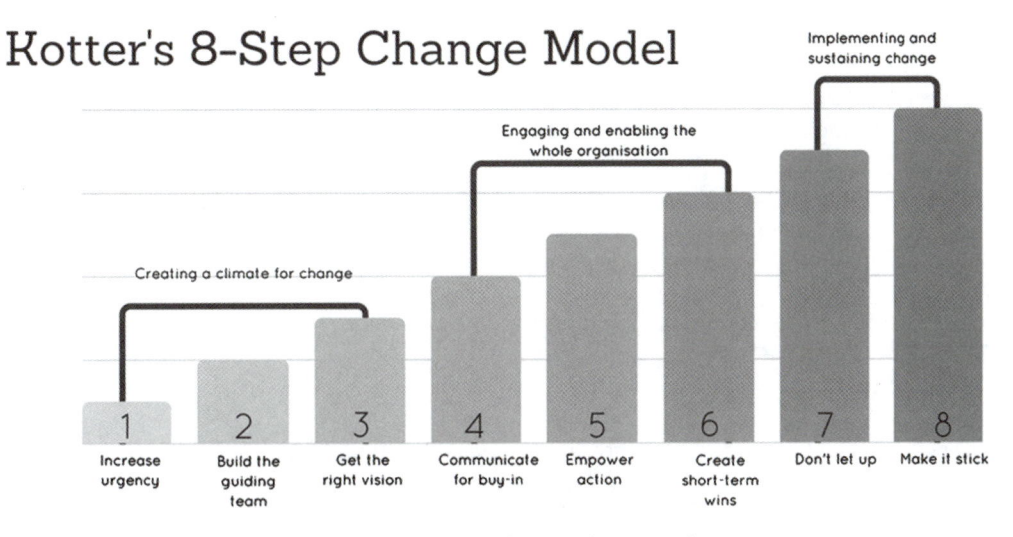

Figure 3.3 Kotter's eight-step change model

in delivering a consistent message. However, in a smaller organization, the individual may have a role to fulfil alongside the change project and time can become a constraint. We need to be realistic about such limitations and how this could affect the schedule for the change programme.

The final stage, as an internal change agent, is probably the most satisfying: seeing the change taking root in the organization. We need to be determined and focused on the outcomes of change during this phase of evaluation. It is very easy to revert to old behaviours and 'ways of doing things'. Our team of ambassadors need to continue to engage with the business long after the change event has been bedded in. Regular reviews should be arranged so that problems that arise can be quickly addressed. Those who can identify issues arising should be able to take action to fix them. As an external agent the opportunity to see change in action will not always be possible as they will have moved on before the change is fully bedded in. This is where the internal change agent team comes into its own.

For those internal agents who are involved or attached to a project throughout its complete life cycle, communication is key and being able to deliver the right message will help engagement, buy-in and create credibility.

Kotter suggests that for change to be successful, 75% of a company's management needs to 'buy into' the change. This means that it is worth spending time planning a communication strategy with the team and reviewing it frequently to check that it is still on track.

Communication

Regardless of the size of the organization or its history, people are key to successful change. Careful consideration of the effects that change will have on the workforce enables a flexible strategy to be adopted. A common derailer is the lack of communication around the need for change – this always gives rise to speculation and uncertainty. Sudden and rapid change can cause anxiety and doubt, leading to resistance. A communication plan can provide an element of review and modify the flow and timing of the information. Information can be leaked and misinterpreted so a blend of information sources is useful to stem the flow of misinformation.

Tools such as FAQ documents, electronic noticeboards, newsletters, drop-in clinics and change ambassadors all aid the flow of information. The communication plan should be distributed to all stakeholders to provide transparency. Consider who the communication is for and what the desired outcome should be. Communication should include:

1. A consistent and clear message to the business
2. The message should come from a senior sponsor/stakeholder; this will help validate the message

3. It should explain the background and why the change is needed
4. What the next steps of the change programme will be
5. Who people should contact if they have questions
6. Timeline for action so that people know what to expect and when

Follow-up communications on a one-to-one basis should include:

1. Explaining your role in the process
2. What's in it for the staff
3. Agree what you expect of them, commitment to the programme
4. Answer questions/concerns
5. Keep them up to date with progress/delays

The strategy adopted for a large private organization will differ from that of a small third sector organization, for example. The style of communication in smaller companies may become more informal. But the essential aspect is being able to talk to people about the change, what the timelines are and what the impact will be and this can be done more easily one-to-one. Sitting down with individuals is time well spent and provides the opportunity to read individual reactions and probe for further information on concerns and answer specific personal questions. We can demonstrate understanding and communicate the need for change more effectively and create stronger loyalty and commitment. You might consider different methods of communicating the same message as an option. Consider that different people require a different focus of detailed change so prepare a summary for those looking for a checklist.

Rather than a top-down cascade approach (which may now be considered a dated approach), the change agent should be able to adopt a strategy to suit the culture of the organization.

Understanding culture

We sometimes describe 'cultural differences' as referring to the different explicit and implicit assumptions and values that influence the behaviour and social artefacts of different groups (Herskowitz, 1948). Yet a company's culture often includes and embraces a considerable number of employees exercising different functions. Those values, principles and attitudes are a way of differentiating themselves from the competition and as Schein suggests those shared norms and values are often created at the start of an enterprise often by the founder of the company. Such leaders create a blueprint for the future but when it is not revisited it becomes 'the way we do things around here' (Deal and Kennedy, 1982). It is worth asking whether or not those who initiated the culture are still in the top-level positions or whether the organization is in a second, third, fourth generation. A recent study concluded that the CEO and top management team's mean conscientiousness were both directly related to organizational performance. Often as an organization grows, particularly in harder times, senior leaders will have been replaced to the point that there is confusion about the direction of the top management team. This can affect commitment to change across the organization. The advantage of being an internal change agent is that insider information about recent company history will allow the enablers of change to be identified early and the internal political system to be navigated more effectively.

Buy-in at the top levels is essential in order to effect sustainable change and therefore the values must resonate with them also. Once this is achieved then the need for change can be supported more easily throughout the entire organization.

Individuals are expected to live the company values day-to-day, at the same time aligning them with their own values. It is therefore pertinent to check the stakeholders' understanding of the values of the staff and how they resonate with them personally. For those who work in the third sector, non-profit, working for a cause whether paid or voluntarily, 'living the values' is very important. The knowledge of a particular area can come from a blend of education, experience, personal experience and personal interest. Staff can be seen working across multiple roles, exceeding contracted hours without pay and sacrificing holidays and weekends for the 'good of the cause'. This can be true of the private sector, but executing change within third sector organizations means keeping alive the beliefs that caused people to feel committed when they joined the organization.

Internal or external change agents can often expect to be given resources (people, budget, space) to plan and execute change but in an organization which depends on government or public funding, finding any resource to assist in implementing necessary change can be extremely challenging. Understaffing due to financial constraints and increasing demand for services can cause change to be delayed or shelved until its neglect becomes critical. This is most likely when external help is engaged. The change agent may be required to work within a tight budget with limited time with the staff. Personal research is key so that time is not spent on understanding what services they provide, for example. Many third sector organizations will accept consultation on a pro bono basis and this can provide added opportunity for the change agent.

Any change agent must understand what is expected of them and be able to deliver. Being armed with a variety of models to showcase and talking in jargon may suit some potential clients/management teams but all are looking for successful transition at the lowest cost with the highest impact.

Change models provide a benchmark or illustration of what we want to achieve but in the fast-paced, changing world people will generally use their own experience of success to evaluate change initiatives. An experienced change agent may provide a plan and strategy for change but if those decision makers have experienced change previously or are biased against it the proposal will be rejected or diverted to suit their preferences. Those who have experienced the early successes of a first-generation company can find it challenging to work within an organization that they now hardly recognize. The requirement for agility once again presents itself, a skill that a small start-up or third sector organization is unlikely to have due to lack of resources. Our challenge as change agents is to help sustain workplace and systems agility during change. The first challenge is to recognize where they are and how to support them through change.

The successful change strategy should align with the culture while developing new ways to respond to changing conditions. This increasing pace and complexity of workplace change means that there is a need for internal change agents to be flexible and adapt the change programme where necessary. Emotional agility enables change agents to be dynamic and able to demonstrate flexibility in dealing with the demands of complex change (David, 2016: 189). Partnering a company to achieve a common goal will demand tolerance at times, understanding and the ability to uncover solutions with people who are under pressure to perform successfully. People are at the heart of change and being able to relate to those you work with, build relationships and trust means that change is not formulaic but is part of a learning and participative experience.

As a change agent, it is important to be comfortable with the work you are being asked to perform, understand whether that comfort comes from a harmonization between the company values and your own and be confident in the skills you possess. Challenges create learning opportunities; be willing to change plans if required and become a good listener. People make change happen and without them it becomes impossible to implement successful change.

CHAPTER SUMMARY

In this chapter, we have explored some of the skills that will sustain the change agent in the challenging opening contact with potential clients. These techniques are offered to facilitate what is a complex process of finding out more about the perceived needs which clients may have and assessing whether there is a synergy between the parties to the opening negotiation which suggests that business may be worth pursuing.

As we explore each chapter topic we will introduce the accounts of practitioners who are or have been internal change agents to give their perspective on the work that they have done. Large consultancies often have a corporate approach to clients in which the team presents, closes and then implements the programme prescribed to bring about imposed change. It will be our contention that for change agents working on their own there is a more difficult task of assessing client need; reviewing whether there is a need-benefit possibility in collaborating in the change; and often facilitating participative change in which the changing perceptions of the client are complemented by continued reflectiveness about the change programme and its required outcome.

For video content relating to this chapter please visit the companion website at **www.macmillanihe.com/Randall-Management-Consultancy.**

REFERENCES

Beckhard, R. (1969). *Organizational Development: Strategies and Models*. Reading, MA: Addison-Wesley.

Beckhard, R. and Harris, R.T. (1987). *Organization Transitions: Managing Complex Change*. Reading, MA: Addison-Wesley.

Bullock, R.J. and Batten, D. (1985). It's just a phase we're going through: A review and synthesis of OD phase analysis. *Group and Organization Studies*, 10(4), 383–412.

David, S. (2016). *Emotional Agility*. London: Penguin Random House.

Davis, G.A., Manske, M.E. and Train, A. (1967). *Training Creative Thinking*. Occasional Paper No. 6, University of Wisconsin Research & Development Center for Learning and Re-Education, Madison.

Deal, T. and Kennedy, A. (1982). *Corporate Cultures.* Reading, MA: Addison-Wesley.

Donleavy, M.R. and Pugh, C.A. (1977). Multi-ethnic collaboration to combat racism in educational settings. *Journal of Applied Behavioural Sciences*, 13, 360–372.

Festinger, L. (1957). *A Theory of Cognitive Dissonance.* New York: Harper Row.

Herskowitz, M.J. (1948). *Man and His Works: The Science of Cultural Anthropology*. New York: Alfred A. Knopf.

Kotter, J.P. (1990). *A Force for Change: How Leadership Differs from Management*. New York: The Free Press.

Kotter, J.P. (1996). *Leading Change.* Boston, MA: Harvard Business School Press.

Kotter, J.P. (2014). *Accelerate – Building Strategic Agility for a Faster-Moving World*. Boston, MA: Harvard Business Review Press.

Lewin, K. (1958). Group decision and social change, in E.E. Maccoby, T.M. Newcomb and E L. Hartley (eds), *Readings in Social Psychology*. New York: Holt, Rinehart and Winston, pp. 197–211.

Louis, M.R. (1980). Surprise and sensemaking: What newcomers experience in entering unfamiliar organizational settings. *Administrative Science Quarterly*, 25, 226–251.

Piderit, S. (2000). Rethinking resistance and recognising ambivalence. *Academy of Management Review*, 25, 783–794.

Schein, E.H. (1978). The role of the consultant: Content expert or process facilitator. *Journal of Counselling and Development*, 56(6), February, 339–343.

Schein, E.H. (1985). Organizational culture. *American Psychologist*, 45(2), 109–119.

Vroom, V. (1964). *Work and Motivation*. New York: Wiley.

Weick, K.E. (1995). *Sensemaking in Organizations*. Thousand Oaks, CA: Sage.

4 Culture and Identity: Exploring a Company's Culture

Julian Randall and Supannee Keawchaum

> **Learning Objectives**
>
> After studying the chapter, you should be able to:
> - Understand how to find out more about the organization, especially its culture
> - Utilize qualitative interviews to surface basic assumptions
> - Develop an interview questionnaire
> - Make sense of interviewees' differing viewpoints
> - Have a better understanding of your role as a change agent

INTRODUCTION

External change agents are unlikely to be familiar with the people who will undergo the change programme. Even familiarity with a sector does not reveal fully the history and experience which a company will have had prior to the change initiative. It is clear that gaining allies who are already on site will be a significant advantage to the external change agent team. In this chapter we will look at ways of achieving this.

Two questions present themselves to the change agent on entering the organization seeking change programmes:

- Who am I dealing with?
- What are they asking me to do?

We have raised these questions during the qualifying interview. Now we need to work out how we can find out what we need to know to explore these questions in greater depth and look at ways in which we might penetrate the background of the company and its people and assess what help is already available to increase our effectiveness in implementing change.

Our aim and purpose is to find out more about the organization from its people, rather than just being dependent on the assessment of the proposers of change. We want to know a little more about the culture of the organization: not just 'the way they do things round here' but also the way people view the value and significance of what they do.

We can begin by reviewing the levels of culture which it is suggested can be accessed by outsiders and then look at ways in which we can explore behaviours and attitudes more deeply.

We have already mentioned Schein's three levels of culture and noted that while visible artefacts may be easier for outsiders to access, probing the deepest level of basic assumptions becomes much more difficult to address directly. To begin with we can revisit some important aspects of **basic assumptions**:

- Deeply held beliefs and norms which come from a cultural background often absorbed prior to employment (teachers' beliefs about how students learn move with them from school to school)
- Some experiences make people less able to cope with uncertainty during change (previous bad experiences of change)
- Many people are **colonisers**: they know what they like and they like what they know (long-term service may indicate this and change may not be welcomed)
- Some people are **isolates**: (pilots, surgeons, salespeople) so they resent being brought in for extra meetings and asked to share their views in meetings with other staff)
- Few are **initiators**: these individuals often welcome change – the more the better. They make good internal change agents

Finding out what different basic assumptions a key group may have in common and those about which they have divergent views is important to uncover before embarking on a change programme. Basic assumptions often embody key beliefs that people have about themselves and the world about them. Researchers who focus on qualitative work often conduct semi-structured interviews (Silverman, 2013) in which they seek to uncover the accounts, stories and narratives which people use to describe who they are and what they are trying to achieve in their work (Jabri, 2017). Commonly held beliefs can be very powerful in shaping the organization and can dictate what individuals and groups will and will not accept at work.

Some writers refer to this as an interpretive process in which the basic assumptions are used to evaluate events going on around us. Gabriel (2000) refers to people as interpretive animals. This means that we define meaning and ascribe value to what we see going on. In this way, we judge whether something is good or bad, or right or wrong. This is particularly crucial during a change programme, particularly when change is imposed. Disconfirmed basic assumptions can often give rise to resistance – where even before change events are implemented, the subjects of the change have already decided that they don't agree with it and will resist whatever the change agents seek to impose (Louis, 1980b). That is why as this book unfolds we will be suggesting that participative change is usually a stronger position to take with the organization and its people – because it can uncover the approach that they find congenial.

> There is a story that a retiring bishop passed over his duties to his successor with the following advice:
>
> This is Norwich and here, if you want to lead, find out where your people want to go and walk in front of them.

While we are not suggesting that people will dictate change, nor that change agents should go along with whatever is suggested to them, most change agents reflect that it is better to identify the expectancies of people before embarking on change programmes than to confront them during the programme itself. At least that way we become aware of why people object to a particular kind of change – especially if it violates deeply held basic assumptions about the job, work or career aspirations of the staff. In this respect time spent in reconnaissance is seldom wasted.

Most jobs, occupations and professions do require the individuals involved in the work to espouse not just acceptable behaviours, but also internalize the values and basic assumptions that the clients expect of those offering the service. This is particularly true of what are sometimes referred to as bounded or embedded communities. A good example of this are members of the medical profession (Nicolini et al., 2008) in which doctors and nurses are in some senses a closed community – even though they may work in a large institution like a hospital. In the case of the medical profession, the basic assumptions they have about their work may even be reinforced by a personal profession to save life and their care and commitment to their patients is always assumed to be paramount. What we have seen in the health sector in the last few years is imposed change, often required by governments to conform to the requirements of the 'internal markets'. This may mean that they are expected to manage bed-occupancy rates, staffing ratios and efficiency factors looked for by the funders. They can be adept at resisting such imposed changes, as the work of Reay and Hinings (2005, 2009) has demonstrated. While appearing to collaborate (collaborating logics) with imposed change, doctors resist and resume practice as normal at the end of the change programme (competing logics) – a process of appearing to comply with the health authorities but resuming normal service as soon as possible.

QUALITATIVE INTERVIEW WORK

So how can we uncover basic assumptions and explore the perceptions and basic assumptions that our change will trigger in the people who we have been asked to assist?

SURFACING BASIC ASSUMPTIONS

As we mentioned earlier, we cannot ask about basic assumptions directly without risking that we will be given an acceptable account which may not address critical factors. Louis (1980a) suggested that there were a number of questions that interviewers could ask which might achieve this objective of probing more deeply into deeply held, and sometimes unconscious, beliefs. This is based on a literature on surprise and sense-making (Weick, 1995), which suggested that during change that violates basic assumptions, surprise is likely to be surfaced. As we noted in the previous chapter, Louis's questions were couched around past change experience:

- What happened that surprised you?
- What happened that didn't surprise you?
- What didn't happen that surprised you?
- What didn't happen that didn't surprise you?

Louis suggested that where there is surprise it is likely that basic assumptions have been disconfirmed and that similarly where there is no surprise then basic assumptions are likely to have been confirmed. So, when constructing a questionnaire suitable for exploring crucial issues with key people inclusion of these questions can be a useful investment.

AMBIGUITY AND AMBIVALENCE

Surprise can also indicate ambiguity as far as individual perceptions are concerned. This has sometimes been referred to as cognitive dissonance (Festinger, 1957). It means that factors presented to an individual seem to conflict with each other. Ambiguity can lead to ambivalence for the individual where this conflict evokes two deferring responses. Piderit (2000) suggests that there are three levels to consider here:

1. **Cognitive level:** What people think about change
2. **Emotional level:** What people feel about change
3. **Intentional level:** What people will do about change

Once again, these are important levels to explore in qualitative interviews with key individuals in the organization.

DRAWING UP A QUESTIONNAIRE

We have already suggested ways of structuring a questionnaire which has about it a logical sequence as far as the interviewee is concerned, but also reveals the levels of ambivalence, surprise, sense making and, therefore, basic assumptions. Usually 12 questions are enough; you may find it useful to split them into three sections:

1. **Establish past experience in work**
2. **The current experience of job, work and career**
3. **Perception of the future prospects at work**

TRANSCRIBING YOUR DATA

Once you have transcribed your questionnaire data you will want to analyse what it offers you. Here are some guidelines:

- Go through your material and mark phrases, sayings and accounts which seem to be commonly held by your cohort
- Make comments in the margin of resonance to theoretical or conceptual references (direct or indirect – expectancy, sense making, ambiguity, ambivalence)
- Make up a table which illustrates how references offer different responses to your questions
- Remember that accounts and stories are not the same as the narrative that you are hearing

Czarniawska (1997) said that organizations are talked into existence. The stories and accounts that we hear sometimes converge in their subject matter and the conclusions which individuals draw from their experience. These become narratives which are often similar in the accounts given by a group. They may include different stories but the essence of what we hear reflect commonly held or expressed beliefs about the job, work, organization, managers, politicians and the world at large.

EXERCISE

The article under discussion here is by Randall and Procter (2008). Entitled 'Ambiguity and ambivalence: Senior managers' accounts of organizational change in a restructured government department', it is the result of research conducted in a part of the Civil Service, specifically with 20 senior managers (Band 11) who between them covered the UK.

As we have noted, people affected by change are not always impressed by the experience of change programmes or the claims made by managers who run them or are responsible for them. This article was written as a result of a change programme run in HM Customs & Excise.

There can be different views about the implications of change and different concerns about the direction which the organization is moving in. Like the first strike of the white billiard ball on the reds assembled at the end of the table, there can be a scattering of what previously looked like a perfectly arranged pattern.

> In this article, we looked at the different stories, accounts and narratives that individuals and groups affected by change gave us. Three different groups emerged from the interview data collected: what we called the long view (staff who had been there many years and remembered the old ways of doing things); the short view (young managers who would not have that memory of the old ways); and the new view (brought about by an influx of accountancy managers who had no previous experience of working in the Civil Service).
>
> So, now, please read the article, then discuss and answer the questions below.
>
> Randall, J. and Procter, S. (2008) Ambiguity and ambivalence. Senior managers' accounts of organizational change in a restructured government department. *Journal of Organizational Change Management*, 21(6), 686–700: www.emeraldinsight.com/0953-4814.htm DOI 10.1108/09534810810915727
>
> **Questions**
>
> 1. Why does change often trigger ambiguity in those who have to undergo it?
> 2. What is the difference between ambiguity and ambivalence?
> 3. What three levels does Piderit define within ambivalence?
> 4. How did older members of staff (the long view) interpret the new directive to go out and visit senior managers in organizations?
> 5. What does that tell you about the staff's interpretation of the meaning of change?
> 6. What were the main concerns of younger managers (short view) during the change?
> 7. Why were they concerned about the appraisals given by their managers?
> 8. What impression did the newly recruited staff (new view) have about HM Customs & Excise in general?
> 9. What was their main complaint about the attitude of the Civil Service to their previous management experience?
> 10. What initiatives did they want to put into place in the way the organization went about its business?
> 11. What does this tell us about the impact of change programmes on culture in organizations?
> 12. How has that affected the culture and what could you do to alleviate this fragmentation?

As you will have noted, even a small body of people sharing the same role in an organization can find themselves responding differently to imposed change than their colleagues. If we had been conducting a change programme there, our interviews would have made us aware that those three different perspectives might indicate different expectancies and probably evoke different responses to change interventions. Managers may all appear to be adhering to company policy, but their basic assumptions about their job, work and the new initiatives may be different and change agents working with them need to take account of those differences and work with them to identify feasible programmes of change. Underlying the work practices, however, there can be deeper beliefs about who I am and my rightful job role in the organization. We can now examine that more closely when we embark on change agency.

IDENTITY AND IDENTITY WORK

Central to this appraisal of the self is the concept of Identity which has attracted much interest among researchers exploring the processes of managing and organizing (Ibarra, 1999; Brown, 2001, 2015; Ybema et al., 2009). It includes identity work (Coupland and Brown, 2012) and is reflected in the distinction between 'who I am' and 'who I think I ought to be' (Corley and Gioia, 2004). This search links the personal (biography) with what is going on in the world (history) and who we take ourselves to be, and is influenced by the person we see reflected in the eyes of others (Goffman, 1968; Watson, 2009). In this respect Identity is sometimes referred to as a dialogic process (Beech, 2008) and is seen as co-constructed through discourse – the way in which we speak about ourselves and what we do. This is often reinforced by the people we work with – our peer group.

Fraher and Gabriel (2014) explore a group of research subjects, furloughed pilots, specifically in the context of occupational identity. They see occupational identity as a narrative web that 'nestles in the identity narratives of each member of the community, blending elements from their profession's past successes and trials, present challenges, and future aspirations and hopes' (2014: 927). The authors also remark on the increasing demands that organizations make on their members. 'Organizations frequently demand that employees go beyond the mere execution of their tasks by embracing their values, brands and narratives – in short they expect employees to identify with the organization' (2014: 928). There may be a disparity between the commitment expected of the individual to the organization while at the same time organizations 'steadfastly refuse to offer employees the security and permanence of stable employment by constantly looking for opportunities to out-source and off-shore' (2014: 28). So, the demands of organizational identity can sometimes conflict with occupational identity – who I think I ought to be.

Identity narratives, it is suggested, are always provisional and reflexive. They are provisional in the sense that they are always open to being recreated by outside change (Ibarra, 1999). What is viewed as a disaster at one point, say a lay-off or job transition, may later come to be seen as a blessing in disguise, as it opens out a new and different chapter in their professional lives. The narratives are reflexive in the sense that the storyteller is also the chief actor in the story. So, 'in telling the story of our lives, we make sense of past events and create a person living in the present as a continuation of the story. It is in this way the story becomes digested and meaningful' (Fraher and Gabriel, 2014: 929). Individuals employ different images of their profession reflecting the different roles that they are asked to fulfil (Fineman, 1996) and this combines with the aspirational elements, the idealized qualities of organizations such as their status, prestige, and excellence which drew them to the organization in the first place. In this way, 'individuals' occupational identities become intertwined with organizational identities' (Fraher and Gabriel, 2014: 930).

In our exploratory work with our clients, interviewing can give us access to basic assumptions, ambiguity, ambivalence and also the identity that people have about themselves, the work they do and the challenges they face in continuing to feel valued in the work they do – in spite of unwanted change.

THE ROLE OF THE CHANGE AGENT

Our work as a change agent lies, then, in facilitating change. We are there to make it easy for people to approach change and challenge by finding out what their aspirations are and how they see what they do and its value. This enables us to be more effective in examining how they see the way forward in the face of that need for change.

THE QUALITIES OF AN EFFECTIVE FACILITATOR

Bullock and Batten's (1985) first phase suggests that **Exploration** is a vital step for implementing emergent change. In the first place this means exploring the need for change: **problem finding**. The problem with top-down change is that the decision has often already been made as to what the problem is that requires change and even sometimes what must be done about it (typically, training and a change in attitudes). In contrast, the participative approach to change requires an open-mindedness to continuing the search for the source of the problem – problem finding.

Map building suggests that the elements of the challenges presented may be linked and this may help in explaining to the proposer what are the findings of the Exploration phase. In this way, the results emerging from initial meetings can illustrate both what the problem is and what solutions are thought to be viable to implement a change programme judging by the support from those consulted.

We have already referred to the role of the consultant and whether we exercise leadership or management roles within the organization. In the strict terms of a specific roles the answer may be not directly. But certainly, indirectly we should both manage the change process effectively and on occasion be the role model for the change, which the organization needs to embark on. To be successful, change is usually a voluntary process and the risk is that enforced change will lead to a loss of the very resources the organization depends on to be successful – its key people. Transformational leaders know this well and so work to secure goodwill from people, who according to HRM theory, are our most important resource.

Good leaders often capture personal details about others in an way that they can consult the information and easily refresh their memory before the next meeting, allowing them to be able to refer to what they were previously told. Peter Drucker used to say that every manager should remember the names of the children of the people who work for her/him. That sounds like a good strategy for gaining commitment.

In summary, we can reasonably say to the group: 'I need to find out more about you in the first half hour than you find out about me.'

From Exploration we can move more confidently to Bullock and Batten's second phase: Planning.

PLANNING THE CHANGE TEAM

Change management requires that we identify three factors to plan a change programme effectively:

1. Content
2. Control
3. Process

This means finding out:

- What we want to do
- Who is in control
- How it is going to happen

This requires the consultant to identify the different roles which members of the change team will play. Here is one such list:

- The **advocate** who proposes change
- The **sponsor** who legitimizes it
- The **targets** who undergo it
- The **agents** who implement it
- The **process owner** – typically the most senior target

(Davenport, 1993: 173)

Think about the likely person required in each of the roles and consider what part they will play in the change team.

The **advocate** is whoever is calling for the change and usually that will be the most senior manager in the organization who called in the change agent. This person will usually be the first to be interviewed during the qualifying interview to discover what the basis of the perceived need for change is. They may also be the flag-flyer of the change and will play a crucial part in the implementation of the change programme.

The **sponsors** will usually be those who have authorized the change initiative and will be responsible for its implementation. Often that will be the Board of Directors. However, it should not be assumed that all members of the Board will be equally enthusiastic about the change. Indeed, it may be that there are some who were less than enthusiastic or even dead set against it.

The **targets** are all those who will be affected by and involved in the change process. That may well be all the staff and should include their managers and directors as well. But behind them usually lie other stakeholders and the effect of change on them should be included too. Most organizations work for the end-user or clients who pay for them or depend on them in some way. Their views should be sought, too, as they will be affected by the change programme. In the case of Leicester Royal Infirmary, UK, for example, the change team set up a focus group of patients who had complained about the hospital in the past. They sought their comments on proposed changes before implementing them.

In case we assume that the targets are passive subjects, our work with initial interviews may well have revealed people are onside with change; have experienced such change elsewhere; are open to becoming involved with change; and have previously shown a dedication to help themselves and others to face change. So, we may find internal change agents whose work will complement our own and eventually who will take over responsibility for evaluating the implementation of the change programme once we have left.

The **agents** who implement the change initially are the external agents. However, as time goes on it will be important to include and engage internal change agents who will help implement the programme and become responsible for ensuring its implementation into the future.

Finally, there is the **process owner** and here the external change agents need someone who will be in overall charge of the programme's implementation once its content has been agreed with the sponsors. Initial meetings need to be scheduled so that mixed groups are established, but also so that departments are not deprived of key staff all at the same time. So, too, training needs to be scheduled so that fill-in staff can be arranged for those who are away developing new skills and knowledge.

- As an external change agent, you belong to the fourth group
- As an internal change agent, you belong to the third and fourth groups (so have a foot in both camps)

INTERNAL CHANGE AGENTS

So, how should we choose internal change agents? Here are some pointers:

- Everyone is now a self-manager (according to Business Process Reengineering)
- Opportunities are presented for individuals to self-select themselves into change agency roles (the internal talent available)
- Change agency requires no particular profile for selection (apart from a willingness to learn) – so choose a cross-section of people

(Doyle, 2002)

EXERCISE

Think of a good teacher whose classes you enjoyed, perhaps in a subject that you would not normally have had a particular interest in.

Make a list of the qualities that distinguished the way that teacher worked with the class and its members (you can include the way in which they put across the subject; the way they made the subject interesting; the way they responded to challenges; and the way they supported struggling or slow learners).

Now go back through your word list and sort them into the four categories we refer to as the personnel profile: knowledge, skill, experience, attitude.

Which of the four categories contain the most words?

You may have found that some of your words coincide with the list that we saw in the previous chapter mentioned by Buchanan and Boddy (1992):

- Sensitivity
- Clarity
- Flexibility
- Tolerance of ambiguity
- Communication skills/Interpersonal skills
- Personal enthusiasm/Motivation and commitment
- Practical awareness
- Influencing skills

It is unlikely that every change agent will be able to demonstrate excellence in every quality listed. But the question of whether they can be developed and training offered is important to consider.

Just for a moment consider how each of the above qualities might be developed.

One way of doing this would be to indicate which factors of the personnel profile might be involved in each quality:

- Knowledge
- Skill
- Experience
- Attitude

Then reflect that training is focused on extending knowledge and/or enhancing skill, and consolidated by experience/practice.

Awareness and perception are more difficult qualities. Sometimes these can be factors depending on aptitude and may not be open to training directly. On the other hand, working with those that demonstrate the quality may be a way of developing it in others. In this case shadowing or mentoring may be a viable option.

Working with the external change agents allows individuals to appreciate the strengths of the others. Sharing (understudying another trainer) training events can help. Good role models reinforce the point that shadowing and mentoring may be a more effective route to acquiring such qualities.

SIGNIFICANT FACTORS FOR PARTICIPATIVE CHANGE

As change agents, we need to overcome the following blocks and alert internal change agency to the challenges they will face:

- Perceptual blocks (can't see the point of it)
- Emotional blocks (afraid but can't admit it)
- Cultural blocks (we've always done it this way)
- Environmental blocks (other people wouldn't like it)
- Cognitive blocks (I could not bring myself to do that)

Knowledge areas for change
Identity

- The way we think about ourselves
- The way we think about our job
- The way we think about our career
- The way we think about the organization

Example

- Sales people might feel that being regraded as 'wholesale merchandisers' was a step down; but 'business consultant' was a step up

Skill areas for change
Skill focused

- What do I have to do?
- What training have I had?
- Have I the aptitude?
- How fast will I assimilate the new behaviour?
- What will help me to reinforce these behaviours?
- What training updates and refresher courses will I need?
- Is success dependent on attitude?

Affective areas for change

- How I feel about my job
- How I feel about my work
- How I feel about my peer group
- How I feel about my boss
- How I feel about the organization

These areas might yield to discussion groups among fellow professionals. Discussion with individuals and groups may make it easier to address these issues with the people facing them.

So, what are the indicators that we might have someone who can fulfil the role of the internal change agent? Here are some indicators:

- Concern for the future
- Concern to develop human resources
- Focus on the product/service being provided to the customer
- Orientation to technologies in use
- A concern for quality, service, excellence and competence
- An orientation to outsiders
- A constant adaptation of reward systems and corporate values
- A focus based on making and selling
- Open to new ideas
- Always interested in learning

The last point is particularly germane. Willingness to train is an essential aspect of the likely profile of the internal change agent.

If you are an observer of groups discussing things among themselves then you can use a form to note how different people put forward their ideas of make their comments:

Names	John	Jill	Fred	Lisa	Mike	Sue
Ask questions	√√			√		
Suggest				√		
Build	√	√				
Summary		√				
Stating difficulty			√			
Aggressive			√√		√	
Silence						√
Other behaviour					√	

Source: Rackham and Morgan (1971)

Team builders tend to stay in the top four rows. Positive interventions tend to build up teams whereas falling into the more negative interventions further down the list can mean that team work is pulled apart by dissention or lack of involvement.

DEMONSTRATING THE CONSULTANCY QUALITIES

What are the qualities you need to be a successful change agent? Rosemary Stewart (1985) suggests some factors which distinguish good senior managers and consultants:

- Exhibit a high tolerance of frustration
- Encourage full participation and permit people to criticize them
- Continually question themselves but without being constantly critical
- Understand the laws of competitive warfare but not feel threatened by them
- Express hostility tactfully
- Accept victory with controlled emotions
- Are never shattered by defeat
- Understand the necessity for limits and 'unfavourable decisions'
- Identify themselves with groups, thereby gaining a sense of security and stability
- Set goals realistically

A tough call certainly, but worthwhile striving for if you are to become a successful change agent.

Internal change agents, then, are vital for facilitating change during change programmes and ensuring that evaluation continues after the external change agents have left the organization. Listening and talking to staff is often the first indicator that they are likely to be able to fulfil this role successfully.

Developing will depend on the external change agents spending time integrating them into the work of supporting the change programme through its different stages. Their knowledge of the culture and acceptance by their colleagues can make all the difference to the implementation of successful change.

CONSULTANCY IN ACTION

WORKING ACROSS CULTURAL BOUNDARIES

Conducting qualitative interviews can be a useful skill to acquire as they often reveal individuals' qualities and beliefs and alert the researcher to those whose basic assumptions will be aligned to the prospect of change and who have been involved with such initiatives in the past.

FINDING OUT MORE ABOUT PEOPLE AND THEIR ASSUMPTIONS ABOUT THEIR WORK, MANAGERS, AND THEIR COMPANY

Supannee Keawchaum, Lecturer in Innovation and Management at Songkhla Rajabhat University, Thailand

Introduction

I have just successfully completed my PhD looking at leadership styles in a company in my home country, Thailand. My research explored how transformational leaders influence organizational learning capability, psychological contract and performance. With ten years' experience in the HR field, I am always curious about how companies achieve their objectives. I realize that leading is the critical factor, particularly in developing and engendering commitment in their people to work for the company.

My research raises the question of how far the work of the transformational leader is like the work of the successful change agent – whether the change agent is external or internal to the company. In this section, we explore this connection in more detail particularly from the point of view of choosing and developing the internal change. The importance of this is to ensure that the work of evaluation continues at the end of the formal change programme after the external change agents have come to the end of their contract.

Transformational Leadership

We are in a turbulent and rapidly changing environment. Customers' needs are not as stable anymore as they may have been in the past. Organizations nowadays cannot remain in a static role any longer. This raises the question of how organizations can respond to, or even predict, such turbulent change in order to survive and be more successful than their rivals.

Transactional leaders push their followers to contribute an expected effort and performance, following the exchange agreement between leaders and followers. In contrast, transformational leaders move followers to generate extra effort, leading to the followers exceeding the performance that they initially believed they could accomplish. Transformational leaders also encourage their subordinates to transcend their self-interest for the sake of team and organizational goal achievement (Bass, 1985). We call this 'strategic integration' which is one of the four outcomes of HRM theory (Guest 1989 cited in Blyton and Turnbull, 1992).

At this point, we can see that the value-added concepts of transformational leadership (TFL) are useful for organizations with a turbulent and rapidly changing environment, because the leaders can try to get the employees to commit to the common goals, leading to performances beyond the followers' original expectations. TFL emphasizes follower development and achievement motivation, which fit the requirements of the working environment in the current knowledge age where people want to be challenged, inspired and empowered to achieve their career potential (Bass and Riggio, 2006; Despres and Hiltrop, 1995). In this way, TFL are involved in change (Levay, 2010) at three levels which are individual, team, and organization. The organizations facing change are looking for internal change agents who have the qualities of TFL.

Methodology

In our study, we used a mixed-methodology case study as its research methodology. The mixed-methodology approach included quantitative and qualitative methodologies. The quantitative research focused on surveys, which helped us understand the overall perception in collective level, the whole organization. In the qualitative research, semi-structured interviews were conducted with surprising cases that the surveys helped us to identify. So, we knew whom we should ask for more information in individual level. Besides, in qualitative research we also used observations and documentary analysis to help us have a clearer understanding of what the interviewees had said. Interestingly, this technique is relevant for change agents. That is because, at first, they may not know who to interview. A survey can be a good tool to help identify the interesting people to talk with.

In our study, we selected a market-leading company in the consumer-electronics business in Thailand as a single case study. The consumer-electronics business is interesting because consumer-electronics devices are based on technology, which never stops developing, rapidly and intensely continuing to revolutionize daily life. Furthermore, consumer demand has increased dramatically, in terms of a demand for innovations that serve to make life easier, and a demand for highly interrelated fashions whereby ownership of one consumer device influences the purchase of another. In this way, the consumer-electronics business is not repetitive, but instead must respond constantly to changes to customers' needs. Therefore, we saw that it was a good platform to evaluate whether a value-added concept of TFL is actually appreciated in this context. It is also worth exploring how far the transformational leader is an internal change agent facilitating change in an organization facing a rapidly changing business environment.

Transformational leadership qualities and the internal change agent

Based on our project, we found that transformational leaders apply their skills of asking the right questions, active listening and observing in an attempt to explore the root causes of problems at work. A service spare parts officer revealed that his manager opened her mind to listen to her subordinates' opinions, particularly the details concerning his job, which he knew in more detail than his manager. He remarked:

> She [manager] always asks the team's ideas and she combines our ideas with hers. ... She always said that she needs our opinions for our effective working. It's not only we that learn from her, but she also learns from us.

The managers respected their subordinates' ideas and that the managers managed to combine different people's ideas together. This suggests a way to learn together in a participative team involving managers as well as team members. This is a facilitating role in team working which is one of the key factors that Weick and Quinn (1999) mention in the profile of the effective consultant. It reflects 'inspirational motivation' whereby the leader provides meaning to their followers' work in a way that also relates to team goals; and the leader also encourages their followers to participate in envisioning attractive future states for the team overall. Such a working team is essential in achieving participative change, which is a bottom-up approach and engenders commitment to change more effectively.

In this sense, change may trigger learning but it may also trigger determination not to be involved in change or to resist the change. The change process at its best is a learning process, particularly in the sense that the managers want to stimulate their team to develop their ideas around the business needs. In this way 'strategic integration' connects organization objectives to departmental goals and then to individual key tasks.

We also found that such leaders act as a role model for the beliefs and values that they want their followers to adopt, rather than directly controlling them – for example, punctuality, honesty and sharing knowledge. The role model can be a useful approach to the voluntarily change process, 'change by example'.

Such role models are more likely to emerge from the internal group of workers than from the external change agent who comes in for a finite time to impose a change programme. This is especially important in bounded or embedded communities such as medical practitioners. So, we need to include such role models as internal change agents if change programmes are to be successful, particularly for the communities who are unlikely to acknowledge the credibility of outsiders as suitable role models.

In our project, we found that the sales function is likely to have a low commitment to change. That is because the nature of their work means they focus on their own targets. For example, their major responsibility is to travel to meet customers, so they do not record their working hours in the way that other employees must do. Yet they do not like to be controlled by too many company regulations. This is a big challenge for a company and requires the sales staff to gain the trust of their employer. So, the role of the manager, as the internal change agent, is to set an example of good practice to those in the field and to bring about the future change. The manager as role model may serve as a catalyst to embed good practice and change. As a sales person with 19 years of service revealed:

I've gained a lot from my manager. He teaches me a lot. ... He is my model. For example, he comes to work early, is dedicated to work, doesn't cheat the company. I've learned honesty from him. This makes me feel committed to the company and want to be like him.

Moreover, as found with our project, such leadership creates a relaxed atmosphere at work, which helps foster, for example, informal chats and discussions about non-work-related topics. This relaxed culture encourages helping behaviour and good relationships within the team and stimulates the generation of new ideas. The role of humour has a place in creating a relaxed atmosphere at work, an atmosphere that makes it easier for the change facilitator to work with teams to achieve change. Humour is usually only available to those who are on the inside of the organization, because it is a part of the culture – the way we do things round here, and the type of humour involved. The role of humour is captured in the following testimony from a finance officer:

She [manager] always talks to me in an informal way. She doesn't blame us when we chat a bit to each other. ... we laugh together. ... I'm not stressed. So, I can work well. ... I like working in the atmosphere like this.

There was another interesting example from our project: an accountant supervisor who at the beginning didn't want to be involved in kaizen activity. She explained that she didn't believe that the activity would be beneficial to her job and her workload did not allow her to become involved in yet another meeting. In her view, kaizen was a burden and she wanted to avoid it. However, kaizen is a compulsory activity. So, her manager tried to motivate and encourage her to become involved in the activity. In a sense, this reflects that her manager acts as an internal change agent who tries to find 'partners and allies'. By attending the meeting, she found that many job processes in her team could be speeded up. Finally, she changed her cognition and perception on kaizen activity. She came to believe that it could be very useful. She told everyone in her team and other departments about her experience and the benefits of kaizen activity. Finally, she volunteered to be a committee member of kaizen activity in the company. This reflects an interesting example of the influential power of change when its benefits are recognized by those who had previously resisted it. As she described her experience, she reflected on the implications for the organization:

People commit to what they believe has benefits for them. ... if people believe that change will provide benefits to them, they will commit to it.

Overall, our research interviews reflected several narratives that suggested managers were role models, providing learning opportunities, creating a productive atmosphere, respecting others' ideas and encouraging a change in perspectives. Such leadership engenders trust and loyalty, which are the integral aspects of the relational part of the psychological contract (Rousseau, 1995). At this point, the increase in organizational commitment is possible, and is reflected in lower staff turnover. It illustrates that people work for people they like and love working in an atmosphere they prefer. This quality of the transformational leader is useful for developing commitment to a change programme. In a sense, the internal change agent is well placed to make this sort of impact on the organization, particularly in the longer term.

THE INTERNAL CHANGE AGENT AND DEVELOPMENT

Based on our project, the management of the company initiated various learning activities that can be categorized into two approaches. Firstly, formal learning activity which is compulsory and directly related to employees' jobs to make them feel more effective at work – for example, kaizen activity, morning meeting, work rotation and training. It is the employee's duty to be involved in formal learning, which is why they are allowed to spend their working hours attending formal learning activities.

Kaizen activity is an interesting example of a formal learning activity which should be addressed here because it can be used as an approach to select and develop skills, knowledge and attitude for internal change agency. Kaizen activity in a company involves a six-month brainstorming activity that allows four to five employees across departments to initiate problem solving or to improve their work. In this way, kaizen can be a good approach to develop sharing knowledge and creating a culture of continuous learning. Kaizen can also be a foundation for recruiting and developing internal change agents. An engineer assistant manager expressed this as follows:

> This activity [kaizen] is great ... They [employees] can pull out the potential of each person and discuss it in their team, not keep it to themselves. ... They felt engaged in the activity because they know that the team tries to solve problems which impact on their work.

Such formal learning activity not only can be a tool for selecting the internal change agent who reflects the qualities discussed above but can also be a good tool for developing skills, knowledge and attitude and engendering commitment to change for the internal change agent.

The second learning activity is an informal or discretionary approach – for example, corporate social responsibility (CSR) activities, exercise classes, cooking classes, sport activities and trade fairs. It is not required that employees get involved in informal learning activities, therefore employees must spend their own time, after work or during weekends, attending informal learning sessions, based on their own preferences. Informal learning does not directly relate to the employee's job. Instead, it provides knowledge that looks beyond their job – for example, flexibility, communication and learning how to deal with people in different situations. The training is formal but attendance is voluntary. A marketing communication officer having 20 years of service stated:

> Good relationships arise from playing football together. The employees talk more to each other. Sports make us have a common topic to discuss. ... I want to come to work because of the friendly atmosphere and after work I can play football with my friends.

The above example reflects social relationships that good companies have always tried to foster among their employees. People are sometimes less willing and able to spend time and money on such activities when profit is the only driver. However, we would argue that enhancing value-added is an important aspect of what we should be developing with the people that work for us. In our research, we found that the informal learning approach contributes to good relationships among employees, leading to an overall positive atmosphere in the workplace, and encouraging the breaking down of social boundaries. Such informal learning activities can be a useful way of recruiting internal change agents from those with the willingness to learn and involve others.

OBSERVING ORGANIZATIONAL CULTURE

As we found in our project, the company's philosophy is 'everyone is equal'. This philosophy is known internally as 'the red brick concept', which means that every employee is like one of the red bricks which the company's building is made out of. Every single red brick is important for the company's building, so each single brick is essential. Each brick is a metaphor for the fact that no single employee can be left out. This is a part of the company mythology. Our research subjects described this as being inherent in the company's philosophy, which is initiated by the company but implemented by managers. For example, work rotation is open to every employee who wants new experience. An interesting case we found was an operator who got a good opportunity for rotating to a marketing co-ordinator. She explained that it was really tough to learn entirely new things but she felt valued for being given this great opportunity. To her, this leads to loyalty. She remarked:

> *It was a great opportunity for me to learn many new things. ... It feels good that the company offered such an opportunity to me. ... This makes me want to come to work because I exist and am valued.*

The change agent should take notice of this to suggest how far the company uses its philosophy and symbolism to foster the desired cultural values. In this case, the company uses them to foster the cultural values of continuous learning and engender organizational commitment by offering work rotation and building career commitment.

Another interesting example about observing organizational culture is language usage. When we conducted interviews, we observed how people verbally referred to their managers and colleagues. Many of our research interviews used the word 'friends', not colleagues or co-workers, to refer to the people they were working with. We could sense that those using the word 'friends' reflected that they preferred to share their free time in conversation and activities beyond working areas. For example, they had dinner after work and shared their holidays travelling together. On the other hand, the words 'colleagues and co-workers' reflect the sense that they only share resources concerning their work. This can link to the atmosphere in the workplace, in which friendship is likely to engender more helping behaviour, a relaxed atmosphere and a commitment to the team. Interestingly, sharing in such conversations helps change agents have more understanding of the workplace and this may help them to appreciate the workplace culture. When the change agents notice this, they can work with the change process more effectively.

THE LINK BETWEEN TRANSFORMATIONAL LEADER AND INTERNAL CHANGE AGENT

Based on our project, we found that the internal change agent can play a role in TFL. This is because transformational leaders do the work that the internal change agent does day by day, often unnoticed and unrewarded. Whether we like the TFL concept or not, the work of the transformational leader and the internal change agent is parallel in some respects because it relies on the same techniques and shares the same qualities. Both encourage, develop and get people involved and engender commitment in those who will be affected by and involved in the change process. They also facilitate people to develop through not just simple training but longer-term development. The company facing change needs such people and will try to develop them to facilitate change.

In the case where a company's management design and run a change programme by themselves, of course, it is possible for them to achieve change effectively. The crucial aspect is that the change team needs to form up with internal change agents who have qualities of TFL. In a case where management want to use consultants from outside, the external change agents need to go in, early enough, with a view to identify those internal change agents to give them effective change teams that facilitate change. It is necessary for the external change agents to look for people who have TFL qualities. This is the way to ensure that the change team can continuously process change after the external consultancy withdraws.

THE CHANGING ROLE OF THE INTERNAL CHANGE AGENT

To make change possible, it is not only necessary for the internal change agents to focus on team achievement. It is also necessary for them to consider individual concerns, which can be very diverse. This is because the individual needs to feel valued and respected which leads to a sense of involvement and commitment by the individual, which are the key factors in facilitating change achievement. Therefore, the internal change agent should focus on both team achievement and individual concerns at the same time, rather than on either the individual or the team. Team achievement is contributed by each individual's efforts. A sales manager reflected this challenge:

> You have to understand them [subordinates] individually. For example, you must know their background and interests, in order that you know how you could lead and motivate them. You, as a leader, know the targets of the team, but at the same time how you can lead your subordinates to achieve the same goals.

Interestingly, this reflects the role of a transformational leader who thinks carefully about the differences among subordinates and individual considerations, and utilizes the uniqueness or self-interest of each individual to contribute to the team's achievement. The internal change agent is in a strong position to achieve this.

Moreover, internal change agents need to change their role to work closely with the external change agents, rather than rely on the consultants throughout the change programme. Working closely means that they should become involved in every phase: Exploration, Planning, Implementation and Evaluation (Bullock and Batten, 1985). In this way, the external and internal change agent can learn together and learn from each other through the process of change. This involvement increases commitment to change. Besides, it leads to an appreciation of the complexity of the problems that will need to be resolved once the external change agents have left the programme. The ultimate benefit of this is long-term improvement. In this sense, consultancy is becoming internalized which means consulting practices are adopted within the role of management (Sturdy et al., 2016) – management as consultancy. At this point, HR plays a major role in selecting and developing internal change agents to give them the confidence to facilitate a change programme.

Linking the HR role to the selection and development of internal change agents becomes a form of management intervention to achieve the company's goals – in this case, the change programme. The human resource development (HRD) list (Randall and Sim, 2014) would include:

- Recruitment and selection
- Induction training
- Supervision
- Management
- Review
- Appraisal
- Reward
- Development
- Structure
- Communication

As we can see the HRD list can provide a useful toolkit for evaluating the change programme after the external change agents have left. It is particularly important to communicate well with employees, and get them involved to foster their commitment to and engagement with change. In fact, commitment and engagement are major factors in the success of change, particularly in the longer term after the formal consultancy programme has concluded.

CHAPTER SUMMARY

Finding out about the culture of an organization means talking and listening to the people who work in it. Identity, as we have seen, is a dialogic process and requires answering the questions, *who am I?* and *who ought I be?* The prospect of change is more than likely to trigger that personal search for those affected by institutional change programmes. So, for the change agents, being part of that self-reflective process is a privilege and something that should be embarked on early on, during the Exploration phase.

Stories and accounts that people give about their work are part of the interpretive framework which defines the past in a present narrative and provides a trajectory into the future. As Polkinghorne states:

> *These studies remind psychologists that people conceive of themselves in terms of stories. Their personal stories are always some version of the general cultural stock of stories about how life proceeds. As narrative forms, these stories draw together and configure the events of one's life in a coherent and basic theme. One's future is projected as a continuation of the story, as yet unfinished.* (Polkinghorne, 1988: 107)

Often, there will be jointly and strongly held beliefs about management's intentions, which it is clear will influence how individuals are likely to respond to imposed change. An example of this would be the belief that their managers are intent on destroying a way of life or changing the basic assumptions of those who are part of a profession. These groups are sometimes referred to as embedded or bounded communities (Nicolini et al., 2008) who are known to be resistant to attempts to breach previously held assumptions about their job, work, career and management expectancies. There can even be examples where professionals appear to collaborate with change but afterwards revert to their originally held basic assumptions about who they are and who they ought to be (Reay and Hinings, 2005, 2009). So, any opportunity to hear what those assumptions are and how people think about their work must be a benefit to the change agent in bringing about acceptable change.

Internal change agents should be in a privileged position as far as knowing the culture is concerned. They have usually shared early training; worked together within the group; and know the history of previous change experience (good and bad).

Kenneth Gergen refers to this exploration as appreciative enquiry. He summarizes it as follows:

> *People carry with them many stories and within this repertoire they can typically locate stories of value, wonderment, and joy. Within an organization these stories are valuable resources, almost like money in the bank. To draw them out, proposed Cooperrider, is to invest in new visions for the future. In sharing these stories confidence is stimulated and indeed the vision can be realized. In effect, appreciative narratives unleash the powers of creative change.* (Gergen, 1999: 177)

We believe that internal change agents are in a strong position both to receive these stories and to discuss their meaning with incoming external change agents. That makes the change team stronger in their awareness of expectancies, basic assumptions and previous experience of change. Thus prepared, they can embark on the change journey together knowing that participative change has begun and that the process of reflecting and listening will continue to inform important decisions throughout the programme of change.

For video content relating to this chapter please visit the companion website at **www.macmillanihe.com/Randall-Management-Consultancy**.

REFERENCES

Bass, B.M. (1985). *Leadership and Performance Beyond Expectations*. New York and London: Free Press and Collier Macmillan.

Bass, B.M. and Riggio, R.E. (2006). *Transformational Leadership* (2nd edn). Mahwah, NJ and London: Lawrence Erlbaum Associates.

Beech, N. (2008). On the nature of dialogic identity work. *Organization*, 15(1), 51–74.

Blyton, P. and Turnbull, P.J. (1992). *Reassessing Human Resource Management*. London: Sage.

Brown, A.D. (2001). Organization studies and identity: Towards a research agenda. *Human Relations*, 54, 113–121.

Brown, A.D. (2015). Identities and identity work in organizations. *International Journal of Management Reviews*, 17, 20–40.

Buchanan, D. and Boddy, D. (1992). *The Expertise of the Change Agent: Public Performance and Backstage Activity*. New York: Prentice Hall.

Bullock, J.B. and Batten, K. (1985). It's just a phase we're going through: A review and synthesis of OD phase analysis. *Group and Organization Studies*, 10(4), 383–412.

Corley, K.G. and Gioia, D.A. (2004). Building theory about theory building: What constitutes a theoretical contribution. *Academy of Management Review*, 36(1), 12–32.

Coupland, C. and Brown, A.D. (2012). Identities in action: Processes and outcomes. *Scandinavian Journal of Management*, 28, 1–4.

Czarniawska, B. (1997). *Narrating the Organization: Dramas of Institutional Identity*. Chicago, IL: University of Chicago Press.

Davenport, T. (1993). *Process Innovation: Reengineering Work through IT*. Boston, MA: Harvard Business School.

Despres, C. and Hiltrop, J. (1995). Human resource management in the knowledge age: Current practice and perspectives on the future. *Employee Relations*, 17(1), 9–23.

Doyle, M. (2002). Selecting managers for transformational change. *Human Resource Management Journal*, 12(1), 3–16.

Festinger, L. (1957). *A Theory of Cognitive Dissonance*. New York: Harper Row.

Fineman, S. (1996). Emotion and Organizing. In: S. Clegg, C. Hardy and W. Nord (eds) *Handbook of Organization Studies*. London: Sage.

Fraher, A.L. and Gabriel, Y. (2014). Dreaming of flying when grounded: Occupational identity and occupational fantasies of furloughed airline pilots. *Journal of Management Studies*, 51(6), 921–951.

Gabriel, Y. (2000). *Storytelling in Organizations: Facts, Fictions, Fantasies*. Oxford: Oxford University Press.

Gergen, K.J. (1999). *An Invitation to Social Construction*. London: Sage.

Goffman, E. (1968). *Asylums*. Harmondsworth: Penguin.

Ibarra, H. (1999). Provisional selves: Experimenting with image and identity in professional adaptation. *Administrative Science Quarterly*, 44, 764–791.

Jabri, M. (2017). *Managing Organizational Change: Processes, Social Construction and Dialogue*. London: Palgrave.

Levay, C. (2010). Charismatic leadership in resistance to change. *The Leadership Quarterly*, 21(1), 127–143.

Louis, M.R. (1980a). Surprise and sense making: What newcomers experience in entering unfamiliar organizational settings. *Administrative Science Quarterly*, 25, 226–251.

Louis, M.R. (1980b). Career transitions: Varieties and commonalities. *Academy of Management Review*, 5(3), 329–340.

Nicolini, D., Powell, J., Conville, P. and Martinez-Solano, L. (2008). Managing knowledge in the healthcare sector: A review. *International Journal of Management Reviews*, 105(3/4), 245–263.

Piderit, S. (2000). Rethinking resistance and recognising ambivalence: A multi-dimensional view of attitudes towards an organizational change. *Academy of Management Review*, 25(4), 783–794.

Polkinghorne, D.E. (1988). *Narrative Knowing and the Human Sciences*. New York: State University of New York State.

Rackham, N. and Morgan, T. (1971). *Behaviour Analysis in Training*. London: McGraw-Hill.

Randall, J.A. and Procter, S.J. (2008). Ambiguity and ambivalence: Senior managers' accounts of organisational change in a restructured government department. *Journal of Organisational Change Management*, 21(6), 686–700.

Randall, J. and Sim, A. (2014). *Managing People at Work*. London: Routledge.

Reay, T. and Hinings, C.R. (2005). The recomposition of an organizational field: Health care in Alberta. *Organization Studies*, 25(3), 351–384.

Reay, T. and Hinings, C.R. (2009). Managing the rivalry of competing institutional logics. *Organization Studies*, 30(6), 629–652.

Rousseau, D.M. (1995). *Psychological Contracts in Organizations: Understanding Written and Unwritten Agreements*. New York: Sage.

Silverman, D. (2013). *Doing Qualitative Research*. London: Sage.

Stewart, R. (1985). *The Reality of Management*. London: Pan Books.

Sturdy, A., Wright, C. and Wylie, N. (2016) Managers as consultants: The hybridity and tensions of neo-bureaucratic management. *Organization*. 23(2), 184–205.

Watson, T.J. (2009). Narrative, life story and manager identity: A case study in autobiographical identity work. *Human Relations*, 62, 425–452.

Weick, K.E. (1995) *Sensemaking in Organizations*. New York: Sage.

Weick, K.E. and Quinn, R.E. (1999). Organizational change and development. *Annual Review of Psychology*, 50(1), 361–386.

Ybema, S., Keenoy, T., Oswick, C., Beverungen, A., Ellis, N. and Sabelis, I. (2009). Articulating identities. *Human Relations*, 62, 299–332.

5 Changing the Culture: What is Feasible?

Julian Randall and Norrie Silvestro

> **Learning Objectives**
>
> After studying the chapter, you should be able to:
>
> - Recognize the difference between culture as 'something an organization is' and 'something an organization has'
> - Understand what is meant by the term 'schema' and how to change it
> - Appreciate the role and limitations of training as a culture change intervention
> - Address factors such as the process of legitimation and the management of meaning
> - Identify factors that adversely affect change, such as perceptual and emotional blocks
> - Identify the need to make and gain alliances

INTRODUCTION

Conducting initial research into the organization and its people puts us in a stronger position to work out what a change programme might feasibly include and areas which may present significant obstacles. So, we can return to the crucial distinction between culture as something an organization is (traits and behaviours) and something an organization has (perceptions and attitudes) (Smircich, 1983).

In all organizations we can become aware of what is sometimes referred to as 'custom and practice' – things that people inside the organization seem to take for granted and which could be putting the organization at risk by delaying change needed to counter the challenges of a changing market or political requirement. The main challenge here, of course, is what is the meaning ascribed to the behaviours that we observe by people inside the organization? How do they interpret what is going on, and what does that mean to the challenge of a change programme? The observer notes, measures, tests and compares the results but is still uncertain to what extent change is incongruous with the culture.

SO, CULTURE CAN BE...

- Behaviour.
- Something we learn or are taught: this can be direct or indirect (children and adults both learn through imitating role models at home and thereafter at work).
- Something we imitate or are trained to do: often this is more formal, particularly if socialization takes place, as when children go to nursery, or as adults during induction training in a company.

- Something we thereafter take for granted: psychologists sometimes refer to this process as internalization – in which we absorb a behaviour and accept its implications without question because it's 'the way we do things round here' and if I want to be accepted by the team, then I need to fall in line, too. After a while it becomes second nature.

Finally, it is a function of competence; and competence consists of three elements:

1. **Knowledge:** Do I know what to do in a certain situation?
2. **Skill:** Can I do what I am expected to do (am I trained)?
3. **Experience:** Has familiarity led to my internalizing the behaviour so that it becomes second nature?

SCHEMAS AND SCRIPTS

A good illustration of this process of forming a culture is the work of Schank and Abelson (1977). Their work concepts consist of schemas – how we learn what we should do in any social situation (such as the way we are expected to meet and greet strangers). The actions can be listed, as we try and get used to a procedure, which is complex, and this list can then act as an aide-memoire. The script is what you are required to say as you go through the prescribed actions. So, on arrival at the restaurant, you should:

- Wait at the door to be seated by the staff
- Choose from the menu (starter and main course NOT the dessert – you do that after you have eaten the main course)
- When you have finished your meal, ask the waiter for the bill
- Pay at the table or till before leaving
- Leave a tip for the service (usually 10% of the bill or more if you are feeling generous or have had more attentive service than you expected)

Changing a script or schema is usually possible as part of a change programme. We can then measure the behaviour and check or validate that it is occurring after the training. It can also be evaluated longer term by exploring the impact on the end-user or customer. Familiar examples include:

- **Retail/telephone interactions:** We are all familiar with the customized responses we receive from our phone enquiries to retail companies. Following a lengthy introduction of the speaker they usually conclude with, 'How can I help you?'
- **Interview procedures:** Usually introduced and conducted according to a preset formula so that each interviewer asks the same question as agreed with the Chairperson to avoid any accusation of bias.
- **Negotiation situations:** Sometimes roles individuals will play during the negotiation have been agreed in advance – for example, leader, observer and summarizer – as well as agreed signals to indicate to the Chairperson a desire to ask a question.
- **Crafting a speech:** Done in a predictive way to ensure that all the necessary parts of the introduction have been covered by the speaker to satisfy the audience's interests or needs.
- **Writing an assignment:** Adhering to the convention that the examiner or marker expects to see observed.
- **Closing situations:** Learned responses to signals or lack of them to gain commitment from a client or correspondent.
- **Handling concerns and objections:** Learned sequence of responses to give the speaker time to think of the real answer.

All of the above strategies can be learned; and this addresses the question of competence. In simple terms, it answers the question, can you do it?

PERCEPTIONS AND ATTITUDES

More difficult for traditional training interventions is the question of changing attitudes. After all, no one can measure others' attitudes directly. We mostly infer or attribute attitudes based on what we have heard or seen going on around us. Questions can easily be parried or avoided sometimes by apparent agreement or compliance, but later lack of change in behaviour may indicate that no change in attitude has occurred.

This is sometimes referred to as the answer to the question, *Do you want to do it?* In other words, your commitment or attitude.

So, training can address behaviours but cannot guarantee changes in attitude directly with the same confidence of success.

ACCESSING BASIC ASSUMPTIONS

So, how do we surface basic assumptions, apart from challenging them unwittingly? It is self-evident that asking for them directly is unlikely to meet with success. As we have seen, the work of Louis (1980a) can help us. She said that when individuals are surprised it often suggests that their basic assumptions have been disconfirmed; and when they are not surprised, their basic assumptions have been confirmed.

Most consultants will be dealing with organizations which have experienced change and certainly the staff may have experienced change programmes in different organizations. So, initial interviews with staff can offer an opportunity to question them about their change experiences and find out whether surprise was triggered or not by things that were done or not done.

Surprise and sense making have long been the focus of researchers' interest in organizations (Weick, 1995). Change itself can often take people by surprise. Lazarus and Folkman (1984) referred to the questions that arise as change programmes are implemented:

1. What is the nature of the threat to me?
2. What can I do about it?

As we have seen, ambiguity between what is said or promises made and what managers do is often a trigger of surprise in staff who witness it. It can give rise to ambivalence in individuals and groups, and Piderit (2000) suggests there are three levels of possible ambivalence that can occur:

1. **Cognitional** (I don't agree with the change)
2. **Emotional** (I don't like the change)
3. **Intentional** (The change should not be happening)

Her point is that there can be occasions when people recognise the need for change (cognitional level) but don't feel comfortable about it (emotional level), and are then left with deciding what they want to do to resolve this conflict within themselves (intentional level). The bottom line may be: Do they stay or do they leave the company? And we can cite here the fact that 70% of change events are perceived to have failed (Wilcocks and Grint, 1997), and that significant numbers of key staff are liable to leave following a merger or acquisition. In other words, the interference costs of change programmes can be high in terms of staff turnover, leading to extra efforts at replacement and the disturbance of customers who may have lost their regular staff contact from the organization and therefore feel less committed and open to consider moving their business elsewhere.

CHANGING BASIC ASSUMPTIONS

There is a well-known belief among management trainers that you can't change attitudes by training. This often comes as a surprise to managers who often believe the opposite. So, management consultants do well to alert prospective clients that quick or early changes to attitudes are unlikely to be achieved using training courses alone. Training providers themselves can sometimes imply that such change is possible. But we need only consider the most popular topics addressed by such courses to realize that early and easy change may be elusive:

- Leadership
- Teamwork
- Customer care

Most training courses in these areas focus on the behaviours and skills and sometimes the underpinning knowledge of these subjects (competence focus again). However, while they can explore ability, potential and aptitude, they cannot make individuals or groups feel comfortable in newly defined roles with which they are unfamiliar. Feeling a new role is uncongenial may lead to lack of commitment and avoidance of the role in the future even when the training seems to have been completed successfully.

EXERCISE

You want to change what a group of administrators do to include cold-canvassing telephoning of potential clients and building up business contacts.

- How would you approach this with them?
- What training would you offer?
- What development would you offer?
- What would you do to support those who can't cope with the change?

Asking individuals to undertake new roles in a business is necessarily dependent on their willingness to undertake risk. Nadler (1993) suggests that such change can easily trigger resistance. Forcibly changing a job description without the compliance of the individual could also give rise to grievance or even a claim of constructive dismissal. So, the answer to the first question would be a consultative approach in the first instance. Change agents expected to manage such an intervention would do well to point this out to managers before attempting to implement any radical change strategy.

Exposure to the new role might be a good investment – particularly talking to those who already undertake the job. Hints and tips of how to go about achieving success in the new role are always more credible coming from those who are already successfully involved in the role.

Acquiring experience in any job requires a path of development and is most easily effected by support during the early stages of acquiring expertise. A buddy system or mentoring scheme may be useful in the early stages. In some cases, what trainers sometimes refer to as 'sitting next to Nellie' may also yield support and assistance from someone experienced who is able to instil confidence during the early stages of acquiring knowledge and skill in a new role.

Finally, for those who are unable to adapt to the new role a fall-back provision will need to be part of the implementation plan.

EMERGENT CHANGE AND SIGNIFICANT AREAS

According to Pettigrew (1987) there are significant factors that should be addressed during change. We have referred to these earlier. Consider how you might address these as a change agent:

> - Processes of legitimation
> - The management of meaning
> - Symbolism
> - Language
> - Ideology
> - Myth

As with all short and pithy statements, some definitions might help in developing these points.

Processes of legitimation may be supported by legal constraints or accepted practices within a working group. Individuals who contravene are liable to experience the disapproval of their peer group and even be excluded from friendship and support.

Similarly, how meaning is managed depends on whose word is accepted as law. And in some cultures the informal power-broker is more influential than the formal leader. Staff may be more influenced by their first-line manager or leading hand than by senior managers or officers who they rarely see and with whom they do not share their working lives.

Symbolism is derived from the work of social anthropology and acknowledges that symbols may be emblemic (a national flag); totemic (a uniform that indicates significant power over others); or even iconic (often individuals whose lives are considered heroic in some way). Once again only familiarity and insider knowledge will indicate just how significant a symbol is within the organization.

Language can be acquired by mixing with and listening to those in the dominant culture. Often they are not themselves aware of how outsiders view the discourses that dominate their working lives. Working in total organizations, often uniformed in different ways, requires internalizing the language and sometimes confining its use to insiders, which can reinforce boundaries for those who seek entry and acceptance and certainly enable the identification of strangers as either 'one of us' or part of the out-group.

Ideology, may include dogmatic positions learned early on in institutional life which again are not challenged without repercussions such as being outlawed or excluded. Such positions are not always open to rational debate and can give rise to what is sometimes referred to as institutional – as in 'institutional racism'. It is sometimes evident in what is referred to as 'canteen culture' in which outsiders are characterized in a demeaning or insulting way.

Eradicating this type of behaviour can be difficult as in the story of the British soldiers who were sent to occupy the Falkland Islands after the 1982 conflict. They found the local islanders rather slow in language and manners and referred to them as 'Bennies' (after a slow-witted character in a then-popular TV soap called *Crossroads*). The officers put up a notice instructing that in future soldiers would not refer to the islanders as Bennies, 'as it was disrespectful'. A little later an officer overheard his soldiers referring to the islanders as 'Stills'. When he asked why he was told: 'Because they are still Bennies.' But at least the officer was practising what is sometimes called management by walking about (MBWA) and did come across what was going on.

Finally, myth often includes iconic figures. In organizations this may be famous founding figures; famous/infamous workers; or influential figures or celebrities relevant to the organization or its workers.

GAINING AND MAKING ALLIANCES

As we have seen, there are a range of people whom we will meet during the opening discussions with staff. Here are some which we have already discussed:

- Partners
- Allies
- Fellow travellers
- Fence sitters
- Opponents
- Adversaries
- Bedfellows
- Voiceless

People take their own time to decide whether they trust others or not. And it should be clear that change agents, especially those parachuted into the organization, are rarely welcomed by the people on whom change is to be visited. So, partners and allies may be sparse to begin with.

Sometimes those who are most stridently against change initially can be the most supportive latterly, once they have bought into the change programme.

What all change programmes need is credible role models in the face of an often-sceptical audience. Specific audiences are more likely to respond to those who have experienced change and survived it and are prepared to share that with others facing the same challenge. As external change agents we will be looking for those who can offer this within the change programme.

In a similar way, visits to organizations who have already demonstrated their ability to undergo change and come up with success may by a good option for staff and managers to experience. British car factories died while German car manufacturing flourished. There had to be a better way of brokering change than confrontation – seeing is believing but it takes lateral thinking and may take courage to embark on that journey.

The last point is particularly germane. Willingness to get involved in change events is an essential aspect of the likely profile of the internal change agent.

OPEN MEETINGS WITH THE STAFF

Your initial meetings with all the staff will be the final aim of the first phase of Exploration. As you do so there are questions that you want to explore. These can include:

- The history of the organization
- The background to the industry and traditional induction training

Then:

- Present job and what it involves
- Work rotation
- Career paths
- Continuous professional development

Then, finally, looking ahead:

- HR involvement
- Union influence
- Outside support (governmental or educational)

Our purpose is to achieve the following objectives:

- Explore basic assumptions about the organization and change in the past
- Identify where there may be opportunity for change agency roles
- Overcome blocks or resistance to change positively

ACTIVITY

The writers have had some experience of talking to and interviewing people. Listening for the signals and indicators lies at the heart of exploring a culture and hearing the narratives that have become part of common coinage among its members.

We are going to offer you the chance of reading excerpts from the scripts taken from four of our research subjects in one organization facing change – in fact a merger between two government departments.

Take time to consider what you are being told (sense giving), and how you respond to what you hear (sense taking). Remember that basic assumptions are revealed when these are challenged (often by imposed change); surprise often suggests that those assumptions have been disconfirmed. Consider whether this might be a factor that would work for/or against change in the future; and ask yourself whether they might be useful internal change agents in the future.

Research subject 1

Our first respondent started out in life as a teacher but transferred to a government department in her late twenties. This was her initial impression of working for the Civil Service:

> *Well, it wasn't a big transition really, because it was less demanding. I didn't have to take my work home with me. Cos when you, you know, you finish at (name of an airport) you finish for the day, that's it. Unless you get a job, and obviously you have to run with that job. I found it quite interesting, obviously dealing with the public and also dealing with oddities as well, restrictions on goods and stuff like that, but it was very different and it was also a lot more physical and it was a good change, for me it was a good change. However, I started to stagnate very quickly because you see you ask the same questions, where have you come from today? Are you travelling with anybody? Blah-de-blah-de-blah. You do start to stagnate. But a lot of people on the bench they stay there for donkey's years until they retire because they get caught in the money trap. That's my personal belief, because obviously when you take promotion, you lose money, because you are going from a basic plus an allowance, to just your basic salary. So, it's. Yeah. But you make sacrifices and change is sometimes good.*

- What assumptions are being expressed about the new job?
- What assumptions are being expressed about the job/work/self-development needs?
- What career aspirations are being expressed?

As time went on our respondent progressed through the organization becoming a manager herself. This is how she describes that change:

Well you'll take on the more technical issues first of all, you'll also manage the work that's been identified to be done and then you'll allocate that to individuals within your team who you think have the skills and are capable of doing it. So for example, inland processing relief is one of the duty reliefs we have whereby goods have come in from outside countries outwith the EU; they are allowed to come in without duty and VAT on the understanding that they are transported outside the Community or to another approval holder. So, we have that method of control... So, individuals I would allocate to that particular work, a lot of that work comes down from the central sift process into various regions and then that's where we divvy it up. But obviously the senior or the team leader would take on the more specialized areas. Also take on the management of individuals as well – the personnel side of things.

- How does she view managing the work?
- How does she view managing her people?
- What are her basic assumptions about the job?

After the merger, she wanted to get on and chose to put herself through training – some of it training courses and some of it online. She did well and passed most of her exams while still working and looking after her family. She describes it as follows:

Well experience obviously, is one thing. At this level, I have undertaken legal and technical training. I don't know if you [know] the legal and technical training department. I have done Excise, Legal and Technical, I have done and I've also gone externally to do the AIIT, so I didn't pass all papers so I will have to re-take... It is the way forward, training, but not a lot of people are keen on training in this sense. Because we have come from a more practical background on the Customs side, Revenue is exam-driven because if you pass your exams you get promoted.

- What assumptions does she express about training and development?
- What rewards does she expect from the extra effort?

But later comes the reality of the dynamics of merged organizations and what can happen to expectancies and promises made by managers:

I have passed two Legal and Technicals, I haven't got promoted. You see? I haven't got promoted. None of my colleagues have got promoted. Some people have got CTA, that's a higher qualification, CTA, and they haven't been promoted and some of them are very capable. But they haven't got promoted.

- What are her responses to this situation?
- What are the implications for her career aspirations?
- What are the implications for future training?

So, what are the final hopes and fears that she has for the organization?

But I've got individuals who ... who ... you know ... even yesterday I was doing a half year review with two individuals and they did not want to take even the Legal and Technical ... Why? What am I going to get out of it? Well your own personal satisfaction, it will help you with your job, it will make it more professional for you in business. What am I going to get out of it? They don't see those benefits. You try and sell it to them and they just ... Well what am I going to get out of it? I had another chap, he has just left and gone to another major, he has gone to a major outside because he got the qualification and was not recognized for it. Got frustrated and he has left. But you know he is going to work for his dollar now. Again, it's what an individual wants, I suppose.

And for herself:

For me it is work–life balance, I have a balance, I have studied three successive years, this is the first year I haven't studied and it's actually quite nice not to study. The last three years I did study because I want the qualification but.. I just didn't have enough in the fuel tank to get through them.

Research subject 2

Our second respondent was also a teacher who moved into the department to work. She describes the change as follows:

I was a physics teacher at the time so there was a, there was the bit of me that, that had decided I didn't really think I wanted to be a teacher for the rest of my career but also because physics teachers then and now of course were always in quite short supply so it was a no risk, it was a no risk ... thing that if I really didn't like it, you know, I could, I could go back to what I'd done before and actually I, I sort of enjoyed it tremendously. I mean that was what, thirty-two years ago, and I've done, you know, lots of different things and the training I received I thought was really first rate, it was, it was, you know, the, what was then the sort of Inspector training course it was, it was one day a week and in a, in a group of people so we had lots of opportunity to discuss issues and there were exams and actually they were really fine, I mean they were degree standard and certainly a degree standard and were far more, a far more need to remember things and learn things than I ever did (laughs) when I was doing my physics degree.

Ask yourself similar questions to those for the previous respondent or make your own comments on what you are hearing concerning basic assumptions and expectations of the career and training provided.
She continued:

I suppose I've just been very lucky because I have progressed and I'm now in quite a senior position in the Department whereas ... there are quite a lot of people who joined in the same way as I did who are still at say grade seven or grade six and so don't have the sort of, you know, whatever power and influence I might have, it's probably more, and, and so I think it's, it's different people respond in different ways don't they?

There is overview about organizational development looking back on her career:

So, it's interesting that there is and I think what, what we're now coming around to thinking is that we do need to be a bit more hands-on in, in actually doing, doing career management. So we've sort of gone from one extreme which is you just sit there until someone rings you up and says we're going to do something to you to the bit that says well actually completely out of our hands, you sort it out for yourselves, apply for jobs and which meant that people hopped around to, to a bit which I mean hopefully is a, a bit more balanced which is that actually we will, we will actually nurture the talent and actually suggest ways in which, in which people can get the, get the experience but clearly we're not going to go back to spoon-feeding people.

She acknowledged the part that others played in mentoring her career:

Dave [her manager] was superb, he really was. He ... you know, he, he identified, you know, a project for me to do, supported me and as I say and then, and then I, people got to know me again and then, you know, I, I found my way in. But it was, it was sort of interesting because, because you do need to have people who care don't you and if you don't have people who care then, then it can be quite, quite difficult.

She reflected on her experience as a female in a predominantly male service when she joined:

I don't really like a sort of gender stereotypes but it is interesting that I think women do on the whole tend to approach their assessment of their abilities slightly differently. You know, I remember someone saying to me that, you know, in a competition for a job a woman is likely to say well actually I'm not, no better than those other people so I don't see why I should get the job. A man would say well I'm at least as good as those people so I think I should get the job. And it's interesting actually I've, I've sort of flagged that with quite a lot of women and it strikes a chord with all of them and it's, it's sort of interesting isn't it cos actually you're saying the same thing.

And the prospects for the future:

I mean we've got to be, we've got to be better at doing things more efficiently. So, so, so the bit that actually looks at what, what, what value do we add I think. Whereas I think … you know, many years ago I think, you know, you just did what you did didn't you cos that's what you did and the bit that says well actually, you know, what value am I adding towards this from, from a sort of UK plc perspective rather than just as an organization.

How far is this narrative similar to or dissimilar from the first research subject?

Research subject 3

Our third respondent also came to the Civil Service with outside experience first. She describes her early career in these words:

I was completely different, I worked in the private sector for Mars in Slough and I was the marketing/market research expert so I dealt in a very different environment. The only reason I gave up that job was because I had children and I stayed at home. It was only when a colleague persuaded me to come and cover a vacancy he had in his organization which just happened to be Customs. He said you're just the sort of person, come and work for me part-time so in I went and I never looked back.

She proceeded through the organization with a determination to progress:

I came in as clerical, way before I joined Mars I had worked two years for Inland Revenue (IR) and I'd also worked for *Times* newspapers but because I'd worked for IR as an EO they reinstated me. I suppose the way I gained promotion every two years, I was jumped up the ladder so every two years I had to change direction and when I got to band 11 and my age was almost against me at this stage, there were no band 11 jobs. A colleague knew that I didn't mind what job I do so a job came up in IR so I went off to IR in 1998. I settled in there very quickly into a totally different culture and different type of work but went straight and managed technical experts without any knowledge of the tax and I just loved it

What were her basic assumptions about her job, work and career in an organization?
She goes on to describe her organizational involvement in change:

I tend to think my life has been one of change all the time and I work in an environment now with a director where I have to face change every day, even if it's … has just been cancelled therefore you have to juggle things and change things. In my life I've had changes, divorce as well and I've just bounced back – it's life isn't it? Part of me I think welcomes change because I think it keeps you very refreshed and on the go and looking forward and I reckon I'm more proactive because I'm always looking ahead to see what may be on the horizon.

How does she approach change in her life? What might this suggest about her approach to the management of change?

She initiated change at work, being unsatisfied with the standard way of approaching client debt:

When I came into the department they had books of instructions and that was incredible. I was one of the ones who rarely looked at them, I didn't do anything that was wrong but when I went into debt management with another person who is a band 11 now, we actually looked at debt differently.

So, she initiated different ways of approaching problems:

We said we have seen notices of distress that come out when the trader has not paid for 40 days or something and by the time you get out to the trader they have been used to you going through this rigid process and they play you at it, they know what you are going to do … instead of waiting for the distress notices we deliberately started this predictive dialling with traders which they are only just bringing in to the department now, we started calling traders who we knew always had a problem but that we also knew would have a large debt with us and we rang them on the first day they had that debt, the day the return came in, and asked them what arrangements they were making to pay so we got them to strike up 'time to pay' arrangements 45 days before we normally touched it, so we looked at the problem differently. There was the rule of instruction that after 45 days you will send this letter, etc. and this was the rule book but we did things differently and we got the debt to the lowest that it had been.

So, what do you think is her approach to change management in business?

She is already looking ahead to the merger in a proactive way, having worked in both organizations:

When you go into their processing centres their managers are so rigid and by the book that they don't spot how they can change that organisation. They recognize their weakness that they aren't an organization that's got leaders because they've never seen the need for them. Also, people keep on about the merger but people are looking into themselves, what is in it for me but I think that modernizing government says we've got to do things differently and that possibly means looking at the customer. Small businesses in this country, for a long time have been saying, bureaucracy is crazy, the rules are horrendous so what the Chancellor is saying is I want a small business focus across revenue departments and I want a large business focus across revenue departments (separation of responsibilities).

And this means managing people to best effect, too:

I brought a band 7 from Reading to the IR to work with me when I was there, she was a resource management system expert and was also a tremendous bookkeeper so she could spot a rogue figure and the IR didn't have that sort of skill, they have tax skills. She went in as a band 7 she is now a band 11 in IR, in three years she has got to band 11, she would never have got beyond band 7 in Customs because she didn't have the right skills to progress, with IR she has never looked back and she has come back and got a load of people from Customs into IR and everyone who has gone to work in IR has said the career, the map laid out is there and you don't need to be a technical expert to get it. I may be a bit off the wall with my reactions but I think that's probably why I do the job I do with the director where we are constantly having to look outside the box and think of something different, or what's in this for us? It makes life very enjoyable.

So, finally, what of the way ahead:

People have never walked across the river in London (between the two divisions), gone to those officers and said tell me about yourself. I have good friends in both Customs and IR who I network with and we are quite open with each other about what is going on and the people in IR I network with really welcome with open arms if we could do more together because they see the sense. You may say it is a bit of a threat to the poor taxpayer out there if you merge two organizations and there are certain things about the data protection but we can do business much better and I think save a lot of hassle, especially to large businesses with having some sort of convergence and I believe a merger of us with a LBG of the IR would be good for business and good for us and the staff aren't going to lose their jobs, the director will lose his job and the support team may lose their jobs but the work will be the same. I think it could be a win-win situation.

So, how would you rate her likely contribution as an internal change agent?

Research subject 4

Our final subject came to the Civil Service from outside organizations and was recruited for his expertise as a Financial Director/auditor.

He describes his early career as follows:

No, I didn't join from school, I worked in industry for many years and I'm a qualified accountant and I joined as a qualified accountant, I joined direct from industry. I've got varying experiences in industry, some of the things I can relate to that you are talking about.

So, how did he adjust to joining the public sector?

You are seen as a specialist and therefore you are not a generalist and therefore you don't meet the criteria, you may not have some of the management skills, not that they are ever tested and not that you had the opportunity to do that but they were some of the issues. I found it a bit galling because I had come from managing 80 and 100 staff and being told that maybe I hadn't got the management skills because I was working as a specialist. I thought, hang on, has anybody ever tested this or looked up my background and what I have got?

What does this suggest about working in different cultures?
He remembers the time before the Civil Service when he had appreciated the support and development of a significant manager in his professional career:

The job just grew, I was very fortunate as I had a very good mentor, the MD, subsequently the Chairman, was my mentor as I worked for him directly right the way through and as he progressed everywhere he went he took me with him so I ended up doing a, it was almost like an incremental job, I started doing one area then I picked up the next bit then I picked the next area and then I ended up as Commercial Manager working for them. I was one below the board, I suppose, in terms of the appointment and then I was I head hunted and I was offered a post as Finance Director.

Interestingly, he was sent away on the three-day assessment course for a senior position in the Civil Service – and failed it. Ironically, he was appointed to the position anyway. But he reflects on the experience:

Yes, it is and I think, one of the things with civil service as a criticism is that it is very closed. It only looks at what you do within, it never looks at what you've done without, it never looks at what you are bringing to it and I think that is something we have got to change, we've got to change that. When they look at you they look at what you've done within the civil service and not what you are bringing to the party in terms of other skills and other things, it is almost wiped out, it is an irrelevance to people's memories in terms of what you bring to the party. And yet other people who have done other things that, I would say, are much less quality and much less developmental are viewed much higher because it has been done within the civil service and I think that needs addressing really.

As far as interactive training and development are concerned he had been sent to Harvard Business School on a course for senior managers before joining the Civil Service so he appreciates interactive developmental courses:

The first session that we did was on creative thinking and it was really about the process, doing different things and it was good fun, I enjoyed it. Then it was on business issues, some of the issues that came up in another session about we were going to deal with them and then we were taking some of the techniques of creative thinking to go away and apply them and come up with the solutions and in a way it was good, we enjoyed it, it was good fun, the creative thinking thing was good fun and some of the exercises were really good and then applying them in the business sense was actually quite productive and actually got what we wanted out of doing.

Discuss how far his approach to training and development would be a benefit as an internal change agent.

Summary

Looking at the four subjects we have included we can identify the knowledge, skill and experience that would contribute to the profile of a potential internal change agent.

ACTIVITY 2 CHANGING CULTURES OVER THE YEARS

The research article 'Understanding employee attitudes to change in longitudinal perspective: A study of UK public services 1996–2007' by Procter and Randall (2015) summarizes work that the authors did together in one organization across 11 years in three different research interventions. It is intended to reflect on constant change in an organization and its impact of perceptions of change among staff. It has implications not just for the individuals but also corporately for the organization. Together they represent the culture of the organization.

What is interesting is to compare and contrast the responses that we had to the same questions in each of the three cohorts.

Please read through the article; it is available at: http://dx.doi.org/10.1108/QROM-01-2013-1127

Questions for you to discuss:

1996 cohort

- What were the main responses to change?
- What did most respondents feel about the way change was imposed?
- What are the implications for the relational part of the psychological contract?
- How should management have conducted the change to avoid resistance and alienation?

2003 cohort

- What was the reason for the change in HMCE?
- How did each of the three groups respond to the change?
- What were their views of the senior managers above them?
- How did the change programme impact on the culture of the organization?

2007 cohort

- What was the reason for the merger between HMCE and Inland Revenue?
- How did IR impose its dominance on HMCE?

- What were the responses of HMCE managers to the reorganization that took place in their work?
- How would you have conducted the change to avoid the disappointment that HMCE staff felt?

CASE STUDY: CHANGING A CULTURE – ROOTING OUT DISCRIMINATION

For most uniformed organizations there are often cultural values that those joining absorb early on in their career. Cohesion within the working group is important, and the team loyalty needed in sometimes hostile environments means that the members need to trust each other implicitly at all times. This can mean 'the way we do things round here' becomes the defining factor of acceptability for new-joiners to the organization. But also, there is the aspect of what we think about what we do; who is 'one of us'; who are our adversaries; and how do we deal with them? This is sometimes referred to as part of 'canteen culture' – what the group takes for granted about other groups, management, outsiders, perceived opposition to group values and objectives, and so on.

You have been employed as a consultant by your local Police College on several occasions and you have noticed that all of the above applies to the way officers relate to each other and those outside the force; the conversations that they have about their work and the challenges they face; their view of management and those they regard as do-gooders, in particular; what should happen to those who break the law; how we treat minority groups and how we deal with them.

You have already conducted programmes for the force in the past and you have noticed that they are very rank-conscious. On one occasion you gave a talk to assembled ranks of volunteers and several times you tried to get them to join in a discussion but had been met by total silence. Afterwards you were told that nobody speaks unless the senior officer present speaks first. On that occasion the senior officer had chosen not to speak – so no one else did either.

You set up and ran a mentoring programme for senior ranks (superintendent or above) chosen to mentor accelerated promotion path candidates (graduates who would be proceeding through the ranks more quickly than non-graduate recruits – from substantive sergeant to chief Inspector in seven years). You noted that mentors had to be of Superintendent rank or above and at that time there were only two female superintendents who fell into this category whereas female trainees were 40% of recruit intake and rising. When you suggested that the rank of a good mentor should not matter, the response you received was that women should accept whoever they were given as a mentor, male or female.

You also discovered that senior officers intending to inspect a police station had to give two weeks' notice to the station sergeant. This raised a question in your mind about how likely inspections were to uncover matters of concern or poor practice.

The McPherson report suggested that the police force who mishandled the enquiry into the murder of a black teenager, Stephen Lawrence, was 'institutionally racist'. Mindful of this rebuke the Head of Senior Division comes to you and asks you to put together a programme for all officers to counter institutional racism for those going forward to senior command posts.

- What issues would you want to raise concerning this request?
- What aspects of deeply rooted attitudes can be changed by training?
- Are there alternative or complementary ways of approaching a radical change to such a culture?
- Who would need to be involved in this programme?
- What role would senior officers need to play?
- How would we measure the programme's success?
- What changes to the organizational procedures might need to be introduced to reinforce a change in values and beliefs?

EXERCISE

Lessons for Change Managers?

Write out a list of six Dos and six Don'ts for managers who want to facilitate change agreeable to those who have to undergo it.

Use your own experience of change at work to compare and contrast with the case study offered here.

CONSULTANCY IN ACTION

WORKING AS AN INTERNAL AND EXTERNAL CHANGE AGENT

Norrie Silvestro began his consultancy career as an internal change agent in the health sector. He then went out as a self-employed external change agent working both in the UK and abroad. He frequently returns to his original employer where his expertise as a change agent is still valued.

GETTING IN, GETTING ON, GETTING OUT AND GETTING BACK: REFLECTIONS OF AN INDEPENDENT CONSULTANT (1993–2016).

Norrie W. Silvestro MA (Hons), Ph.D., C.Psychol., AFBPsS, C.Sci
Chartered Occupational Psychologist
NWS Assessment & Development

Introduction

No one is born or brought up to be an independent consultant. It was not even a 'normal' work role aspiration where I grew up. Clearly, it requires dedication and determination. It also needs a solid foundation of relevant qualifications, skills, experience and motivation to be successful with the purchasing client, or their gatekeepers. However, when I was a very small child (aged about seven), I can remember thinking to myself: 'I will never work for large companies because they move you around whenever it suits them!' I do not know where that observation came from. My mother worked as a cleaner and my father was a van driver. We did not ever have any conversations about jobs, careers or the politics of work.

However, when I was approaching 21, this strange 'not fair' notion came back to me. Consequently, I never applied for any of the Graduate Schemes during the University 'Milk Rounds' (in the pre-social media and internet eras when large companies went around university campuses to recruit new graduates). Instead, I preferred to keep my independence by undertaking a PhD in Occupational Psychology. I was also determined to create my own 'applied' research focus rather than be part of a 'PhD factory'. I worked hard to explore many areas that could become the focus of my research. Initially, I was attracted to the puzzle of why negative information did not travel up from the shop floor to the top of the organization. I was also interested in how meeting room configurations might impact the level of engagement, communication and decision-making in business meetings. After a lot of reading and thinking, I finally settled on investigating the psychological challenges associated with introducing worker-directors into the Board Rooms of private sector companies. This was a part of a European Union legislative proposal, which became the UK Committee inquiry of Industrial Democracy report (Bullock, 1977).

In this section, I intend to offer an overview of my experience as an internal and an external consultant over a period of more than two decades. I have loosely framed this narrative within a structure first offered by Buchanan, Boddy and McCalman (2014) when they described the key steps and the core skills required

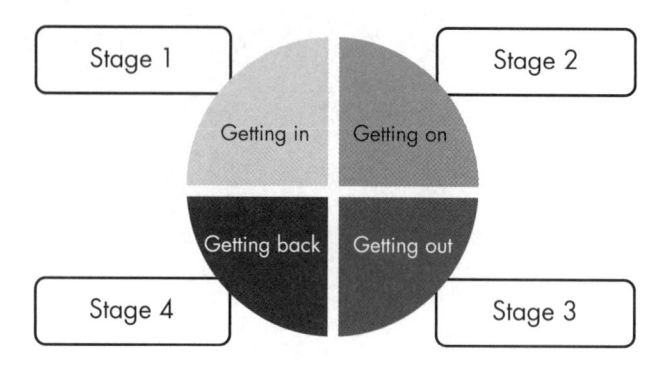

Figure 5.1 A consulting reflection framework
Source: After Buchanan, Boddy and McCalman (2014)

to conduct effective qualitative field work for researchers. The active labels in this model had a strong resonance with me when I was looking for a framework to share my career experience for my presentation to postgraduate students studying for an MSc in Consulting. It also captured the sense of dynamic uncertainty that I experienced during this period. The framework can be applied to the consultant role level and to the career and consulting industry levels too. This chapter is not offered as a 'best practice' example. It merely offers some personal reflections on the journey of one consultant, on what helped and hindered my functioning and survival as a consultant. It is a personal and professional reflective case study.

The model in Figure 5.1 provides a structure to share my anecdotes and experiences about learning to work and survive as a consultant. Inevitably, like any model, it is a simplification of what actually happened in my career. Additionally, some of the stages have quite a degree of overlap and interdependence. Indeed, it operates more like a series of overlapping spirals as different client projects coexist in the different stages.

Getting in: How to identify and connect with prospects

I got 'into' psychology by accident. My school career advisor suggested that this might be a good subject for my foray into a university qualification. Becoming an independent occupational psychologist is a common route for occupational psychologists who have worked for the large UK Occupational Psychology consulting businesses. This typically provides these practitioners with a good foundation with a range of work projects with increasing responsibility for complex business development, design and delivery. It also has the potential for these individuals to build up a broad and deep subject matter expertise and high visibility across a wide range and levels of businesses. Additionally, it also allows them to build a professional and client network (before the days of LinkedIn) that they can draw on to extend their reach and visibility into other projects and assignments as independent Associates. Once qualified as an Occupational Psychologist, I still did not seek out this 'large company' route to employment as I wanted to retain control and influence over where I worked and what I worked on.

My first professional consultant assignments were typically obtained through informal work connection or through recommendations by people who knew me. As I moved towards operating as an independent consultant, I began to get into organizations via formal procurement bids and tenders. I also made progress into getting new business via informal networking, and scanned the literature and the professional magazines looking for tenders and new work opportunities.

My first professional assignment came through a friend of mine who had a client contact. They wanted a new secondary school intake to be assessed using a psychometric ability tool to help them to assign the pupils to different class cohorts. They needed this support service quickly, and I was able to propose a tool and a group administration process that was acceptable to them. They did not know that this was my first consultancy assignment. They might have guessed this from my nervousness. I spent a lot of my time getting to know the technical strengths and weaknesses of the tool and how to administer, score and report the results.

My lack of experience meant that I was only partially prepared for the challenges in the context of the group admin of this psychometric test. The school hall had about 200 nervous new secondary pupils seated in rows of desks. I stood at the front and provided the welcome and the verbal instructions about what the task was and what they needed to do within the time available. However, I did not anticipate that a proportion of the pupils would not be able to understand what I was saying. This problem arose, not because I spoke with a Scottish accent but because several of the pupils did not speak English (or understand my version of it!). I had no contingency plan for this situation because I did not have the experience to anticipate this issue arising.

My first real full-time job was when I was hired to lead a small team of trainers to support the transition of young unemployed people into work through structured work experience and college-based training. I did this job for a couple of years (while I was writing up my PhD thesis). Then I became a 'proper' internal consultant to support a broader culture change programme at a local university to help the academic staff seek out new income streams. I was hired to help them market and sell their expertise to employers for specialised training products and services.

A year later, I switched to a Head of Organization Development (internal consultant) role with my local health care provider. This was also a culture change role to support the organization to become more service-orientated and to improve how it planned and used its staffing and its physical resources to deliver better services. The vision was to create a 10-year Service and OD strategy. I did this role for about five years. I described some of the challenges there through some case study reports that I wrote with two of my direct reports (Grubb, Silvestro and Ward, 1994a, 1994b). As part of an ongoing restructuring within health care, I became the Management Development Manager responsible for the identification and development of the top 200 managers and clinicians.

At the age of 40, I decided that I wanted to 'get out' of my internal consultant role and 'get in' to become an independent consultant. I had a couple of goals behind this 'plan'. Since I was a post-graduate student for a long time, I set a financial target to double my income within a year of going independent. I also had a professional goal of testing the extent to which my previous 'success' at work was largely down to my skills and experience, or whether I was just fortunate to work with really good HR colleagues.

Most of my 'getting in' meetings have been set up and created through my informal network of professionals who I had worked with and who had then moved on to new roles and new organizations. They were often meetings with HR stakeholders to explain the context and the challenges that they were facing. This 'chemistry session' first contact typically led to a formal proposal and bid process (mostly without competition). I have also benefited by approaching larger organizations that I discovered were building up consultant capability for large national and international contracts. I have worked as an Associate consultant for several large consultancy businesses. In the last year, I have been approached by two consultancy businesses who wanted to extend their Associate pool. This contact was made by them through LinkedIn, and they both led to very interesting and challenging Associate work.

This is the most challenging phase of the consultant work cycle. It requires constant market vigilance to seek out opportunities to meet with potential clients or their gatekeepers. In the public sector it has also become even more demanding through the growth in formal procurement hurdles. These often consume time and effort to write and submit proposals as bids just to get onto a 'preferred' shortlist. After many failed attempts to win new business through this process, I concluded that it took up too much time and effort and it was not a reliable way to win new business. I made the commercial decision to stop participating in any future bids through these formal procurement channels (unless I had an internal stakeholder that could help me navigate the way in!).

Weiss (2003) is also clear that he needs to meet with the 'economic buyer' to ensure that his needs and expectations are clear and realistic and that he can deliver against them. One of the main helping traps that Schein (2011) identifies in this phase is that inexperienced consultants often try too quickly to satisfy the

Turnover by Year

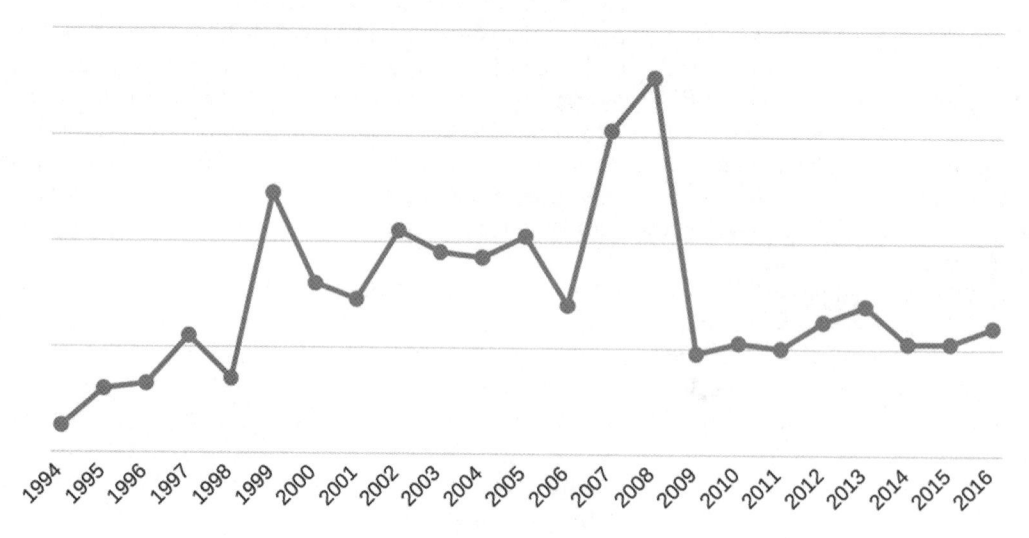

Figure 5.2 Turnover by year

client's needs by suggesting new solutions, being sure that they have enough pertinent data and without the guarantee that they will win the new business.

Once, when I was making a presentation to MSc students in the Occupational Psychology degree at the University of Leicester, on what it was like to work as an independent psychologist, I showed them a graph of the variation in my earnings over a 10-year period. It was highly variable! I invited them to interpret what this graph meant. I interpreted it as stress, and it also reflected that my post-graduate degree had nothing in it that prepared me to become an independent business operator. I was not taught how to market or sell my skills. I also did not know how to be commercial and business focused. I had to learn these skills by just 'diving in'.

I have reproduced this chart for a longer 20-year period. When I reviewed my accounts over this longer period, I was still surprised at the extent of the annual variation. Even within each year there was often considerable variation across the four business quarters. Access to work though Associate assignments reduced the anxiety of income variation. It meant that I did not have to market or 'sell' my services actively as this was not a strength of mine. The income flow pattern was still 'feast' or 'famine' as a solo consultant (Figure 5.2).

Getting on: How to build effective rapport and trust with clients

In terms of the work profile of who I was aiming my services at in organizations, I saw myself as a peer support to the Senior HR specialists in OD, Training, Performance Management, Recruitment and Assessment, Succession Planning and Coaching. I also saw myself as the 'professional's professional'. Someone that they could call in when they were stuck, either because they lacked experience and expertise or else they did not have the time to deliver specific work projects, or because they lacked the credibility as internal HR staff with the senior stakeholders due to the 'professional glass ceiling' that I had also experienced as an internal advisor. I was careful to position myself in the initial conversations as a partner and not as a threat.

Clarifying the key requirements and needs associated with each project typically occurred through meetings with the key stakeholders. I used questions to clarify the outcomes required and the timescales for delivery. I also developed a way of working that sought to involve and engage a wide range of stakeholders on key projects. I did this to check that I had a clear understanding of the work context. I also took this approach to validate the issues and to assess the likelihood that the planned solutions would be capable of addressing the context and the potentially different interpretations of the problems.

For Block (2011), this is the critical part where 'contracting' about mutual wants and expectations needs to occur and to build trust and rapport. To further enhance the need to build trust at this phase, Weiss (2003) advocates that the consultant should focus on offering what is in the client's best interest and focusing on building rapport rather than closing a sale.

I also learned to include 'dissidents' in project teams as I believed that their concerns and frustrations usually contained a 'nugget' of insight that others in the organization had rejected or stopped listening to. It also provided some insights about what concerns and obstacles that might exist in the broader organization. However, I also 'contracted' with these 'dissidents' that they would need to be full participants in the change projects, and that they would not be allowed just to use the project as a disruptive 'soap box' for their discontent. Collaboration and respect were critical in creating these new projects working relationships. For me, it was also about ensuring that the internal project team and managers were given the credit for the progress and the success of the initiatives. I was happy to be influential by 'leading from the back'.

When I was an internal OD consultant working in the NHS, I remembered an incident when I observed the most senior Board General Manager 'requesting' a time in the diary when the external consultant was available. This surprised and confused me at first because it did not reflect my model of who had the power in the consultancy – client relationship. Clearly, it was not as simple as I had imagined. Later, as I mentally prepared for becoming an independent consultant, I created a future scenario picture of my diary being full with client projects. This felt really good. I was also anticipating feeling good about the prospect of being able to turn down potential work because I was too busy or because I did not want to work with a particular client or project.

Weiss (2003) also advocates offering clients three options with different levels of complexity and costs rather than offering a single specific set of proposals. He regards this as the best way to give clients the choice and ownership of how to proceed.

Getting out: How to ensure effective service delivery and handover

So, I had to 'get out' of being an internal consultant and employee before I could 'get in' to become an independent consultant. One night at the dinner table when I told my family that I was going to become 'self-employed', my daughter was shocked as she thought that I said that I was becoming 'unemployed'.

There were other practical reasons behind my decision to change my work identity. There was a major restructuring of the organization and I had been relocated from a strategic corporate role to a more operational role within a smaller part of the service. My job title changed from the Head of OD and Training to become the Management Development Manager. There was still good and interesting work to be done, but the influence associated with the role had been reduced substantially. I also felt that there were issues within the new Board and the Senior Management Team that I was not being invited to advise on. This felt like a 'professional glass ceiling'. At one level, although it felt uncomfortable, I also interpreted it as a structural issue that was not directly related to my skills and ability. It might have just been about the internal senior stakeholders needing the space to identify and work on their development needs without feeling observed (and judged) by their subordinate.

When I started doing some networking and sharing of my plans to go independent with another experienced independent psychologist, he congratulated me. He also mentioned that I would need about 20 clients. I nodded in agreement, but I did not know what he was referring to with his 'cryptic' 20-client observation. It took me many years to realize that he was alluding to the need to have a 'pipeline' of clients that ranged from prospects to active projects and to the completion of projects. I realized this when I quickly experienced the 'feast and famine' aspects of not having an established client pipeline.

I set the transition from being an internal consultant to becoming an external consultant by making an outrageous proposal to my new HR Director. In a one-to-one review meeting, I shared with him my plan to leave and to become an independent external consultant. I made a case that it would be better for him and the organization to keep my services on a part-time (half-time) basis rather than losing my expertise and support. He agreed. I also proposed that my skills and experience compared well with external consultant support and that there should be a premium on the cost of retaining my services. He agreed. I then proposed that I should move to a half-time contract and still retain my former full-time salary. There would be no employer benefits costs such as holidays, sickness, car or pension payments and so this proposal represented a reduction in his costs. He agreed. In some ways, I guess that I was proposing a retainer deal with my employer to ensure that he had regular access to my skills and my added-value. This is useful for the client, too, as there was less need for them to need to 'onboard' a new consultant when they continued to work with me. There was also less risk for them in terms of the likely speed and quality of the deliverables from me as a known resource.

After working this new part-time contract for six months, I decided that it was time for me to become a fully independent consultant. I advised my employer of my plan, and I supported him to design an assessment centre process to select and appoint my replacement. When we were building the job analysis to identify the key skills required for success in the role with key stakeholders, the Chief Executive was very positive about my legacy. He just wanted someone else like me who just got on with designing and delivering the required OD interventions for his large and complex organization. This was the first time that I had actually received any specific feedback from him. Even then, it was still indirect feedback through the HR Director.

Again, Weiss (2003) is very clear that the independent consultant also needs to be willing to turn down potential business to succeed. This can have the professional advantage of not becoming 'stuck in a rut', and it can indicate when 'fresh pastures' and new learning are overdue. I have declined several potential work assignments particularly when I felt that there was a discrepancy between the level of integrity and openness being shown by the potential client and the level of transparency that I thought was required for effective organizational interventions.

For example, I have turned down a work assignment in the NHS when a newly appointed Board General Manager wanted me to provide him with 'off the record' access to confidential conversations and observations that I was having with other senior managers in his service. I declined to work with him as it was a violation of my confidentiality agreements with these other senior managers. I would not operate as his 'spy'. I also declined to get involved with a potential client when it became clear that his approach to leadership development was incompatible with my values. He wanted a design that woke the participants up with a fire alarm in the middle of the night just to see how they reacted to this pressure. This General Manager came from a specialist military background. We did not work together.

I also had to exit early from a major Talent Management role in the Middle East after 18 months due to domestic health pressures and because of a major breakdown in trust in the working relationships with some key stakeholders. I described the frustrations and the learnings from this experience in Silvestro (2016).

Getting back: How to get more business

Weiss (2003) is a strong advocate of keeping in regular contact via emails and notes and shared information to 'get back' and to stay visible and connected with clients. Cope (2003) is also clear about the needs and benefits of 'stage-managing' a 'look back and learn' review meeting with the client to ensure that the deliverables have been met with the explicit handover of responsibility to the client to implement and support the project changes. He also sees this final stage needs to be handled sensitively so that the client–consultant relationship does not become unbalanced and overdependent.

Even when this type of 'walk away' and 'transfer of skills and knowledge' had been agreed formally in a change management project that I had inherited, there was a silent 'conspiracy' between the external consultants and the senior managers that kept the external consultants returning to the organization to design and lead further change management initiatives. I challenged this ongoing dependency because it was not what we had originally agreed, and on the basis that it meant that the internal consultants (change agents) would never have the opportunity to build their skills and status with the senior managers if this overdependence was not stopped. The Senior Managers agreed reluctantly to cut back on their use (and their dependency) on the external consultants.

Cash flow is a constant issue when you are working as an independent consultant. That is why having a 'full-time' income from my previous internal consulting role was a great platform from which to seek out new work assignments. The longest that I have had to wait for payment was six months. This was for an Irish college when I was hired to design and write an innovation manual for family businesses. This delay created a lot of stress and frustration when I could not get them to acknowledge that my payment was severely overdue. I also could not find anyone who seemed to care about the cash flow impact on me as a small business for this delay. Needless to say, that once my invoice was eventually paid, I decided that I would end my working relationship with them.

I have probably spent more time and money investing in my professional development since I became an independent consultant than compared to when I was an internal consultant. My budget for purchasing new books went from zero to about £500 in my first year of business. My accountant asked why I was spending so much on books and I had to explain to him that I was a consultant in the 'knowledge management' business and that I had to keep fully abreast of the best practices and the new developments in order to be competitive and of value to my clients. In recent years, it has also been relatively easy to participate in online webinars at no cost to keep my knowledge and skills up to date. When I do this, I always set myself a target of asking several questions of the host to ensure that I remain actively engaged in this learning session.

As part of my 'vision' of going independent, I had a pleasant feeling of how wonderful this type of work would be because I would be able to work more on the complex strategic projects that challenge me the most. About 30 seconds later, 'reality' kicked in again. I quickly reminded myself that I would need to work on those 'operational' projects that clients wanted (and trusted) me to do. The latter thought was more valid than the strategic work fantasy.

However, in the early years of my independent business practice, it always felt like either 'feast or famine' as I needed to set aside time to find new work and then deliver it. It also felt that I was working for the Government when I had to hand over large chunks of my turnover for value added tax (VAT) and income tax each year. Sometimes, it was a worry to ensure that I had enough cash reserves to meet these bills. In a typical year, I issued about 30 invoices across five different clients. About 50% of this was based on repeat business and about 50% of work income through Associate contracts. On average, across the years, I managed to achieve my initial commercial target of doubling my income. I have also managed to sustain an independent consultant role. This satisfied my second target to test the market to see if my previous success was down to me or my HR colleagues. Although I still relied on their support for repeat business.

I have been working in my career rather than working on my career (Gerber, 1995). I was more focused on the content of the work rather than trying to build a business or a career. One unintended benefit of becoming an independent consultant was that I could be at home when my children were sitting their key exams. I was able to distract, joke and motivate them to go to their exams to do their best.

Having access to a computer, a printer and a mobile phone enabled me to work a lot from home doing research, preparing materials for workshops and creating reports. I also had the necessary IT and internet skills to set up and operate these tools from my post-graduate research experience. And I had the discipline to manage my own time and effort to ensure that my work was delivered in time to the quality required.

I also had to learn how to create financial records and to produce invoices and to find an accountant to submit my income tax returns and to produce my annual business audit. I learned to complete my own VAT returns.

I have also walked away from assignments that tried to lock me into a commercial rate that I thought was below the market rate for my skills and expertise. Some other independent consultants in my network take a different view on this type of decision. Their line of reasoning is that it is still better to have some income (even at a lower rate) than run the risk of having no income in a specific period of time. For them, it is better to sell a day of their expertise than to have a day without any income. I typically turned down these potential work assignments. I did not want to reduce my availability for other more suitably compensated work assignments. I also did not want to get dependent on doing assignments that were below my skill and market levels as I would 'resent' being attached to this type of work. I have taken a lower day rate only under two conditions. The first is where there is a relatively high volume of work guaranteed or when the work was of a high quality or complex and required me to develop my skills.

There are many advantages of becoming an external consultant, such as greater autonomy, more responsibility, enhanced learning and a higher degree of choice about when you work, and on what and with whom. Once you become an independent consultant it can be very difficult to go back into regular employment.

Working as an Associate reduces the need for marketing and it also can reduce the risk of impaired cash flow. It will also likely mean that the level of the work assignments is below your capability level as you are effectively working as a 'bit part player' in someone else's play.

Working as an independent means that there are fewer opportunities to work collaboratively with peers and other stakeholders. This can be lonely.

However, working on complex and large-scale projects as an Associate can bring useful learning and development and networking opportunities. They can also allow learning by seeing and hearing other professionals in action and by training alongside them and getting feedback. It also boosts your network, and this can be useful in getting recommendations for new work and for support and advice on tricky assignments. This network can also be an asset when bidding for larger and more complex projects where the staffing levels have to be 'scaled up' for delivery across large numbers of staff or multiple sites. However, they are also 'competitors'.

I have performed eight different roles in the past two decades. I have been a part-time Lecturer, a Training Manager, a Training Co-ordinator, a Head of Organization Development, a Management Development Manager, an Independent Occupational Psychologist, a Head of Talent Management and an Associate Psychologist. Sometimes, these roles have been full-time. At other times, there have been overlaps. I spent about a quarter of this time as an internal consultant and three-quarters as an external consultant. For me, the learning challenges have been associated with those roles and projects that had the biggest strategic focus.

There are several advantages of becoming an independent consultant. It allows a degree of autonomy from 'office politics' and the pressure for more responsibility, pressure and status associated with the 'up or out' expectations within big consultancies. It also allows more control over my own workload and workplace than conventional employee roles; and has allowed me to offer bespoke solution options to my clients rather than just offer what they consultancy business has to offer. As an independent, I can research and select the best tools and the best processes for the client's context.

Weiss (2011) is also clear about the need to be systematic in allocating time equally to 'marketing, sales and delivery' in order to have a regular 'pipeline' of work and potential work. He is also committed to 'creating solutions so that the problems remain fixed'. So, in some ways, this approach is less about seeking 'repeat business' than it is about seeking 'new business'.

I would definitely choose this career again if I was starting out all over again. Only, the next time, I would do it quicker and smarter with a stronger focus on the acquisition of marketing and business development skills and expertise. I might even decide to work within a large organization as part of my professional apprenticeship!

CHAPTER SUMMARY

So, now we can review the implications for choosing and using internal change agents during a programme of managing change. Use the following questions to clarify your thoughts on what makes an effective change agent.

> **STOP AND REFLECT**
>
> - What are the qualities required of an effective change agent?
> - How can a change agent enter the culture of the organization?
> - Is prior knowledge of the sector a benefit or not?
> - How can internal change agents be identified in the organization?

Of course, competence is complemented by commitment and the attitudinal qualities also count. Over and above that our own experience suggests that prospective internal change agents will be:

- Self-reflective of their own experience of change
- Appreciative of help from managers and mentors in the past development
- Willing to understudy any sessions or training that you want them to run
- Good at helping others identify learning opportunities
- Helpful and supportive with feedback to others
- Willing to monitor the effects of change programmes on company performance in the future

Any person exhibiting these qualities would make an excellent internal change agent.

The consultant as trainer and developer

The role of the external change agent is a demanding one not just in the supporting knowledge of business, people and change but also in the skills of identifying the need for change; exploring important issues with people throughout the organization; asking relevant questions to uncover basic assumptions and culturally based narratives; deciding on the feasibility of change aspirations; and communicating that to the proposers of change.

It also means being a talent spotter; identifying potential internal change agents; involving them in the change; opening out and airing company-wide and individual perceptions of change; and exploring feasible approaches to change which will work with those undergoing change.

There may be patterns of change laid down for processual change programmes but each receiving company will approach the need for change differently. Remaining aware of the changing perceptions of those involved in change will facilitate understanding and encourage flexibility in how the change programme is implemented.

> For video content relating to this chapter please visit the companion website at **www.macmillanihe.com/Randall-Management-Consultancy.**

REFERENCES

Block, P. (2011). *Flawless Consulting: A Guide to Getting Your Expertise Used*. San Francisco, CA: Jossey-Bass/Pfeiffer.

Buchanan, D., Boddy, D. and McCalman, J. (2014). Getting in, getting on, getting out and getting back. In E. Bell and H. Wilmott (eds), *Qualitative Research in Business and Management: Practices and Preoccupations*. London: Sage.

Bullock Report (1977). *Report of the Committee of Inquiry on Industrial Democracy*. London: Her Majesty's Stationery Office.

Cope, M. (2003). *The Seven C's of Consulting* (2nd edn). London: Financial Times and Prentice Hall.

Gerber, M.E. (1995). *The E Myth Revisited: Why Most Small Businesses Don't Work and What to Do About It*. New York: HarperCollins.

Grubb, I.M., Silvestro, N.W. and Ward, D.F. (1994a). Stop the organization, I want to change it! Part 1. *Industrial and Commercial Training*, 26(1), 23–27.

Grubb, I.M., Silvestro, N.W. and Ward, D.F. (1994b). Stop the organization, I want to change it! Part 2. *Industrial and Commercial Training*, 26(4), 15–21.

Lazarus, R.S. and Folkman, S. (1984). *Stress, Appraisal and Coping*. New York: Springer.

Louis, M.R. (1980a). Surprise and sense making: What newcomers experience in entering unfamiliar organizational settings. *Administrative Science Quarterly*, 25, 226–251.

Nadler, D.A. (1993). Concepts for the management of strategic choice. In C. Mabey and B. Mayon-White (eds), *Managing Change*. London: Open University and Paul Chapman Publishing.

Pettigrew, A.M. (1987). Context and action in the transformation of the firm. *Journal of Management Studies*, 24(6), 649–670.

Piderit, S. (2000). Rethinking resistance and recognising ambivalence: A multi-dimensional view of attitudes towards an organizational change. *Academy of Management Review*, 25(4), 783–794.

Procter, S.J. and Randall, J.A. (2015). Understanding employee attitudes to change in longitudinal perspective: A study in UK public services 1996-2007. *Qualitative Research in Organizations and Management: An International Journal*, 10(1), 38–60, https://doi.org/10.1108/QROM-01-2013-1127

Reid, R.S. and Silvestro, N.W. (2008). *Positive Solutions for Female Leaders: An Innovation Qualification*. Glasgow: Caledonian Family Business Centre.

Schank, R. and Abelson, R. (1977). *Scripts, Plans and Knowledge*. Hillsdale, MI: New Jersey Erlbaum.

Schein, E.H. (2011). *Helping: How to Offer, Give and Receive Help*. San Francisco, CA: Berrett-Koehler Publishers.

Silvestro, N.W. (2016). Embedding a talent management strategy in the Middle East: Cultural and consultant obstacles and levers. In B. Burnes and J. Randall (eds), *Perspectives on Change: What Academics, Consultants and Change Managers Really Think about Change*. London: Routledge.

Smircich, L. (1983). Concepts of culture and organizational analysis. *Administrative Science Quarterly*, 28, 339–359.

Weick, K.E. (1995). *Sensemaking in Organizations*. London: Sage.

Weiss, A. (2003). *Million Dollar Consulting: The Professional Guide to Growing a Practice* (3rd edn). New York: McGraw-Hill.

Weiss, A. (2011). *Million Dollar Consulting Proposals: How to Write a Proposal That's Accepted Every Time*. New York: Wiley.

Wilcocks, L. and Grint, K. (1997). Reinventing the organization? Towards a critique of business process organization. In I. McGloughlin and M. Harris (eds), *Organizational Change and Technology*. London: ICP.

6 Identifying the Role of Training in Achieving Strategic Outcomes

Julian Randall and Elaine Mottram

Learning Objectives

After studying the chapter, you should be able to:
- Know how and where to gather information on strategic plans and operational objectives
- Gather information on how an organization communicates its strategic vision
- Define the difference between standards and targets as they apply to behaviour
- Appreciate how to change standards and targets and what effect such changes can have
- Analyse and implement training needs

INTRODUCTION

The need for training is often assumed to be the first outcome of a change programme. Change proposers can take it for granted that people are transformed by training events. The problem is that this may not be possible, in which case other ways of developing people need to be considered.

There is a second challenge which will sometimes present itself to the external change agent: the organization's strategic plan. Such documents are written from a variety of backgrounds, sometimes planners; sometimes PR people; and sometimes strategic plan-writers. Such plans are only as good as the accuracy of the information they include.

Even good journalists are dependent on what insiders tell them about a market and its prospects. Often it is clear to the experienced reader that assumptions have been made which are probably not justified by the facts known to those who have a wider and current experience in the sector.

This means that the change agent presented with the strategic plan will need to ask penetrating questions about the content of the strategic plan and compare it with alternative sources of information from outside the company. The assumption that there will be incremental growth in market share, for example, is dependent on many factors – including the competition. And yet traditionally salespeople are much less confident about what the opposition offer, largely because they have no deep knowledge about alternative products and services nor have they been trained in them – hence the temptation to dismiss the opposition. As one sales manager said on being asked about the competition by trainees: 'Don't worry about them. We are the best.' In fact, the company were living on their brand name and market share. They went out of business in the early 1980s to competitors with better products penetrating the UK from overseas.

So, we are looking for realistic assessments of current progress and well-founded forecasts of future growth prospects based on accurate assessment of a market's prospects before deciding whether competence is an issue for change or not. Our challenge is to identify where the links are between the declared aims and objectives of the organization and how everyone plays their part in making those corporate goals happen in their own jobs. Once this is established then how to achieve it becomes necessary.

If people are our most important resource, as the HRM strap-line alleges, then investing in them so that they can grow and develop the business ought to be a primary concern to those who run the enterprise. In this chapter, we examine how the links between individual effort and corporate objectives can be supported and how training and development can offer the future direction which focuses on both individual efficiency and supporting corporate effectiveness.

LINKS BETWEEN STRATEGIC OBJECTIVES AND INDIVIDUAL KEY TASKS

The challenge of linking the strategic objectives to individual key tasks predates HRM and can be found in earlier attempts to link what organizations want to achieve and how their people achieve it. One example can be found in management by objectives.

Management by objectives

1. Set the **organizational objectives** (increase profit by 2% over the next 12 months of trading)
2. Break this objective down into the **departmental goal** areas within the organization (what will sales/marketing/production have to do to achieve their part of the organizational objective?)
3. Break down the departmental goals into the **individual key tasks** that support them (so for each member of the team, what are their revised targets to achieve that departmental goal)

Setting organizational objectives is difficult enough to get right and putting figures on expected growth will always be a something of a surmise. Shareholders want to be assured that the company is performing well, if not above-average in the sector. But how realistic are such targets for those required to deliver them? Demanding more sales will have implications for production and supply; for the marketing budget; for sales activity; and for finance to support extra activity in all these areas. This will be the focus of departmental goal changes and it will often give rise to strongly held conflicting views between competing departments – something that will usually come out during the first interdisciplinary group discussions during the **Exploration phase** of participative change.

Then there are the implications for the individuals in each disciplinary team. How much more will they have to do to make this happen; are there commensurate rewards for extra effort; what support will be needed to achieve these new objectives; where exactly is the extra business to be found?

Finding out what you need to know

So, how easy is it to define these links in practice? For external change agents coming into the organization, identifying the evidence to support the links can be elusive as most departments and individuals have their own views and ideas (particularly in a blame culture). That does not mean that the right questions are not being asked, but it could mean that the evidence of their existence is more difficult to identify. Companies tend to count what is countable and that becomes the basis of their accountability. They are less comfortable with looking for what is not so countable – so that becomes assumed rather than assessed. As we have already mentioned, interference costs are largely invisible in most organizations, which is why they are frequently overlooked in day-to-day decision-making by managers. It is the challenge of the external change agent to explore these areas more fully and begin to put a cost on, for example, staff turnover, wastage rates, accidents and so on.

STOP AND REFLECT

- Where would you expect to find organizational objectives?
- Who would you ask about departmental goals?
- Where would you expect to find individual key tasks listed?
- Which department(s) ought to have the overview of these links?

You may have examined the formal and written sources that can be found in organizations, particularly the strategic plan agreed with the Board. Often the CEO will offer this early on to consultants and it will repay detailed examination and committal to memory. After all, if they are as important as their sponsors suggest, then everyone should know about them and be aware how the organizational objectives apply to their jobs. So, this is a good opportunity for the visiting consultant to find out what people know about how they play their part in implementing the strategic plan effectively.

Who might we ask about the departmental goals? You may have identified the director responsible for the department and certainly they usually have a clear idea of the implications of strategic plans for their own department, and often for the other departments on whom they depend. So, for example, sales may have views about the marketing strategy and whether the decisions made on promotional activities will facilitate their new sales targets or not. Strategic plans can propose the way ahead, but those tasked with implementing them are not always convinced of their feasibility, sometimes based on previous experience of lack of appropriate support.

Then finally, there are individual key tasks. As we would expect, most staff are aware of what is expected of them – that is why they were engaged by the company in the first place. But new targets are not always welcome, nor are they always thought to be achievable; or even revised when organizational objectives are revised. Perceived discrepancies between company rhetoric and reality in a marketplace may often give rise to uncertainty about feasibility and the sooner this is surfaced the better it can be addressed. There is often a perceived gap between effectiveness and efficiency: what the company aspires to achieve is not always perceived as realistic by those tasked with implementing it.

Finally, who is the primary stakeholder in the HR field? We know that the answer should be the HR department. They are the custodians of the employment contract – often responsible for drawing them up in the first place and the first port of call when there are questions raised about the fairness of implementing them at work. So, one question to ask is: How up to date are the records held about people and their employment contract? The answers can sometimes be that records are often surprisingly lax or even non-existent ('as everybody knows what they are').

IMPLICATIONS FOR CHANGE

For consultants, calculating the interference costs will be important in reinforcing the value of a change programme. The costs of consultancy are always perceived as expensive as far as clients are concerned so our intervention will need to reduce any areas of identified loss to offset the cost of the change programme.

The interference costs being generated by the business can be calculated by such indicators as the incidence of staff turnover; intermittent absence; sick absence and accident rates; and loss of sales while sales territories are uncovered. Change agents should examine how much these have changed over the past year. What does the trend of the figures show and how does it compare with other companies in the same sector?

We will examine these elements one by one and explore what the consultant can do to clarify what is in place already and what needs to be put in place to ensure that the system is secure and capable of achieving what the company wants to achieve. Added to which, the cost of implementing the programme is always more acceptable if the yield or benefit is going to be higher than the cost of the programme.

COMMUNICATING A VISION

We need to be careful about the word 'vision'. It can have different meanings for those that use it. Company visions, like mission statements, often seek to capture in a sentence or two the essence of the message the organization wants to put out about itself to those it wants to work with. The aspiration is reasonable but too often has about it the vagueness of a general statement and omits the detail of how the vision is to be realized. To be 'the best at what we do', or 'to make our clients happy by being the best in our sector' may be worthy aims, but it is probable that competitors are making the same claims with equal justification. Such statements can too easily be dismissed as an earnest hope that most companies advertise about their business aspirations while those inside the organization are likely to view such statements sceptically.

The challenge lies in the second half of the statement: 'to all employees'. These are the people we need to convince that the vision is realizable. They are the people who may have reason to doubt whether such broad assertions can be achieved, given the compromises that staff often need to make as they attempt to satisfy the customer that they are 'the best in their sector'. So, our questions might be: How focused is the vision on what staff have to do to achieve it? Does it focus on the competencies of the staff? Are those competencies distinctive in the sector?

> ### EXAMPLE
>
> An example of this would be the Customer Charter initiative in the early 1990s, which for one organization dictated that all phone calls should be answered within five rings. Staff became fixated by answering the phone as soon as it rang – often then finding that they had to pass the call to someone else to answer the caller.
>
> For the customer, being passed through several hands and repeating the question became irksome and time-consuming. So, while answering within five rings improved efficiency, customer satisfaction (effectiveness) diminished.

SOURCES OF INFORMATION ABOUT COMPANY PRACTICE

Everything that is written by the company should reflect the links between the company's strategic objectives and how they seek to implement it through their departments and groups to individual workers who implement it. We should look at different sources of information. These may include:

- Policy, procedures and practice documents generated by the company
- Operations directories
- Training manuals
- HR handbooks
- Staff handbook

These sources will enable us to look more closely at the second element.

Relating performance targets to the strategy

We will look in more detail at standards and targets later in this section. However, suffice it to say that references to departmental goals and individual key tasks should be clearly stated if staff are to be engaged in achieving the organizational objectives in day-to-day operational detail. Here we can find ourselves at the heart of the distinction between objective standards and subjective, aspirational goals. As we will see, quality – one of the outcomes of HRM theory (Guest, 1989) – is dependent on the perceptions of those who make the judgement that they have had a quality service. Sometimes expectations held by potential clients are unrealistic or unrealizable. So, although staff delivered to the efficiency standards set down by the company, the target set by the client was not achieved as far as that client was concerned (effectiveness). The more clearly standards are stated by the company, the less likely it is that confusion will arise for clients and customers. In other words, everyone is clear about what is being offered.

Linking review with these targets

For most organizations, there are regular appraisals in place, though staff are not always convinced about their value (Fletcher, 1993). Less often do such reviews include the end-user or customer. So, one point of enquiry might be whether there are regular reviews which include those who use the service. In some organizations, for example, there are regular customer focus groups. Some hospitals use such groups to gauge how change to the service affects the patients and monitor patients' response on a regular basis. It may be that this review is ongoing through the customer service department, in which case there should be records of customer complaints and how they were dealt with and error/wastage/accident rates, which the company has dealt with.

Identifying training, development and reward outcomes

People management should always include training and development strategies and reviews and appraisals should be an excellent opportunity for assessing the implementation of such plans. How much the company spends on training is always a significant indicator of its commitment to developing its staff. Organizational commitment, which HRM theory features as an outcome, is reinforced by a proactive **continuing professional development** strategy for staff. It is also worthwhile looking at any of the initiatives such as **Investors in People** to discover how the organization allocates resources for training to individuals and how far that coincides with the strategic objectives that are published yearly.

- All critical performances should be subject to standards
- All standards should be related to the company's strategic objectives
- All critical performances should be monitored so that we all know what we have achieved and how much more we need to do to achieve our targets

Only in this way can **strategic integration** be achieved in the company.

Evaluating effectiveness

One of the most enduring complaints about change at work voiced by those who undergo it is that change is never-ending and that one change initiative is never assessed to see whether it worked because the company has moved on to another change initiative before it evaluates the effectiveness of the previous programme. For external change agents, this is one aspect of change which will rely on **internal change agents** to carry on the work of the change programme after the external consultants have left. Evaluation involves not just the efficiency factors that govern performance but whether the service offered is now fulfilling the expectancies of those the business seeks to serve – in other words, effectiveness for the client.

Regular review of performance requirements

There is much that has been written about appraisal and its effectiveness and many companies, while having an appraisal system set up, are less proactive in using it to develop staff over the long term of their career (Fletcher, 1993). This can mean that staff address their own personal development plans and often the company is unaware of courses of study that they are undertaking in their own time. Similarly, companies are often work-focused to the exclusion of exploring where staff want to be in their longer-term career – for example, helping them to plan their progression by offering time and financial support. How much HR knows about such personal initiatives – **Personal Development Plans** – can be a significant indicator of their concern to work with their people by linking these aspirations to continuing professional development at work.

Identifying realistic standards will not only be important to the links between strategy and individual key tasks but can often reveal underlying problems which the company may have overlooked.

> **EXAMPLE**
>
> A company minting coins was housed in a draughty factory where staff were employed to insert sheets of metal and manually bring down the stamping machine head, removing the sheet once the coins were deposited down a chute. Daily targets of 76,000 coins per operative would put an operative into the bonus bracket. The best worker produced 56,000 coins per day.
>
> A visiting consultant asked the supervisor why such a high target was offered when it was clear that no one could reach it. The supervisor's answer was: 'They could, if they wanted to.'

STANDARDS AND TARGETS

One of the important functions of the initial research on company data is to access the accuracy of their wording of standards and targets. Failure to get this right can be a source of confusion and possible contention later when employment contracts are implemented or when their provisions are challenged, particularly during change.

- A **standard** is a level of behaviour or performance that applies to everyone
- A **target** is a level of behaviour or performance that applies to an individual

This simple distinction can illustrate the difference between a standard and a target. For those involved in sales, the standard requires that all sales people achieve the same output to retain their job. But there will be different targets for individual salespeople depending on the potential yielded by their territory, their own expertise and their previous sales record. These are sometimes referred to as 'stretch targets'.

To be correctly worded a standard has three parts:

- It is stated in **behavioural terms**
- It contains the **condition** that applies to that behaviour
- It contains the **standard** that applies in the context of that behaviour

We can look at these elements in detail.

BEHAVIOURAL TERMS

The words used to describe the standard should trigger an action – concrete verbs, for example. This makes it easy to measure or test the behaviour and should be validated during training in the way in which it would be expected to be achieved at work.

It is important to avoid abstract words – words which do not trigger a concrete action but could be internalized – meaning that there is no demonstrable action which can be observed.

One example of this would be to test whether someone knows the national anthem: you might ask 'Do you know the National Anthem?' to which they might give the answer 'Yes'. However, we would not have evidence that they knew it solely from that response alone. To trigger the evidence, we should have asked a question that required a demonstrable performance – '**recite** the national anthem', for example.

Here are two lists to illustrate the distinction:

Concrete terms (use)

- List
- State
- Describe
- Assemble
- Draw
- Write down

Abstract terms (avoid)

- Know
- Acknowledge
- Grasp
- Appreciate
- Consider

Just to reinforce this distinction we may think about the word 'appreciate'. For example, for a music course to indicate that one of the learning objectives would be that students 'appreciate good music' would certainly be unsupportable in measurable terms. 'At the end of the training trainees will understand' is often used in company training documents and once again it requires a demonstrable performance to validate the knowledge – how would they demonstrate the knowledge?

Which of these statements is correctly worded?

- Understand the powers of arrest of a police officer
- Assemble a type-A engine
- Address an undergraduate student group
- Appreciate good music
- Manage your people effectively

As we can see, the first and fourth statements need to be changed to a more concrete verb to validate a performance. Two and three would trigger a behaviour. The fifth statement would need development through the other two parts of the standard to enable us to use it to measure effectiveness. So, you might say:

> Working within the company budget provided, manage your work to achieve your business targets, without contravening Health & Safety or Employment Law.

CONDITIONS

The second part of the standard includes the conditions under which the behaviour is to be conducted. These can include the four efficiency factors of:

- Time (how long have I got?)
- Quantity (how much/many must I produce?)
- Quality (to what standard must I perform?)
- Cost (any budget constraints on costs?)

Obviously, the more elements included the tighter the standard becomes. So, on approach to landing the pilot must adopt a 3-degree flight path to the runway threshold; +/– 50' of the flight-path; no more than 2½ degrees either side of that flight path. Pilots are regularly tested to these standards and this reinforces an important element of flight safety for all flying professionals to validate their licence, with simulator checks required if pilots have been inactive for a stated period.

STANDARD

The legal context of the standard should be cited specifically to ensure that no infringements take place for any other reasons. So, for example we might cite:

- Error rate
- Wastage rate
- Accident rate

Or the legal context itself:

- Without violating Health & Safety
- Without violating Air Law
- Without violating Employment Law

Example of correctly/incorrectly worded standard

Incorrect

- Improve your sales performance as soon as possible

Correct

- Increase your sales by 10% over last year's figures, in the next 12 months, completing all company order forms correctly

A quick review of the company's key documents should alert you to how far the company's policies, procedures and practices adhere to an accurate description of what their key tasks, departmental goals and organizational objectives require and whether they link together, so that the individual's efforts can deliver what is required corporately to achieve the success defined by the organization.

Note that some companies use the word **goals** in their contracts leaving it unclear whether the goals are targets or standards. In this case you would need to probe further to clarify whether the goal is mandatory (a standard) or discretionary (a target). Companies that fail to make this distinction clearly in their terms and conditions risk legal action should matters between parties involved be legally disputed.

To test that you are confident you can return to the exercise in the above section, 'Communicating a Vision' and extend the five statements into fully developed standards containing correct wording, adequate conditions and the legal contextual reference for the standard.

Changing the organizational standards

As we have said, changing the organizational objectives will usually have implications for both departmental goals and individual key tasks. How far this is likely to affect the individuals involved should now be the focus of the change agent's attention. As we know from research, individuals can sometimes resist change because of fears about the future demands which may be made on them. There are questions of enhancing competence; supporting the achievement of more demanding results; mastering new procedures; and losing status under the newly promulgated standards (Nadler, 1993). There is also the question of jobs changing as they are undertaken by competent staff doing more than their contract but this expansion of those standards is not reflected in their employment contract (Stewart, 1991).

Overcoming concerns and objections during the change programme is yet another reason why initial meetings need to explore what staff have found helpful during change in the past; what they prefer by way of training and support; and how new practices are best supported back at work. This discussion will often need to explore changes to the way things are done; how these will affect competencies; and clearly defining the knowledge, skill and experience required to achieve the newly promulgated standards and targets.

TRAINING AND DEVELOPMENT

Standards and targets, then, are particularly important to all organizations during change. Our investigation should include checking that existing standards are adhered to consistently in the organization – examining the wording of standards in company documents; inspecting the validation methods used during the training given; and exploring how far training interventions have had a significant effect on the achievement of business effectiveness in the past. These steps can then inform the traditional training cycle (Figure 6.1).

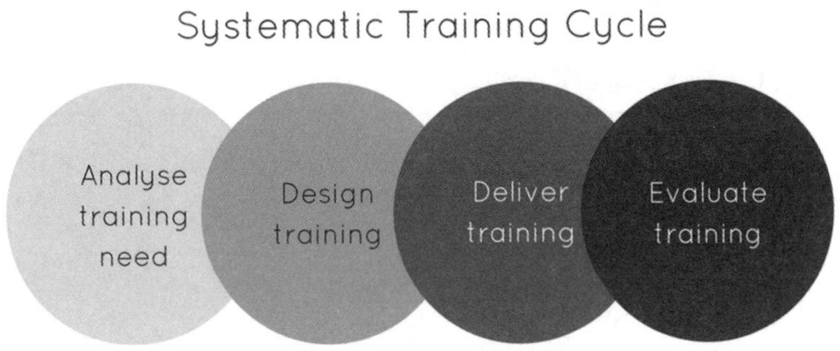

Systematic Training Cycle

Analyse training need — Design training — Deliver training — Evaluate training

Figure 6.1 *Systematic training cycle*

It may be that part of the change programme will include designing and running training programmes for staff. So, it will be important to identify the implementation stages and ensure that they have a logical sequence, regardless of whether the consultants intend to run the training events themselves or subcontract them to others.

ANALYSING A TRAINING NEED

In HR practice, we refer to the personnel profile when considering a training need. In other words, we identify the human factors which we will need to influence during the training to achieve success through our people. They can be listed as follows:

- Knowledge
- Skill
- Experience
- Attitude

The first three are a function of **competence** and generally answers the question, 'can I do it?' The fourth element is a function of **commitmen**t and answers the question, 'do I want to do it?'

In broad terms knowledge and skill may be enhanced by training, and experience (practice) consolidates the knowledge and skill acquired. Once we can list the factors which the trainee needs to master, we can draw up learning objectives for the training session.

List what the trainee sales person will be able to do at the end of the training session (some training providers state: 'At the end of the training you will be able to…'):

1. Conduct a qualifying sales interview
2. Present the product or service to the prospect
3. Put together and explain a proposal/estimate for the prospect
4. Conduct a negotiation to cover prospect's needs
5. Close the sale successfully
6. Handle concerns and objections

Each of these elements would be the subject of separate training sessions run successively to build up the sequence of expertise areas in a logical order so trainees acquire competencies in a way that develops the tasks around the work cycle within which they will operate.

As we said earlier, we need to make sure that the learning objectives are correctly worded before embarking on designing the training event.

DESIGN THE TRAINING

There are many ways of conveying knowledge and wherever possible adults usually prefer a choice in the methods that are used. A lot of training is now subcontracted and may increasingly be offered online. However, not everyone responds well to distance learning and it may be that alternative support is also valued involving interacting with others, asking questions, and receiving support and guidance.

So, training might include various options such as:

- Knowledge/skill/practice sessions
- Role play/filming/play back
- Feedback on performance from others in the peer group
- Accompanying a more experienced salesperson in the field
- Conducting an interview in the field supported by mentor/manager

What matters is that people have time to access and absorb training material in a way that suits them best. So, beware of sessions in which observation of a professional is followed by individual attempts unsupported by adequate feedback (experience suggests that IT training often fails for this reason: too many trainees and not enough support). Experts are not always the best people to convey knowledge or support the first tentative steps at acquiring a new skill (those who have struggled themselves are often more sympathetic to those who take longer to learn).

VALIDATION

Testing what we have taught is an important part of assuring ourselves that standards have been successfully met during training events. So, after training in negotiation skills the validation might include the following items:

- Answering questions about the features of the product/service
- Handling concerns and objections

- Asking probing questions to extend knowledge of customer need
- Responding to customer signals during negotiation
- Working out what the range of negotiation should be
- Using appropriate closing techniques at critical stages of the negotiation

It is important to test so that the knowledge/skill is demonstrated in the field. So, for example, avoid written tests when the trainee would be expected to answer verbally face-to-face with the client.

EVALUATION

This is the element most often neglected by organizations investing in training and change interventions. It needs to take place over a time period sufficient to ensure that our business objectives have been achieved successfully. The next appraisal and/or year-end may be a good opportunity to assess how effective individuals have been at achieving the company's objectives.

How we conduct ourselves is a question not just of efficiency but also of effectiveness. The customer/end-user/colleague is the sole gauge of this aspect of our performance. Here are some possible evaluation tools:

- 360-degree appraisals (where peer group/colleagues are involved)
- Customer feedback sheets
- Colleague assessments
- Professional appraisal (Fletcher (1993) suggests a blank sheet of paper)
- Customer focus groups
- Exit interviews

Interference costs need to be monitored to ensure that the trends which we based the training needs on have been addressed successfully. So, for example, has staff turnover or accident/error rates reduced?

Level of evaluation	Evaluation question	Evaluation method	Staff involved
Reaction level	What do trainees believe they have learned?	Discussion Observation Questionnaire Diary/log book	Trainer/tutor Trainees Client or sponsor
Learning level	What have trainees actually learned?	**Knowledge** (exam) **Skill** (practical test/role play/simulation) **Attitude** (observation/role play/mystery shoppers)	Trainees Sponsors Trainers External assessors
Job behaviour	What has been the impact on job performance?	Observation/interview Logs/appraisals/continuing professional development	Trainees Supervisor/manager Colleagues Clients/customers Sponsor
Team/department	What has been the impact on team or departmental performance?	Organizational benefits: staff turnover/absence/Accidents/productivity Cost–benefit analyses	Management team Sponsors Training manager HR manager
Organizational level	Does it represent value for money? Was it cost-effective? Contribution to the business	As above	As above

So, finally, we can put together the factors to be evaluated. They will include all those who have been involved in developing the competencies. Trainers are often excluded from the management review loop. It should be borne in mind that trainers see people develop and overcome challenges. People often exhibit qualities which managers may not have been aware of previously in the workplace. They can benefit from this awareness of potential and aptitude in their staff from the trainer who has supported the new learning. In that way, they can use the newly acquired skills at the workplace before those skills and knowledge are forgotten.

Potential internal change agents can also be identified during training events. Again, it is the trainer or external change agent who will often identify individuals with this potential first. It will be important to gain management agreement for such people to be released for this additional role, which is crucial for the success of the change programme evaluation.

SUMMARY

What a change programme is trying to achieve requires the links between the strategic aspirations of the company and the final outcomes for the end-user to be clearly identified and addressed at each stage in the process of development. Clarity about standards and targets allow all those involved to implement the programme aware of how those links will support a successful outcome in the business. The proposers of change are not always clear about the feasibility of what they are asking the change agents to achieve. Early clarification of the learning objectives will ensure that those involved will be alerted to the need of what needs to change to achieve success.

EXERCISE

Training an internal change agent

Your task is to put together a training plan for a three-day course suitable to prepare your internal change agents to undertake stand-up instructional training sessions
  It should contain:

- Learning objectives for each day (At the end of the training the trainees will be able to...)
- Timed sessions (morning and afternoon)
- Content of each session
- Breakdown of timings for each session (Introduction; syndicate groups; plenary session)
- Validation (How you will test each session)
- Evaluation (how you will know when the trainees are effective)

Knowledge

Often transferred through lectures/talks, etc.

Skill

Often conveyed through exercises and role plays.

Experience

Combination of the two (consolidation). Videos, films, visiting speakers, etc.

Validation

Tests, quizzes, multiple-choice exercises, etc.

Evaluation

Sitting next to Nellie
Understudying
Getting feet wet with supervision
Going solo

Suggested points to address

- Writing correctly worded learning objectives
- Session(s) on why people learn (motivation theory; recency effect; attention span; biorhythms)
- Session(s) on how people learn (I hear and I forget; I see and I remember; I do and I understand)
- Lectures (timing and content)
- Activities to check understanding
- Discussions (syndicate groups/plenary sessions and timing)
- Validation sessions (instructional technique sessions filmed and played back with feedback)
- Evaluation plans (future use within the change programme/mentoring/shadowing)

Two days should be enough to cover the important theoretical and practical supporting material with a third day validating the knowledge and skills in interactive workshops.

CASE STUDY: CHANGING A CULTURE

Becoming competitive

For most organizations in the public sector the move into the private sector is still a threat rather than an opportunity. Long-serving employees will often have set views about their job, their work, their career, their managers and their organization. Culture rests on the basic assumptions of the members: what they expect and accept will be governed by those beliefs. Such assumptions can include:

- Job security (in return for loyal service)
- Promotion through the ranks (as their career develops there will be increased status and rewards)
- Training and development will be a continuing provision during their working lives
- Holidays, sick absence and time off for other activities will be part of their terms and conditions
- There will be a generous pension with the option of early retirement

The list here covers the belief that staff have about their work lives and any changes will be stoutly resisted. So, radical change will be difficult to initiate and follow through on for the change agent.

The Government has embarked on a programme of compulsory competitive tendering and the Director of a local area within a government department has asked for your help. The tax collection specialist teams will have to compete for their work with outside providers for inspection and collection work and the senior managers in charge of each of the 12 teams are concerned about the threat to their own and their team members' jobs.

He asks you to develop a programme which will give them a chance to:

- Examine the privatized industry's way of doing business
- How independent providers manage their business
- The costs they work to and the prices they charge
- How they train their staff to work in a competitive world

> - The benefits which are looked for by those choosing the new contractors
> - How to put their proposal together in a business plan
> - How to present it convincingly to the assessors
>
> You might also like to think about the distinction between training and development and the different routes that you might use to establish competence and commitment from staff in the face of this organizational challenge.
>
> How might you prepare the senior managers to:
>
> - Prepare their teams for the challenge of compulsory competitive tendering
> - What difference might it make to the way they need to do their work?
> - What competencies might they need to acquire to enable them to achieve this?
> - How could these best be trained?
> - What development programmes might support this long-term change?
> - How would they evaluate the change to ensure future effectiveness?
>
> All radical change can involve people reviewing whether they want to continue in the organization or look at alternatives.
>
> So, finally, what provision should the organization make for staff who feel they cannot change in the way that the organization needs them to in this new challenging environment?

CONSULTANCY IN ACTION

LEADING AND MANAGING CHANGE: MAXIMISING THE CONTRIBUTION FROM EVENTS AND INTERVENTIONS

Elaine Mottram, Pensando Consultancy

Introduction

Working in the field of organizational development and change management inevitably involves facilitating events. At their best, events can be the most influential part of a change process but at their worst they can be another brick in the wall of 'we've been here before and nothing ever changes' and indeed do more harm than good.

My own experience of events has been varied in terms of size, complexity, purpose and location – the most interesting took place on the Moray coastal path on a glorious summer day; and the most challenging included guide dogs and wheelchairs in a room intended for half the number attending. While my initial training to work in the field of organization development included an extremely sound theoretical basis regarding behaviour in organizations (Beckhard and Harris, 1987), responses to change and leadership, there was very little that equipped me to design and facilitate events. My impression is that this is still a neglected area, yet it has the capacity to bring huge benefits to a change process. At the same time, however, there can be significant risks, related not simply to the opportunity cost of people attending the event but also to the risk of jeopardizing the potential impact of future events.

There are several set processes for example, World Café and Open Space, and if these are to be used in their entirety there is little scope for detailed design. However, if the event does not lend itself to a pre-scribed process there is a need for careful design with perhaps some reference to elements of set processes.

This chapter will offer a number of areas to be considered and results from my own experience, my reflections about what makes for a successful event, feedback from participants and learning from attending events designed and facilitated by others. Much of what I will cover can be found in different texts as part of different topics, for example learning styles or facilitation, but I have tried to bring together as many of the components as possible which should be considered when asked to design and facilitate an event.

Running an event is a bit like squeezing a tube of toothpaste: once the top has been removed it is never clear quite how much of the content is going to emerge and at what speed. And of course, it is an irreversible process – the toothpaste cannot be put back in the tube. It is therefore important to consider whether an event is the most appropriate intervention for the client's requirements. The real world can involve a request from a client to facilitate an event which is already scheduled, participants have already been invited and an 'agenda' has already been distributed. In this situation understanding clearly what the client means by 'facilitate an event' is crucial. Do they mean manage the time? Do they want someone to keep notes and record outcomes? Do they want a chairperson? Or do they really mean facilitate, i.e. ensure a set of outcomes is achieved? What you decide to do next for your client depends on the answer to these questions: how much is already fixed; and how much might be negotiable.

In the same way that changing the management structure can provide the illusion of managing change, delivering an event can be a seductive option. Like a change in structure, an event may not help and indeed, it may hinder a process. If the purpose of an event relates to some change being planned, then it should be part of a process and the timing should be considered. If it is stand-alone and not part of a change process it may be worth trying to help your client place it into a process, perhaps of delivering strategy or of improving productivity, so that the overall process can be planned and supported. This situation has arisen on many occasions for me. A simple request to deliver an event has, through discussion, often been converted into an important part of a change process being led by the client. One client who experienced this said to me by way of feedback 'I didn't realize I was going to get some leadership development and support for change management. I thought I was just getting someone to run an event for me.' No ethical considerations arose in this case, for example of extending the contract beyond what the client wanted. The provision of the leadership development and change management support became, through discussion, an integral part of the planning process for an event for approximately 80 staff.

These topics and others will be explored in the sections that follow.

TO RUN AN EVENT OR NOT TO RUN AN EVENT?

As touched on already, if involvement with a client is established at an early enough stage, it is crucial to clarify whether it is the right decision to run the event. Asking the client questions such as 'what do you want to be different as a result of the event?' and 'what are the risks that might result from running the event?' will provide important clues to the level of consideration that has already taken place. The answers to the questions may result in confirmation that the event will be useful or necessary, they may indicate a better timetable than originally proposed or indeed they may result in a decision that the event is not appropriate now or at all (Block, 2011).

In other words, it is wise to use all the questioning that would normally be used when contracting with a client. For some reason, these can often be overlooked in the context of a training event.

In line with any other contracting, a thorough approach at this stage will bring benefits. So, clarity about purpose, aims and objectives is important to establish. There is no intention here to become obsessional about the difference between purpose, aims and objectives but they can be very useful prompts and different clients may respond and engage with different terminology.

In broad terms the purpose of the event will be very high-level. A method which has always worked for me is to complete the sentence, 'The event is to do … so that …' An example may be: 'The event is to bring all staff together so that they have the same information and we have the opportunity to make sure that there is reasonable understanding of the implications for them.' Such a description would provide a clear platform from which to design a timetable and process for an event. An alternative description might be: 'The event is to lay out the challenges we are facing and seek ideas about how we might address those challenges, so that staff are engaged and involved and as a result take ownership of the plan.' Clearly a different design and process would be required here.

Another way of teasing out information from the client might be to ask: 'What do you want to be different as a result of the event?' This may elicit an unrealistic answer such as 'We want everyone to be committed to the plan' and so open the door to a discussion about what the event might realistically do (allow staff the opportunity to hear the plan and ask questions about it) and what process would be required to develop commitment further (Isaacs, 1999).

Once there is clarity at this strategic level then the conversation about aims and objectives can begin. So, an aim may be to create an environment in which everyone feels free to speak without fear of judgement or the risk of recriminations. Another aim may be to facilitate the sharing of ideas among groups of staff who don't normally spend time together sharing their different perspectives.

Objectives are 'what it says on the tin' – objective; in other words, an agreed action plan containing clear responsibilities and timescales or a set of weighted criteria to enable comparison of options that would both qualify as realistic objectives for an event and provide the basis for appropriate design and implementation. Examples which might be relevant to a training event might be the aim of beginning the process of equipping staff to use a new system and objectives may be that by the end of the session everyone will be able to identify the main components of the system and have practised using it. An objective to become competent in one session may well be overambitious and lead to failure with all the consequences which can result from a failed event – so be realistic about time required for practice.

Outlined above is the ideal situation where the freedom to establish purpose, aims, objectives and outcomes exists. However, in the real world of competing priorities and deadlines a degree of pragmatic accommodation may be required. A very common situation is that a client may ask you to facilitate an event scheduled for a particular date and the participants have been invited in order to manage diaries and maximize attendance. So, the audience is fixed but the purpose is only sketchy and there is no design. Alternatively, an agenda may have been prepared with lectures from several Directors who feel the need to 'tell' everyone a great deal of information, though little thought has been given to the purpose of the session. All your consultancy skills will be required to decide how to manage these situations but having the personal commitment to make sure that 'form follows function' as far as possible will be a valuable part of your professional competence.

Finally, clarity about purpose, aims and objectives will ensure that everyone, client and participants as well as facilitator, share the same expectations. Experience has shown me that even with a well-designed and facilitated event, where there are different expectations, the outcome can be compromised by disagreements about intended results.

DESIGN, PROCESS AND FLOW

It is very common to begin the process of planning or designing an event by considering inputs – who needs to speak; what ground should be covered. Starting from the desired outcomes and working backwards is more likely to deliver these outcomes. Working backwards in this way also ensures that both process and content receive equal attention.

As already mentioned, it is very common for a number of senior managers or Directors to want to speak because they have something they want to say. However, the starting point should be what we need to be said (what information is necessary) and who would be best placed to do it, if we are to achieve a successful outcome. It is much easier successfully to challenge a Director who wants to speak at an event if the desired outcomes are used to influence the discussion, rather than simply to say they are not needed. If an outcome is about 'knowing' certain things then having a lecture may be appropriate; but if the outcome is related to understanding or exploring implications then simply providing the information will not be sufficient, and providing it at the event via a lecture may not be the most efficient process either. Pre-event information or 'homework' may be a useful alternative with a very short briefing of key issues on the day by the Director in question. There may be an assumption that because staff have been sitting in the same room while you are giving certain information, you can have confidence that the information has been received and retained. This needs to be challenged and contrasted with the assumption that 'no one will read anything we send out in advance'. Both are assumptions to be challenged and a process which gives the most confidence that what is required will be achieved should be prepared. A very valuable aim may be to provide everyone with exactly the same information at the same time and under the same conditions. If this is the case, then careful preparation of the input is necessary. Be creative and keep an eye to 'form follows function' always.

Expected outcomes may often be very difficult to measure. Energy, commitment and motivation are examples; but this should not be a barrier to attempting to design a process which will lead to these more abstract outcomes. Similarly, if the generation of ideas is the aim, the creation of an environment in which such ideas are likely to flow and participants will have confidence to express them will be crucial. If an outcome is the development of a sense of a team or the sharing of perspectives then, again, the process must make this possible.

A third factor alongside design and process is now emerging as important and that is the climate in the room or the environment which will be conducive to what is to be delivered. As facilitator, you may well have one of the most important roles in that you can take responsibility for creating the environment. This may be how you speak but more importantly how you listen and the example offered of the kind of listening and valuing of each other's opinions. Ground rules is the term often used but to some extent this may be confusing. The language of rules is the language of what is not allowed, of constraints and of sanctions if rules are broken. It is more often the case that the desire is to facilitate trust and openness and confidence to speak. The language of 'creating the right environment' in which the event can take place is much more consistent with what is being aimed for. This language reflects a space albeit with boundaries.

Another aspect of an aim may be to encourage participants to think and to think in some depth and for this to happen the 'container' is very important. One of the most important factors which facilitates thinking is the quality of our listening and indeed the listening throughout the group (Kline, 1999). Role modelling good listening and poor listening as a contrast can be a very effective way of demonstrating what the 'container' might usefully look like.

A model which can be useful when considering design is to separate outcomes into knowledge, skills and attitudes. Inputs can then be developed which will target each of these. It is very easy to design an event which is part of a change process and geared towards changing attitudes, which paradoxically contains inputs mostly focused on developing knowledge. This can be an easy mistake to make but some degree of rigour around the kinds of issues already described can reduce that risk significantly.

The flow of an event can be a factor that goes unnoticed when it is right but if the process does not flow there are significant risks. To help achieve 'flow' it is worth beginning the design process at a high level. For a one-day event this may be by dividing the day into four 'chunks' or sessions; for a week-long event it may be about thinking about the days as 'chunks'. Using a one-day event as an example:

- Session 1: Establishing the environment – introductions; aims and outcomes; outline of the day; scene setting/background; creating the mood, e.g. ice breaker and agreeing the 'container' (up to coffee time)
- Session 2: Exploring the issues – sharing views; opening up the topic; identifying risks and benefits (coffee time to lunchtime)
- Session 3: So what session? – agreeing the implications of session 2; options for going forward (lunchtime to teatime)
- Session 4: Pinning things down and action planning – what will happen next?; who will do what?

From this strategic plan, it is easy to develop some detail about the actual process and to think about when energy levels will be low and what sort of activity might be required to sustain interest. Experience over many years and events has shown that little 'real' work is done in the afternoon of a one-day event or in the final day of a several-day event. Awareness of this can influence design and expectations of client, participants and facilitator alike.

Being clear about the 'opening up' stage of an event and the 'pinning down' or moving forward phase offers another way of tackling strategic planning for an event (Whitney, Trosten-Bloome and Rader, 2014).

FACILITATION STYLE AND ENGAGING PARTICIPANTS

Many books and articles cover in-depth the topic of facilitation and the skills entailed but this chapter would be incomplete without a brief overview relevant to the requirements of facilitating an event. The bigger the event, the more diverse the participants are likely to be and the more challenging it will be to maintain the level of engagement needed to achieve the outcomes. Much of the responsibility falls on the facilitator who might be considered to be the guardian of the process, making facilitation a very active and assertive activity.

It is likely that the facilitator will be aiming to achieve certain outcomes on behalf of their client. Provided there has been a good design for the event resulting in a well-thought-through process, the facilitator will be able to focus on the process and ensure maximum inclusion and engagement of those attending. The more independent they can appear on the day, and the more focused on the process, the more likely they are to achieve their client's expectations.

Clarifying expectations of the client with regard to the role of the facilitator will avoid some potential problems. A client may base their requirements on previous experience of facilitators, and if that previous experience has been entirely with a facilitator who has assumed the role of expert and timekeeper, then their expectations are likely to reflect that. Confusion or even conflict may result from the old adage of the client 'not knowing what they don't know'. Sorting out at an early stage whether the client expects and/or requires the facilitator to act as chair or timekeeper or expert advisor or trainer or as I have suggested above 'guardian of the process' to achieve desired outcomes is advisable. For the purposes of exploring the skills and attributes required to facilitate an event let us assume that the required role is one of 'shaping and guiding the process to achieve the outcomes'. Success in this regard will need a facilitator who is able to suspend their own judgement and views and be equally accepting and valuing of contributions from others. Taking sides is something a facilitator should never do but challenging views in a respectful way can be an extremely important part of the process. The facilitator must have the ability to simultaneously observe and listen to what is happening at any given time and maintain an overview of the overall process and the entire group. The ability to be aware of atmosphere and mood in the room and to notice non-verbal activity and signs are important skills in this respect.

This capacity to pay full attention to both the interactions that are taking place and the overall mood in the room (Bushe, 2009) may lead to a need to make judgements about allowing a topic to be pursued beyond the time allocated, curtailing a conversation in order to shift the focus to an emerging issue, or about making robust interventions to manage the situation. Good understanding of the topics being addressed and the likely perspectives that will surface in the room can equip the facilitator to make good judgements but there is always a risk of 'getting it wrong'. The better the design and the more trust and confidence there is in the room, the more challenge will be possible and tolerated by participants. Being willing and able to draw on a subtle combination of curiosity, humility, compassion, assertiveness and confidence is a crucial mix of skills for a facilitator, especially in a difficult situation.

If the facilitator can achieve a situation where all or most participants are comfortable and the design of the event is such that input from everyone is possible, the conditions are in place for a successful event. Positive emotions such as feeling valued, respected and supported can lead to more flexible, open-minded and co-operative behaviour as well as more creativity and innovation – often this is required from an event. As a result of involvement any decisions or plans made are likely to have ownership of the group and the likelihood of a smooth and sustainable change project (if that is what the event is part of) is increased.

The diversity of participants has already been touched on. Some of the areas of diversity can be predicted and accommodated – for example, different learning styles and Myers-Briggs Type Indicator preferences. Other areas may be associated with the existence and visibility in the room of 'human' as well as 'work selves'. It must be remembered that participants may not all know each other and that their interactions are normally very work-based. The potential level of physical inactivity involved in spending a day at an event can be a huge contrast for some groups whose job is physical. Building in some requirement to move around at intervals, perhaps by working in different groups, or moving round the room to look at flip charts or information on the walls can be useful to maximize engagement over the period of the event.

LAST BUT NOT LEAST THE VENUE!

Choosing a luxurious venue with attractive facilities and good catering can sometimes be seen as a way of rewarding staff and this might be received well. Alternatively, it may be perceived as excessive or lacking in sincerity if it is in contrast to normal working conditions. If travelling to and from the venue introduces a degree of difficulty for staff, the intention behind the choice of venue may be lost or indeed perceived negatively, jeopardizing the event. So, getting the venue right for the culture of the organization is important.

However, even though the culture of the organization may indicate that the use of an existing room would be best, it is wise to consider what preconceptions and what patterns of behaviour might be associated with such a room. An example would be where a Board Room is suitable in terms of size but the experience of many participants is that it is a room where formality is expected and innovation and creativity are discouraged. Similarly, if the aim is to do some strategic thinking, long-term and visionary, a room which is associated with quick-fire operational problem-solving will be less than ideal.

There are a number of what might be termed hygiene factors which, if they are right, attract no attention. These include access and parking, toilet facilities, temperature of the room, comfort of the chairs, being able to see and hear, and the quality and availability of refreshments – a problem in any of these components can create a disproportionate risk to the success of the event.

The capacity of the room is another very important factor. Allowing 70 into a room designed to be comfortable for 60 may seem like a good idea but it may be a disaster because of the impact on the hygiene factors above. A notable example of this was a time when I was persuaded to allow late applicants to attend a public involvement event. Alongside the extra 20 participants were a number of guide dogs, several wheelchairs, some participants accompanied by carers and as a result a huge distraction for facilitator and participants and dogs!

CONCLUSIONS

Preparation is the key to success when delivering an event and while it may not be possible to have an ideal lead-up to an event starting from a 'blank sheet', the discipline of addressing the areas I have outlined will increase the likelihood of success. It can be tempting to take the programme for a previously run event 'off the shelf' and with hindsight many programmes that I have prepared have looked very similar. However, the discipline of going through a planning process can ensure that risks are minimized and both you and the client can have confidence that the event has a high likelihood of success. The resulting effect on the quality of leadership through this visible confidence may be inspirational for participants.

Demonstrating leadership at an event is important, but if the style, behaviour and atmosphere on the day of an event contrasts significantly with 'normal' ways of working then confusion among participants is likely (Goleman, Boyatzis and MacKee, 2003). New approaches may be welcomed by staff but will not be trusted unless and until they become commonplace. The importance of sustaining the same style of leadership beyond an event is a key factor in the success of the overall change process of which the event is a part.

While compromise and pragmatism are inevitable requirements in the lead-up to an event it is wise never to overlook 'hygiene' factors. The practicalities of physical comfort and access to a venue have a major influence on the ability of participants to engage fully with an event. However inspiring and interesting an event may be, if the chairs are uncomfortable and the room is cold it is likely that a proportion of the participants will disengage. Of course, everyone is different and there are different levels of tolerance for physical discomfort and the maxim 'you can't please all of the people all of the time' could have been invented for this very situation. In spite of that, making the effort to do the best possible event and to value the differing experiences of participants, and perhaps even engender a collaborative approach to maintain comfort, are very worthwhile.

The multiple areas covered in this chapter demonstrate that a wide range of consultancy skills will be invaluable to be an effective designer and facilitator of events. The challenge presented by an unknown group of participants and the inability to anticipate exactly what will emerge at an event are among the most energizing and professionally satisfying aspects of working in consultancy. Falling into the trap of thinking that events are a boring part of consultancy work risks missing out on some extremely fulfilling assignments.

CHAPTER SUMMARY

The change agent needs to evaluate the client's need, not just the espoused need but the underlying problems which require resolution. Imposed change is rarely the best way of addressing change programmes, largely because it often ignores the views, opinions and experience of those who will be expected to achieve the change.

Participative change will allow the exploration of previous experience; acceptable approaches to change events; the need for support back at work; and long-term development paths – particularly continuing professional development.

Consultancy is expensive, so is training; we need to ensure that our investment will not be wasted and that the benefits we proposed at the outset of the change programme will be achieved successfully by delivering what was promised at a cost outweighed by the benefits.

For video content relating to this chapter please visit the companion website at **www.macmillanihe.com/Randall-Management-Consultancy.**

REFERENCES

Beckhard, R. and Harris, R. (1987). *Organizational Transitions: Managing Complex Change*. Boston, MA: Addison-Wesley Publishing Company.

Block, P. (2011). *Flawless Consulting*. San Francisco, CA: Pfeiffer.

Bushe, G. (2009). *Clear Leadership: Sustaining Real Collaboration and Partnership at Work*. Mountain View, CA: Davies-Black Publishing.

Fletcher, C. (1993). *Appraisal: Routes to Improved Performance*. London: IPM.

Guest, D. (1989) Personnel and HRM: Can you tell the difference? *Personnel Management*, January: 48 – 51.

Goleman D., Boyatzis, R.E. and MacKee, A. (2003). *The New Leaders Transforming the Art of Leadership into the Science of Results*. London: Sphere Books.

Isaacs, W. (1999). *Dialogue: The Art of Thinking Together*. New York: Random House.

Kline, N. (1999). *Time to Think: Listening to Ignite the Human Mind*. London: Ward Lock.

Nadler, D.A. (1993). Concepts for the management of strategic choice. In C. Mabey and B. Mayon-White (eds), *Managing Change*. London: Open University and Paul Chapman Publishing.

Stewart, R. (1991). *Managing Today and Tomorrow*. Basingstoke: Macmillan Press.

Whitney, D., Trosten-Bloom, A. and Rader, K. (2014). *Appreciative Leadership: Delivering Difference Through Conversation and Inquiry*. Chichester: Kingsham Press.

Further reading: Other writers that have influenced me

Bridges, W. (1980). *Transitions: Making Sense of Life's Changes*. Cambridge, MA: Perseus Books.

Drucker, P.F. (1992). *Managing the Future*. Oxford: Butterworth-Heinemann.

Kouzes, J.M. and Posner, B.Z. (2011). *The Leadership Challenge*. San Francisco, CA: Jossey Bass.

Kurtz, C.F. and Snowden, D.J. (2004). *The Cynefin Mode*l. London: IBM.

Stavros, J.M. and Hinrichs, G. (2011). *The Thin Book of SOAR – Building Strengths Based Strategy*. San Francisco, CA: Pfeiffer.

7 Negotiating Successfully Through Change

Julian Randall and Allan J. Sim

> **Learning Objectives**
> After studying the chapter, you should be able to:
> - Define what is meant by the term 'negotiation' as it applies to organizational change
> - List the nine steps of negotiation
> - Define the content of a negotiation
> - Understand the strengths and weaknesses of different negotiating styles

INTRODUCTION

Change agents are frequently involved in negotiations, especially if they want to achieve participative change. Asking people what they think and feel about their job, work, career and the prospects for successful change raises as many questions as it does answers so probing, listening, observing and deciding are the key skills which enable us to succeed in exploring options and preferences and thus gaining commitment. In this chapter, we will look more closely at the dynamics of the negotiation processes and stages which can make it easier to find a mutually acceptable solution to the problems and challenges experienced during change.

If we accept that the word negotiate means conducting business, then we might reasonably assume that the skill of negotiation is a specialist area, which such people as sales personnel are trained in but which most people do not become that closely involved with on a day-to-day basis. There are those who enjoy visits to countries where local markets still encourage bargaining between seller and buyer, but for the most part the rest of us look at the price, decide whether we want to pay it, and then either click to proceed online or pay up and take the goods purchased if face-to-face with the vendor. We associate negotiation as largely to do with price and may dislike the confrontation or manipulation that bargaining face-to-face requires of us.

The present writers believe that this does not do justice to the extent to which all of us are dependent on negotiation to succeed in life. There are few situations where some form of negotiation does not enhance our experience with people we deal with in our everyday lives. Most of us, for example, like to feel that we had a choice in decisions made about us and that we were consulted about things affecting our lives day-to-day. So, finding out what others want is part of accommodating their needs and hopefully making that process a more pleasant experience. In this way, it is more likely that we will agree to co-operate willingly with others and feel committed to the outcome. Rewards do not have to be confined to who came away with the best deal (at the expense of the other party). There can be many reasons for wanting to reach agreement with someone about what happens next in a shared experience – happiness and peace of mind can be important to gain too.

Learning about others requires that we are aware of the signals which are coming to us. They may be audible or visual, but we need to read and interpret what they mean to be successful in our day-to-day negotiations. Give-and-take is the basis of a civilized life. Doing others the favour of listening to what they want to say and having the courage to say thoughtfully what we think in return, is the basis of being at ease with others – hopefully most of the time. In this respect, then, we usually value exploring a range of negotiated options in decisions affecting our lives.

In this chapter, we take the view that negotiation is central to most interactions with others that consultants undertake, not just the initial agreement on what is to be undertaken during a change programme, at what price and over what duration – important though that is. If change is to be freely entered by both parties, both change agents and the change participants, then negotiation will be an important part of how we propose options for proceeding; how we respond to what others tell us; and how we agree to proceed to secure the successful outcome that everyone wants.

Firstly, we examine the elements involved in the negotiation in the context of what change agents are likely to become involved in during the successive stages of the change programme. We will then look at the steps which negotiators prepare for; the field of negotiation that needs to be explored; and the clarification of detail that determines whether we can agree to do business or not. In some ways, these steps may appear to be self-evident. However, other people always have the capacity to surprise us by responding in ways that we could not have foreseen, and that means that we will have think on our feet and sometimes approach problems from a completely different direction to reach successful agreement.

In this chapter, we will look at four areas which cover the context of negotiation; its dynamic content; the styles of negotiation; and the way in which they contribute to the organizational outcomes addressed by change agents as they seek to implement change programmes in organizations. We will link the theoretical context of negotiation with practical examples of situations that can arise during change programmes to show how negotiation can be both general to the consultancy contract and specific to the implementation of its provisions.

THE CONTEXT OF NEGOTIATION

What we see here are the stages of a traditional negotiation beginning with qualifying the prospect or client and uncovering the need, which lies at the heart of the negotiation. This emphasizes that a negotiation should never start just with a presentation made about the product or service or a firm proposal dictated at the outset. Except for routine fast-moving consumer goods, where customers merely repeat-buy, there is always a need to uncover client need before attempting to make a formal presentation and the more complex the product or service, the more exploration is usually required.

The reason for this is that if presentations are to be successful, they need to address the benefits that the customer will derive from the service being offered. Mere repetition of what is a list of features about the product cannot be targeted towards advantage unless the benefits are apparent to the potential client. So, before moving on, it will be worthwhile examining the three elements underpinning an effective negotiation:

FEATURES

Most of what we buy is governed by a list of features, which have been designed into what is produced or is part of the service. Cars are detailed with their top speed; fuel consumption; 0–60 in x seconds; and so on. Electronic and computer equipment is even more complex and expert sales people delight in memorizing these details and delivering them to their prospective customers, though not always with the intention of simplifying matters.

Most customers, however, only want to know what the product will do for them, rather than listen to an extended list of features. To enable this to happen, the presenter needs to ask questions about what that is and listen carefully to the answers, and this is the first step in the qualifying process. Once these details have been uncovered, the presentation can be focused on what the client wants done to bring out the advantages which can be offered by a proposed product or service and link it to the unique aspects which only working with you can offer.

ADVANTAGES

Advantages are mostly comparative in the sense that they allow comparison to be made with the other options available. If a buyer is interested in a new car's acceleration, then 0–60 in x seconds information becomes relevant, once it is established that this makes it the fastest car in its class. Here, then, the knowledge of what competitive vehicles will do complements what our own product or service is capable of. For this reason, good presentation includes skill in targeting comments usually aware of what the competition is currently offering. Potential customers surveying the market will usually be starting to find out what the opposition offers for themselves, as they make enquiries about what is available. It is rare for companies to approach only one consultant. They will usually want to make their choice from several proposals made. So, identifying your own distinctiveness from other consultancies will be a benefit for you to identify and mention (though do remember: Do not knock the opposition. If asked about them say: 'I am sure they offer a good service. But let me tell you what we can offer you.').

One more step needs to be taken to include the most important aspect of a presentation: the benefits of using what is being proposed.

BENEFITS

Benefits are what the features and advantages together can do to support the business needs and aspirations of the prospective client. This means knowing what the client does currently in their own business. These can be usefully summarized in the efficiency or productivity factors which are as follows:

- Time
- Quality
- Quantity
- Cost

In other words, the benefit will lie somewhere within this list and needs to be identified early in the presentation stage of the negotiation. Can the company produce greater quantities more quickly; to a higher standard; at a more reasonable cost as a result of the change programme? These aspects will need to be brought out clearly so that the client is aware that we understand their business and the impact that our service will need to have on their business outcomes. Emphasizing what we know competitors would find difficult to do is also worthwhile pursuing at this point – and far better than being negative about them. So, for example, the small consultancy can reinforce the message that those presenting will also be conducting the change programme – knowing that this is much less likely to happen using large consultancy teams.

We cannot state too early that our presentation will benefit from including the calculation of **interference costs** within a business. Often, managers themselves are unaware of these costs. They need to be made aware of how and where they are likely to arise in a business; how they are calculated; and the impact that an effective change programme will have on reducing them.

Consultancy costs always sound prohibitive to managers who need to authorize the budget and agree the programme of change. So, reducing a recurring loss will be an important benefit of what we as consultants can offer. The well-known saying 'If you think training's expensive, try ignorance' alerts the client to the fact that **accidents**, for example, are extremely costly and represent a significant interference cost, which is rarely calculated by the company but nonetheless reduces their efficiency. A common interference cost is **staff turnover**. So, calculating the cost of staff turnover can be crucial in making a presentation linked to benefits of the change programme to reduce such costs. Reduction of interference costs is a major benefit and one which consultants do well to focus on during their presentation. Some of these issues can be uncovered during the **qualifying interview**. As we have seen, the key questions will have included:

- Previous experience of change programmes
- What was liked about the change programme(s)
- What was disliked by the change programme(s)
- Expected standards of what is now being sought
- Summary of the benefits

PRESENTATION

We have already mentioned the link between the qualifying interview and the presentation phase of the negotiation cycle. We will return to that in this chapter as we look at examples that can arise during the change programme. The next step in the negotiation cycle brings us to the costing aspect which is a relevant place to examine in more detail the steps of negotiation. Once again, we can note that clarifying important aspects of a change programme will require negotiation both before, during, and after the programme itself and each of these steps needs to be clarified and agreed – closing for commitment in other words. Each aspect agreed brings closer the final closing agreement.

HANDLING CONCERNS AND OBJECTIONS

Clients are usually sceptical about the claims made by consultants and presenters in general. We are justifiably known for making claims which are not always realized later during the experience of a change programme. Clients who raise concerns and objections are rarely welcomed by those who make presentations or negotiate final contracts. However, they should be viewed as a bonus, as they are an opportunity to probe the basis of the concern; allow the consultant to examine what has been said; and respond to something that might otherwise become a block at the final agreement stage. Concerns and objections should always be accepted, probed to establish the details of the claim made, and then used as an opportunity to solve the problem and reinforce the benefits of the service being offered.

Here is a summary for handling concerns and objection:

- Accept the objection (I can understand your point)
- Now state the compensating benefit (let me go back to something you raised when you spoke about...)
- Rework the feature(s) that supports the benefit which you know you can deliver
- Reinforce the USP that only you can offer
- Check (Have I answered your question? Is there anything else that I can tell you?)

THE CONTENT OF NEGOTIATION

There are many step approaches to the elements of negotiation and they cover the stages through which the negotiation will normally proceed. So, for example, Douglas (1957, 1962) suggests three phases:

- **Phase 1**: establishing the negotiation range
- **Phase 2**: reconnoitring the range
- **Phase 3**: precipitating the decision reaching crisis

These are general, prescriptive phases which do not always offer detailed explanation of what sort of activity is being offered. More detailed steps are offered by Gulliver (1979) who suggests eight phases:

1. Search for an arena
2. Composition of the agenda and definition of the issues in dispute
3. Establishing maximal limits to issues in dispute
4. Narrowing the differences
5. Preliminaries to final bargaining
6. Ritual affirmation
7. Execution of the agreement
8. Implementation

Although these extend the sequence of the steps involved they do not make clear the different functions that will be played during the negotiation. So, for the benefit of both clarity and detail we have chosen to use the eight-step approach of Kennedy (1998):

1. Prepare
2. Argue
3. Signal
4. Propose
5. Package
6. Bargain
7. Close
8. Agree

We will take each step and consider how they may be relevant in the context of consultancy work.

Prepare

We have already mentioned the need to explore and examine the sources of potential information about our potential client before a first meeting if possible. This process itself may already have raised questions that a consultant will want to probe during the qualifying interview. This may focus on the company's performance in its sector; the competition the company faces; the changing perceptions of customers in that market; critical issues such as falling market-share and eroding profits (important to probe in more detail). It will usually be the case that the company will be looking at your own position in the consultancy market; whether you have any track record in their sector; and what previous clients have said about you. It is likely that there will be probing from both sides of the negotiating table. Be careful not to make claims which you cannot substantiate.

The first, **qualifying interview** should have explored and established what potential clients know about their own business and the sector they work in; what experience they have had of change management programmes in the past; how they evaluate a worthwhile and effective change programme; and what they want to achieve from their present quest for an external consultancy in the proposed change.

At the same time, clients will usually want to find out as much as they can about your consultancy business and your track record in the sector. As with TripAdvisor, there will be plenty of information which they may already have come by – not all of it accurate. Be prepared to accept the comments; probe them; and modify them where necessary.

Most clients are sensitive about revealing their budgets early on and are more interested in what your charges will be. You may want to think about the way you will answer questions posed during this opening interview. There are three ways you can take:

- Honesty
- Deferral
- Avoidance

If you cannot answer, you will say so and explain why – perhaps offering to come back with the requested information at a later stage.

Rather than go firm on a cost at an early stage, you may want to use deferral strategy, explaining that you will be in a better position to answer once you can both establish exactly what needs to be done and then calculate what the cost implications will be.

Finally, there are some areas that you need to avoid. If asked about your competitors, always adhere to the principle of 'Do not knock the opposition'. If you have worked for them it is always tempting to show how much you know about them – resist that temptation.

The purpose of the opening interview is to explore the limits which your potential client has in mind and compare that with you own assumptions about the business offered before you focus more closely on the detail.

It may help to think about the **range of negotiation** which is sometimes summarized as three stages (Walton and McKersie, 1965):

- **L** – Limit beyond which you would not be prepared to operate
- **I** – Your intended position
- **M** – Your most-favoured position

Bear in mind that your prospective client will have similar positions in their range of negotiation. You will each be seeking to explore these as you negotiate in the opening phase of your discussions.

One thing that you will be looking out for is indicators that continuing with the negotiation would not be in your best interests. For example, taking business that is marginal in the hope of getting more in the future (a sprat to catch a mackerel) is usually a flawed strategy.

It may be that the way in which the meeting is conducted is uncongenial to you – frequent interruptions; negative comments; inappropriate humour; failure to listen – any of these may indicate that this could be a difficult client for you to deal with. It is better to draw the right conclusion early on and agree to part amicably before commitment locks you into an unfavourable partnership. Intuition represents 75% of what managers do according to Stewart (1991). You can rely on your own perceptions. They will not usually be wrong.

Argue

The second of Kennedy's steps of negotiation suffers from a word whose meaning is commonly associated with having a row or confrontation with someone. In the context of negotiating we would suggest that the popular meaning should be abandoned as it can set people at variance early on and become an obstacle to reasonable outcome.

A more useful definition is to put on the table your own position and listen to the response. You should already have worked on the position that you will take and, as far as possible, worked out what you think is the likely position of those you are negotiating with. So, a better idea would be to put forward your own position. One way of doing this is to start with the summary of the **qualifying interview** – particularly what you were told about the client's previous experience of change; the likes and dislikes of that experience; and the expected outcomes of the current quest for support.

But, before embarking on the details of this section, we should consider the roles that can be adopted by the negotiating team. Interviewing and by extension, negotiating is usually found to be far more taxing than making a presentation (though in truth the latter is more often feared than any other intervention). At least in a presentation if the preparation, notes and aids have been properly prepared, the speaker will usually be given a respectful hearing before being subjected to questions. In negotiations and interviews this is not nearly as likely. From moment to moment the other parties to the negotiation are likely to answer in a way that no one could have planned for yet requires an instant response. That prospect will always present a feeling of unease in those taking part. Working with others on your team means that there is someone else to share the burden with in an interactive way, if you plan it before you go into negotiations. So, here are some suggested roles which are sometimes used by negotiating teams:

Leader: The leader can introduce each item you want to raise and present your position clearly before hearing the response of the other side. The leader must listen and be prepared to probe or ask supplementary questions to clarify responses made and similarly offer explanations for any queries made by the other side.
Observer: If there are three of you then one person can position themselves between the other two team members and make notes which are visible and legible. There is no need for the observer to say anything. The role is solely to alert other team members to what has been said and indicate where a probe may be necessary, if a signal has been missed by the team.
Summarizer: The role here is to summarize at appropriate points what has been agreed and what has yet to be agreed by both sides. This gives the leader time to think about follow-up suggestions and can be facilitated by referring discreetly to the notes made by the observer.

You may want to agree a signalling system beforehand indicating when you want to intervene or ask a question. It might be removing your glasses or moving a pen. But watching each other will be as important as watching the other side.

Remember: What you learn in the first interview will inform the subsequent steps in the negotiation so it may be that an adjournment would make sense where the profusion or complexity of detail needs to be assimilated and a thoughtful response prepared.

Some questions that may shape your negotiation

- What do you want to achieve (from a change programme)?
- What will that do for you and the company?
- What will it be like when you have achieved it?/How will you know when you have achieved it?
- What outside resources do you need?
- Who can help you?
- What will this goal confirm about you and the company?
- What other benefits might there be?
- What is the first step to getting what you want?

The answers apply to both sides of the table. So, at the adjournment you will need to check how far you can answer the questions about yourselves.

Signalling

Here we touch on the third element which Kennedy includes in his list and we mentioned in the chapter on the qualifying interview. Observation is important here. Closed gestures; negative humour; unflattering comments; rare or no eye contact; breaking eye contact before answering a question; mannerisms indicating uncertainty, all may indicate that the client is uneasy and cause you to find out why or conclude that there is nothing to be gained in continuing with the negotiation. Early agreement to conclude allows the development of more positive business elsewhere.

On a more positive note, however, it is open to any party to a negotiation to give signals, which though they may sound uncertain or sceptical, invite probing to establish whether there is ground for negotiation or not. Here are some examples. How would you probe these comments to discover what lay behind them?

> - The board would find it difficult to accept that
> - Our suppliers accept a 90-day payment period
> - We have a standard agreement with the unions
> - We expect all work to be completed within the contracted time
> - We expect to have the final say on which consultants you send in to do the work

In general, straight probes can be made choosing the key word that lies in the statement or question asked. So, in the first statement we might ask:

'Why would they find it difficult?'

Bearing in mind the four factors of efficiency we already mentioned, the second statement invites the question:

'What do you negotiate on?'

The third statement should be probed to discover what exactly the Local Authority discount is that they have been receiving.

The fourth statement may invite several questions:

'What do you mean by 'nonsense'?'
'Which Unions do you work with?'

The fifth question can be sharp-angled closed:

'Why do you ask that?'
'Is that what you want?'

Alternatively, you might probe for further details:

'What do you mean by extended hours?
'Which jobs are we referring to here?'

The fifth statement did occur with the closed culture of a well-known IT company. The training consultancy used agreed to the vetting of their staff before they were allocated to any training role. It will equally apply to organizations in which signing the Official Secrets Act is a required practice.

In short, signalling is part of every step in any negotiation. What is spoken, what is done, even what is implied or inferred should be open to those taking part to explore and evaluate. Those good at negotiation are usually observant of other's behaviour and aware of their own; good at listening and probing; making it easy for others to contribute to the process; working for goodwill rather than being confrontational or challenging.

Propose, package and bargain

The following three steps are key to the central part of negotiation. Having looked at the issues you think will arise and tried to work out what the position of your potential client is, you can embark on planning how you will go about closing your negotiation.

We have already mentioned the key factors of time, quantity, quality and cost and at this stage you may want to consider what it is that you can offer as a package to best facilitate the change programme. You may find it useful to pursue the following points with the client:

- What do they see as being the need for change (do you agree with their initial diagnosis)?
- What do you propose as the best way forward (are you intending to work for participative change)?

- If so, how long will this take (Time)?
- What will be the major interventions (Quantity)?
- What are the business outcomes they want to achieve (Quality)?
- What are the cost implications (Cost)?

At this point you may want to consider how you will deal with the contentious issue of cost. The cost always seems to be high to potential clients. There are several ways that you might approach this:

1. The overall cost broken down into the main activities you will undertake

Or

2. You build up the costs, itemizing the main activities you will undertake one by one

In some cases, it may be appropriate to mention what the market rate is and then indicate that you are more reasonably priced than that rate. Alternatively, you may want to mention your charging bands and then build up a cost calculation so that the client can understand what they are asking for and what that involves in terms of cost.

Either way, you would be well advised to mention contingency allowances for cost overruns and the implications of your team being asked to do more than was agreed – which can happen easily once the programme has begun and can often lead to misunderstanding if not dealt with before the change programme begins.

Close

Our final steps include closing – which we have looked at in Chapter 3.

Here is a summary of the 13 classic closes and how they might fit into the negotiation steps:

Opening:

1. Order-book close (use your notes)
2. Sharp-angle closing (clarifying a question with a probing question to clarify what has been asked)
3. Alternate closing (either … or …, which do you prefer? Useful for gaining commitment for follow-up)
4. Under/over technique (asking for something in return for a requested favour

Middle of your negotiation:

5. Puppy-dog close (offer a pilot scheme, for example)
6. Handle concerns and objections (always be ready for this one)
7. Dutch auction close (go up to come down technique when you are asked about price)
8. T-square close (write down all the things that are agreed benefits, then summarize on what has yet to be agreed)

Closing stages:

9. Summary close (use your notes to read off what has been agreed)
10. Closing on an objection (is this the only thing that stands between us…)
11. Major and minor close (first choice to be made and then the second choice straight after)
12. Disaster close (describing the consequences of not adopting change programme)
13. Silent close (exactly what it says. The first to break loses the initiative)

Closing is part of clarifying as you go through the steps of negotiation – not something left to the end of the process. In training, these are sometimes referred to as **testing questions**. They are usually closed questions but they have the benefit of focusing on specific answers and are generally factual:

- Who?
- What?
- When?
- Where?
- How?
- Why?

Agreement

You will want a written agreement to be exchanged and signed as soon as you have reached agreement with your new client. Ensure that it includes all that you have discussed. The role of the observer and summarizer will be crucial here.

It will be important to ensure the all conditions are expressed as objective criteria – sometimes referred to as **SMART**:

- Specific
- Measurable
- Attainable
- Realistic
- Timely

You should seek legal advice about the sustainability of the terms and conditions that you have included and ensure that you have covered all likely eventualities. We will expand on the implications of legal contracts and agreements in Chapter 9.

The range of negotiation

One interesting piece of research suggested styles of negotiation and how they vary according to assertiveness and co-operation see figure 7.1. How we feel about others we meet can sometimes be an instant impression that causes us to adopt a position which is difficult to move away from later. For example, competition often leads to confrontation and we would be better probing concerns early rather than becoming defensive. Agreement to disagree is perfectly acceptable and such a compromise may lead more easily to collaboration.

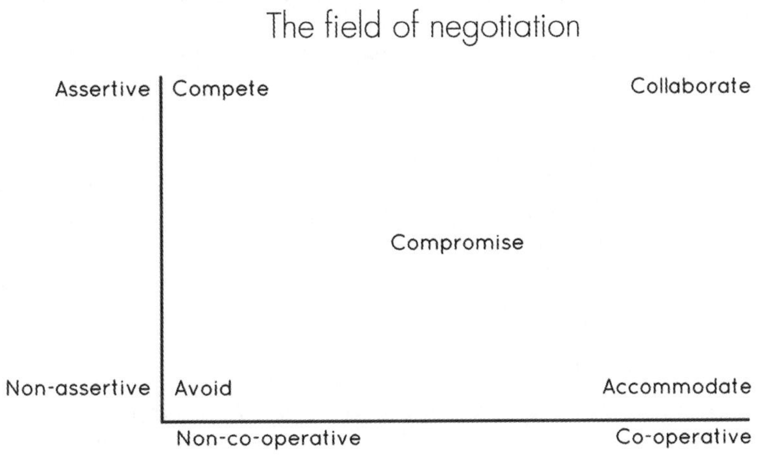

The field of negotiation

	Non-co-operative	Co-operative
Assertive	Compete	Collaborate
	Compromise	
Non-assertive	Avoid	Accommodate

Figure 7.1 *Styles of negotiation (Rubin and Brown, 1975)*

Most people would agree that the ideal position would be collaboration. However, sometimes the approach of the party we are negotiating with may mean that we have some work to do before it is possible to move to that point.

Senior managers can sometimes adopt a dominant approach to others (competing – especially with consultants). Getting such people to slow down and adopt a more discussive approach may be necessary (asking closed or sharp-angled questions may help you to achieve this).

Aggressive people take time to relax and be frank about their own business prospects. Asking open questions and showing interest in their responses may make a constructive discussion more likely.

Avoiders, by contrast, take time to become involved and will need more careful handling: being confrontational will usually meet with more passive resistance such as silence or feigned uncertainty. Finding a way in will require observation, responsiveness and patience. Again, questions that demonstrate interest and awareness of issues faced may be a useful way in.

As far as the style of conversation to achieve a reasonably balanced agreement is concerned negotiators may find that a dialogue rather than an adversarial approach achieves the best response.

Adversarial/Assertive negotiation

Debate	Dialogue
Knowing the answers	Finding out
Winning or losing	Discussion
Unequal power	Questions
Proving a point	Sharing
Defending a position	Respect Exploring new possibilities Listening and responding

Source: Zohar and Marshall (2004: 177)

Table 7.1 Adversarial/Assertive

Findings from early research (Karass, 1968, 1970) into what makes effective negotiators suggested the following points. The researchers concluded:

- First, we discovered that skilled negotiators were very successful when they had high aspirations or were lucky enough to face unskilled opponents with equal power.
- Second, we found that skilled negotiators were benevolent when they had power.
- Third, we found that unskilled negotiators were losers except when they had power and high aspirations.
- Fourth, we discovered that successful negotiators made high initial demands, avoided making first concessions, conceded slowly and avoided making as many large concessions as their opponents.
- Fifth, our results indicate that successful negotiators used concessions in a dynamic way. They applied the above techniques to test the validity of their assumptions and the intent of the opponent. Losers did not test reality in the same way.
- Sixth, all negotiators, successful or not, expressed equal satisfaction with the final agreement.

Mutual satisfaction with a deal is a truest measure of the success of a negotiation.

(Kennedy, 1998: 306)

> # EXERCISE
>
> **Toughness and Honesty**
>
> How do you get groups in a conflict to reach an agreement that is in their mutual interest when it is in each individual's interest to hold out for as favourable an agreement for their side as possible? It is worth noting that by holding out the groups may in fact prevent the achievement of any agreement and thus end up in a position that is advantageous to neither. This problem is often called the *toughness dilemma* (Zartman, 1981: 279). The argument is that the tougher the group acts the more likely they are to reach an agreement closer to what they want *but* they are also more likely to not reach an agreement at all by this tough stance. So, there is the dilemma: act too tough and perhaps get nothing, or be too accommodating and reach an agreement that isn't good for you. It is a fundamental problem in negotiation and is closely linked with the question of honesty.
>
> Is it good to be honest? It is an interesting ethical question, should you always tell the truth? Certainly, Kant may argue so: 'by a lie a human being throws away and annihilates his dignity as a human being' (Kant, 2003: 430). However, have you ever told someone that their new outfit suits them, even if it does not? As an ethical person you should be honest in negotiations but much like the toughness problem, how honest? I would argue that while you should not practise to deceive, absolute honesty like absolute truthfulness may not always be the best path to a happy result either.
>
> What follows here is an exercise in negotiation where you can consider how tough and how honest you must be. Remember, tough does not mean aggressive and when I say 'how honest' I am not talking about an action to deliberately deceive. Rather, I am discussing how many of your cards do you put on the table for the other side to see and when do you do it?
>
> You may like to consider that it follows on from an inspection visit that was paid to a potential client after which you wanted to raise the issues you uncovered and explore the implications with the parties involved.

NEGOTIATION TASK FOR TWO GROUPS

Auditor

You recently completed a fairly routine site audit of a factory in a foreign country that was undertaking production for your company. What was particularly troubling to you was the disparity between the foreman's reports of activity at the factory and what you found. Based on the reports, you didn't expect to find any problems. Not only were there a number of audit findings but the behaviour of the factory owner and the foreman confused you. Except for a brief welcome and an assurance that everything was well, the foreman was not to be seen. While very pleasant, the owner seemed hesitant about sharing information. When you asked him about some of the issues you had discovered, he indicated that he was aware of them but had no more information. You got the feeling that there had been problems between him and the foreman, but you weren't able to identify anything specific. He seemed to be in a very difficult position and was obviously uncomfortable with what he should or shouldn't say to you.

The problems you identified were the following:

- There were a number of exceptions to the guidelines previously set by your company, for which there was no documentation. The foreman indicated that these exceptions were approved by your company.
- A number of Adverse Events were identified, but the only ones reported were those that the foreman felt were directly related to your production run.
- Production counts were off.

- There were discrepancies in dates as to when staff began working on your company's project.
- The signatures on the Health and Safety assessments are not clear. You are not sure if the foreman has signed them or if someone else has.

At the conclusion of the audit, you discussed your findings with the owner and let him know about the issues you identified. You attempted to meet with the foreman, but he only made a brief appearance, saying he had another appointment. He said that he would be back shortly, and indicated that if there are any problems, you should wait for his return.

Your meeting with the owner took around 30 minutes and you waited a further 45 minutes for the foreman. When he did not return, you left. You informed the owner that either the senior manager or one of her staff members would get back to them. You then contacted the senior manager to schedule a meeting so that you can report your findings. It will be held shortly.

Aims

- You want your concerns expressed in the final report and you feel that it needs to be released urgently.
- You want to ensure that the company's senior management is aware of the conditions at the factory and the risk that they represent.
- You are particularly concerned over the Health and Safety issue and are concerned that it may go public.
- You want to ensure that your reputation as a fair and objective auditor is maintained.
- You want to keep your job.

Senior manager

The compliance team recently completed an audit at one of the overseas factories that your company has product manufactured at. As is frequently the case, the auditor raised issues that you don't consider to be either important or that will have any serious impact. Moreover, the auditor fails to consider the broader context of the importance of the factory's production to the company. However, before you had a chance to call the owner with the findings, he called you and was clearly upset. He pointed out a few things:

- 'These are typical start-up problems in a production run, and they'll be taken care of. It's still early in the process.'
- 'My foreman is relatively new and they shouldn't have put him under this type of pressure. If there were concerns, they should have insisted that I be there. It wasn't the right way to handle this type of issue. I am very surprised at how this was done.'
- 'Based on our initial conversations with your company, I wasn't clear about what the auditor needed or would be looking for. I know they sent a written notice of their visit, but they should have spoken directly with me.'
- 'If there were problems, your people should have said something to me at the conclusion of the visit. I came by while they were meeting with my foreman, and I figured everything was okay.'

He went on to point out that his factory has done numerous jobs on this scale, and always comes through. You are aware that he is correct in this. In fact, you have heard that the factory's work is usually first-rate. While they have never previously done any production for you, they have done work for several of your rivals, that is why you gave them the job.

In your own mind, you're not clear about the importance or purpose of these audits. It's really the end result that counts. You were once a foreman yourself and you know how time-consuming and difficult these audits can be. It's a real problem at some of the busier factories, where there might be several production runs for multiple firms occurring at the same time. In your opinion, the problems identified are pretty minor. The owner is someone you feel deserves trust due to his record of successful delivery, and you are not looking to create problems. Besides the factory is integral to production of the product on time and Marketing is breathing down your neck about the product launch.

You haven't yet seen the final report. Basically, you know what the owner told you: the problems were minor, his foreman is new, and not to worry, everything will be fine. You are troubled, not only by the possible findings of the final report but by how the audit was handled. You are concerned that the auditor may not have treated these people with the due degree of respect and care.

Aims

- You are anxious that the final report does not damage your links with the factory owner.
- You want to ensure that the report in no way slows down production because you have a lot invested in the success of the project.
- You don't want anything coming out that could embarrass you or the company but you also don't want to be seen as whitewashing the report.
- You hope to get the auditor to be reasonable and either change the report or delay it until after production is completed.
- You want to keep your job.

Feedback

Remember that the way negotiations are conducted is as important as what is achieved. There should be no 'winners or losers' approach. And where people get stuck or have a blank moment the negotiation exercise can be paused while those involved discuss among themselves what should be the next step.

In some cases, we have used a 'tag' approach in which a negotiating team sends forward their first representatives but can choose to substitute a team member if they think this would be helpful. The advantage of this approach is that everyone can be involved at some point in the negotiation. But also, that people learn from watching others, so the different styles extend understanding of different approaches to negotiation.

Remember to praise first what you liked about what was achieved, and then offer options for handling situations which were less successfully handled during the role play.

It should be said that professional negotiators, however experienced they may be, usually consult each other after a negotiation and exchange their impressions of how things went; what was successful; what was less successful; how they would approach a similar situation in the future.

CHAPTER SUMMARY

Formal negotiation is an art that requires practice and working with colleagues who are reflective and responsive to other people. But informally the opportunities for negotiation are extensive in the life of the change agent.

It would be rare for a change programme to move from its beginning to its conclusion without the need of amendment or change. Indeed, if we are embarking on emergent change, then we should welcome the opportunity to discuss different ways of approaching the steps involved in the programme – especially when they require the active involvement of company staff. Training and development issues would be a typical example of involving those involved both before, during and after any planned events. Solving problems means finding solutions. Consultants should be used to that.

As we noted earlier, mutual satisfaction is a win-win situation which allows all involved to feel that they made progress – even if they did not get exactly what they would have liked. Similarly, most change programmes reach situations which can threaten the success of the programme. Again, it is important that these are addressed with the proposer of the change programme as soon as the situation surfaces.

It has often been said that 'people buy from people they like'. So, gaining support for change throughout its stages will require a high level of awareness of how people are responding to change events and intervening early to resolve situations amicably.

For video content relating to this chapter please visit the companion website at **www.macmillanihe.com/Randall-Management-Consultancy.**

REFERENCES

Douglas, A. (1957). The peaceful settlement of industrial and inter-group disputes. *Journal of Conflict Resolution*, 1, 67–94.

Douglas, A. (1962). *Industrial Peacemaking*. New York: Columbia University Press.

Gulliver, P.H. (1979). *Disputes and Negotiations: A Cross-Cultural Perspective*. New York: Academic Press.

Kant, I. (2003). *The Metaphysics of Morals*. Cambridge: Cambridge University Press.

Karass, C.L. (1968). A study of the relationship of negotiator skill and power as determinants of negotiation outcomes. PhD thesis, University of Southern California, Los Angeles, CA (unpublished).

Karass, C.L. (1970). *The Negotiating Game*. New York: Thomas Y. Crowell.

Kennedy, G. (1998). *Kennedy on Negotiation*. Aldershot: Gower Publishing.

Rubin, J.Z. and Brown, B.R. (1975). *The Social Psychology of Bargaining and Negotiation*. London: Academic Press.

Stewart, R. (1991). *Managing Today and Tomorrow*. Basingstoke: Macmillan Press.

Walton, R.E. and McKersie, R.B. (1965). *A Behavioural Theory of Labour Negotiation: An Analysis of a Social Interaction System*. New York: McGraw-Hill.

Zartman, I.W. (1981). Explaining disengagement. In J.Z. Rubin (ed.), *Dynamics of Third Party Intervention: Kissinger in the Middle East*. New York: Praeger, pp. 148–167.

Zohar, D. and Marshall, I.N. (2004). *Spiritual Capital: Wealth We Can Live By*. San Francisco, CA: Berrett-Koehler.

8 Internal Change Agents and Participative Change

Julian Randall and Dave Sherrit

> **Learning Objectives**
>
> After studying the chapter, you should be able to:
> - Understand the rise of the internal change agent
> - List the elements of an effective change programme
> - Facilitate participative change
> - Define the role of an internal change agent
> - Appreciate the skills and competences required of an internal change agent

INTRODUCTION

As we have noted in previous chapters management consultants have not always enjoyed the appreciation they might have expected for their work, if the academic accounts are to be believed. There is little about the demands of entering an organization and braving the waves of mistrust from groups and individuals; the demands of senior managers; and the sometimes unrealistic expectations of those requiring change. There is little about the work of the facilitator who spends time listening and learning about a culture and receiving the messages of despair in the face of perceived insuperable marketplace and political challenges. Neither is there an appreciation that much work was done to enable individuals and groups to fine-tune their competencies and extend their career prospects in ways that they could not have imagined without the support of those trained to give them that support, encouragement and advice. Rather, there are two groups: managers who defer to consultants' claims; and consultants who overawe managers and persuade them that their intervention is essential to staying in business.

So, we hear messages that suggest that:

It is their (consultants) search for control and predictability which renders managers vulnerable to the quasi-magical solutions management gurus offer as relief to their sources of frustration.

(Clark and Salaman, 1998: 142)

Gurus are masters of the art of presentation:

Guru performance has major elements of display and conversion with a focus on the irrational, emotional and symbolic aspects of organization.

(ibid.)

Consultants themselves, it is suggested, often indulge in specific behaviours which reinforce fears in managers and encourage them to embark on the desired course of action prescribed:

1. (They) create disequilibrium by challenging audience members' normative world views
2. Induce guilt by the threat of damnation and promise of salvation
3. Enable the audience to see familiar ideas and concepts in new ways (ibid.)

The imagery here sometimes borders on the religious and reinforces the view that consultants indulge in the dark arts of manipulation, implied threats and the possibility of redemption – if the prescriptive path of change is undertaken.

Gurus are manipulators of myths and strategies for managing meaning and extending management control (Willmott, 1993). They know how to win management acceptance by becoming an obligatory passage point (Callon, 1986). Rhetoric is the core of guru work: the degree of elaboration of the language code through which one describes one's organization, regulates client-orientations as well as identity (Alvesson, 1993). The focus of this language is the claim to mastery of, and experience in, valued managerial behaviours, skill and knowledge (Clark & Salaman, 1998).

Consultants, according to this view, are myth-makers and storytellers. These myths and stories are rationality-surrogates (Alvesson, 1993). They help managers convince themselves that consultants know what they are doing and are drawn from the brightest and best. Managing is itself an art of performance – the reading and interpretation of events – and the expression and embodiment of that reading in action on the part of the manager (Mangham, 1994). Labels, metaphors and platitudes are building blocks for more complex control machinery: world views, philosophies, ideologies, cosmologies, business ideas (Czarniawska-Joerges and Joerges, 1990).

What we see here are interpretative repertoires in action (Whittle, 2006). They are exercised in paradoxical ways. There is a range of behaviour which can encompass the way in which the role of the consultant can be exercised:

1. Advocate and advisor
2. Interested and independent
3. Scientist and storyteller
4. Bespoke and standardized
5. Ally and enemy
6. Facilitator and leader

This, it is suggested, is a skilful use of discourse (Potter and Wetherell, 1987), part of the habitus of the consultancy field and the 'ability of actors to manoeuvre in a culturally competent way' (Alvesson, 1993). It is all a part of situated learning in the client–consultant relationship. Their identity – who we are and what potential we have (Lave and Wenger, 1991) – is continually evolving through participation in multiple communities of practice (Giddens, 1991). So, consultants 'may seek to project a coherent identity which they believe their clients want to see (being an expert; being in control) which is regulated by the managerialist discourses at the workplace and more generally' (Handley et al., 2007). In this sense, consultants are 'experimenting with provisional selves' (Ibarra, 1999).

The work of the consultant is 'knowledge commodification' (Heusinkveld and Benders, 2005). They are continually introducing new knowledge products which makes the existing seem old and less attractive (Kitay and Wright, 2007). The occupational rhetoric of management consultants is that of the professional; prophet; partner; business person; service worker. And the three key issues on which they depend are legitimacy (the right thing to do); efficiency (improving business performance); and vulnerability (exposing this in the client).

THE RISE OF THE INTERNAL CHANGE AGENT

In more recent years there has been an increasing emphasis on the changes which businesses have undergone. The breakdown of large organizations and the rise of subcontractors and consultants replacing core workers has been highlighted for 30 years (Handy, 1989). There has been a breakup of once unitary organizations into what is sometimes referred to as neo-bureaucratic/hybrid organizations (Sturdy, 2017). There has been fragmentation of organizations through outsourcing, external networks and diffuse occupational boundaries. In some cases, internal expertise (HR and IT, for example) is viewed as a service to staff within the organization whose staff are now viewed as clients of internal consultancy. Business Process Management referred to such managers as expertise managers (Champy, 1995). This emerging market-led structure within the organization leads to managers becoming leaders or facilitators rather than directors of operations (O'Reilly and Reed, 2011) and leads to the move of managers into the role of consultant within the organization (Schein, 2004; Wright, 2008).

This trend suggests a more concerted move into change management with a more strategic advisory role (Caldwell, 2005) for the internal consultant manager (Czerniawska, 2011). This new role indicates the 'mechanism, forms and tensions of neo-bureaucratic management' (Sturdy, 2017: 191). It also opens the door for collaboration with external change agents. As we will see, internal change agents can make an important contribution to the continuing impetus of a change programme. It offers a chance that once the external change agents have left, there are those left behind who can continue to validate and, more importantly, evaluate the impact of change in the organization.

In this chapter, we will look at the elements of change programmes and the qualities required of the effective change agents. We will also look at how external and internal change agents can work together to make it easier for change events to succeed. Teams can complement the skills and knowledge which each member has by tapping into perceptions, knowledge and skills, which others in the group have developed.

STARTING AT THE BEGINNING

Imposed change always has about it a risk that it will be resisted by those who are directly affected by the change programme. It is not just a question of industrial democracy in which we seek to reach agreement and gain consensus. It is clear that in some situations a change is something which is not voluntary and has to be undertaken regardless of how its subjects feel about it. Nor do those who are the subjects of the change have the expertise to dictate what the content of change should be, especially when technologically driven change is involved. However, what the proponents of participative change see is that there is a benefit in drawing people into the change process at the outset, so that their views about how best to implement change events can be taken into account and greater commitment to change can be supported.

In this respect, the role of the internal change agent comes into its own. Formal meetings to explore what will be viewed as workable can then be complemented by the experience of those who are part of the peer group and more likely to know what is being said informally behind the scenes about the proposed change.

So, what should the change team focus on initially? Here are three areas that will be important to clarify early on.

EXPLORING THE CHANGE ENVIRONMENT

How can the external and internal change agents work together to clarify the foundations of change (Nadler, 1993)?

Motivate change: Change, as we have remarked, is not usually welcomed, especially if it is imposed from outside. Internal change agents are a part of the predominant culture and should be able to tap into the assumptions of their fellow workers more readily than outsiders. However, the need for change can come from market-led or outside-in strategies, and external change agents may well be aware of these elements and how they work – particularly, if they have worked in the sector recently in other organizations. So, motivating change benefits from both internal and external perspectives to appreciate the dynamics of the drivers of change.

Manage the transition: Finding out where people are ought to be more readily within the knowledge and experience of internal change agents – especially those who have experience of working outside the organization or sector. Transitions make people feel exposed to unwanted change and lead to feelings of inadequacy and threat (Nadler, 1993). On the other hand, external change agents may have experienced such change in the past and experienced successful strategies for overcoming them. Once again exchange is significant for both groups.

Shape the political dynamics: Internal change agents are in a strong position to identify where there are disparities between groups and factions within the organization. Knowledge-sharing early on can be invaluable for incoming external change agents – though again, they may have experience themselves of overcoming such differences in the past which offer options for different approaches to change events. Allaying fears that such differences are insurmountable can be useful to share early on.

Overall, then, we might say that internal change agents can offer a ready way into the organization for change agents coming in from outside. External change agents can offer a window of opportunity to sharing perceptions and experience drawn from outside the organization and relevant to the sector in which they work.

In summary, we could say that working together provides a congruence model drawn from both the inside and outside experience and knowledge of change agents:

Congruence model of organizational behaviour

- Environment (outside-in/market-led approach)
- Resources (inside-out/resource-led approach)
- History of the organization (where have they come from)
- Strategy (where do they want to go)
- Think holistically
- Look for cause and effect (Nadler and Tushman, 1979)

Both the external and internal change agents can offer part of the jigsaw which can make the difference to starting the change programme from a secure base of comprehensive knowledge and experience.

ADVANTAGES OF EXTERNAL AND INTERNAL CHANGE AGENTS WORKING TOGETHER

Finding out which are the key power groups will be a useful start for the group. External change agents will benefit from the knowledge of their internal colleagues here.

Leaders think about the strategic frame of change and it is here that the external change agents may have much to give their internal colleagues. The vision of the future which leaders create should also be considered at this point: What is it that we are aiming to achieve for all those involved in the change programme? Is there a vision that we can share that could then take us forward?

Language is itself symbolic. So, following on from the preceding point, the title of the programme could make all the difference to its acceptance and will merit careful consideration before the launch. There may also be other symbolic behaviours which will signify change as led by the change agents. It might be informality during the programme sessions; an invitation for individual volunteers to contribute to the change team; the emphasis on participative change and what that will mean for the change initiative.

Finally, what's in it for those taking part? Evaluation begins not at the end of the programme but at the beginning. From the outset, we need to be clear what is the desired goal which people will work towards and provide the reward for taking part in the change programme.

NEED TO MOTIVATE CHANGE

> **STOP AND REFLECT**
>
> **How would you?**
>
> - Surface dissatisfaction with the present state
> - Gain participation in change
> - Reward behaviours supporting change
> - Find time and opportunity to disengage from the present state
> - Disengage at the right time

Lewin's early work in T-groups have always led the way for those embarking on emergent change strategies. The quality of those facilitating the initial interdisciplinary group meetings is the gauge of the success of the sessions.

Gaining participation will depend on asking the right questions; listening to the responses; acknowledging important ideas; encouraging everyone to take part; using summary skills; and keeping the session moving forward.

Involvement and interest are the gauge of rewarding behaviours supporting change. From the outset, look out for likely recruits for the internal change agent team and approach them directly if need be.

MBWA (management by walking about) provides opportunities to liaise with everyone throughout the organization. It disengages from the formal work setting and allows the airing of more general discussions. Meetings socially can be useful too – though once again an informal setting may be best. But listen, learn and don't outstay your welcome.

MANAGING THE TRANSITION

> **STOP AND REFLECT**
>
> **How would you?**
>
> - Develop and communicate a clear image of the future (what is it going to look like?)
> - Use multiple and consistent leverage points
> - Develop organizational arrangements for the transition (learning and development; visits to successful sites)
> - Build in feedback mechanisms (can people say what they think from time to time?)

We have already mentioned the need for a vision of the future that the change programme is seeking to achieve. How we put that across is an important point to consider. Based on starting where people are and leading them to where you want them to be, how we describe the present situation will need careful consideration. Sometimes internal staff may be better placed to do this particularly if they have experienced similar changes in the past.

The second point we have already mentioned: there will be external factors (outside-in) and internal factors (inside-out) both of which will affect the success of the change programme. A similar approach can address the rewards which will reinforce the evaluation of the programme. What are the benefits for the individual as well as the benefit for the group?

The third element is most often missed out by change agents. Where are the lived examples which could influence people to embrace change? The hollowing out of the psychological contract is a significant risk in all change programmes, which will often be perceived as organizations wanting more for less (profit-focused). We are looking for value-added approaches that will work for both staff and customers – they are our principal stakeholders, and this is something that needs to be reinforced with the shareholders.

In summary then:

GUIDELINES FOR FACILITATING PARTICIPATIVE CHANGE

- Be open in your questioning
- Show you listen and understand
- Don't make any judgements yourself
- Only intervene to restore order
- Use sharp-angle closing to check questions (Why do you say that?)
- Seek examples of general complaint (Is there a story here you want to share…?)
- Summarize (what we have achieved/what we haven't achieved)

Don't be afraid to speak up and reflect what you think you are hearing back to the audience in an assertive way.

SKILLS WHICH CAN ENHANCE AND DEVELOP DIALOGUE

- Sensing needs (I get the sense that you disagree with that…)
- Amplify understanding (Tell me more about that…)
- Build awareness (From what you say you feel strongly about that – tell us more)
- Create credibility (I think most people in your position would feel that, too)
- Legitimize viewpoints (What you say makes perfect sense. However…)
- Generate potential solutions (Suppose we were to…)
- Broaden support (How many others would agree with this?)
- Identify indifference and opposition (You don't seem very impressed by what's been said so far. Why is that?)

(Quinn, 1980: 51)

IMPORTANT CHANGE INTERVENTIONS

STOP AND REFLECT

How would you?

- Change perceived risks
- Build in flexibility
- Put forward trial concepts

- Create pockets of commitment
- Eliminate undesirable options
- Crystallize consensus
- Manage coalitions
- Formalize agreed commitments

Altering perceptions depends on influencing beliefs and for most people that will mean informing a discussion with crucial information that may not have been explored previously during imposed change. In this sense, previous experience may come more readily to external change agents who have facilitated relevant change events elsewhere.

This point may also lead to the second point of structuring needed flexibilities. People can negotiate when they see realistic options laid out clearly before them. So, time spent in exploring such issues is always worthwhile – particularly if change will affect terms and conditions of service significantly.

In the same way, groups may accept pilot schemes or trials more readily if they feel involved in choosing how these are implemented. Indeed, that may well be a useful starting point for gaining commitment of volunteers willing to engage in such an initiative.

Eliminating undesirable options may be more difficult to handle. The implications of embarking on perceived undesirable outcomes depends on the skill of the facilitator and their experience in the planning and implementing of such change.

The rest is gaining consensus – by using summarizing skills and drawing out positive points made to support change; deferring decisions on any contentious matters; gaining commitment for what has been achieved and agreement to discuss other matters later.

DIFFERENT ROLES FOR CHANGE AGENTS

As we have seen there are traditionally five roles which need careful consideration at the start of the change programme:

- The **advocate** who proposes change
- The **sponsor** who legitimizes it
- The **targets** who undergo it
- The **agents** who implement it
- The **process owner** – typically the most senior target

(Davenport, 1993)

Part of the challenge of a balanced programme is to ensure that the key roles are covered by the company. There should be no occasion when the senior managers/CEO opt out completely and leave it all to the external change agents. Tempting though that is for them, it will present problems later when those resisting change look for support to executives who are perceived as being uncommitted to the change.

So, from the outset the CEO needs to take a lead role of **advocate** in key meetings with staff: introducing the consultants; explaining why they were invited to come; explaining the brief which they have been given to institute the change programme; answering questions that staff may have about the future of the organization and the prospects for the people working in it.

The **process owner** will have day-to-day responsibility for working out who can be released for initial interdisciplinary meetings and training events so that the business needs are covered and this will be a crucial role to be covered by the company's staff.

The **agents** will be the external change agents complemented by the internal change agents who will become more responsible for the long-term impact of the change as the programme unfolds. They are taken from the target group so they can fulfil a bridge-building role between staff and external providers. They provide the change initiatives with a credibility which external agents cannot command and so become critical for the successful adoption of change initiatives.

- As an external change agent, you belong to the fourth group
- As an internal change agent, you belong to the third and fourth groups (so have a foot in both camps)

Just as HRM theory sought to engage managers in day-to-day interventions with staff, so too with consultancy. So, these roles are not confined to external change agents parachuted into the organization to implement change. Participative change emphasizes that.

CHANGE AGENTS

- Everyone is a potential change agent (even the persistent questioner at the back of the room)
- Opportunities should be presented for individuals to self-select themselves into change agency roles (encourage and support volunteers)
- Change agency requires no special consideration for selection (learning and listening skills is all – the rest you will provide training for)

(Doyle, 2002)

CRUCIAL ROLES FOR CHANGE AGENTS

> **STOP AND REFLECT**
>
> How would you develop the following skills in internal change agents?
> - Clarity in communicating with groups and individuals
> - Defining their role clearly
> - Gaining commitment to ideas and action
> - Establishing leadership and authority
> - Working across groups effectively
> - Understanding and working with working cultures
> - Managing change events

Most of the initial work that you do developing internal change agents will be involving them in the activities and change events which you undertake. Understudying others more experienced is always a useful means of developing those who are taking their first steps in interactive developmental work with others.

Communication is the key word here but, as is often said, listening is as important as making announcements or getting into explanatory mode. Indeed, looking at the three points involving groups we would say that discussion is an important means of stimulating reflection and developing confidence. In this respect, opportunities to reflect with the external change agents after a shared event is good practice to explore how others more skilled reflected on the events and why they responded in the way that they did. The ability to answer concerns and objections is best acquired by witnessing how others more experienced deal with it. Sometimes remembering what other effective operators did or said can then become internalized and inform responses at critical moments in the future.

As far as **leadership and authority** are concerned, the change agent is in a partially negotiated situation. Teamwork requires acceptance that others may have knowledge, skill and experience that will lead the group and a good facilitator will recognize and encourage that rather than be challenged by it. This approach means that there is a judgement to be made from moment to moment about how far any intervention is providing leadership and will make a positive contribution. The only time that the facilitator will need to use a formal leadership role will be when interventions are inappropriate or uncalled for. How those are dealt with will need to be carefully crafted to uphold what is legally correct, while working for goodwill in the group. This requires a high level of tact and diplomacy.

Intergroup work is a part of managing change events when interdisciplinary teams are the basis of change programme events. Hearing what others think is not always possible in a concentrated working group and working across boundaries will be an opportunity to hear different viewpoints rarely shared. More broadly composed groups can be the occasion for expressing strongly held views about other colleagues in different parts of the business and such frankness is not always welcomed. For the facilitator, this will present a challenge of keeping the balance between free speech carefully exercised to ensure that personal antipathy is not vented. Again, experience is the gauge of deciding when to intervene and what to say. It may be that a word to the wise after an event is better than an open challenge in front of the group, which may lead to long-term resentment.

Finally, summarizing will be the important skill to use at the end of each session, so that everyone is aware of what has been agreed and what remains unresolved.

DEVELOPING SKILLS AND COMPETENCIES IN INTERNAL CHANGE AGENTS

In the box below are 14 skill areas mentioned by two well-known researchers into the management of change. Thinking of what can be trained means focusing on:

- Knowledge (K)
- Skill (S)
- Experience (E)

Some qualities are a function of aptitude, which may not be so easy to acquire through the training route.

Go through the list and discuss which of these qualities can be enhanced by training and say what sort of training might be appropriate. As you will see we have indicated where K & S (knowledge and skill) apply, and where we might be seeking to develop A (attitude). This may indicate whether training or development might be the preferable route to take.

- Sensitivity (A)
- Clarity (S)
- Flexibility (A)
- Team building (K & S)
- Networking (K & S)
- Communication skills (K & S)
- Interpersonal skills (K & S)
- Personal enthusiasm (A)
- Motivation and commitment (A)
- Selling (K & S)
- Negotiation (K & S)
- Practical awareness (A)
- Influencing skills (K & S)
- Helicopter perspective (K, S & E)

SPECIALIST SKILL

> **STOP AND REFLECT**
>
> Here is a list of situations which you might face as a change agent. Discuss how you would approach each one:
>
> - Getting action/support from a manager who doesn't want to go public
> - Reconciling expected with actual resource levels
> - Gaining co-operation from key people in difficult situations
> - Modifying unreasonable demands (tactfully)
> - Diverting needed staff and resources when required

All change programmes should be supported by the Board and therefore they are the ultimate source of the consultant's authority. Coverage by a Board decision should make it easier to gain the support for what clearly has been agreed with the company.

Promises of support, time or money can be an issue on all programmes: training rarely finishes on time and can involve cost overruns that could not have been foreseen at the outset of the change programme. This reinforces the point that some contingency funds should be worked into the programme at the outset by the clients and this is a point you may want to make before embarking on the change event. Unexpected gaps in support or funding can give rise to a loss of trust so are best raised as soon as a shortfall is spotted.

Negotiation is an ongoing skill which is required by all change agents. Getting willing co-operation is a function of shrewd negotiation but its exercise needs to be thought about carefully. Raising critical issues at the wrong time will usually meet with resistance from senior managers, especially if they are challenged publicly.

We have already spoken about a word to the wise discretely. If requests are unreasonable we need to assume first that it is not perceived that way by its proposers. This means that we may need to alert them that their public interventions are causing problems and would be better dealt with in another way.

The final point is covered by the above points but reinforces that early warning should be given of the need to move staff and resources and not left for discussion and decision until the last minute.

ISSUES THAT NEED IMMEDIATE ACTION

Here in summary are the points we have raised so far. Spotting them early on as they occur will enable them to be addressed sooner rather than later:

- Lack of goal clarity
- Badly managed reorganization
- Misunderstanding of what has been delegated to whom
- Insufficient authority to carry out a programme
- CEO too busy to see the principal change agent
- Inadequate resources
- Unanswered concerns

Resistance is normal and not a threat and its basis can be probed and addressed early on during the initial interdisciplinary meetings.

Resistance will be lessened if

- Participants feel the project is their own (not imposed from without, therefore emergent change may be preferable)
- Project has wholehearted support from the top (CEO tops and tails sessions with staff; no one from the Board is allowed to opt out)
- Participants see change as reducing their present burdens (What's in it for them...?)
- Projects accord with values/ideas of participants (reinforces the culture)
- Project offers new experience which interests participants (working towards career development)
- Participants feel their autonomy and security is not threatened (particularly bounded communities within the professions)
- Proponents are able to empathize with opponents (internal change agents are invaluable here)
- Provision is made for feedback during the project (positive and negative)
- Participants experience acceptance, support, trust and confidence between each other (working in interdisciplinary teams can help)
- Project remains open to revision and accommodation to amendment (Bullock and Batten's change phases approach helps here)

(Watson, 1966)

Addressing these points will encourage participative change and increase the chances that those involved will collaborate rather than obstruct the change.

CREDIBLE LEADERSHIP

In summary, we have raised the following points:

- Know their business (use internal change agents)
- Share their values (take time to find out through initial meetings)
- Be symbolic (you represent the change which you are promoting)
- Be inspirational/aspirational (your enthusiasm and belief must be palpable)
- Be a prophetic voice (where will they be in five years' time?)
- Been there? (draw on experience of the change agents)
- Listener (probe; listen; observe; decide)
- Be positive (commitment; enthusiasm; good humour)

We may be magic-makers; charismatic; storytellers; and the other epithets observed by researchers. However, what we do is grounded in a jointly held belief that the future can be better, and that it will happen through the people involved – especially the well-chosen and developed internal change agents.

CONSULTANCY IN ACTION

Dave Sherrit, HR consultant at Chevron (UK)

In this section, I explore how the role of the change agent has been present throughout my 31-year career in learning and organization development and how much the term 'change agent' has played a conscious and sometimes less conscious role in shaping my practice in the organizations where I have worked.

I intend to do this by examining my experiences in the organizations I have been employed in throughout my career and how a wide range of factors associated with the role of the change agent have influenced my practice. Before I embark on this retrospective review I will also define what the term change agent means to me.

WHAT IS A CHANGE AGENT?

The term 'change agent' is not exclusive to those in the field of learning and organization development and can equally be applied to a range of roles and professions, either assigned or emergent in almost any organization. The nature of working in the realm of change does mean you tend to hear the phrase more often especially in the large global organizations I've worked in.

The first time I heard the term was when I joined the National Health Service (NHS) (UK) and I worked closely with a team of change agents who were plucked from key clinical posts where they already had credibility in their chosen professions. Their purpose was to deliver part of a larger plan of change ultimately focused on patient care. Back in 1988, as a fairly naïve 23-year-old, these modern-day shamans who managed to move effortlessly through the hierarchy of the organization with their toolbox of tricks, totally mesmerized me in comparison to my very limited practice as a training officer. I was very fortunate to work alongside these seconded professionals who had been intensively trained in the tools and techniques of organizational change.

As I look back on this period of my career, the one key learning point that seems very obvious now is the concept of 'self as instrument' as popularized by Mee-Yan Cheung-Judge (2001) in which she proclaimed:

> *The premise underlying my approach is that OD consulting necessitates a high degree of self-knowledge and personal development that must engage OD practitioners throughout their professional lives.*

In 1988, this concept hadn't really been talked about in this frame, but looking back on what I observed in the change agents of the NHS, this was very much part of the way they engaged all their stakeholders. Their ability to integrate the way they communicated using their own personal style and work with almost any stakeholder from the very bottom to the very top of the organization was very much down to not just their competencies as change agents but also how they navigated the wide range of stakeholders (tribes) that existed in the NHS in the late 1980s. This demonstrated the benefit of being an internal consultant over an external, and the 'here today gone tomorrow interventionist', who neither had credibility nor affordability in the then, as it is now, cash-constrained NHS. That is not to say an external consultant cannot occupy the role of a change agent, but in this instance the cards would certainly have been stacked against them. This learning has influenced my practice today in the way I use the power of relationships with my clients in many aspects of my own personal practice.

AM I A CHANGE AGENT OR AM I NOT?

In defining the concept of the change agent I'm drawn to Havelock and Zlotolow (1995) who see the function as having four key roles. In this section, I will take each role in turn and provide an example of where I fulfilled the role from my own work experience and also what I learned from that experience.

THE CHANGE AGENT AS CATALYST

Most change needs help from within to initiate it and start the process, and sometimes to even be the standard bearer – whether that's simply, as Havelock and Zlotolow (1995) state, by prodding and applying pressure to the system or by challenging the status quo to create dissatisfaction. Even in some of the more transactional roles I occupied in my career in training and development, the topics I delivered were connected to a bigger picture. As a result, I definitely occupied the torchbearer role especially in the delivery of how we wanted leaders to practise as defined in the many leadership programmes I have delivered over the years. Many of these programmes I have been involved in were linked to the company's cultural values. In Baker Hughes INTEQ, a drilling services company, the organization's core value had been defined to give clarity to employees on the kind of culture we wanted to build. How we trained leaders was critical to embedding these core values through the way people were led. Given the biggest resource in Baker Hughes was the competence and capability of the people, this became a significant priority in delivering the core values which essentially became a belief system on a global basis across the many regional locations where Baker operated. We did this through the expectations we set leaders and how we wanted them to lead.

Another example where I unwittingly ended up in this role was when I was delivering a two-day course in the NHS which was part of a rollout for a new Management by Objectives performance appraisal system. In 1989, this was a significant change in how goals were managed from the very top of the organization to the bottom and was viewed very cynically by the unions and clinicians of the NHS who saw it as a corporatization of the long-standing institution they worked for. Having joined from Debenhams as a training officer, I was viewed by some as part of the problem, entering the NHS from the private sector. On many occasions, I co-tutored these events with a change agent who came from the clinical profession. They provided 'credibility by association' allowing me to deliver and run the events to meet the key learning outcomes. Looking back, that partnership was essential to the delivery of a new system, and the coaching I then delivered to assist ward managers was only possible because of this 'credibility of association' that gave me permission to enter this world without too much emphasis on my being seen as the hand-of-management, especially given that I was a non-clinician.

THE CHANGE AGENT AS SOLUTION GIVER

This is not just about giving solutions but assisting others in creating energy to be more receptive to new ways forward. The change agent plays a key role in opening thinking and can often be a mirror, especially for those who already think they know the answer to the problems.

My practice as a coach has been very extensive over the last 20 years of my career. Often my role as a coach was part of a larger plan in the use of this intervention as it was when I joined Chevron in 2003. One of the first assignments I had was leading and working with several other coaches on a programme aimed at increasing the impact leaders had on people in the areas of safety, reliability and cost. We used a model called performance-based leadership as popularized by Aubrey Daniels (2000) and, after training, each leader went on to provide in-field coaching support to increase their fluency and practice of the ABC (antecedent, behaviour, consequence) model of human performance. Coaching was the intervention in this instance but the coaches did occupy the role of change agents, despite the perceived stand-alone interventionist role they had been assigned. I was the only coach that was employed directly by the business unit. The other two were external coaches. At the time I would not have described the role as a change agent, but the process we employed and the relationships that developed in the coach–client relationship resulted in a much deeper involvement in the organization for me than an external coach interventionist could occupy, simply because of their role and the nature of their short-term relationship with the business unit. In reality, we were in part trying to create an army of change agents indirectly through the focus on coaching, with the then top 50 leaders in Chevron Europe. The change agent role in this instance was less about one individual and more about a hive-mind approach to change. We all had a part to play but in reality none of us would have called ourselves a change agent.

THE CHANGE AGENT AS PROCESS HELPER

The change agent should never get too deeply into the detail or what I would refer to as the content of change. One of their roles is to champion a process that helps those either involved or impacted by change to see their way through the challenges they face. By investing time in relationship building and awareness of the needs of different stakeholders, the change agent helps the client navigate a process that can deliver the change as envisioned and do so by themselves. Ultimately, this creates sustained change.

Most people who are wanting to initiate or create change are not often very expert in what is involved in making change work. Havelock and Zlotolow (2005) refer to this as the 'how to's' of change. Helping the client look at a process of how to implement change based on the work of the gurus in the field of organizational development. Out of the many models and approaches that exist the two that most readily feature in my own practice and thinking are Kotters 8-step model by John Kotter (1996) and Burke-Litwin's model of systems and organizational change (Warner Burke, 2011). Both of these models are useful lenses in assisting with analysis of a major change and how to make it happen. Additionally, they also help establish that change has a level of complexity and discipline that if applied correctly can significantly increase the chances of success.

THE CHANGE AGENT AS RESOURCE-LINKER

A change agent can play a powerful role of bringing the right resources together of directing clients toward the appropriate resource. They can often have the line of sight to see what is needed and clarity of thought on who best can fulfil that need.

As a fairly young training officer in the NHS I recall being set the challenge of bringing multiple groups of stakeholders together to focus on a single issue. This issue in 1991 was the movement of individuals with long-term psychiatric care needs from the institution of the hospital, to the being cared for by a patchwork of services in the community. The challenge at first seemed obvious, and in reality, my naïvety of the complexity of it all somehow carried me through. Bringing together diverse groups such as the police, the Local Authority, the NHS, social workers and the voluntary sector to explore this issue and the way forward was an interesting task. My role was to meet with each stakeholder, understand where they were coming from and build an agenda to facilitate dialogue on how this transition would happen. If only I knew then what I know now. My oversimplification of the situation didn't help in the end and sadly I left the NHS in early 1992 before this project was complete. Looking back, I definitely was in the role of a resource-linker between some very opposing and polarized stakeholders. It certainly wasn't my job to solve the problem but to try to help those facing this complexity to begin to unravel its nature. I, of course, wasn't alone in this task and the project continued after my departure from the NHS. In retrospect, the most significant learning for me was that all viewpoints are valid no matter how diverse they may seem at first.

CHANGE AGENTS ARE EVERYWHERE

In the penultimate section of this chapter I want to examine the impact a change agent can have on a system no matter how small their contribution might be, and how an industry without realizing it can have a hidden army of change agents focused on a single aim.

In 1998 the single worst loss of life occurred in the North Sea Oil and Gas industry. Piper Alpha was a step-change event that would create ripples of transformation for years to come. My journey into the oil and gas sector happened nearly four years after this catastrophic event. However, working in the company that operated Piper Alpha, and then its replacement Piper Bravo, gave me a line of sight on the impact this event had on many hundreds of thousands of people, possibly today even millions.

Even though I was a single individual I was part of an industry that was determined to see change and continue to innovate in making this kind of disaster something that would never happen again. For me, having worked inside the oil and gas sector for nearly 25 years, I have witnessed a phenomenon I would refer to as 'hive-mind change'. There are many change agents in oil and gas focused on the same thing but with multiple agendas. If you explore the many and varied stakeholders across the industry that includes oil and gas operators, service companies, the unions, regulatory authorities, and of course those people who work in the sector, and you find individuals focused relentlessly on making this an industry where fatalities and failures can be engineered out of the system.

I've never worked in safety, nor do I have any safety background or qualifications, but for much of my career in oil and gas the focus of my role has been in creating thinking, beliefs and behaviours that support and create safe working through the application of my skills in learning and organizational development. With the incredibly strong drive which comes from the very top of the industry it results in an army of change agents across a wide spectrum of roles focused roughly on the same goal. This change is initiated by people, by individuals who most likely would not recognize the term change agent readily but in fact are fulfilling that very role.

This hidden hive-mind approach is infectious. Even organizations that may be described as laggards are eventually pulled or even pushed into becoming part of this wider change movement. In 2017 it is still happening, whether it is the focus on creating a belief that we can eradicate fatalities or simply being extra cautious when a near miss occurs, such as the recent incidents that involved fatalities during helicopter flights in both the UK and the Norwegian sectors of the North Sea.

This raises the question which started this chapter, 'what is a change agent?' During my career, I have been involved in both roles, consciously acting out the role of a change agent and also unconsciously assisting organizations with change no matter how small the intervention might have been. Everything we do as people in organizations creates ripples that impact others. We are all agents of change yet many do not recognize the energy and impact they make, whether it is to steer fellow workers towards finding the ideal, or likewise look for ways to erode entrenched barriers and work to achieve the opposite effect in an organization. Some organizations as they reach their desired objectives quickly become less aware of the need for continuous change, and so the learning journey, perhaps after a disaster, begins once again. The boom and bust hiring of the oil and gas sector is a great example of capitalist economics driving a cycle of damaging change, that until recently had resulted in the UK North Sea being the most expensive industry basin in the world. However, if we harnessed the energy of this secret change agent army as we do on safety with boom and bust, surely we could counter this cycle and create more stability.

Pascale and Sternin (2005) talk about secret change agents and how they could move mountains not just in our corporate and public sector organizations but also on a global basis. They refer to the power of the 'positive deviant' in the organization. They define this as 'isolated areas of change that break from the norm and bring improvement in performance'. For me this is like discovering cold fusion, a way we can generate energy from within.

CONCLUSIONS

Drawing on my own experiences I have discovered that change agents exist in many forms. You don't need the job title 'change agent' to be defined as one, yet many of us may not even realize we are part of making that change happen. If organizations could harness these armies of change agents, imagine the power that could be unleashed to create a win-win environment for all stakeholders.

Change agents may create a hive approach and may enact beneficial or less beneficial change in an organization, however this is a recipe that requires the right ingredients. The missing ingredients are engagement and clear leadership. Pascale and Sternin (2005) said:

The key is to engage the members of the community you want to change in the process of discovery, making them the evangelists of their own conversion experience. This means that as a leader, you will take on a very different role from the one you have played in previous change management scenarios.

This leads me to my final conclusion and possibly the most obvious. No one can do this alone. Change agents need to be part of a wider system that supports their role and ideally should be aligned with the aims of the organization. The concept of positive deviance is incredibly powerful but like all discoveries needs to be harnessed in order to transform change events from having a minor impact to a major force.

We must also not forget the role leaders have in this recipe for success. They play a critical role of aligning and engaging the whole system to convey impactful and lasting change through their example and inspiration.

I've been very fortunate in my career to experience the many faces of the change agent and in my current role I continue to learn about what this means for my own practice, and the ability of an internal consultant to make a lasting and meaningful impact in large organizations. I hope some of my reflections help to focus on where the internal change agent can make an impact in any system irrespective of how challenging it may seem.

CHAPTER SUMMARY

Reading the accounts of those experienced in change agency is always enlightening and the account we have here reinforces much that we have covered in this book so far. It links the work of individual change agents with the people they work with and acknowledges that culture can only be changed by internal initiatives. Change initiatives work when those who engage in them internalize the messages needed to reinforce and ensure success. Internal change agents can play a crucial role in the framework of successful change programmes. Their work is only now becoming recognized. The academics who have researched this work are to be applauded for making that work known to a wider audience of managers and OD specialists.

The need for internal change agents will continue in a world of work that is no longer as supportive of the individual as it once was. Global capitalism has privileged the making of profit at the expense of its impact on HR development and the pursuit of traditional career aspirations at work. The promise of HRM theory that people are our most important resource may well ring hollow for those who are trapped in low-tech, no-tech jobs; and as the prospect of home ownership eludes the up-and-coming generation, the claims that we have a society that works for all sometimes seems a tired and overused claim used by public speakers and politicians – unsupported by practical support to those who struggle to cope with and benefit from globally led change initiatives.

Ignoring the added value that individuals bring to a profession, trade or occupation does not make long-term sense for developing a society that aims to be caring, supportive and developmental of its citizens. The efforts of good parents, teachers, managers, mentors and guides are a constant need in connecting the development and growth of the individual with commitment to a civilized society. The internal change agent shares in all those roles and promotes the link between individual aspiration and its fulfilment in the wider community of service beyond self and development of others for a better world for humanity.

For video content relating to this chapter please visit the companion website at **www.macmillanihe.com/Randall-Management-Consultancy.**

REFERENCES

Alvesson, M. (1993). Organizations as rhetoric: Knowledge-intensive firms and the struggle with ambiguity. *Journal of Management Studies*, 30, 997–1015.

Caldwell, R. (2005). Things fall apart? Discourses on agency and change in organizations. *Human Relations*, 58(1), 83–114.

Callon, M. (1986). Some elements of a sociology of translation: Domestication of the scallops and the fishermen of St Brieuc Bay. In J. Law (ed.), *Power, Action and Belief: A New Sociology of Knowledge?* London: Routledge and Kegan Paul, pp. 196–233.

Champy, J. (1995). *Reengineering Management: The Mandate for New Leadership*. London: Harper Collins.

Cheung-Judge, M.Y. (2001). The self as instrument: A cornerstone for the future of OD. *OD Practitioner*, 33(3), 11–16.

Clark, T. and Salaman, G. (1998). Telling tales: Management gurus' narratives and the construction of managerial identity. *Journal of Management Studies*, 35(2), 137–161.

Czarniawska-Joerges, B. and Joerges, B. (1990). Linguistic artefacts at service of organizational control. In P. Gagliardi (ed.), *Symbols and Artefacts: View of the Corporate Landscape*. Berlin: de Gruyter, pp. 339–364.

Czerniawska, F. (2011). Consultant-managers: Something else to worry about. *The Source blog*, 3 May. Retrieved from http://www.sourceforconsulting.com/blog/2011/05/03/consultant-managers-somethingelse-to-worry-about/

Daniels, A.C. (2000). *Bringing the Best out in People: How to Apply the Astonishing Power of Positive Reinforcement*. New York: McGraw-Hill Education.

Davenport, T. (1993). *Process Innovation: Reengineering Work Through IT*. Boston, MA: Harvard Business School.

Doyle, M. (2002). Selecting managers for transformational change. *Human Resource Management Journal*, 12(1), 3–16.

Giddens, A. (1991). *Modernity and Self-Identity. Self and Society in the Late Modern Age*. Cambridge: Polity.

Handy, C. (1989). *The Age of Unreason*. London: Century Hutchinson Ltd.

Handley, K., Clark, T., Fincham, R. and Sturdy, A. (2007). Researching situated learning: Participation, identity and practices in client-consultant relationships. *Management Learning*, 38(3), 173–191.

Havelock, R.G. and Zlotolow, S. (1995). *The Change Agents Guide* (2nd edn). Englewood Cliffs, NJ: Educational Technology Publications.

Heusinkveld, S. and Benders, J. (2005). Contested commodification: Consultancies and their struggle with new concept development. *Human Relations*, 58(3), 283–310.

Ibarra, H. (1999). Provisional selves: Experimenting with image and identity in professional adaptation. *Administrative Science Quarterly*, 44, 764–791.

Kitay, J. and Wright, C. (2007). From prophets to profits: The occupational rhetoric of management consultants. *Human Relations*, 60(11), 1613–1640.

Kotter, J.P. (1996). *Leading Change*. Boston, MA: Harvard Business School Press.

Lave, J. and Wenger, E. (1991). *Situated Learning: Legitimate Peripheral Participation*. New York: Cambridge University Press.

Mangham, I.L. and Pye, A. (1991). *The Doing of Managing*. Oxford: Basil Blackwell Business.

Nadler, D.A. and Tushman, M.L. (1979). A congruence model for diagnosing organizational behaviour. In D. Kolb, I. Rubin and J. McIntyre (eds), *Organizational Psychology: A Book of Readings*. Englewood Cliffs, NJ: Prentice Hall.

Nadler, D.A. (1993). Concepts for the management of strategic change. In C. Marbey and B. Mayon-White (eds), *Managing Change*. London: Paul Chapman and Open University.

O'Reilly, D. and Reed, M. (2011). The grit in the oyster: Professionalism, managerialism and leaderism as discourses of UK public services modernization. *Organization Studies*, 32(8), 1079–1101.

Pascale, R.T. and Sternin, J. (2005). Your company's secret change agents. *Harvard Business Review*, May 2005. https://hbr.org/2005/05/your-companys-secret-change-agents

Potter, J. and Wetherell, M. (1987). *Discourse and Social Psychology: Beyond Attitudes and Behaviour*. London: Sage.

Quinn, J.B. (1980). *Strategies for Change: Logical Instrumentalism*. Homewood, IL: Richard D. Irwin.

Schein, E.H. (2004). *Organizational Culture and Leadership*. San Francisco, CA: Jossey Bass.

Sturdy, A., Wright, C. and Wylie, N. (2016). Managers as consultants: The hybridity and tensions of neo-bureaucratic management. *Organization*, 23(2), 184–205.

Warner Burke, W. (2011). *Organizational Change: Theory and Practice*. London: Sage.

Watson, G. (1966). *Resistance to Change*. Washington, DC: National Training Laboratories.

Whittle, A. (2006). The paradoxical repertoires of management consultancy. *Journal of Organizational Change Management*, 19(4), 424–443.

Willmott, H.C. (1993). Strength is ignorance; slavery is freedom: Culture in modern organizations. *Journal of Management Studies*, 30, 515–552.

Wright, C. (2008). Reinventing human resource management: Business partners, internal consultants and the limits to professionalization. *Human Relations*, 61(8), 1063–1086.

9 Consultants, Ethics and the Law

Allan J. Sim and Thom D. Young

Learning Objectives
After studying the chapter, you should be able to:
- Distinguish the ethical from the legal constraints of consultancy work
- Understand excusing conditions and mitigating factors
- Explore the dangers of ethical relativism
- Understand the legal implications of your consultancy contract
- Check the legal basis of your consultancy brief

INTRODUCTION

A man without ethics is a wild beast loosed upon this world. – Albert Camus

Consultants are expected to be knowledgeable about business in general, not just the area of their own expertise. Change can trigger many different emotions and responses in those who are subjected to it without warning and the questions which arise very often require answers about what the terms and conditions of changing a working contract, for example, are for those affected. It is likely that the change agent will be quizzed about this and asked for advice.

There can also be occasions when custom and practice accepted by everyone in the organization looks to the incomer as at least questionable if not misguided and likely to lead to legal challenge in the future. Again, the change agent is expected to be aware of such constraints and willing to intervene to alleviate the problem.

As change agents, we can be asked to do things which are questionable both by senior managers and by members of staff. We know that we should not do them but we need to find the right words to avoid being put on the spot without sounding judgemental or high-handed in our response.

In this chapter, we will look at some of the legal and ethical issues that can impact consultancy. We'll look at ethical and legal considerations on why consultancy projects may fail or why they should not start to begin with. These are complex issues but they are issues that cannot be ignored. Your reputation and that of your client will rely upon the choices that you make.

The role of consultant is one which continues to attract discussion and debate. For some, consultants provide an essential service to their clients but to others they charge enormous professional fees for providing advice that was startlingly obvious. The very language of the consultant has become for some a maxim for inconsequential narrative and near valueless recommendations. In other words, they see the consultant as one who practises to deceive while charging high prices for it. These perceptions are not something that the consultancy sector can afford to ignore. As the proverb goes, the reputation of a thousand years may be determined by the conduct of one hour. What we do as consultants, what we propose and the actions we say we will take may benefit or damage not just ourselves but the sector in general. Hopefully this chapter will assist you in avoiding the worst of the pitfalls and guide you along the, often difficult, path of ethical decision making.

WHAT IS ETHICS?

In 1968 Raymond Baumhart conducted some research on ethics and business. As part of this research he asked Business Managers the simple question, 'What does ethics mean to you?' and some of the responses he received are quite telling.

- 'Ethics has to do with what my feelings tell me is right or wrong.'
- 'Ethics has to do with my religious beliefs.'
- 'Ethics consists of the standards of behaviour our society accepts.'
- 'Being ethical is doing what the law requires.'
- 'I don't know what the word means.'

(Baumhart, 1968)

While most people will focus in on the last response, with some good cause, all of these responses are wrong. All of them display a fundamental misunderstanding of what ethics is. Ethics cannot be what you feel is right, nor is it always correct to assume that your religious beliefs are ethical, nor are the social norms always ethical and lastly the law itself is not always ethical. We may consider that the law can be an ethical minimum but that does not mean that all laws are intrinsically ethical. But more on the law later.

Ethics can be seen as the practice of making a choice between right and wrong. Ethics isn't really concerned with how people act but rather with how people should act. It is our actions that define who we are. So, the consideration of whether those actions are ethical or not defines us not just as moral actors. What we use to assess situations and events we encounter during our lives and how to react to them is at the core of ethics. By the nature of their work, consultants will have to make numerous decisions throughout the consultancy process. They will be asked to undertake many tasks by their client at the initial consulting opportunity and throughout the consultancy project. Without a firm grounding in practical business ethics they may find themselves in situations that can produce extremely damaging consequences for their client, their employees and themselves.

The very nature of what we mean by ethics in the context of business can be unclear. Some elements of observed business behaviour single themselves out: fraud, deception, false claims concerning products/services, the exploitation of labour and damage to the environment are clearly unethical to the majority. However, the question of whether there is an underlying set of values or philosophy against which more normally observed individual or corporate performance can be easily and objectively assessed is a more difficult one. While legal frameworks in the majority of nations will provide boundaries beyond which behaviour is clearly not acceptable, increasingly there is a sense that some of what is legal may not be generally accepted as ethical.

HOW CAN WE BE ETHICAL?

How do we avoid these damaging consequences? How can we act ethically? Before moving on to some potential answers to these questions I would like to briefly look at **excusing conditions** and **mitigating factors**.

What do we mean by an excusing condition and mitigating factors in relation to ethical action? It is generally agreed that there are only two excusing factors for unethical action: ignorance and inability. These are two things, I would argue, that no consultant wants to own up to. There are two forms of excusing ignorance: ignorance of fact and ignorance of ethical standards. Here are the differences: ignorance of fact eliminates moral responsibility because a person cannot be responsible for something which he or she cannot control; and ignorance of ethical standards removes responsibility because a person is not responsible for failing to meet obligations of whose existence he or she is genuinely ignorant (Velasquez, 2012). What it is vital to remember here is that in both cases it must be **true ignorance** and not simply an effort to remain unaware of facts or standards. In other words, not the 'plausible deniability' so beloved of some politicians. The second excusing condition, inability, only applies if the person or persons could not have prevented the unethical action. So, you are only excused if there was no possible way to avoid the action. But what of mitigation?

There are more mitigating factors than excusing ones and they are:

1. Circumstances that minimize a person's involvement in an act
2. Circumstances that leave a person uncertain about what they are doing
3. Circumstances that make it difficult for the person to avoid doing it
4. Circumstances that show the matter involved was of a minor nature

The extent to which these mitigating circumstances can diminish your ethical responsibility depends on the seriousness of the consequences of the action. Generally, the more damage your action will cause lessens the mitigating circumstances. Now if you are reading this and thinking *but how do we calculate the extent of ethical responsibility?* I have to tell you that there is no easy answer. There is no single ethical theory upon which all people or philosophers agree, but two basic approaches to moral reasoning have prevailed over time: the teleological approach and the deontological approach. Simply put, the teleological approach suggests that you look at the end result of your actions to make an ethical judgement; and the deontological says that you don't. Deontology is a more difficult approach in some ways because it essentially argues that some things just are right and some are wrong and that you have a duty to do the right thing.

The classic example of the teleological approach to ethics is Utilitarianism. This is an ethical theory that holds that an action is right if it produces, or if it tends to produce, the greatest amount of good for the greatest number of people affected by the action. Nice and simple, at least on the surface. It is effectively a cost–benefit analysis approach to ethics. It is often popular because the cost–benefit approach isn't alien to most people as it is widely used in many forms of general decision making. The problems arise when we start asking awkward questions like, what do we mean by good? Is my good the same as yours? So, while it is appealing in its simplicity, it can be difficult in its equivalencies. How much bad to produce? How much good is ethical?

The deontological approach I think is best summed up by Kantian Duty ethics. Duty ethics holds that an action is ethically right if it has a certain form; it is ethically wrong if it doesn't. Perhaps the best way to consider it is to look at Kant's Categorical Imperative. For Kant, an action is ethical if: it is amenable to being made consistently universal; it respects rational beings as ends in themselves; and it must stem from, and respect, the autonomy of rational beings (Brown and Patton, 1949). What Kant meant by universality, in a simple form, was that you should act only in a way that you would be happy with others acting towards you.

Okay, but how do you act ethically? What you can do is try to follow an ethical checklist to determine if your action is ethical. In his 2011 book *Business Ethics* Richard T. DeGeorge provides what I consider a useful checklist to determine the ethicality of your action which I have simplified here:

1. Get all the facts about the case.
2. Determine the ethical issue or issues to be resolved.
3. Use your moral imagination to consider the possible alternatives.
4. Determine all those affected by the action who should be considered in your analysis.
5. Determine if the action you are considering is ethically required or whether it constitutes an ideal towards which you aspire. If the latter, the action is good but not required.
6. If required, in the most promising alternative(s), does some clear prima facie obligation apply, such as don't steal or lie? If so, apply it.
7. Is there still an ethical issue? If no, act appropriately. If yes, go to step 8.

8. If there are two or more prima facie obligations that apply and they conflict, does one clearly take preference? If so, act on it. If not, go to step 9.
9. Does the action lend itself more clearly and obviously to a teleological approach or a deontological one of duties? Use the approach that applies most clearly or obviously.
10. Consider how someone who disagreed with your analysis might argue for the opposite ethical conclusion.
11. Determine whether you would be comfortable if the actions you are presently contemplating were to be made public. (Sometimes called the Headline Test.) (DeGeorge, 2011)

Perhaps we could just draw step 11 and ask the question of our actions, would we be happy if everyone knew about what we were doing? It is a simple but powerful question to ask oneself and very pertinent for the consultant. It is often said that ethics is what we do when no one is watching us. So clearly if you have any concerns about what people would think of what you are doing then there is an issue in your own mind as to the ethical correctness of your action. For many, the problem will be that there is no easy answer; the process of ethical reasoning is a continuous individual and social endeavour. Always changing and never ending, but no one ever claimed that being an ethical consultant would be an easy task.

WHY BOTHER?

If it is so hard to be ethical why are we doing it? We have a mortgage to pay and a life to lead. Can we afford to be limited by ethical concerns? Will our competition? Anyway, who is to say what is ethical? It could be different from place to place.

All of the above are good questions and ones which you may think about yourself or encounter as you work. You may look around you and see others who are clearly not acting ethically and who will give you reasons for their actions that are not those of ignorance or inability but rather based on ethical relativism.

Ethical relativism is the concept that every culture has its own ethics, values and ideas about what is right or wrong. It is an argument that no culture is inherently superior to any other and thus we cannot make judgements on another culture's ethics. It is an argument that there is no universal standard for ethics, that ethics and morality are relative. In many ways, it is an appealing argument. How can we judge other cultures? But how far does this go? We need to ask a simple question, what is culture?

Geert Hofstede defined culture as 'the collective programming of the mind which distinguishes the members of one group or category of people from another' (1991: 5). Therein lies the problem for relativism. Since we speak of organizations as having a culture (Schein, 1992) must we say that we cannot judge unethical behaviour in an organization because its culture is different from ours? What of individuals? Do they each have their own culture and would that mean that everyone is entitled to decide what is ethical based purely on their own programming? Ethical relativism sounds appealing but its danger is that it leads us as consultants to act in a manner which the organization, area or individual you are currently engaged with may consider ethical but that would not be considered ethical by a wider community. This can have a very negative impact on our reputation.

To the consultant, reputation is extremely important. It is what we are judged on. If we narrow the role of the consultant down to four core areas I would argue that they are:

1. Information gathering
2. Analysis
3. Provision of advice
4. Assisting implementation

I would further argue that the quality essential to all four of these is trust. If we consider the first area, information gathering, I would argue that the most common ethical issues concern questions of the disclosure of personally sensitive data on the performance of individuals within the organization. For those from whom the information is being sought, the risk is that the gathered information may be manipulated in order to serve the perceived needs of the organization. So, it is vital for the consultant to come to the work with a reputation for ethical action that engenders trust. There is no point in saying, 'Oh well, where I last worked what I did was considered ethical.' Indeed, it is possible that some clients may specifically seek to employ consultants as a means of securing confidential information about their employees in a covert way. While the client may see no issue with this it presents to the consultant an unethical prospect.

If we are perceived as unethical then the advice we provide may be seen in the same light. Since this involves the definition of options, the exercise of judgement and the formulation of recommendations we must strive to ensure that they are not tainted by negative perceptions. If we consider the example of human rights, these have come far more into focus for business with the continuation of globalization. Businesses competing in the global marketplace seek ways to reduce costs to remain competitive. One of the popular ways of cost reduction is the use of cheap labour in developing nations. While this is generally accepted as a legitimate strategy, and one which is clearly legal, there is increasing ethical criticism. Much of this pertains to the idea that the labour is cheap because the developing nation does not possess the same laws governing health and safety at work and employee rights as the home nation. So, while a consultant could give a recommendation for outsourcing to reduce costs that would benefit the company financially, not considering the ethical dimension could have consequences for the company as well as the consultant's reputation. It needs to be remembered that there is more at stake than just increased return to shareholders.

THE STAKEHOLDER PROBLEM

According to Milton Friedman (1970) the only social responsibility of business is to increase its profits for its owners (shareholders) while staying within the *rules of the game*, which means staying within the relevant laws. So, if a company wanted to reduce costs by using cheap labour in a country with poor laws governing worker safety, for instance, then this would be fine because they are still within the rules of the game as established by the host country's government. But an alternative view to this shareholder approach exists: the stakeholder approach.

Freeman proposed that 'any group or individual who can affect, or is affected by, the achievement of the organization's objectives' (1984: 46) should be considered as a stakeholder of that organization. These stakeholders would include government, shareholders, suppliers, civil society, employees, customers and competitors. This would mean that the company, rather than just having to consider the laws in the country of its operation, would need to take multiple concerns into account. So, what does that mean for the consultant?

The web of stakeholders can be complex, as can be seen from the above short list, so how do you ensure that you are considering the needs of all stakeholders? The honest answer is that you can't. Some of their needs may be conflicting. The best a consultant can do is to attempt to make ethical decisions.

People will tell you that ethics and business do not go together; indeed, there is an assumption among many that to be ethical in business is to be a failure at business. The old adage 'good guys finish last' seems to be widely believed. However, ethics and a sense of morality are very necessary in managing people – especially when you are in the spotlight, as all consultants are.

Ethics examines the moral rights and wrongs of situations. If we consider the fact that HR managers are frequently required to negotiate salaries and contracts, then managing conflicts and ensuring compliance with ethical standards within the organization is vital. Ethics and the monitoring of ethical behaviour are challenges in management but challenges that must be addressed in every organization.

DISCUSSION

Managers

Here are six requests that you may be faced with when dealing with managers as a consultant.

> **EXERCISE**
>
> Discuss in your group how you would deal with each one. You need to decide first:
>
> - Whether you can do what is asked
> - Whether you can do it if you modify what is being asked of you
> - Whether you need to close off the option completely

Now you can decide how you would say what you need to say to the person who asked you. Remember that you need to be assertive.

1. The Managing Director says that he is a bit busy at the moment so can't make it to open the first session and introduce you and your consultancy. Can you do it for yourself? (He will come in at a later stage.)
2. The Sales Director says, 'That manager of mine, Roger, is a funny bloke, isn't he? How is he getting on in your group?'
3. The Managing Director's PA says, 'You want to watch out for some of these directors. It's them that need the training not the workers.'
4. The union representative says, 'You don't know what you have let yourself in for here. It really is a snake pit. But if you need the low-down on any of the characters we've got here, just come and see me.'
5. The Board tell you that if any of the staff want to know about redundancies to tell them that there won't be any.
6. The Managing Director says, 'Before you publish your report I want to see the recommendations to make sure I agree with them.'

Staff

You will also be assailed by members of staff. Discuss the implications of these situations and decide what you would say in response.

1. The staff ask you to tell the directors that everyone is worried about the change programme and to ask whether there will be any redundancies.
2. Salespeople drop a hint to you that everyone is fiddling their petrol allowances – it's just custom and practice, apparently.
3. The staff ask you to sign a farewell card to Fred who has been dismissed by the company.
4. During a session, the staff ask you about the number of people who are on zero-hours contracts. They say, 'That's not fair, is it? What do you think?'
5. The HR manager comes up and says, 'They're an odd lot on the Board, aren't they? How do you get on with them?'
6. A female member of staff comes to you and reveals that she is being passed over for promotion. She believes it's a case of gender discrimination. Can you help her at all?

EXERCISE

You may find it helpful to follow the three steps to assertiveness:

1. Show you listen and understand
2. Say what you think or feel
3. Say what you would like to happen

Remember, forewarned is forearmed. But be assertive and diplomatic.

GUIDANCE

Managers

1. You may want to defer the meeting or ask for another Board member to attend and fulfil that role.
2. You can say, 'I hear many opinions expressed during the course of my work. Forgive me if I cannot remember who said what.'
3. Just say, 'Thank you.'
4. Just say, 'Thank you.'
5. Explain that you think it important that they say that themselves (offer them the chance to come into one of your meetings to do that, if appropriate).
6. Not an unreasonable request. What happens thereafter may become a matter for negotiation between you.

Staff

1. You will need to discuss with them how they can approach this themselves and discuss with them how they might put it. But it is not your role to become the staff spokesperson.
2. Say that you will need to explore this and refer it back to the company (You cannot afford to ignore this as later those who spoke to you may say, 'We did tell the consultant, but he/she did nothing.')
3. You can say that you did not know Fred well enough to sign the staff card but that you will convey your good wishes when you next see him.
4. Definitely use avoidance: 'What I think does not matter, it is what you think that counts.'
5. Use a vague answer here: 'They are much like any other group that I have worked with.'
6. Probe and make any notes that will record what was said. Go with her to HR and ensure that she speaks to the right person there.

Keeping the balance between stakeholders will be crucial. An ethical approach will aim to safeguard the rights of all stakeholders while taking account of the responsibility and obligations the consultant has undertaken to fulfil the change contract.

Once again, we can summarize responses to the questions about ethics as we would any other queries about the change programme:

- Be honest (say what you know to be factually correct without divulging your own opinions).
- Use deferral (this means coming back with an answer when they have said you will).
- Use avoidance (when you are being led into making comments that are inappropriate for a consultant to engage in).

FAITH, ETHICS, DUTY AND THE LAW

A Consulting Conundrum

Derrial Glass the CEO of Let the Children, a successful church-run Children's Home and Adoption Organization found himself with a major problem. He was caught between faith and law and had to decide how best to lead the organization into the future.

Let the Children had been set up with the funding by the church. Although the church continued to fund the organization, their representatives, the bishops, delegated day-to-day running of the organization to Derrial and his staff. This approach was clearly effective as over the previous years Let the Children had helped place many troubled and abused children in foster homes as well as acting to place these children with new families through their adoption service. All of this contributed to the organization's good reputation and had led to some very positive media coverage.

Derrial and his small staff had continued running the organization secure in the knowledge that they enjoyed the support of the bishops. However, this began to be threatened by the introduction of two pieces of new legislation.

The first concerned recruitment of staff. In future, Let the Children would be required to employ social workers with adoption experience. While this was not in itself an issue, what was a potential issue was the legal condition that competence be the only recruitment requirement. What this meant for Derrial was that should a non-Catholic homosexual, for example, be the most competent candidate they would have to be employed.

While the bishops were not pleased with this recruitment situation, they reluctantly agreed that they would have to comply with the law. So, while Derrial knew that the Board was unhappy, he was also confident that funding would continue despite this reservation so that he and his staff could continue helping children in need.

The second piece of legislation concerned the legalization of the marriage of same-sex partners. While these marriages would occur outside the church it did mean that legally married same-sex couples could apply to Let the Children to adopt and that to discriminate against them on the grounds of their being a same-sex couple would be illegal. This proved more of a problem for the bishops. They had long discussions about it and ultimately decided that, rather than see such adoptions occur, which went against their faith, they would close down Let the Children.

This placed Derrial in something of a dilemma. How could he continue to support the vulnerable children at the home and secure the jobs of his staff? He found himself wondering if the bishops could legally act to close Let the Children for the reasons they had stated. Would that not also violate the law? But could the organization survive without the Board's support?

Questions

- Given his own faith where does Derrial's duty lie? Is it to his faith or the children and his staff?
- Can Derrial challenge the bishops' decision?
- Suppose Derrial and the bishops genuinely consider that adoption by a same-sex couple is not in the best interest of the children. How should they then proceed without incurring the risk of an action against the organization on the grounds of discrimination against same-sex couples?
- In what ways is this a legal issue and an ethical issue?
- As a consultant called into this organization, what advice would you give Derrial on how best to proceed?

CONSULTANCY IN ACTION

DEALING WITH LEGAL IMPLICATIONS

Thom D. Young, Worklegal

The relationship between ethics and the law may not always be clear and the law may sometimes seem like an ass. However, 'ignorance of the law is no excuse' is a maxim that applies absolutely (i.e. there is no defence) in most modern legal jurisdictions. It may derive from philosophical underpinnings of ancient systems in which legal rules were regarded as self-evident and were well promulgated, but it now applies even where laws are inordinately complex, not readily available and incomprehensible to non-lawyers.

This brief section is not intended to diminish your ignorance directly, but rather to raise your awareness of it. It will give you some appreciation of the benefits that developing your understanding of legal implications will bring to your consultancy and to your clients. I will not deal with actual legal rules, but rather aim to guide you generally. Management consultancy projects inevitably involve issues that have legal implications. I will encourage you not to become bogged down in legal issues, but to see them set in a wider context. References to UK law are by way of examples only. You must consider the law applicable to your projects.

There are three general ways in which the law may be relevant to your work as a consultant, namely:

- In demonstrating enough knowledge of the client's environment to get the work
- In managing your relationship with the client
- In assisting the client during a project

CLIENT ENVIRONMENT, REGULATORY CONTEXT

To get work, you should aim to impress prospective clients with an understanding of their environment, their sector and where they fit into it. As part of that it is at least useful and it may be essential to be aware of ways in which the law impacts their business. There are some areas of law that affect most businesses. Among the more obvious areas in the UK are Employment Law, Health and Safety Law, and Environmental Law. Some businesses will be impacted to a much greater extent than others by the law in specific areas. Some businesses will be affected also by regulation that is specific to their sector. You may not need to be an expert in any of these areas of law, but you must be sufficiently aware to anticipate how they might affect your client in relation to a project.

Please refer to the 'Online Resources' at the end of the chapter for examples of where you might start to look for information on business regulation in the UK. It is a good idea to start with official government or regulatory authority sites, but there may be others, including business representative organizations and specialist legal firms that make useful information freely available on the internet. You should be able to differentiate quickly those that are useful in practical ways from those that are merely self-promotional.

In the UK many sectors are highly regulated. Some, such as education and health and care services, are also regularly inspected, sometimes by multiple agencies. Understanding this will require time but the internet holds a wealth of information. For example, if you need to get information on the care sector in the UK, a Web search on 'regulation of care in UK' will quickly reveal over 45,000 results. Among them you would see, for example, a link to a page on the Health and Safety Executive Website – http://www.hse.gov.uk/healthservices/arrangements.htm. Although focused on Health and Safety, this includes references to the other agencies with responsibility for regulating aspects of the care sector and links to their online resources. You will quickly get an overview of the regulation of the sector from which you can drill down via other links for more detailed information. In the UK context, remember that legal provisions may vary across the three separate jurisdictions: England and Wales; Scotland; Northern Ireland.

You should do some research on the target firm and industry sector before discussing a project with a prospective client or submitting a proposal. You will only have one chance to make a first impression and showing complete ignorance about something that is crucial is probably not the best way to start. Don't overstate your knowledge, however. It may be far more impressive to say that you are not an expert (unless expertise is a prerequisite) and to immediately demonstrate some knowledge about the legal constraints that apply or the challenges they face. If you claim to focus your consultancy on an industry or sector, you will be expected to demonstrate a more in-depth knowledge of the relevant legal environment.

Your understanding should extend beyond the practical impact that relevant regulations have. You should consider the practical implications of non-compliance with legal requirements. In some cases, the damage to reputation or to financial security of breaching obligations imposed by the law can be devastating. Failure to fully recognize these implications can easily lead to underestimating the danger of cutting corners. Acknowledging regulations but justifying avoiding them in the interest of efficiency or profit is a feature of some organizational cultures. This is not necessarily obvious without an understanding of what is really happening in an organization and why. It may not be understood by those who are responsible for overall corporate governance. You should not assume that regulations that are well documented or that appear to be implemented by internal protocols, processes or procedures are necessarily followed across the firm. Don't be fooled by 'value statements' prominently displayed on reception walls; they may be completely embedded in the culture or they may be no more than works of art that create widespread cynicism in the workforce. You must tread warily, however. There may be some pride in the extent to which regulatory requirements have been documented and apparently promoted and are believed to be followed. Any suggestion of underlying failure may create friction unless there is concrete evidence. For a view on dissonance between espoused values and behaviours, please refer to Argyris (2010).

YOUR RELATIONSHIP WITH YOUR CLIENT

In most legal jurisdictions, your relationship with a client will be a contractual one. You must check for any restrictions in the relevant legal system. There may be specific terms that are stipulated by law. There may be some terms that are prohibited or regarded as invalid and of no effect, even if agreed between you. There may be some that are illegal and that may render the entire contract unenforceable by either party to it. In the UK, for example, any term of a contract that has as its intention or natural consequence that there would be any kind of tax fraud, including tax evasion, is likely to render the whole contract illegal and unenforceable.

Yes, you do need legal advice on contractual terms and it is worth having standard terms drafted professionally if you are likely to be in a situation where you are able to stipulate the terms. If you are dealing exclusively with large corporations or responding to tenders, it may be that the contractual terms will be dictated by the client and you will have little or no say.

It is not possible to even begin to give a detailed breakdown here of all the issues that should be dealt with in a contract with a client. An online search of management consultancy contract templates will give you an insight into the range. You can also find the standard terms and conditions of large management consultancy firms online. Do not give in to the temptation to cut and paste, however! Words and phrases may have very specific legal meanings and joining them together to make sentences may not create the outcome you intended.

Be aware of 'the battle of the forms', in which parties to a proposed contract try to use conflicting terms. If, for example, an Invitation to Tender document sets out conditions that are to apply to the execution of the tender project, you are unlikely to be able to override those conditions simply by submitting your own terms and conditions. The tender conditions may even state that no alterations will be accepted. Do not accept tender terms without making sure that you really understand the implications. This may require legal advice.

Where you can stipulate what the contract terms will be, your standard terms and conditions are a good place to start, but always consider the individual project and what additional issues need to be addressed specifically in a contract. It is important to ensure that the contact deals with everything that can be covered reasonably. Any prior documents that are necessary to understand what has been agreed should be referred to and attached. You must ensure that you understand what wording the relevant legal jurisdiction may require in the contract for effective incorporation of such documents into the contract.

It is far better to have one document (with attachments, if appropriate) that sets out the contract, is signed by all parties to the contract and can only be changed in writing agreed by all parties. It may seem obvious but do ensure that you know exactly who you are contracting with and that the name of the firm is correctly stated and is set out in sufficient detail to comply with any legal requirements.

It is important that the actual work to be carried out is expressed in sufficient detail to avoid any dispute later. Keep an eye on the specification of the work as the project proceeds. Make sure it remains accurate as it develops. If there is an agreed change to the specification, set it out in writing even if there is no change to payment. If there is additional work that you intend to charge extra money for, get approval in writing. It is a good idea to discuss changes first, get agreement on what is to be done and when, and what change there will be; then get the client's confirmation in writing before you proceed. Make sure that the documentation complies with the contractual requirements for amendment. It is a good idea to have a standard 'Contract Variation' document that refers to the original contract by parties, date(s) and project description, and which sets out the details of the variation. Use it, even if it is to record something like a change to the delivery timing or order of task completion. If managed properly with an explanation that it is to keep everyone clear on what, when or how things are to happen, it should impress the client that you are well organized – provided everything else points to that!

You should provide for assessment of legal implications at appropriate intervals. Set this out in your proposal. Make sure it is clear who will be responsible for obtaining legal advice and who will pay for it. You should not be responsible or liable for costs unless you are either a legal consultant or you have included a legal advisor as part of your project delivery team.

Depending on the jurisdiction, legal liability for compensation by you to your client may typically arise either because you have breached a contractual term and you are liable for damages or because of negligence on your part that causes loss to the client. You can be protected to some extent by Professional Indemnity insurance. You must ensure that the insured cover limit is sufficient for the value of the contracts you are likely to enter into. Typically, that limit relates to your liability for loss suffered by a client. Such loss could, however, be out of all proportion to the payment you receive under a contract. You should consider a contract clause limiting your liability to the sum you are insured for or even the payment you are to receive, although the latter is likely to be resisted. Again, you must check what legal rules apply in the relevant jurisdiction. Make sure you understand the terms of your insurance cover.

When considering obtaining legal advice yourself, bear in mind that it might be useful to have a relationship with an appropriate legal firm with relevant experience that you might be able to have informal chats with in relation to projects. I will return to this later.

ASSISTING YOUR CLIENT IN RELATIONSHIPS WITH OTHERS

In terms of your consultancy practice, recognizing your own limited understanding of the law and being able to assess the level of knowledge of your client is vital. You should assess the normal practice of your client in terms of obtaining legal advice. This will depend to some extent on the size of the organization, but also on the perception of decision makers. Do they have internal lawyers or other experts? Do they have a close relationship with external lawyers? Do they take advice as a matter of course or only in exceptional circumstances? Do not assume that a suggestion of obtaining legal advice at intervals will be warmly received.

Lawyers may be regarded as an expensive resource to be avoided wherever possible – or worse! In this case, you must be able to justify the need for incurring the cost. If it is perceived as your being unnecessarily cautious, it may not be well received. You need to portray it as having the positive benefit of protecting the business. However, you must consider whether it is better to get advice at a relatively early stage to avoid making a proposal that results in wasted time, since a proposal by you that is subsequently dismissed as legally impossible will not impress your client.

I dealt earlier with the possibility of your having a relationship with a legal firm from which you can get overviews or pointers. You should expect to pay for advice, but it could give you a distinct advantage. You will always have to be careful not to breach obligations of confidentiality to your client. Your advisor must not know your client's identity or have any information that would give that away, but it could be extremely helpful to you to be able to provide an outline of an issue. For example, if you explained that a project you are working on or tendering for in the UK might result in an entire shift pattern changing and a likely reduction in the number of employees required in certain sections of the workforce, you could very quickly be given an overview of potential issues relating to workers' existing contractual obligations and statutory consultation requirements. You would not have to understand the details, but you would have a clear justification for informing your client that you are aware of complex legal implications that must be understood before any option is worked into a firm proposal, to avoid wasting time and costs. In other scenarios, you might be advised that there are no obvious significant issues that are likely to require advice until a firm proposal has been worked up.

One way for you to gain an increased knowledge is for you to be present when advice is being obtained on the legal implications of a project. This also means that you can ask questions that might not occur to anyone else. You may be able to develop a relationship with your client's lawyers or other advisors, internal or external, which will allow you to sound them out quickly as you go through a project.

The level of commercial awareness among lawyers varies enormously. Some will think only in straight lines and be completely bound by legal analysis, so that if an apparently straightforward set of circumstances is presented, perhaps only one outcome will be considered. Others may start from an understanding of where you want to get to and they may assist in searching for a route to get you there. Make sure advisors are encouraged to think outside the box that only contains the legal analysis of what is presented to them and that they are aware of the commercial issues.

WHY SOME PROJECTS MAY FAIL

There is much empirical evidence that the clear majority of corporate change programmes and strategies for enhancing effectiveness, including reengineering, **TQM** and downsizing, as well as management development programmes, show little or no gain. Campbell and Quinn's conclusion on this, based on extensive empirical studies, was that

> without another kind of fundamental change, namely, a change in organizational culture, there is little hope of enduring improvement in organizational performance. Although the tools and techniques may be present and the change strategy implemented with vigour, many efforts to improve organizational performance fail because the fundamental culture of the organization – values, ways of thinking, managerial styles, paradigms, approaches to problem solving – remains the same. ...
>
> This dependence of organizational improvement on culture change is due to the fact that when the values, orientations, definitions, and goals stay constant – even when procedures and strategies are altered – organizations return quickly to the status quo. (Cameron and Quinn, 2011)

There may be a temptation to see issues in purely legal terms and to envisage a legal problem as simply having a legal solution. Culture change is beyond the scope of this consideration of legal issues, but you should be very wary of simply complying with legal requirements. Legal solutions imposed on people without regard to their perceptions and emotions and the perceptions and emotions of others, who may be regarded as unaffected bystanders, may well comply with legal requirements, but will not change culture. It will also often have unintended, far-reaching consequences in the existing culture. Focusing exclusively on those people directly affected by a proposal can easily lead to unexpected and often hidden reactions among other groups. Failing to communicate as fully and meaningfully as possible with everyone who is or will be aware of actions taken, or to be taken, can easily result in perceptions of a lack of trust or apparent disregard for organizational justice (fairness). This may be unjustified if the full facts were known but allowing ignorance to prevail can destroy relationships and co-operation in delivery of a change project. For an overview of the importance of Trust and Organizational Justice in the context of co-operation in organizations, please refer to Tyler (2011).

Legal advice should guide a project, not dictate it. Lawyers acting for a company, presented with details of a proposed change, may engage immediately in an analysis of legal implications and provide possible processes intended to avoid or minimize negative legal outcomes for the company. Lawyers will tend to indicate what is required by the relevant legal provision. As an example, let us take an obligation to consult on a proposed redundancy in the UK. To comply does not generally require much information to be provided and it may only have to be given to a small number of people. There is often a reluctance on the part of management to divulge any information that is not strictly necessary or to inform someone to whom there is no legal obligation to inform. Some consideration should be given as to whether leaving the rest of the workforce in the dark would be in the best interests of the business. This may affect trust and morale, and perceptions of organizational justice, as well as encouraging rampant rumour-mongering that can be destructive to performance.

FORESEEING THE CHALLENGES

Risk management and positive project management will be central to your work. There are challenges in respect of your relationship with your client and in respect of your client's relationships with others.

A practical change strategy should incorporate a legal risk assessment and a process designed to comply with legal requirements, if any. It is a good idea to have this included in a standard project template and to have a heading 'Assessment of legal implications' at each stage, even just as a reminder as you progress.

If the project requires physical changes to the work environment, there may be regulatory issues ranging from building regulations and planning consents (even for external signs or a flagpole!) through Health and Safety implications and very specific regulations relating to all manner of things including, for example, ventilation, floor signage for pedestrians and fork-lift truck routes or ways in which particular machinery must be sited or fitted together. If there are changes to the way people work, this may dictate that certain steps, for example, information provision or consultation, must take place at a certain stage or defined time or it may suggest that it would be better to follow a particular route involving set stages. Expert input will be required on such matters.

EVALUATING THE STRATEGY

There is no doubt that what people think of you is vitally important. Managing your own brand is central to your success. Think about the impact that your demeanour, your communications and your actions will have on those with whom you are interacting. Do not assume that everyone will react in the same way. You do not have to change your personality, but you do need to manage the ways in which you express yourself for the particular people with whom you are engaged. That means you have to understand enough about them to be able to interact appropriately.

Specifically, in the context of legal issues, you must evaluate the impact of your approach with regard to:

- Your knowledge of the legal environment
- Obtaining legal advice
- Dealing with the implications of legal advice

You should understand enough to be able to perform a useful conduit between practical needs and protecting the organization from failure to comply. To do that, you must assess your client's normal approach. If you intend to suggest a different approach, you must express and justify it in ways that will convince clients that what you are suggesting is appropriate to their interests.

Decision makers may well have their own ideas of levels of trust and fairness in their organization, although it is equally likely that they may never have considered such matters other than incidentally or in relation to specific incidents. It would be unusual for them to have carried out any meaningful enquiry of the workforce. Few of them will be aware of the potentially serious implications for the business of lack of trust or perceptions of unfairness. If pressed, they may suggest that they do everything by the book, that is, that they follow legal due process. For the reasons already alluded to and as explained in detail by Tyler (2011), focusing on legal process without understanding the wider context, may be quite damaging. Your strategy should include assessment of the impact of project outcomes on Trust and Organizational Justice and ways of building and/or maintaining positive perceptions of these. You should assume a limited understanding on the part of management and that your concerns will have to be explained and justified as being of positive benefit to the business.

HANDLING PEOPLE PROBLEMS

The complexity of people problems may vary substantially depending on the relevant legal jurisdiction(s).

Proposed organizational change may not involve any specific legal changes or it might involve, for example:

- Changes to employees' terms and conditions of employment (such as work patterns, hours of work and reduction in benefits)
- Reorganization of roles
- Reduction in numbers of employees
- Integration of groups of employees because of merger, acquisition, disposal or outsourcing

The role of change agent will depend on the way the project is managed and what part the agent is playing in the overall scheme. Management communication will be central to these issues. Some general questions may be useful:

- When, what and how should those who may be affected/may not be directly affected be told?
- How can expectations and perceptions of different groups be 'managed' positively?
- How might perceptions of trust be affected? How might they be 'managed' positively?
- How might perceptions of organizational justice be affected? How might they be 'managed' positively?

Challenges continue after change is implemented and focus must be on all employees, not just those directly affected. Who will be responsible for this?

There is a tendency in the UK to pigeonhole people issues at work in contractual and therefore legal terms. Legal problems are generally conceived as having legal answers. Legal answers are often seen as final solutions. This can lead to intense and exclusive focus, perhaps on one person or on a group. This may be appropriate in some instances. If it results in a failure to focus on the wider picture, the apparent solution may lead to unforeseen and potentially totally unappreciated consequences, perhaps pervading the workforce.

When a legal solution is proposed, the possible implications of that solution beyond dealing with the direct issue should be considered in answering the following questions. How should it be progressed? Should it be consulted on and, if so, how? How should any proposals, processes or decisions be communicated? In terms of legal requirements, these questions are likely to be answered by reference to legal proscriptions.

You should understand these, but then consider how those directly involved might react, how those not directly involved might react and whether there is a better way to proceed in the overall interest of the business. This is not to suggest in any sense that management decisions should be hostage to anyone else or that confidential issues should be revealed inappropriately, but rather that perceptions and knowledge must be managed in a sensible and practical way, so that everyone has a sufficient understanding to avoid unnecessary damage to the operation of the business.

For example, let us consider a situation in which a loss of a contract means that there is not enough work to do for certain people in a UK business. A lawyer advising on this is likely to immediately explain that this brings about what is generally referred to as a redundancy situation and that it requires a fair procedure for consultation with anyone who might be affected and a selection from among them of those who will be dismissed by reason of redundancy. It may be far more complicated than this as it progresses, but that is the essence. Managing perceptions optimally requires ensuring that everyone has an appropriate amount of information to appreciate why the situation has arisen, what options are open to management, what legal process must be followed, how decisions will be taken and what the implications will be for the business. Failure in this may create conditions that lead to rumour-mongering, lowering of morale, perceptions of unfairness and lack of trust, which can either create or exacerbate a dysfunctional environment. Your challenge is to anticipate this and encourage consideration of the delivery of proposed legal solutions in the wider context of the system of people in the organization.

CHAPTER SUMMARY

This chapter reinforces many of the points that we have addressed throughout this book. Consultancy requires change agents to be adept at assessing organizational need for change; defining the objectives which the change programme needs to address; exploring the means by which the change programme may be pursued; involving people in decisions about their own career choices; understanding the legal and ethical issues of the change programme's impact; and ensuring that the change is embedded in the organization and that there are internal change agents in place to evaluate its effective implementation in the business.

Change agency requires an awareness of the business dynamics involved in a change programme. But it is also an art in that it repays sensitivity to the responses of others; awareness of political constraints in the organization; reflectiveness with all those involved in the change programme; and moral courage to address fairly and objectively the challenges that face the organization and its people.

For those who enjoy challenge and change in their professional lives there are few professions or occupations that can equal consultancy for professional learning and personal development. Legal and ethical considerations are essential to the probity of consultancy work. While we are not expected to be the conscience of the organization, we cannot disregard the legal and ethical implications of any aspect of the work in which we are asked to be involved. As consultants, we are expected to have expertise power and that expertise includes moral integrity and care for the legal rights of all those involved in programmes of change in which we are involved.

For video content relating to this chapter please visit the companion website at **www.macmillanihe.com/Randall-Management-Consultancy.**

REFERENCES

Argyris, C. (2010). *Organisational Traps*. Oxford: Oxford University Press.

Baumhart, R. (1968). *An Honest Profit: What Businessmen Say About Ethics in Business*. New York: Henry Holt & Company.

Brown, S.M. and Paton, H.J. (1949). The categorical imperative. *Philosophical Review*, 58(6), 599–611.

Cameron, K.S. and Quinn, R.E. (2011). *Diagnosing and Changing Organisational Culture* (3rd edn). Englewood Cliffs, NJ: Jossey-Bass.

DeGeorge, R.T. (2011). *Business Ethics* (7th edn). Englewood Cliffs, NJ: Pearson.

Freeman, R.E. (1984). *Strategic Management: A Stakeholder Approach*. Boston: Ballinger.

Friedman, M. (1970). The social responsibility of business is to increase its profits. *New York Times Magazine*, 13 September.

Hofstede, G. (1991). *Cultures and Organizations: Software of the Mind*. London: McGraw-Hill.

Schein, E.H. (1992). *Organizational Culture and Leadership: A Dynamic View* (2nd edn). San Francisco, CA: Jossey-Bass.

Tyler, T.R. (2011). *Why People Cooperate: The Role of Social Motivations*. Princeton, NJ: Princeton University Press.

Velasquez, M.G. (2012). *Business Ethics: Concepts and Cases* (7th edn). Englewood Cliffs, NJ: Pearson.

ONLINE RESOURCES

These specific links may change and are simply examples current at time of writing.

Health and Safety Executive – http://www.hse.gov.uk/legislation/

Healthy Working Lives – http://www.healthyworkinglives.com/

Government UK – https://www.gov.uk/browse/employing-people

10 Organization Development and Future Challenges

Bernard Burnes and Julian Randall

INTRODUCTION

As we conclude our book we would like to summarize some of the points that have been raised under four headings:

- The nature of change
- Traditional commentaries on the work of change agents
- The learning approach to change and the role of the internal change agent
- The future challenges facing management, consultancy and change

THE NATURE OF CHANGE

The respective roles of managers and workers in change interventions have been a topic of much debate ever since modern organization forms began to emerge in the Industrial Revolution and it will no doubt remain so in the future. The path between planning and implementing change successfully is a complex one and can take many unexpected and not necessarily beneficial paths. The motivation for change most often arises from efficiency factors and this is sometimes referred to as performativity. The organization needs to react faster, be more productive and achieve lower costs to outwit the opposition. Needless to say, the biggest cost is people, so either squeeze them out or squeeze what you pay them. It is unsurprising that for some commentators performativity is a pejorative term implying that 'the employer-employee relationship is inherently exploitative' and is certainly not emancipative (Thompson and Warhurst, 1998; Willmott, 1993). However, in this book we have taken a more optimistic view of the work of change agents and have argued that change can and should be a participative-learning process. And when it is conducted fairly and openly by people who care about those affected, it can be just that.

It would be fair to say that many consultancy interventions have been perceived by those affected as directive and tended to be imposed by those in charge. Taylor's Scientific Management is perhaps the best-known example of this approach. His low-skill, high-control approach to designing work systems is still influential today, as is the time and motions approach pioneered by the Gilbreths, which is a central feature of Taylor's approach to job design.

In contrast, the architect of organization development (OD), Kurt Lewin, emphasized that change is a participative-learning process for the group of workers concerned (Burnes, 2004). He argued that, in a situation where change is necessary, firstly the group must unfreeze its current behaviour. We can accept that the imagery is rather overused here while appreciating that it is achieved by the work group studying and learning about the appropriateness of current behaviours and working practices. This was intended to explore the continued relevance of current arrangements (an unfreezing of support) and a willingness to consider alternatives. Lewin's approach to change has captured the imagination of many practitioners and consultants in the years since he pioneered it. It marks a shift from the focus on controlling the behaviour of the individual, as epitomised by Scientific Management, to a situation where groups are given the freedom to challenge their own beliefs and practices by learning about the underlying assumptions that influence what they do at work and how they view efficiency and effectiveness as they face future challenges.

It also marks a blurring of the line between the disciplines of psychological and sociological research – the individual responses to working conditions and the group's beliefs about 'the way we do things round here' (Deal and Kennedy, 1982). Lewin advocated listening to what people say, rather than telling them what they have to do, which marked a significant difference in how change was approached in organizations. This is one reason why Lewin is such a significant figure and why he has influenced generations of change scholars and practitioners, including leading figures such as Chris Argyris, Barbara Bunker, Marvin Weisbord, David Cooperrider, Edgar Schein, Douglas McClelland and many others (Burnes and Cooke, 2012).

By drawing attention to the importance of group beliefs and norms, Lewin paved the way for the later interest in the influence of organizational culture on organizational behaviour. As the academic community, in its exploration of the role played by culture in change programmes, ventured into areas which had been confined previously to positivistic approaches in research analysis, the value of qualitative research began to be recognized.

In the years since Lewin's death in 1947, there have been many developments whose roots can be traced back to his work. They not only laid the foundations for OD but gave rise to an impressive and thoughtful range of OD-related approaches to change. Process consultation is an outstanding example of one such OD-related approach to change (Schein, 1967). However, there are many others including socio-technical systems (Pava, 1986), strategic change (Pettigrew, 1987), appreciative enquiry (Cooperrider and Srivastva, 1987), organizational design (Greiner and Schein, 1988), organizational learning (Senge, 1990) and dialogical change (Bushe and Marshak, 2009). The focus on connecting the structural and processual change elements to the human subjects of change has become mainstream in the developing tradition of OD.

As we mentioned, what is perhaps most significant about Lewin's contribution has been the emphasis on involving working groups in the changes to be implemented by the organization (Bullock and Batten, 1985). This in turn gives the change agent scope to explore workers' attitudes to change and the assumptions that underlie these. This learning approach is an important part of any change initiative. It may take time and resources to achieve, but it is intended to engage people in change; reduce resistance to change; lead to the prospect of evaluation of the change initiative for organizational outcomes; and connect with continuous change through continuing professional development for the individuals involved.

The search for the soul of the organization in its people has had many sponsors, some of which predate as well as post-date Lewin. The forerunners of the Institute of Personnel Management began work in 1919 and the Human Relations tradition can be traced back to the Hawthorn Studies that took place in the 1920s. In the 1950s, the Tavistock Institute's socio-technical system approach advocated change based on employee involvement. At the same time, Reg Revans (1980) was developing his Action Learning approach, which sought to bring groups of staff together to learn collectively about change and how to implement it. So, we could claim that this tradition privileged the agency side of the structure – actor debate (Billig, 1996; Reed, 1997). Once again, this approach contributes to the view of change as a learning process.

There have been concerns about the relevance of Lewin's 3-step model; it has also received a great deal of support (Burnes, 2004). While there are those who challenge the time involved in and necessity of 'unfreezing', many others point to the knowledge that is surfaced and the learning that is derived during this step. Similarly, the 'moving' step is seen as overcomplicated and long by some, but the case for management-imposed change is viewed as arbitrary and unhelpful. As for Lewin's final step, 'refreezing', the issue is how the new behaviours and practices can or should achieve a degree of permanence. It is worth noting that Lewin tended to define refreezing as achieving a state of 'quasi-stationary equilibrium'. This approach recognized that as contexts changed, so the new behaviours might lose their appropriateness and would again need to change. However, for the period in which they were appropriate, they would need to be relatively safe from regression. Many organizations have found to their cost that it is very easy for workers to slip back into old habits once the change agents have left. Therefore, just as the old behaviours had needed to be unfrozen, the new ones need to be refrozen if regression was not to recur.

N-STEP APPROACHES TO CHANGE

The propensity of consultancies and change organizations to use prescriptive approaches to change can probably be accounted for by pragmatic considerations: it is easier to control teams of external consultants by adhering to a preset template for action. The sequence of steps frequently becomes a problem-solving approach in which the challenge faced is investigated by the incoming expert; the solution is identified and agreed between the external change agents and the change proposers; the change programme is implemented and validated; and then concluded and reinforced instrumentally – through changes in working practices, processes and the redrafting of employment contracts.

The assumptions lying behind these approaches would seem to be that there is a problem that can be fixed; incoming experts can find out what the problem is more readily than the managers of the organization themselves; experts have the skills to bring about change more easily than the organization's managers; once the change programme has been completed the consultants can leave and the managers can resume their day-to-day running of the newly established routines. As we have seen, that set of assumptions would seem to run counter to the perceptions of the effectiveness of change initiatives – 70% of which are perceived to have failed. That could be because expectancies of change were unrealistically high; or that the working group failed to rise to the challenge of change; or that the change agents were not effective in implementing the promised programme. Whatever the answer, it does raise important questions which need to be addressed.

PROBING EFFECTIVE CHANGE AGENCY

Here are some key questions which are worth addressing before change is embarked upon:

Firstly, how can change agents explore the issues underlying the need for change effectively?

At very least that suggests the need for an open-mindedness, which is not always apparent by those commissioning change, or by those coming in to undertake the change initiative from outside the organization.

Secondly, how can the subjects of change be engaged in a way that gives them a stake in their own future development as well as that of the company?

Most accounts of change concentrate on the benefits for the organization and subsequent turn-round in efficiency and effectiveness (often meaning profitability). There is less evidence of the benefit individuals can derive from change initiatives.

Thirdly, what is the best way of facilitating a change programme?

Training can often look like the obvious solution, but is it necessarily the best way of promoting long-term development for individuals and that organization? Perhaps longer-term development strategies would be more effective.

Fourthly, how can change be effectively evaluated?

Perhaps there is a preceding question that requires an answer: why is change rarely evaluated effectively following a change programme? (For many organizations the answer was often that they had embarked on another change initiative so didn't have time.)

Answering these questions can put change agents in a stronger position to mediate change not only in what people do but in how they think about what they do. If identity is the answer to the questions *who am I?* and *who ought I to be?* (Corley and Gioia, 2004), then during change these questions will probable re-emerge in the minds of those who are subjected to programmes of change. The dialogic work that identity requires (Beech, 2008; Watson, 2009) can resonate with those being asked to rethink their answer to those key questions during change but it needs time and sympathetic encouragement. This need for identity work should privilege the learning approach to change, allowing those affected by change to reconsider who they are and how they can be who they ought to be. For professional workers, the erosion of their self-belief in the value of what they do is vital to address during change. Medical professionals will be demoralized by attempts to erode the value of what they do (Reay and Hinings, 2005, 2009). Employers who impose change unilaterally invite the demoralization of key people and may find the service they offer increasingly unsustainable due to key people leaving and the difficulty of attracting replacements.

TRADITIONAL VIEWS ABOUT THE WORK OF CHANGE AGENTS

It would be fair to say that traditional practices of external consultants have attracted less than favourable comments from either managers or academics. We have already seen that the views about them range from unjustified claims to expertise to offering self-evident solutions and should be within the capability of any experienced manager established in the business (they borrowed our watch to tell us the time). Consultants have been described as myth-makers and storytellers (Alvesson, 1993); they help managers manage meaning and so extend control over the workers (Willmott, 1993); they claim mastery in key management knowledge skill and experience (Clark and Salaman, 1998); they use labels, metaphors and platitudes as building blocks for more complex control machinery: world views, philosophies, ideologies, cosmologies, business ideas (Czarniawska-Joerges, 1990). They are also adept at developing new ideas, which will appeal to managers seeking to appear familiar with the latest management fad or trend. The work of the consultant is thus sometimes described as 'knowledge commodification' (Heusinkveld and Benders, 2005). As we see, there is nothing new about the comments that we read here.

The question that we have tried to illustrate in the present volume has been the work of facilitation focusing on what thoughtful change agents attempt to achieve through working with people during change programmes. This coincides with an emerging interest in the trend to use insiders as change agents (Sturdy et al., 2016) and these we have referred to as internal change agents.

Internal change agents have a significant contribution to make to the work of achieving acceptance of change and involvement in change programmes. As Sturdy points out, they are often from an HR background, perhaps with training expertise in their profile. They offer several advantages to those organizing change events:

- Awareness of the inner workings of the organization

Previous experience of change events may be something that they can contribute from a staff perspective. This is an area which ought to be a benefit to the incoming team of external consultants.

- Prior involvement in successful environments

Sturdy mentions the increasing number of internal change agents who have previous experience of working for the large consultancies as external change agents. Their experience of different approaches to change and successful change environments can give credibility to claims made about the prospect of successful change outcomes.

- Mixed teams for training and implementation

Implementation teams benefit from a combination of external and internal change agents. Internal change agents can give their view of the likely acceptability of change initiatives based on experience. This can be valuable to outside trainers.

- The work of evaluation

Most external consultants have a time limit to adhere to and it may not include involvement in the long-cycle task of evaluating the change event. This is where internal change agents can provide the support for monitoring organizational outcomes and supporting the continuing professional development of staff.

- Mentoring, shadowing and development

Most companies encourage and support continuing professional development for their staff and internal change agents can actively support these initiatives. This combination of individual development opportunities and organizational evaluation outcomes is important in retaining the confidence and commitment of staff that 'people are our most important resource'.

BOUNDARY SPANNERS

There is an emerging recognition in current academic discussions of managers who support change that coincides with change agency. It is the term: boundary spanners (Schotter et al., 2017). Douglas (1966) suggested that if we want to study change we should focus on boundary-related dynamics. The boundaries referred to relate not just to the traditional differences between the silos in the organization where sales, marketing, production, finance all have their own disciplines and are sometimes less aware of those working around them. Hernes (2004) suggests these boundaries can be physical, social and mental differences and says that groups that have what he describes as tight mental boundaries, in the sense of high thresholds of understanding, are generally reluctant to learn from newcomers or outsiders. This resonates with the work of Nicolini (2008) who notes that the medical profession is one such community which resists outsiders and tends to compete rather than collaborate with change initiatives (Reay and Hinings, 2005, 2009). So, boundary spanning relates to the work of those who can negotiate knowledge and relationships across disciplines and cultures (Roberts and Beamish, 2017).

The case studies supporting these findings are often based in multinational enterprises, frequently involved in engineering and IT-based disciplines (Tippman et al., 2017; Klueter and Monteiro, 2017). Their success depends on individuals with the requisite knowledge to span groups, the skill to negotiate across boundaries, and the experience to facilitate learning within hierarchies, functional domains, and geographical territories (Schotter et al., 2017). The authors suggest that 'a small number of managers with unique skill-sets emerge as critical facilitators of cross-boundary coordination' (2017: 404). But they admit that little is known about the characteristics of boundary spanners and how far their capabilities are inherent or can be developed.

Some researchers suggest that it is a combination of ability, persistence, willingness and opportunity which links the boundary spanner with a learning perspective based in educational theory (Lecusay et al., 2008). In this way boundary spanners can help members 'learn from foreign knowledge practices and engage in meaningful ways with foreign stakeholders' (Roberts and Beamish, 2017: 511). They suggest that R & D managers are in a good position to balance the expectations, practices and concerns of managers and scientists in R & D intensive firms and raise the idea of 'scaffolding' by which they mean that knowledge absorption requires temporary support while knowledge practices and relationships are transferred and transformed within the organization from an external field of practice. It includes the need to overcome emotional attachment to previously held practices; mediating where conflict occurs; and building competence across boundaries. Such competence is ideally suited to the role of the internal change agent.

FUTURE CHALLENGES

The rise of zero-hours contracts

Increasing numbers of people are struggling to survive on zero-hours contracts. To put it into perspective, in one academic institution known to the authors of 1,300 academic staff, 489 are now on such contracts – mostly the younger, newly recruited members. There is a debate to be had as to how committed to the organization staff on such contracts can be. Higher management in the sector speak of their dedication to improving the student experience, at the same time as they reduce the number of permanent staff and increase the number of insecure contracts whose holders will struggle to be committed to the institution. In the many organizations that have moved to such 'flexible' forms of working, the question must be asked whether such workers have any stake at all in seeing change initiatives succeed and what are the implications for future personal development for those joining on such terms and conditions. It is important to take account of future needs in the sector and that organizational members require an individual focus on continuing professional development to consolidate their experience and expertise.

Kane and Levina (2017) ask how far the boundary spanner needs to be 'one of us'. They answer that, firstly, a familiarity with the groups involved and the expertise required are important. Secondly, that they should be recognized as negotiators for the group. Thirdly, they themselves should feel inclined to be engaged in the role. Finally, they suggest that this only occurs 'when you go beyond taking orders and instead question why certain decisions have been made' (2017: 554).

The present writers believe that internal change agents play a similar role to the boundary spanner. They may be managers who have had experience of consultancy and development roles themselves, perhaps in HR, as Sturdy and colleagues (2016) suggest. Their knowledge and skills enable them to bridge the gap between the present and the future aspirations that need to be realized to secure a successful future for the organization and everyone in it. We hope that the nature of the work that they engage in will be further researched and that this work will evaluate the benefits they achieve in enhancing the effectiveness of the organization and its people.

CONTINUING TREND OF INTERNAL CHANGE AGENTS

In summary, then, it would be fair to say that unpredictability in global markets will continue to impact on work practices requiring flexibility and responsiveness to change. This uncertain time for individual workers will privilege continuous change as a means of enhancing the value-added of what they can offer at work. Monitoring where people are in their development will become more important for reviewing the potential that the company depends on and encouraging its people to stay. This connection between individual development and organizational outcomes seems to be lost on some proponents of change and may indicate how privileging short-term company gains may ignore long-term issues of developing aspiration, potential and aptitude which alone can offer value-added to its clients.

All the above points would suggest that internal change agents play a crucial role in ensuring that people and systems together can rise to the challenges of answering the future needs that challenge any business. As we have suggested, for future researchers, there is a challenge to find out what successful change agents do in their organizations and how those skills can be mobilized more readily for all workers who want to be part of a society that works for everyone.

TENSIONS APPARENT FOR OD PRACTITIONERS

The structure-actor debate lies behind much that change practitioners seek to achieve (Reed, 2003). Are organizations as powerful and deterministic as some would have us believe? If individuals are so locked down by discourses which then become frameworks of power (Clegg, 1990), then where does the potential for change lie? How do some individuals and groups, small though they are, influence the majority view in a way that change to basic assumptions becomes not just desirable but also necessary?

Behind these questions lies the long-running debate on culture as something an organization is or something an organization has – behaviour or attitudes (Smircich, 1983). The assumption that training can change attitudes is still believed by many change proponents, though those tasked with implementing it are often less confident that this is a path for successful change as easy as is sometimes claimed.

If we return to Schein's three levels of culture, we can accept that at their deepest level basic assumptions need to be surfaced if change initiatives are to have a realistic chance of addressing long-term change. Lewin's group learning approach is a credible attempt to achieve this, though Schein himself believed that outside change threats were also likely to surface previously unacknowledged beliefs. Similarly, a researcher can do the same using semi-structured interviews, which include questions on surprise and sense-making (Louis, 1980). This then gives us a link to Gabriel's (2000) assertion that we are an 'interpretive animal' in that basic assumptions are themselves used to interpret events and derive meaning and ascribe value to proposed change. In this sense, Bevir's (2005) assertion that the qualitative researcher's work is 'the interpretation of interpretation' also encapsulates the work of the effective change agent. Within this work we can distinguish sense-giving – management's attempt to justify change, for example – and sense-taking – how staff hear what is said and interpret it according to their own beliefs of why change is being introduced (Gergen, 1991; Polkinghorne, 1988).

At the heart of structure (the organization's intentions in changing what we do) there lies the actor's interpretation (how does this affect who I am and what I ought to be doing?). Changing the DNA (basic assumptions) underpins all radical change initiatives and no one can be certain that any particular approach is likely to be successful or not. What we can say is that developing people is a long-term investment and convincing the proposers of change that though change initiatives are likely to meet with scepticism and initial resistance – surfacing uncertainty is an important part of addressing and exploring the implications of change.

CONSULTANCY AND CHANGE: THE FUTURE

It has sometimes been said that nothing is certain except that nothing is certain. But in uncertain times, the knowledge and skills of the change agent will continue to play an important part in bringing assurance to people during change events. We have tried to show through the chapters of this book the wide range of areas in which the consultant must be able to operate successfully. Business needs to be flexible not just to keep pace with political, social and economic changes but to look ahead and initiate change effectively in a world with a growing population, decreasing resources and a less predictable ecological and climatic environment. The change agent has a significant role to play in an era of change and while one could argue that this has always been true, we can assert that the impact of global change has become more pronounced in its impact on individuals at work. In short, the abilities, knowledge and skills of the consultant, internal and external, have never been more needed and, we believe, will be part of the profile of the effective manager in the future.

For video content relating to this chapter please visit the companion website at **www.macmillanihe.com/Randall-Management-Consultancy.**

REFERENCES

Beech, N. (2008). On the nature of dialogic identity work. *Organization*, 15(1), 51–74.

Bevir, M. (2005). *New Labour: A Critique*. Abingdon: Routledge.

Billig, M. (1996). *Arguing and Thinking: A Rhetorical Approach to Social Psychology* (2nd edn). Cambridge: Cambridge University Press.

Bullock, R.J. and Batten, D. (1985). It's just a phase we're going through: A review and synthesis of OD phase analysis. *Group and Organization Studies*, 10(4), 383–412.

Burnes, B. (2004). Kurt Lewin and the planned approach to change: A re-appraisal. *Journal of Management Studies*, 41(6), 977–1002.

Burnes, B. and Cooke, B. (2012). The past, present and future of organization development: Taking the long view. *Human Relations*, 65(11), 1395–1429.

Bushe, G.R. and Marshak, R.J. (2009). Revisioning organization development: Diagnostic and dialogic premises and patterns of practice. *Journal of Applied Behavioural Science*, 45(3), 348–368.

Clark, T. and Salaman, G. (1998). Telling tales: Management gurus' narratives and the construction of managerial identity. *Journal of Management Studies*, 35(2), 137–161.

Clegg, S.R. (1990). *Frameworks of Power*. London: Sage.

Cooperrider, D.L. and Srivastva, S. (1987). Appreciative inquiry in organizational life. In R.W. Woodman and W.A. Pasmore (eds), *Research in Organizational Change and Development*, Vol. 1, pp. 129–169.

Corley, K.G. and Gioia, D.A. (2004). Identity, ambiguity and change in the wake of a corporate spin-off. *Administrative Science Quarterly*, 49(2), 173–208.

Czarniawska-Joerges, B. (1990). Merchants of meaning. In B. Turner (ed.) *Organizational Symbolism*. Berlin: De Gruyter.

Deal, T.E. and Kennedy, A.A. (1982). *Corporate Cultures: The Rites and Rituals of Corporate Life*. Reading, MA: Addison-Wesley.

Douglas, M. (1966). *Purity and Danger: An Analysis of Concepts of Pollution and Taboo*. Abingdon: Routledge.

Gabriel, Y. (2000). *Storytelling in Organizations: Facts, Fictions, Fantasies*. Oxford: Oxford University Press.

Gergen, K. (1991). *The Saturated Self: Dilemmas of Identity in Contemporary Life*. New York: Basic Books.

Greiner, L.E. and Schein, V.E. (1988). *Power and Organization Development: Mobilizing Power to Implement Change*. Prentice Hall: Organization Development Series.

Hernes, T. (2004). Studying composite boundaries: A framework for analysis. *Human Relations*, 57, 9–29.

Heusinkveld, S. and Benders, J. (2005). Contested commodification: Consultancies and their struggle with new concept development. *Human Relations*, 58(3), 283–310.

Kane, A.A. and Levina, N. (2017). 'Am I still one of them?': Bicultural immigrant managers navigating social identity threats when spanning global boundaries. *Journal of Management Studies*, 54, 540–577.

Kleuter, T. and Monteiro, F. (2017). How does performance feedback affect boundary spanning in multinational corporations? *Journal of Management Studies*, 54(4), 483–510.

Lecusay, R., Rossen, L. and Cole, M. (2008). Cultural-historical activity theory and the zone of proximal development in the study of idioculture design and implementation. *Cognitive Systems Research*, 9, 92–103.

Louis, M.R. (1980a). Surprise and sense making: What newcomers experience in entering unfamiliar organizational settings. *Administrative Science Quarterly*, 25, 226–251.

Nicolini, D., Powell, J., Conville, P. and Martinez-Solano, L. (2008). Managing knowledge in the healthcare sector: A review. *International Journal of Management Reviews*, 10(3), 245–263.

Pava, C. (1986). Redesigning sociotechnical systems design. *The Journal of Applied Behavioral Science*, 22, 201–221.

Pettigrew, A.M. (1987). Context and action in the transformation of the firm. *Journal of Management Studies*, 24(6), 649–670.

Polkinghorne, D.E. (1988). *Narrative Knowing and the Human Sciences*. Albany: State University of New York Press.

Reay, T. and Hinings, C.R. (2005). The recomposition of an organizational field: Health care in Alberta. *Organization Studies*, 25(3), 351–384.

Reay, T. and Hinings, C.R. (2009). Managing the rivalry of competing institutional logics. *Organization Studies*, 30(6), 629–652.

Reed, M. (1997). In praise of duality and dualism: Rethinking agency and structure in organizational analysis. *Organization Studies*, 18(1), 21–42.

Reed, M. (2003). The agency/structure dilemma in organization theory: Open doors and brick walls. In H. Tsoukas and C. Knudsen (eds), *The Oxford Handbook of Organization Theory*. Oxford: Oxford University Press.

Revans, R.W. (1980). *Action Learning*. London: Blond and Briggs.

Roberts, M.J.D. and Beamish, P.W. (2017). The scaffolding activities of international returnee executives: A learning based perspectives of global boundary spanning. *Journal of Management Studies*, 54(4), 511–539.

Schein, E.H. (1967). *Process Consultation: Lessons for Managers and Consultants*. Reading, MA: Addison-Wesley.

Schotter, A.P.J., Mudambi, R., Doz, Y.L. and Gaur, A. (2017). Boundary spanning in global organizations. *Journal of Management Studies*, 54(4), 403–421.

Senge, P.M. (1990). *The Fifth Discipline: The Art and Practice of the Learning Organization*. London: Century Business Publishers.

Smircich, L. (1983). Concepts of culture and organizational analysis. *Administrative Science Quarterly*, 28(3), 339–358.

Sturdy, A., Wright, C. and Wylie, N. (2016). Managers as consultants: The hybridity and tensions of neo-bureaucratic management. *Organization*, 23(2), 184–205.

Thompson, P. and Warhurst, C. (1998). *Workplaces of the Future*. Basingstoke: Macmillan Press.

Tippman, E., Sharkey Scott, P. and Parker, A. (2017). 'Boundary capabilities in MNCs: Knowledge transformation for creative solution development'. *Journal of Management Studies*, 54, 455–82.

Watson, T.J. (2009). Narrative, life story and manager identity: A case study in autobiographical identity work. *Human Relations*, 62, 425–452.

Willmott, H. (1993). Strength is ignorance, freedom is slavery – Managing culture in modern organizations. *Journal of Management Studies*, 30(4), 515–552.

Index

A
Abelson, R., 88
accidents, 134–135
Action Learning, 9, 182
Action phase (Bullock and Batten), 18, 61
action research (Lewin), 3
active listening *See* listening
Adair, J., 18
advantages, in negotiations, 134
adversarial/assertive negotiations, 142
advocates, 73, 153
agents (change team role), 73, 74, 153–154; *See also* change agents; change teams
aggressive people, 142
agreement, in negotiations, 141
alternate closing, 57, 140
ambiguity, 60, 69–70
'Ambiguity and ambivalence: Senior managers' accounts of organizational change in a restructured government department,' 70–71
ambivalence, 60, 69–70, 89
appraisals, 46, 115, 116, 121
appreciative enquiry, 182
arguing, in negotiations, 137–138
Argyris, Chris, 3, 174, 182
assembly lines, 8
assumptions *See* basic assumptions
attitudes, changing, 2, 89
authority, forms of, 7, 154–155
automation, 5
avoiders, 142

B
Baker Hughes INTEQ, 158–159
basic assumptions, 20, 51, 187
changing, 90
examples of, 93–99
facilitating change, 61
in interpretive process, 68
surfacing, 59–60, 69, 78, 89
Batten, D.
Exploration phase, 20, 33, 39, 40, 72
Planned approach (four-phase model), 17–18, 61, 157
Planning phase, 18, 61, 73, 83
Baumhart, Raymond, 166
Beckhard, R., 61
behavioural change, 2, 18, 20–21
force field analysis, 4
and organization standards, 116–117
'refreezing,' 4–5
Benders, J., 25
benefits, 13–14, 134–135
Bevir, M., 187
Block, P., 105
blocks to participative change, 75–77
Board of Directors, 74, 156

Boddy, D., 75, 101
body language, 52
bottom-up approach, 79
boundary spanners, 47, 185, 186
bounded communities, 68, 80, 84
Branson, Richard, 14
Buchanan, D., 75, 101
budgets
of change programmes, 34, 53, 65, 156
in negotiations, 136–137
in Planning phase, 62
Bullock, R.J.
Exploration phase, 20, 33, 39, 40, 72
Planned approach (four-phase model), 17–18, 61, 157
Planning phase, 18, 61, 73, 83
Bunker, Barbara, 182
bureaucratic approach, 8
Burke-Litwin, 160
Burnes, Bernard, 1–22, 25–47, 181–187
Business Ethics, 167–168
Business Process Management, 149
Business Process Re-engineering (BPR), 11, 14–18
business regulations, 173–174

C
Caldwell, R., 27
Campbell, K.S., 176
'canteen culture,' 91, 100
case studies
change agents, 101–108, 157–162
change programmes, 123–124
employees and managers, 93–99
ethics, 172, 173–179
organizational culture, 93–99, 100, 123–124
Categorical Imperative, 167
CEO
in change teams, 153–154
influencing organizational culture, 64
role in change programme, 41–42
change, 1–3, 6–7, 19, 42–43; *See also* change agents; change programmes; change teams; consultants; organizational development (OD)
ambivalence to, 89
approaches to, 8, 11–18, 61–65
assumptions facilitating, 61
behavioural, 2, 4–5, 18
blocks to, 75–77
bottom-up approach, 40, 79
boundary dynamics and, 185, 186
Business Process Re-engineering (BPR), 11, 14–18
contexts of, 30–32, 42–44
drivers of, 5–6, 14, 25–26, 181
eight-step model, 62–63, 160
emergent approach, 18

evaluating, 18, 184
failure rate of, 3, 26–27, 89, 176–177, 183
financial implications, 113–114
four-phase model (Bullock and Batten), 17–18, 61, 62
interventions for, 152–153
interpretive process, 68
learning approaches, 3–5, 182, 187
as learning process, 19–20, 79, 81
map-building for, 72–73
market-led, 14, 186
motivating, 40, 151, 162
n-step approaches, 16–18, 183
nature of, 1–2, 181–183
performance-based leadership approach, 159
Planned approach to, 3–5
prescriptive approaches to, 147–148, 183
problem-solving approaches, 2, 183
process consultation approach, 58–59
resources for, 11–14, 65
Scientific Management, 181
systems and organizational change model, 160
tied to success, 46–47
time and motions approach, 181
Total Quality Management (TQM), 11–14
change agents; *See also* change teams; consultants; external change agents; internal change agents
case study, 157–162
choosing, 76–77, 108–109, 154
as coaches, 159
communicating, 38, 63, 114, 154
defining, 158, 161
developing strategies, 38, 43, 65, 159–160
driving change, 40, 158–159
effectiveness of, 183
as facilitators, 21, 35–37, 72–73, 154–155, 160
forming alliances, 92
future role of, 187
interference costs, calculating, 113–114
as leaders, 38–39, 78–82, 154–155
legal position of, 165
listening by, 37, 65, 79, 127, 154
managing transition, 41
map-building, 72–73
models for, 27
in negotiations, 132, 134, 135
open meetings with staff, 92–93
organizational culture, learning, 42–44, 59–60, 67–68
and process consultation, 58–61
resources, finding, 65, 160
as role models, 30

role of, 10–11, 38–39, 61, 72, 149, 154–155
skills and qualities, 77, 156
traditional views of, 184–185
change initiatives *See* change programmes
change programmes
Board of Directors supporting, 156
budgets of, 34, 53, 65, 140, 156
case study, 123–124
changing schemas and scripts, 88–89
communication plans, 63–64
evaluating, 115, 121–122, 183–184
events as parts of, 124–130
facilitating, 72, 152, 183
failure rate of, 26–27, 89, 176–177, 183
immediate action issues, 156–157
legal issues of, 165–166, 177
necessity of role models, 92
need for vision, 151
negotiation as part of, 145
participation in, 19–20, 58, 181–182
phases for, 61
proposing packages for, 139–140
resistance to, 68, 90, 149, 156–157
training programmes in, 111, 119–121
value-added approach, 152
change teams; *See also* change agents; consultants; external change agents; internal change agents
advantages of, 150–151, 185
as congruence model, 150
vs. individual concerns, 83
initial focus of, 149–150
intergroup work by, 155
managing transitions, 150, 151–152
motivating change, 79, 151
roles in, 73–74, 153–154
shaping vision, 150
charismatic authority, 7
Charter Mark, 14
Cheung-Judge, Mee-Yan, 158
Chevron, 159
clients; *See also* consultants; interviews
communicating with, 32
concerns and objections from, 135
creating pipeline of, 105
designing events for, 125–128
expectations of, 53, 128
legal relationships of, 173–176
meeting with, 39, 50–57, 106
negotiating with, 56–57
preparing to meet, 32–34, 51–52
in process consultation approach, 58–59
qualifying prospective, 51, 136
sending out wrong signals, 57–58
staying connected with, 106
tailoring negotiations to, 133–135
as targets, 74
closing techniques, 57–58, 140–141
sharp-angle, 55
cognitive dissonance, 60, 69
colonisers, 68
commitment
creating, 19, 44, 149
interventions for, 152–153

leaders gaining, 73
training influencing, 119–120
transformational leadership (TFL) for, 79
'commodification' of organizational development (OD), 25
communication, 8, 38
by change agents, 62–64, 154
with clients, 32
in hierarchies, 8
as intervention, 46–47
companies *See* organizations
competencies
cultural, 88
developing, in internal change agents, 155
influenced by training, 119–120
competition
awareness of, in negotiations, 134
as context, 43
driving change, 14, 25–26
concerns and objections, handling, 135
congruence model, 150
consultancy, 25, 26; *See also* organizational development (OD)
academic approaches to, 147–148
and ethical issues, 165–166
framework for, 102
future challenges for, 186
internalization of, 83
and legal issues, 165–166
prescriptive approaches to, 183
presentations *vs.* open approaches, 55
risk management in, 177
three aspects to, 28–29
consultancy in action *See* case studies
consultants, 25, 26; *See also* change agents; clients; internal change agents
Associates *vs.* independent, 108
challenges faced by, 33–34, 186–187
change programmes, developing, 41, 65, 112–113, 134, 135
client relations, 32–34, 39, 50–58
communicating, 32, 38, 114
coping strategies of, 34–35
creating events, 125–129
creating profile, 104–105
as doctors, 11
employees, interacting with, 20, 35–37
ethical considerations, 166–168, 170–171
as facilitators, 21, 35, 37, 72–73
income, 107
interference costs, calculating, 113–114
knowledge, applying, 16, 19, 38–39, 158, 166–167
as leaders, 29–30, 38–39, 73, 109, 157
in learning approach, 5, 38
legal considerations for, 173–179
as managers, 29–30, 34–36, 73
managers' relationships with, 147–148
map-building, 72–73
in mitigating circumstances, 167

and n-step approaches, 17
networking, 103
and organizational cultures, 28–29, 67–68
organizational politics as strategy, 37–39
presentations by, 54, 55
qualities needed, 77
reputations, 168
responsibilities, 179
role of, 1, 2, 10–11, 26–27, 61, 72, 148
as storytellers, 148, 184
three aspects of work, 28–29
using strategic plans, 113
views of, 147, 165–166, 184–185
consumer demand, as context, 43
contingency allowances, 140
contingency funds, 156
continuing professional development *See* professional development
contracts
closing, 51, 55, 57–58
for events, 125
legal aspects of, 174–175
negotiating, 51, 56–57, 174–175
tender terms, 174–175
Cooperrider, David, 182
coping strategies, 34–35
costs
of change programmes, 12, 140, 156
driving change, 5–6, 12
interference, 113–114, 134–135
justifying legal, 176
as type of flexibility, 44
cultural differences, 64; *See also* organizational culture
culture, ethical definition of, 168; *See also* organizational culture
custom and practice, 6, 87, 165–166; *See also* organizational culture
Customer Charter initiative, 114
customers, 5
evaluation tools for, 121
as judges, 13
satisfaction, in Total Quality Management, 14
setting standards for, 115
tailoring features to, 133–134

D

Daniels, Aubrey, 159
Davis, G.A., 61
Dawson, P., 2, 6
Deal, T.E., 19
deferral strategy, 137
DeGeorge, Richard T., 167–168
Deming, W. Edwards, 11
denial, 33, 34
deontology, 167
development *See* professional development
dialogical change, 182
dialogue; *See also* facilitators; negotiation
vs. debate, 142
enhancing and developing, 152
disaster closing, 140
distancing, 34

diversity, in event participants, 129;
    See also organizational culture
Donleavy, M.R., 61
Douglas, A., 135
Douglas, M., 185
Drucker, Peter, 5, 29, 73
Dutch auction closing, 57, 140

E
eight-step model (Kotter), 61, 62–63, 160
Elrod, D.P., 4
embedded communities, 68, 80, 84
emergent change, 18, 40, 72, 91, 157
Emotional Intelligence, 36
employees, 9, 10, 20–21; *See also* managers
    age of, in Business Process Re-engineering, 14
    ambiguity and ambivalence in, 60, 69–70, 89
    appraisals of, 116
    in assembly lines, 8
    basic assumptions of, 20, 59–60, 68–69, 71, 90
    case studies of, 93–99
    communicating vision to, 114
    and cultural values, 64–65, 68–69
    empowerment in Business Process Re-engineering, 14
    first meeting with, 39
    flexible, 9, 186
    identity, 31–32, 72
    and legal issues, 178–179
    participation by, 19–22, 40, 92–93, 182
    positive responses from, 35–37
    raising ethical issues, 170, 171
    as 'red bricks,' 82
    resistance in, 30–32, 90, 119
    as resource, 73
    socializing, 20, 81
    as stakeholders, 183
    as targets, 74
    types of, 59, 68, 92
    validating after training, 120–121
    on zero-hour contracts, 186
environment of events, 127
equilibrium, 'refreezing' as, 183
ethical relativism, 168–169
ethics, 165–166, 169
    case study, 172, 173–179
    checklist for behaviour, 167–168
    deontology, 167
    excusing conditions, 166–167
    mitigating factors, 166–167
    responses to issues, 170–171
    and stakeholders, 19
    teleology, 167
evaluation, 45, 121–122
    from beginning of programme, 151
    change agents for, 83, 185
    effective, 184
    as part of communication, 46
events, 124–130; *See also* change programmes; interventions
    contracts for, 125
    designing, 126–128

diverse participants in, 129
facilitating, 127–129
'hygiene' factors in, 129, 130
leaders' role in, 129
listening at, 127
venues for, 129
working backwards for, 126
excusing conditions, 166–167
exit interviews, 121
expectancy theory, 53
Exploration phase (Bullock and Batten), 18, 20, 33, 39, 40, 61
    emergent change via, 72
    internal *vs.* external change agents, 62, 83
    open meetings during, 92–93
    setting objectives, 112
external change agents; *See also* change agents; consultants; internal change agents
    case study, 101–108
    on change teams, 74, 153–154
    finding onsite allies, 67–68
    vs. internal change agents, 27, 46, 62, 83, 105–106, 149–152
    linking objectives to tasks, 112–113
    motivating change, 40
    qualities needed, 77
    role models for, 92
    traditional views of, 184–185
    as trainers, 109
    using strategic plans, 113

F
facilitators, 21–22
    change agents as, 154–155, 160
    consultants as, 35, 37
    of events, 127, 128–129
    for groups, 154
    guidelines for, 152
    leaders as, 82, 155
    managers as, 79
    skills needed, 37, 72–73
failure rate of change, 15, 26–27, 89, 176–177, 183
features, in negotiations, 133–134
field theory (Lewin), 3, 4
Fincham, R., 26
first meeting *See* interviews
flexibility, types of, 44
focus groups, 6, 115, 121
Folkman, S., 89
Follett, Mary Parker, 29
force field analysis, 4, 19
Ford, Henry, 8, 25
four-phase model (Bullock and Batten), 17–18, 61, 157
    Exploration phase, 20, 33, 39, 40, 72
    Planning phase, 18, 61, 73, 83
four-step process, 83
Fraher, A.L., 72
Friedman, Milton, 169
future
    in change programmes, 31, 33, 157
    consultants envisioning, 26, 39, 150–151
    focus on, 36, 40–41, 60

    in Planned approach, 3–4, 21
    success, tying change to, 46
future challenges, 186

G
Gabriel, Y., 68, 72, 187
generalizability, 16
Gergen, Kenneth, 84
Gibson, S.K., 27
global capitalism, 162
goals, 118
    breaking down into tasks, 112
    leading to achieve, 78, 83
    in Planning phase, 18
    setting realistic, 77
group dynamics (Lewin), 3
group learning approach, 3, 187
groups
    embedded communities, 68, 80, 84
    facilitated by change agents, 39, 143, 154, 178
    focus, 6, 115, 121
    interdisciplinary, 21, 43, 74, 126
    intergroup work, 155
    responding to, 35, 43
    T-, 6, 20, 151
Growth Model, 61
gurus, 147–148

H
Handy, Charles, 10
Harris, R.T., 61
Havelock, R.G., 158, 160
Hawthorn Studies, 9, 182
Hendry, C., 4
Hernes, T., 185
Heusinkveld, S., 25
Hinings, C.R., 69
Hislop, D., 26
'hive-mind change,' 160, 161
Hofstede, Geert, 168
honesty, 32, 136–137, 143
Human Relations tradition, 9, 182
human resources (HR)
    awareness of employee initiatives, 116
    developing internal change agents, 83
    in organizational structures, 10
    as primary stakeholder, 113
    role in change process, 27, 46–47
    strategic integration as outcome, 78

I
Ice Model, 61
identity, 71–72; *See also* organizational culture
    as block to change, 76
    in change programmes, 184
    as dialogic process, 72
    occupational *vs.* organizational, 72
ideology, 91
ignorance of consultants, 166–167
implementation, 28, 41
Implementation phase (Bullock and Batten), 83
In Search of Excellence, 25–26
induction training, as intervention, 46
Industrial Revolution, 2, 181

initiators, 59, 68
inner context of change, 42
innovation, as context, 43
inside-out approach, 11–14
Institute of Personnel Management, 9, 182
institutional racism, 91, 100
intangible benefits, 13
Integration phase (Bullock and Batten), 18, 61
interference costs, 113–114, 134–135
intergroup work, 155
internal change agents, 10, 39; See also change agents; consultants; external change agents
　advantages of, 184–185
　as agents, 153–154
　boundary spanners as, 185, 186
　case study, 101–108
　challenges facing, 62, 75–77
　change programmes, shaping, 61–63, 83
　on change teams, 74, 149–152
　choosing, 22, 74–77, 81, 108–109
　continuing trend of, 186
　creating commitment, 149
　developing strategies, 44, 65
　evaluation by, 41, 45, 115, 185
　vs. external change agents, 27, 46, 62, 83, 105–106, 149–152
　and four-phase models, 62
　initiators as, 68
　managing transitions, 41
　as role models, 79–80
　role of, 45, 83
　as targets, 154
　training for, 83, 122–123, 155, 185
　transformational leaders (TFL) as, 82
　understanding culture, 64
internalization, 88
'interpretive animal,' 68, 187
interpretive process, 68
interventions; See also change programmes; events
　events as, 124–130
　important, 152–153
　maximising contributions from, 124–130
　negative, 36, 77
　positive, 33, 44, 77
　types of, 46
interviews; See also clients; change agents; consultants
　closing, 55, 57–58
　exit, 121
　exploring objectives in, 52–54
　follow-through, 54–57
　negotiation in, 56–57
　preparing for, 51–52
　presentations vs. open approaches, 55
　qualifying, 135, 136, 137
　qualitative, 59, 60, 69, 70
　signals in, 55
　surfacing basic assumptions, 68, 69
　transcribing data, 70–71
introductions, 52
intuition, 137

investors, 5
Investors in People, 115
isolates, 68

J
just-in-time approaches, 14

K
kaizen activity, 80, 81
Kane, A.A., 186
Kant, Immanuel, 143, 167
Kanter, R.M., 4, 16, 17
Keawcahum, Supannee, 67–84
Kennedy, A.A., 19, 137, 138
Kitay, J., 26
knowledge
　developing, in internal change agents, 155
　management of, 179
　'scaffolding' to support, 185
　testing, 121
　via training, 120
'knowledge commodification,' 184
Kotter, John, 61, 63, 160
Kubler-Ross, E., 33

L
language, 91, 150
Lazarus, R.S., 89
leaders, 29
　as change agents, 78–82
　in change teams, 73–74, 153–154
　consultants as, 29–30, 38–39, 73, 157
　as facilitators, 82, 155
　gaining commitment, 73
　in negotiation teams, 138
　role in events, 129
　as role models, 79–80, 80–81
　shaping organizational culture, 64, 80
leadership, 78–82, 154–155, 161
learning approach, 3–5, 19–20
legal contexts of organization standards, 118–119
legal issues, 173
　and consultancy, 165–166
　insurance for, 175
　organizational culture and, 176–177
　periodic assessments of, 175
　vs. trust, 177
legitimation process, 91
leverage points, 41
Levina, N., 186
Lewin, Kurt
　approach to change, 3–5, 19, 21, 61, 181–182
　Bullock and Batten elaborating, 17
　concerns about, 182–183
　criticisms of, 4–5
　Ice Model, 61
　T-groups, 20, 151
　unfreezing stage, time spent, 40
listening
　active, 79
　by change agents, 37, 65, 79, 127, 154
　at events, 127
　in negotiations, 133
Louis, M.R., 31, 59–60, 69, 89

M
major and minor closing, 57, 140
management
　as intervention, 46
　by objectives, 112
　organizational politics as strategy, 37–39
　theories of, 15–16
Management by Objectives (Drucker), 5
managers, 8, 29
　basic assumptions of, 19, 71
　as boundary spanners, 185, 186
　case studies of, 93–99
　consultants as, 29–30, 73
　as facilitators, 79
　influencing culture, 64, 73
　interim, 10
　in negotiations, 142
　involving, 12–13, 41–42, 73–74, 153–154
　raising ethical issues, 170, 171
　relationships with consultants, 83, 147–148
　role of, 36, 149
　as role models, 80–81
　skills and knowledge in, 15–16, 37, 77
map building, 72–73
market research, 12
Markham, C., 28
McCalman, J., 101
McClelland, Douglas, 182
McGregor, Douglas, 3
meaning, managing, 91, 184
medical profession, 68–69, 158, 160
mitigating factors, 166–167
Mottram, Elaine, 111–130
moving phase (Lewin), 4, 21, 182–183
　as Action phase, 18
Myers-Briggs Type Indicator, 129
mythology, 82, 91, 148, 184

N
n-step approaches, 16–18, 183
Nadler, D.A., 17, 40, 90
narratives, importance of, 70, 84
identity, 72
National Health Service (NHS), 158, 160
Need Satisfaction Model, 61
negative interventions, 77
negotiations, 132, 135–143
　approaches to, 135–136
　change agents in, 132, 137–138
　closing, 140–141
　context of, 133
　dialogue in, 133, 137–139, 141, 143
　listening in, 133
　managers in, 142
　preparing for, 136–137
　presentations in, 135
　propose, package and bargain, 139–140
　qualifying process, 133–135
　questions for shaping, 138
　range of, 137, 141–142
　as specialist skill, 156
　task for two groups, 143–145
　three elements underpinning, 133–135
Nicolini, D., 185
nostalgia, 40

O

O'Mahony, J., 28
observers, in negotiation teams, 138
occupational identity, 72
occupational psychology, 102
Open Space, 124
order-book closing, 57, 140
organizational change, 2, 3, 5–6; *See also* change; change programmes; organizational development (OD)
organizational culture, 6, 64–65, 87–88, 187; *See also* identity; organizational politics; organizations
   basic assumptions, 51, 59–60, 68, 69, 89, 90
   in Business Process Re-engineering (BPR), 15
   'canteen culture,' 91, 100
   case studies, 93–99, 100, 123–124
   and choosing consultants, 28–29
   as context, 43
   elements of, 91
   and ethical relativism, 168–169
   event venues, 129
   failure to change, 176
   interventions for, 46–47
   'is' *vs.* 'has,' 87
   language, 82, 91
   legal issues, 176–177
   legitimation process, 91
   mythology, 82, 91, 148, 184
   qualitative interviews revealing, 78
   'red brick concept,' 82
   schemas and scripts for, 88–89
   staff shaping, 64, 80
   'the way we do things round here,' 19, 43, 51, 64, 67, 88, 100
   three levels of culture (Schein), 19–20, 59, 64
   understanding, 6, 19–21, 51, 64, 67–68
   values, 20, 51, 88
   visible artefacts, 51, 59, 68
organizational design, 182
organizational development (OD), 3–5, 27; *See also* change; change programmes; consultancy
   approaches to, 3–5, 18
   'commodification' of, 25
   competition influencing, 25–26
   consultants' role in, 5, 26–27
   evaluating, 18
   events as part of, 124–130
   failure rate of, 26–27
   human relations role in, 27
   vs. organizational structure, 8
   as participative process, 181–182
   self-knowledge for, 158
   tensions in, 186–187
organizational identity, 72
organizational justice, 177, 178
organizational learning, 182
organizational politics, 6, 37; *See also* organizational culture; organizations change teams shaping, 150
   as context, 43
   driving change, 6
   as management strategy, 37–39

organizational structure, 7–8
   increasing flexibility, 9–11
   as initiative for change, 6
   as intervention, 46
   modern *vs.* postmodern, 10
   vs. organizational development (OD), 8
organizations; *See also* organizational culture; organizational politics
   choosing internal change agents, 28–29
   goals of, 111–113
   global capitalism's impact, 162
   information sources, 114–116
   interference costs, 113–114, 134
   performance targets, 115, 116
   researching prior to negotiations, 136
   standards, 116–119
   strategic integration in, 115
   structure of, 149
   traditional hierarchy of, 7–8
   training and development, 115
   transformational leadership (TFL) for, 78
   understanding, 20–21
   values, 68–69
outcomes, of events, 127
outer context of change, 42
outside-in approach, 11, 14–18

P

participation, 38, 40, 161, 181–182
   basic assumptions for, 68
   diverse, at events, 129
   facilitating, 21–22, 79, 152
   interventions for, 152–153
   in Planned approach, 3–4, 19–20
   for problem finding, 72
   significant factors for, 75–77
Pascale, R.T., 161
performance standards, 115, 117
performance targets, 115
performance-based leadership approach, 159
performativity, 181
Personal Development Plans, 116
Peters, Tom, 16, 26
Pettigrew, A.M., 91
phases
   in change models, 61
   in eight-step model (Kotter), 62–63
   in negotiation (Douglas), 135
   in negotiation (Gulliver), 136
   in Planned approach (Bullock and Batten), 17–18
Piderit, S., 31, 60, 69, 89
Piper Alpha, 160
Planned approach, 3–5, 17–18, 19
   Bullock and Batten (four-phase model), 17–18, 61, 157
   criticisms of, 4–5
   Exploration phase, 20, 33, 39, 40, 72
   participation in, 3–4, 5
   Lewin, 3–5
   Planning phase, 18, 61, 73, 83
Planning phase (Bullock and Batten), 18, 61, 73, 83

politics *See* organizational politics
Polkinghorne, D.E., 84
positive interventions, 44, 77
power relations, 6
presentations, 54, 55, 135
problem finding *vs.* top-down change, 72
problem-solving approaches, 2, 183
Problem-Solving Model, 61
process consultation, 58–60, 182
process owners, 73, 74, 153
processual change, 2
Procter, S.J., 70–71, 99
professional associations, 41
professional development, 46, 115
   vs. change, 186
   for internal change agents, 185
   as intervention, 46
Professional Indemnity insurance, 175
propose, package, and bargain, 139–140
psychology, 2–3, 30–32, 182
psychometric test, 103
Pugh, C.A., 61
puppy-dog closing, 57, 140

Q

qualifying interviews, 135, 136, 137
qualitative interviews, 59, 69
   questionnaire for, 60, 70
   surfacing basic assumptions, 78
   transcribing data, 70–71
quality, 12–13, 14, 115
questionnaires, 60, 70–71
Quinn, J.B., 43
Quinn, R.E., 79, 176

R

Randall, Julian, 1–22, 25–47, 50–65, 67–84, 87–109, 111–130, 132–145, 147–162, 181–187
range of negotiations, 137, 141–142; *See also* negotiations
rational-legal authority, 7
Reay, T., 69
recruitment and selection, 46
'red brick concept,' 82
redundancy, 34, 170, 179
refreezing phase (Lewin), 4, 18, 183
regulations, 173–174
'Reinventing HRM: Business partners, internal consultants and the limits to professionalization,' 27
research, methodologies for, 79
resistance, 68, 90, 149, 156–157
resources, 11–14, 20, 65, 150, 160
Revans, Reg, 9, 182
rigidity, via standards, 13
role models, 30, 79–80, 80–81
Ruona, W.E.A., 27

S

sales cycle, 50–51
Schank, R., 88
Schein, Edgar
   basic assumptions, 20, 51, 68, 187
   helping traps, 103–104
   process consultation, 58–59
   responding to Lewin, 3–4
   three levels of culture, 19–20, 59, 64

values, 20, 51
  visible artefacts, 19, 51
schemas, 88–89
Scientific Management (Taylor), 8, 181
scripts, 88–89
sectional benefits, 13
selection criteria, 46
'self as instrument,' 158
Shamrock organizational model, 9–10
shareholders, 5
sharp-angle closing, 55, 57, 140
Sherrit, Dave, 147–162
signals, 55, 133, 138–139
silent closing, 57, 140
Silvestro, Norrie, 87–109, 101
Sim, Allan J., 132–145, 165–179
Six Sigma, 14
skills
  as block to change, 76
  developing, 120, 155
  for dialogue, 152
  testing, 121
Smith, Sarah, 50–65, 61
social anthropology, 2–3, 91
socio-technical systems, 182
sociology, 2–3, 182
sponge phenomenon, 13
sponsors, 73, 74, 153
Sports Direct, 6
stability, importance of, 42
staff *See* employees; managers
staff turnover, 89, 113, 135
stakeholders
  communicating with, 63–64, 104, 160
  employees as, 183
  and ethical considerations, 169
  identifying primary, 113
  as targets, 74
standards, 116–119
  behavioural terms, 116–117
  effect on employees, 119
  vs. goals, 118
  legal contexts of, 118–119
  rigidity of, 13
Sternin, J., 161
Stewart, Rosemary, 37, 137
stories, importance of, 70, 84
storytellers, consultants as, 148, 184
strategic change, 182
strategic integration, 78, 79, 115
strategic objectives linked to tasks, 112–113
strategic plans, 111, 113
structural change, 42–43
Sturdy, A., 27, 184, 186
subcultures, 21
success, change tied to, 46–47
summarizers, in negotiation teams, 138

summary closing, 57, 140
supervision, as intervention, 46
surveys, 79; *See also* interviews
symbols and symbolism, 91, 150
systems and organizational change (Burke-Litwin), 160

T
T-groups, 6, 20, 151
t-square closing, 57, 140
targets, 73, 74, 153
  defined, 73, 116
  vs. goals, 118
  internal change agents as, 154
tasks, objectives linked to, 112–113
Tavistock Institute, 9, 182
Taylor, Frederick Winslow, 25, 181
teams *See* change teams
technology, 1–2, 28–29, 43
teleology, 167
'Ten Commandments for Executing Change,' 4
tender terms, 174–175
testing questions for closing, 140–141
'the way we do things round here,' 19, 43, 51, 64, 67, 88, 100
three levels of culture (Schein), 19–20, 59, 64
  basic assumptions, 20, 51, 68, 187
  values, 20, 51
  visible artefacts, 19, 51
three-step approach *See* Planned approach
time and motions approach (Gilbreths), 181
timely arrival, 51–52
Tippett, D.D., 4
top-down change, problem finding *vs.*, 72
top-down communication, 8
Total Quality Management (TQM), 11–14
toughness dilemma, 143
traditional authority, 7
training
  designing programmes for, 119–121
  evaluating, 121–122
  events for, 124–130
  identifying need for, 111–112, 119–120
  for internal change agents, 122–123, 155
  spending on, 115
  systematic cycle for, 119
  validation after, 120–121
transformational leadership (TFL), 78–82
Transition Model, 61
transitions
  change teams managing, 150, 151–152

  managing, 41
  stage model of, 33
true ignorance, 166–167
trust, 20, 92, 104–105
  budget issues undermining, 156
  context for change, 30, 65
  vs. ethical relativism, 168–169
  vs. legal implications, 177, 178
  politics undermining, 37
Tyler, T.R., 178

U
Uber, 6
ultimatum closing, 57
under/over closing, 57, 140
'Understanding employee attitudes to change in longitudinal perspective: A study of UK public services 1996-2007,' 99–100
'unfreezing' (Lewin), 3–4, 21, 181–182
  as Exploration phase, 18
  time spent on, 40
unions, 41
Utilitarianism, 167

V
validation, 45, 120–121
values, 51; *See also* organizational culture
  employees living, 64–65
  of organizations, 68–69
  workplace, 6, 20
venues for events, 129
visible artefacts, 19, 51, 59, 68; *See also* organizational culture; three levels of culture
vision, 114
  change teams shaping, 150, 151
  communicating, 114
  creating, 62

W
wages, 5–6, 9, 46
wastage in production, 11
Weber, Max, 7
Weick, K.E., 31, 79
Weisbord, Marvin, 182
Weiss, A., 103, 105, 106, 108
Wilson, D.C., 12
workers *See* employees
workplace culture *See* identity; organizational culture
World Café, 124
Wright, C., 26, 27

Y
Young, Thom D., 165–179

Z
zero-hour contracts, 186
Zlotolow, S., 158, 160

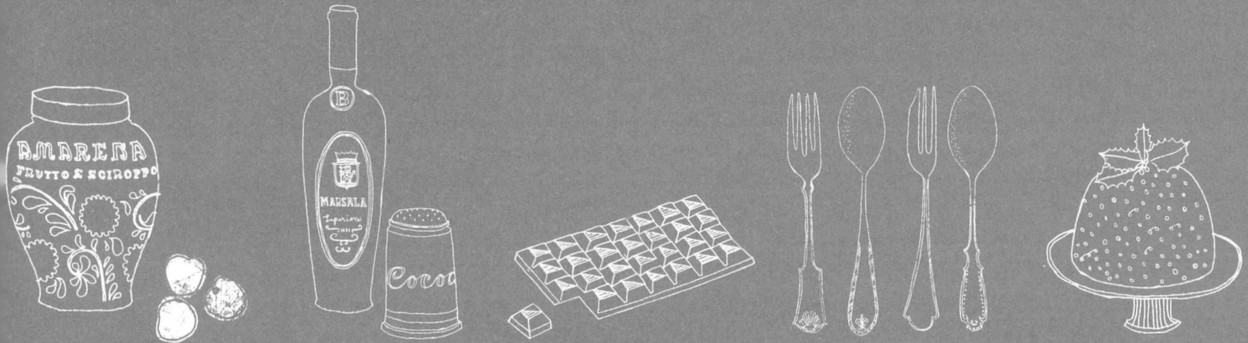
AMARENA
FRUTTO & SCIROPPO
MARSALA
Coco

PATISSERIE *Maison*

PATISSERIE *Maison*

RICHARD BERTINET

EBURY PRESS

Contents

About the author 7

Introduction 9

Basics 13

1 Small
A COLLECTION OF SWEET THINGS MADE IN INDIVIDUAL PORTIONS 61

2 Shared
MOUSSES, CAKES AND TARTS TO SLICE AND SHARE 111

3   Treats
    MOUTHFULS, MORSELS AND MUNCHIES   157

4   Festive
    EVERY YEAR I AM ASKED FOR MY CHRISTMAS RECIPES – SO HERE THEY ARE   191

Index   212

Suppliers   220

Online resources   221

Acknowledgements   223

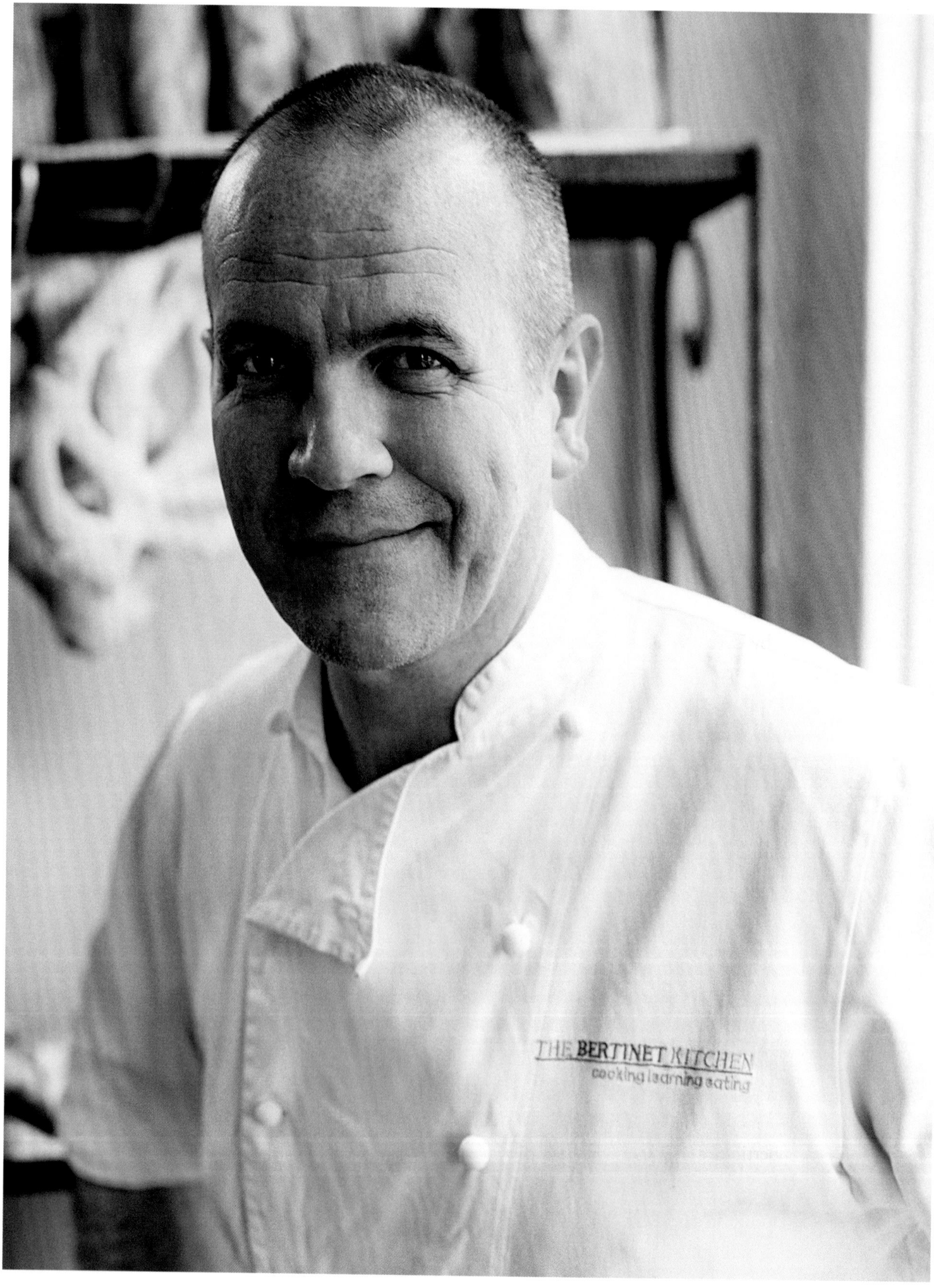
THE BERTINET KITCHEN
cooking learning eating

About the author

Originally from Brittany, France, Richard Bertinet trained as a baker from the age of fourteen. Having moved to the UK in the 1980s, he is now very much an Anglophile.

With twenty years' experience in the kitchen, baking, consulting and teaching, Richard moved to Bath in 2005 to open The Bertinet Kitchen cookery school. The school attracts people from all over the world to participate in Richard's classes and has been highly praised, including recognition by US *Gourmet* magazine and the television series *Adventures with Ruth* [Reichl], in which it featured as one of the best cookery schools in the world.

As well as instilling passion through his teaching, Richard works as a consultant for major manufacturers developing speciality products throughout the industry.

The Bertinet Bakery started life as a weekly pop-up shop above the cookery school in 2007 but has grown to a much larger affair, producing breads and pastries for restaurants, hotels and food stores in the South West and further afield. It also supplies the bakery's own shops in Bath. The bakery's signature sourdough loaf was the winner of the Soil Association's award for Best Baked Good in 2010 and 2011.

Richard's first book, *Dough,* received a host of accolades, including the Guild of Food Writers' Best First Book Award, the Julia Child Award for Best First Book, a James Beard Award for Best Book Baking & Desserts and the International Association of Culinary Professionals Cookery Book of the Year Award. His second book, *Crust,* was also published to critical acclaim and received a World Gourmand Award. His third book, *COOK,* focused on many of the dishes taught at the cookery school. His most recent book, *Pastry,* was published in 2012.

Richard was named BBC Food Champion of the Year 2010 at the BBC Food & Farming Awards. For more information about Richard, The Bertinet Kitchen and The Bertinet Bakery, visit www.bertinet.com.

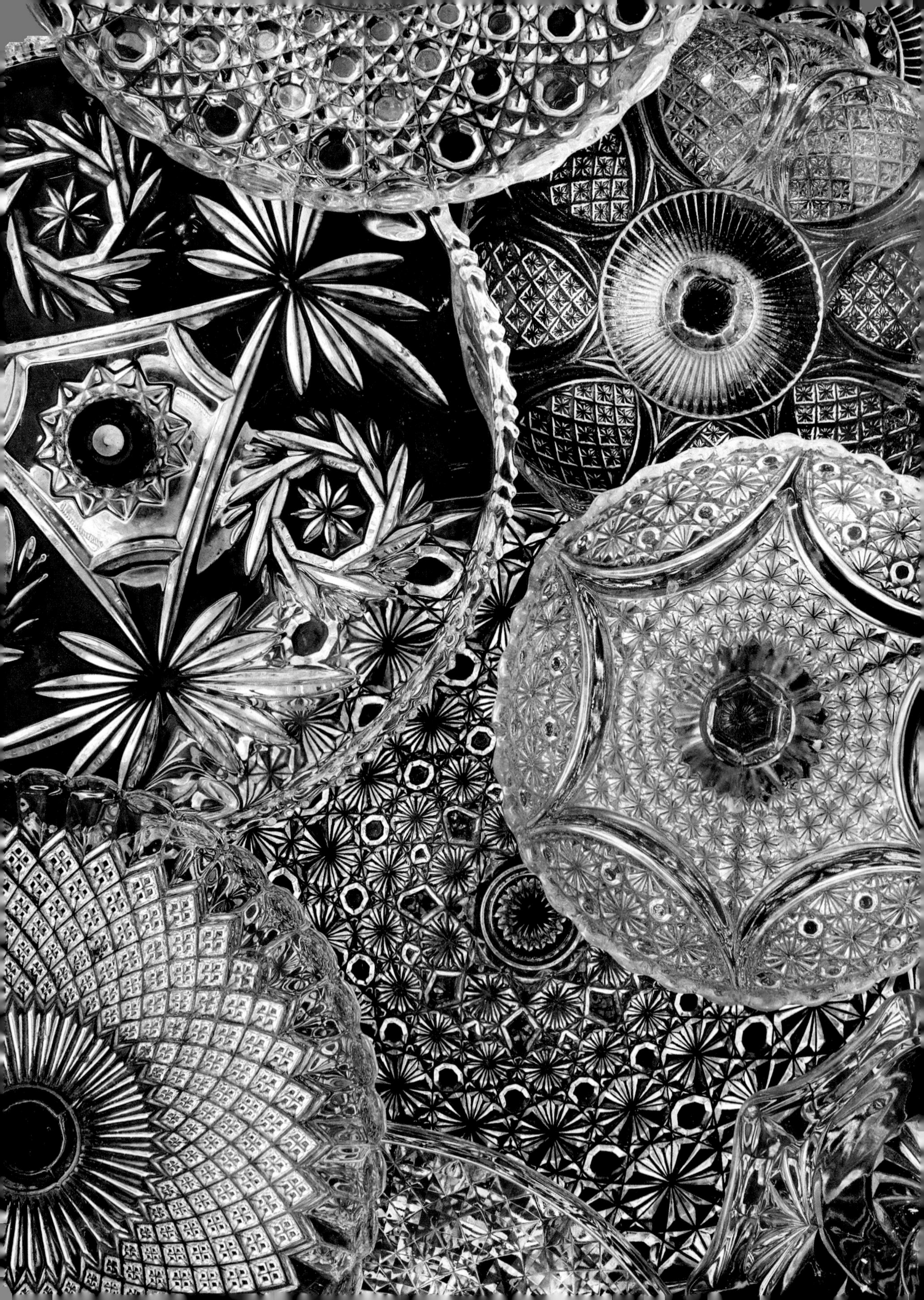

Introduction

When I began my apprenticeship in Britanny I had the choice of training as a baker, patissier or chocolatier. In France each one is a distinct profession with its own set of qualifications. Even though I knew that at heart I was a baker, I was always fascinated to know what my friends the patissiers were up to in the next room. Because bakers start work at two in the morning and finish at about midday, I was able to put in a double shift helping them out with the tarts and genoise sponges.

From being covered in flour and working with simple ingredients in the serenity of the bakery, where I had only one other person for company, it was such a contrast to be in the frenetic atmosphere of the patisserie, where half a dozen people seemed to do a thousand things at once. Whisks were constantly on the go and there would be fruit, cream, chocolate and sugar everywhere, and so much more washing up than in the bakery! Sunday was always the busiest day, when everyone came in to buy their desserts for Sunday lunch.

The very finest patissiers, who have risen to the top of their profession, are phenomenal artists, incredibly skilled and dedicated to the art of construction and perfect presentation – but I want to show you that at a simpler level you can still achieve great-tasting and great-looking patisserie. The recipes in this book are a mix of those that we teach in our cookery school in Bath, and the kind of thing that you would find in a small boulangerie-patisserie in France. They are what I call patisserie 'maison': simple tarts, mousses, meringues and pastries that you can make in your own kitchen, with a little practice. I have tried to keep the ingredients accessible, and the techniques as simple as possible, using only basic equipment.

Most of the recipes rely on a combination of classic base recipes: genoise sponge, sweet pastry, meringue, a selection of creams and syrups, chocolate ganache, and so on. The key to making life easy is to be forward thinking and organised. When you make a sponge or pastry, for example, make double, triple or quadruple the quantity and put what you don't need immediately into the freezer. And read the recipes through first, as sometimes, especially when you are working with mousses, glazes or jellies, you will have to set each layer in the fridge before you can move on to the next. So, although a recipe might not be complicated, it might mean you need to start making it the day before you want to serve it.

We all taste with our eyes before we even put food into our mouths, so I have given a few ideas on simple, smart presentation. Sometimes just a minimal dusting of cocoa powder over a chocolate glaze, a thread of coffee run through a meringue, or a cleverly piped cream inside an éclair can make the difference between ordinary and eye-catching.

Most of all, I hope that once you get to grips with the various techniques, you will have the confidence to personalise the recipes by experimenting with different combinations of flavours, textures and decorations – and just have fun.

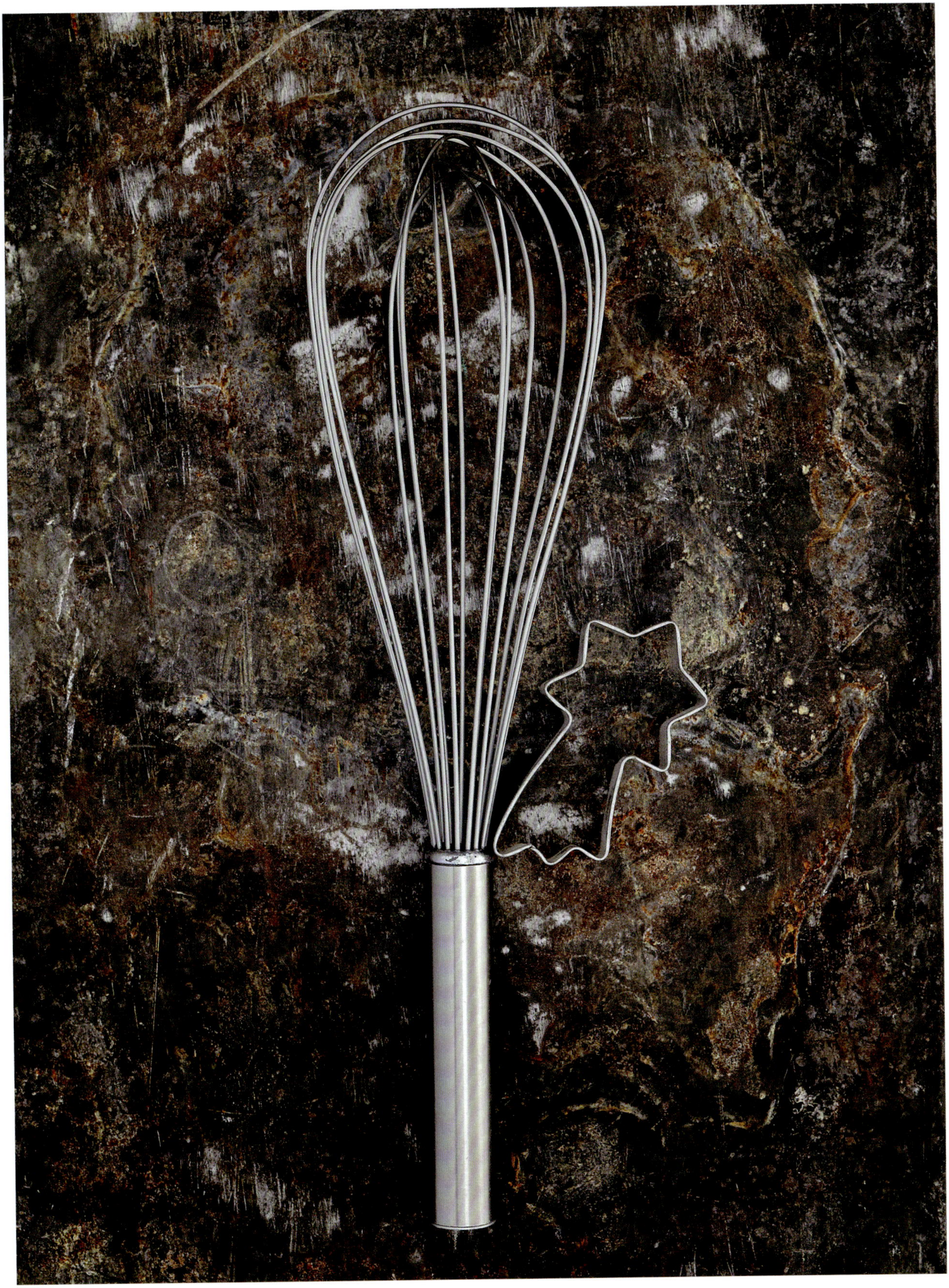

Transfer to a food mixer with a whisk attachment, or use a hand-held one, and whisk at high speed for about 4–5 minutes until the mixture has cooled down and clings easily to the whisk, which will leave ribbon patterns in the mixture as you lift it.

Very gently fold in the flour a little at a time with a metal spoon – you want to keep as much air in the mixture as possible.

Put the sugar and eggs in a bowl (use the bowl of your food mixer if you have one), and stir with a whisk, then put the bowl over a pan of barely simmering water (don't let the base of the bowl touch the water).

Whisk for about 3–4 minutes, until the mixture is foamy and has tripled in size.

(Continues overleaf)

Genoise sponge

A good genoise sponge is one of the fundamentals of patisserie. You will find a layer of plain or chocolate sponge being used in many of the recipes in this book, such as Tiramisu (see page 84), Fraisier (see page 93), and the Blackcurrant and Passion Fruit Mousses on pages 112 and 115. I suggest you bake a few trays at a time and freeze what you are not using immediately, ready to defrost when you need it. The quantity below will make enough for two shallow (2cm) rectangular sponges baked in a tray approximately 35cm x 27cm.

You could also use this recipe to make one 21cm round or equivalent square cake (7cm deep), which will need around 20 minutes in the oven until it is golden and springs back if you touch it gently in the centre. A skewer inserted into the middle should come away clean.

Once the cake has baked and cooled, you could simply halve it horizontally, brush each cut surface with sugar syrup flavoured with a dash of kirsch (see page 35) then sandwich the two halves together with whipped double cream or crème Chantilly (see page 42) and fresh raspberries or strawberries. Finish with a dusting of icing sugar on top.

125g caster sugar
4 medium eggs
125g plain flour, sifted
25g butter, melted
a little butter for greasing the tin

Grease two 35cm x 27cm x 2cm baking trays with a little butter and then line them with baking paper.

Preheat the oven to 180°C/gas 4.

Basics

Then, again very gently, fold in the melted butter.

(Continues overleaf)

With a spoon, turn the mixture into your trays and tilt it so that it spreads into the corners.

Bake in the preheated oven for 12–15 minutes until golden and the centre is springy to the touch. With shallow tray sponges like this you can tell easily when they are done, so there is no real need to do the skewer test – though you can, if you prefer.

When the sponge is baked, turn out onto a cooling rack. Now the sponge is ready to use in your chosen recipe. Or to freeze, leave the sponge on its greaseproof paper, put another layer on top, and wrap well in clingfilm before putting into the freezer, where it will keep for around three months.

Variations:

For chocolate genoise
sieve 1 tablespoon of cocoa powder with the flour.

For coffee genoise
sieve 1 tablespoon of very fine instant ground coffee with the flour.

For vanilla genoise
add either 1 teaspoon of vanilla extract, 1 teaspoon of vanilla bean paste, or the seeds of one vanilla pod to the mixture with the egg and sugar.

For orange genoise
add the grated zest of one orange, and a drop of orange essence or orange flower essence to the mixture before folding in the flour.

For lemon genoise
add the grated zest of one lemon and a drop of lemon essence to the mixture before folding in the flour.

Choux pastry

Choux is so fashionable – in every pastry class we run at the cookery school it is the technique that most people want to learn. It is the great versatile classic that any apprentice patissier must master, and the more often you make it the easier it will become. Don't be afraid to double or even quadruple the recipe below, pipe it into different shapes from round buns to little éclairs, bake them and then keep them in the freezer, to bring out any time you need a last-minute dessert.

This recipe makes around 500g of dough, enough for the Paris Brest on page 69, éclairs on page 73 and Gâteau St Honoré on page 128. For the Croque en Bouche on page 206 – the festive tower of choux buns – you will need to triple the quantity. One quantity of dough can be made easily by hand; however, if you are making bigger quantities, I suggest you use a food mixer with a paddle attachment.

MAKES 500G

125g plain flour
4 medium eggs
225ml water
60g butter
½ teaspoon salt

Sieve the flour into a bowl and have the eggs ready in another bowl.

Bring the water, butter and salt to the boil in a large pan.

Tip in the flour, whisking all the time.

(Continues overleaf)

Continue whisking until the mixture clings to the whisk and resembles mashed potato.

Swap the whisk for a wooden spoon and beat over the heat for 2–3 minutes until the mixture is glossy and comes away from the edges of the pan cleanly. Then, if using a food mixer with a paddle attachment, transfer the mixture to the bowl now, otherwise leave the mixture in the pan and take the pan off the heat.

Add the eggs, one by one, either beating them in by hand or with the motor running. Whether mixing by hand or by machine, go carefully with the eggs. Add them one at a time, making sure each one is well incorporated before adding the next. Before you add the last one, check the texture. You are aiming for a mixture that is smooth and glossy but that will hold its shape for piping (it is better to be slightly too stiff than too runny). If it is almost at this stage you might not need to add all of the last egg.

Now the dough is ready to use.

Piping choux pastry

One of the things I am asked about most in my classes is how to fill a piping bag cleanly, whether for piping choux pastry, cream or icing. The best way to do it is to turn the bag inside out over one hand and, with the other hand, fill it half full only. This helps to stop the mixture smearing over the outside of the bag as you fill it. Pull up the sides of the bag and twist the top so that the mixture is forced down towards the nozzle.

To pipe, hold the bag in one hand, with the other hand underneath to steady and guide it. Squeeze with the hand that is holding the bag, pipe, then turn the bag anticlockwise, squeeze again, applying the same pressure all the time, and pipe again.

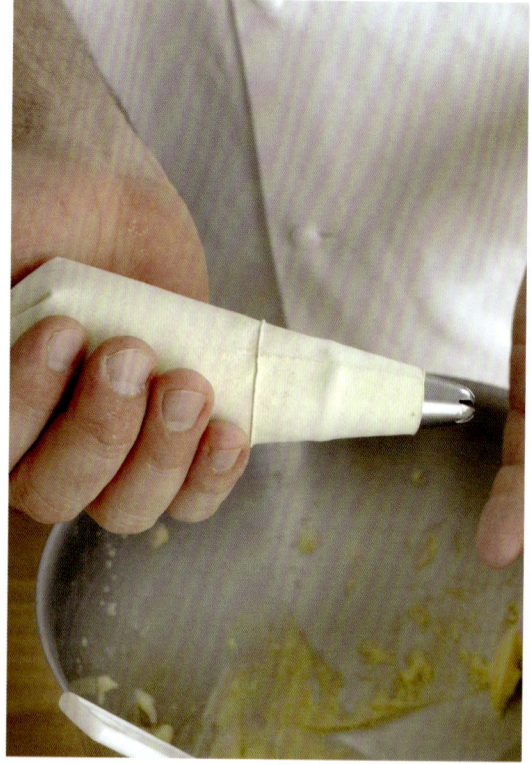

A note about baking choux pastry

When you bake choux pastry, the heat of the oven causes the pastry to expand and become hollow inside. The trick to keeping choux buns, éclairs, and so on, puffed up and crispy so that they don't deflate (crucial for something like the Croque en Bouche on page 206) is to dry out the pastry well during baking. Don't be scared of leaving them in the oven longer than you might expect. I have seen recipes that suggest taking out éclairs and buns halfway through baking, then making a little hole in the base for the air to escape, before putting them back in. I think a better way is to mimic what happens in a professional bakery, where you can press a button and allow steam to escape from the oven. You can do this quite simply by leaving the door of your oven open just a little for the last few minutes of baking.

BASICS 25

Sweet pastry

Some of the recipes use sweet pastry as a base. Although you can mix it by machine (see page 31), it is such a quick and easy process that I suggest you do it by hand, especially if you are new to making pastry as this helps you to get the feel of what you are looking for in terms of texture.

The pastry will keep for up to a week in the fridge and up to three months in the freezer, so it makes sense to make at least double the quantity and then freeze what you don't need immediately. A good tip to stop the pastry from discolouring slightly in the freezer is to add a couple of drops of lemon juice or vinegar to the dough during mixing – you won't taste it in the pastry.

I wrap pastry for the freezer in greaseproof paper, followed by a tight layer of clingfilm. When you take out the pastry and defrost it ready to use, you will find that it is beautifully easy to roll.

MAKES 360G

175g plain flour
pinch of salt
60g sugar
1 medium egg, plus 1 medium yolk
60g butter

Put the flour and salt in a mixing bowl. Have the sugar in a separate bowl and break your eggs into yet another bowl – there is no need to beat them.

The key to good pastry is to keep the butter very cold but still soft and pliable. I leave the butter in the fridge until I am ready to use it, then put it between two pieces of greaseproof paper and bash it with a rolling pin until it is about 1cm thick.

Put the whole piece of butter into the bowl of flour so that it is well covered, then tear it into large pieces and rub into the flour, with as light a touch as possible. The way to achieve this is to keep the pieces of butter constantly covered in flour, as you repeatedly scoop them up in both hands and just flick your thumbs over them in a soft skimming motion, as if you were dealing a pack of cards. Don't press or grind the butter or it can become clumpy.

(Continues overleaf)

Recipes often say to rub the mixture until it looks like breadcrumbs, but I find that people often overdo it trying to achieve this, and end up with pastry that is quite sticky and difficult to handle. Instead, I always say to stop when the shards of butter are still the size of your little fingernail.

Add the sugar, mixing it in evenly.

Tip the egg and yolk into the flour and butter and mix everything together.

(N.B. the pictures show double the quantity being made)

You can use a spoon, but I always use one of the little plastic scrapers that I have for bread making, as it is easy to run it around the edge of the bowl, pulling the mixture into the centre until it forms a very rough dough, that ideally shouldn't be sticky.

Press down on the dough with your thumbs, then turn it clockwise a few degrees and press down again. Repeat this a few times.

Now turn the pastry out onto a work surface. If it isn't sticky, you don't need to flour your work surface, but if you do, just very lightly skim it with the finest film of flour as you are going to work the pastry very briefly and any extra flour that goes in at this stage will make it heavier. Holding the dough with both hands, press down again gently with your thumbs and then turn the dough clockwise a few degrees, as before. Repeat this four or five times.

(Continues overleaf)

Finally fold the pastry over itself and press down with your fingertips. Repeat this a couple of times until the dough is like plasticine and looks even and homogeneous.

Pick up the piece of pastry and tap each side on the work surface to square it off so that when you come to roll it, you are starting off with a good shape, rather than with raggedy edges.

To make the sweet pastry by machine

WITH A MIXER: use a paddle attachment. Before putting the cold butter in the machine, bash it with a rolling pin, as on page 27, then break it into four or five pieces. Put it into the mixer with the flour and salt and mix at a slow speed until the pieces of butter are about the size of your little fingernail. Stir in the sugar. You will need to scrape the butter from the paddle a few times, as it will stick. Add the egg and mix very briefly until a dough forms. As soon as it does, turn it out onto your work surface with the help of your scraper and follow the rest of the method on pages 29–30.

WITH A FOOD PROCESSOR: go carefully, as it is very easy to over-process pastry. Take the butter straight from the fridge and cut it into small dice, then put it into the bowl with the flour and salt. Use the pulse button, in short bursts, so that the flour just lifts and mixes, rather than whizzes into a greasy ball that will result in dense, tense pastry. Add the sugar and pulse in the same way. Add the egg and again just press the pulse button briefly until the pastry dough comes together. Turn it out with the help of your scraper and follow the rest of the method on pages 29–30.

32 PATISSERIE MAISON

Resting the pastry

Wrap the dough in greaseproof paper rather than clingfilm (as this will make it sweaty) and put it into the fridge for at least an hour, preferably two, or better still, overnight. The point of resting the dough is to allow the gluten in the flour to relax, so that the dough becomes more elastic and easier to roll. This also helps to stop it shrinking when it goes in the oven.

If you are in a hurry to use the pastry, flatten it by half with a rolling pin before wrapping it in greaseproof paper. This will help it to chill more quickly. Or you can put it into the freezer for 15–30 minutes.

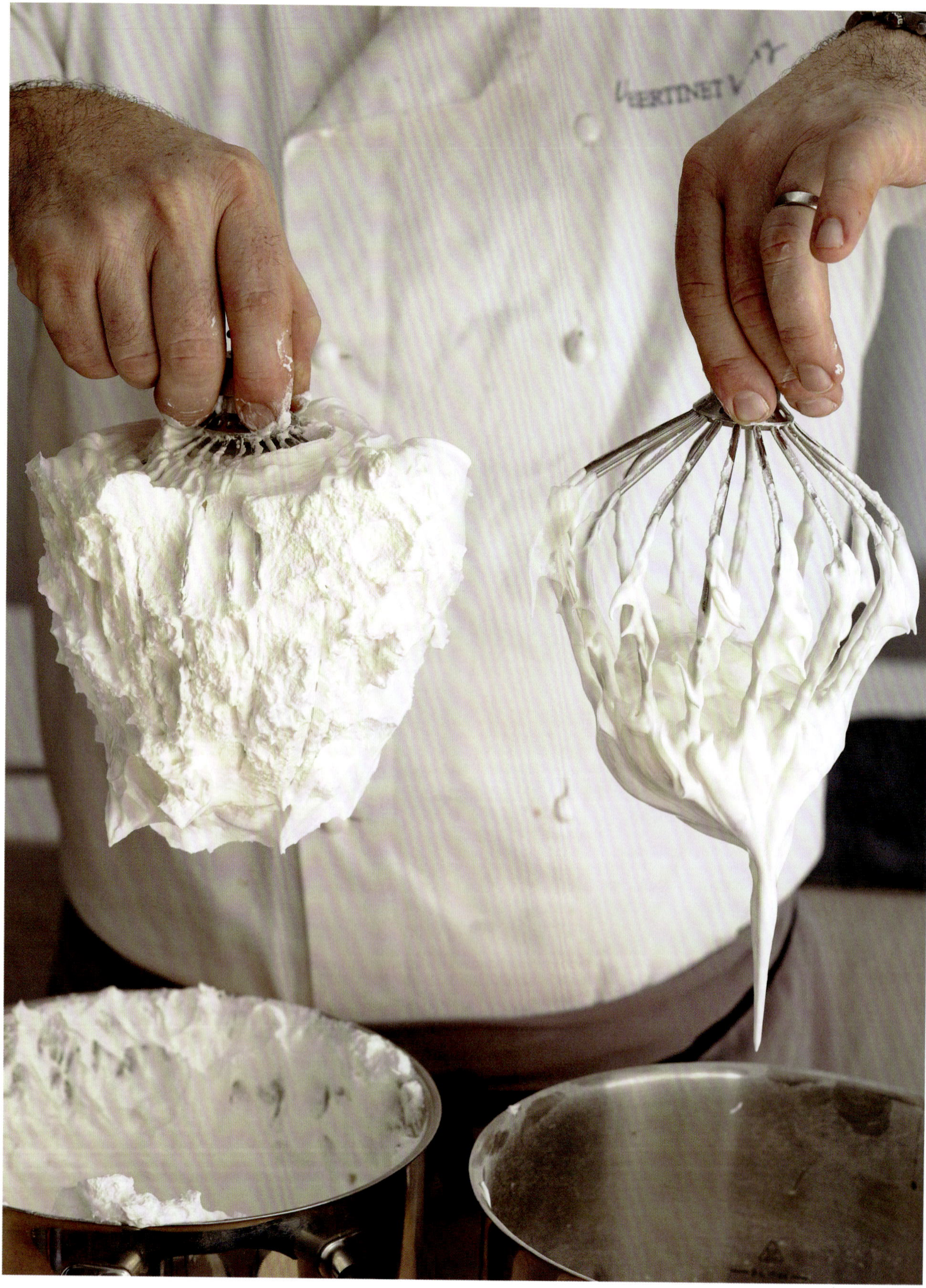

Meringue

The two most widely used styles of meringue are French and Italian. French meringue, which is the one most people are familiar with, is made by whisking egg whites and then adding sugar and continuing to whisk until the mixture forms stiff peaks. The Italian recipe is made with a hot sugar syrup, rather than sugar, and people tend to shy away from it, thinking it is harder to make – but if you use a sugar thermometer to take the syrup to just the right point, the rest is straightforward.

You can see the difference between the consistency of the two different styles in the photograph opposite: on the whisk the French meringue (on the left) is more compact and dry, whereas the Italian meringue is more 'stringy' with a glossy, silky shine to it.

I generally prefer the Italian-style meringue because it is more versatile to work with, and while it is firm on the outside, it retains a wonderful gooey softness in the centre, whereas French meringue is light, but a little drier and more brittle. However, it really is an individual choice, and though I have suggested Italian meringue in the recipes, you can substitute French meringue if you prefer.

The quantities I have given for each style will make around six big individual meringues, or one tart case, which you can use for the recipe for Chocolate Meringue Tart on page 142, or simply fill with Chantilly cream (see page 42) and fresh fruit.

Working with sugar

Some of the recipes in this book involve sugar syrups or caramel, which are really only about boiling sugar and water, but to different stages. I know from my classes that people find the idea of working with sugar daunting, usually because they have come across terms like thread, soft ball and hard ball, soft crack and hard crack, so I have deliberately kept things simple.

Most of the sugar syrups are simply equal quantities of sugar and water boiled until the sugar dissolves and you have a colourless syrup that can be flavoured with an alcohol such as rum or kirsch. I use these syrups for brushing over genoise sponge, to keep it moist and infuse it with extra flavour, when I am using it as a layer with various creams and fruit.

A slightly more dense sugar syrup, made with less water, and some glucose added to the sugar, is needed for making Italian meringue (see page 37) and for this and the few recipes that require caramel, the way to make your life easy is to invest in a sugar thermometer. These are inexpensive, and the best are those with digital displays that you can pre-set to a certain temperature and just wait for them to bleep when it is reached. I use mine for much more than working with sugar – for anything that I want temperature-controlled, for example deep frying.

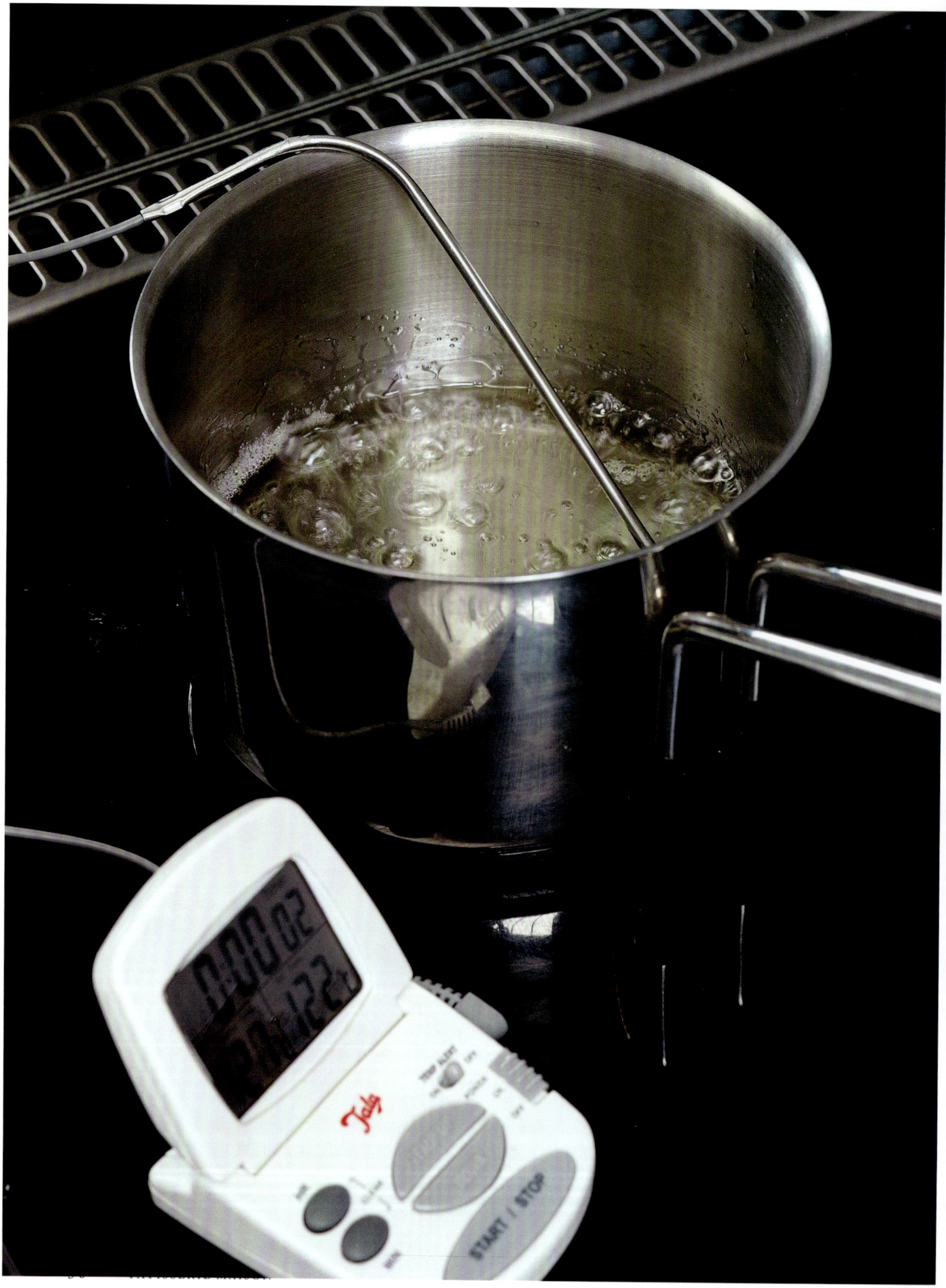
TEMP ALERT
START / STOP

Italian meringue

MAKES 6 LARGE INDIVIDUAL
MERINGUES OR 1 TART CASE

190g sugar
45ml water
20ml liquid glucose
3 medium egg whites

Put the sugar in a pan with the water and heat gently for about 5–8 minutes until the sugar has dissolved and formed a colourless syrup, and small bubbles are breaking the surface. The syrup is ready when the temperature reaches 121/122°C maximum, so I always set my thermometer to 122°C.

Now you are ready to whisk your egg whites. You can do this using a food mixer with a whisk attachment, or a hand-held whisk, but whichever you use, make sure your bowl is absolutely clean and dry, as water or grease can prevent the egg white from stiffening. Whisk the egg whites until soft foamy peaks form, then stop as soon as you reach this point, as if you over-whisk, the air bubbles that you have created will burst and the egg whites will collapse back into liquid.

Next you are going to pour the hot syrup onto the egg whites. Since you need both hands free – one to whisk, one to pour – if you are whisking by hand, then before you start, wrap a tea towel around your bowl and wedge it into an empty saucepan to hold it steady.

Pour the syrup in a slow, steady stream, whisking continuously until the meringue has cooled down to room temperature, and is silky and glossy.

Now the meringue is ready to use according to your recipe.

French meringue

MAKES 6 LARGE INDIVIDUAL MERINGUES OR 1 TART CASE

4 medium egg whites
125g caster sugar
125g icing sugar

Whether you use a food mixer with a whisk attachment, or a hand-held whisk, make sure your bowl is absolutely clean and dry, as any water or grease can prevent the egg white from stiffening. Whisk the egg whites and caster sugar until soft foamy peaks form, then stop as soon as you reach this point, as if you over-whisk, the egg whites will become liquid and you will have to start again.

Before you add the icing sugar, if you are whisking by hand, wrap a tea towel around your bowl and wedge it into an empty saucepan to hold it steady. You need both hands free – one to whisk, one to sieve in the sugar.

Sieve in the icing sugar slowly, whisking continuously until the mixture forms firm, shiny peaks.

Now the meringue is ready to use according to your recipe.

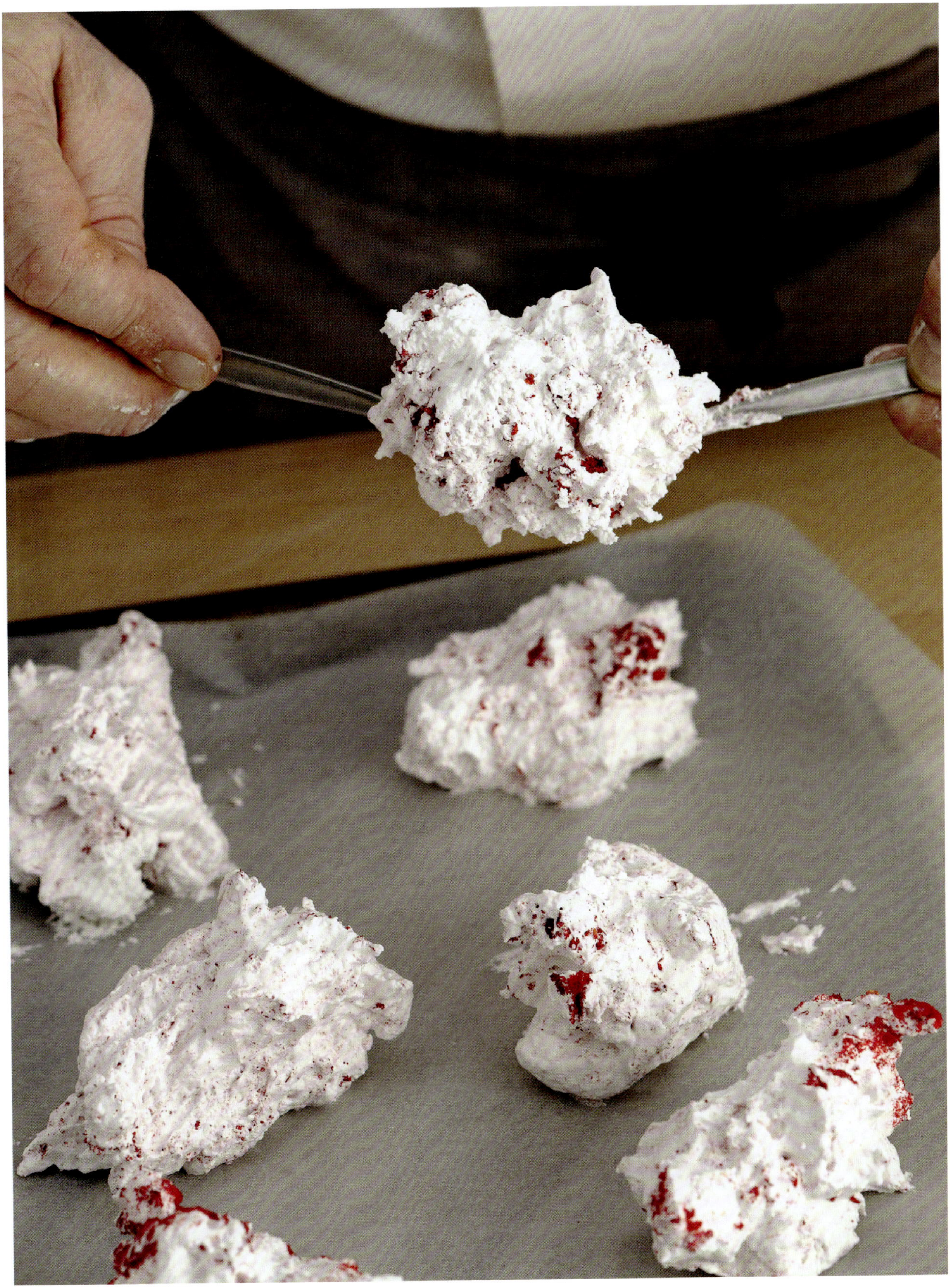

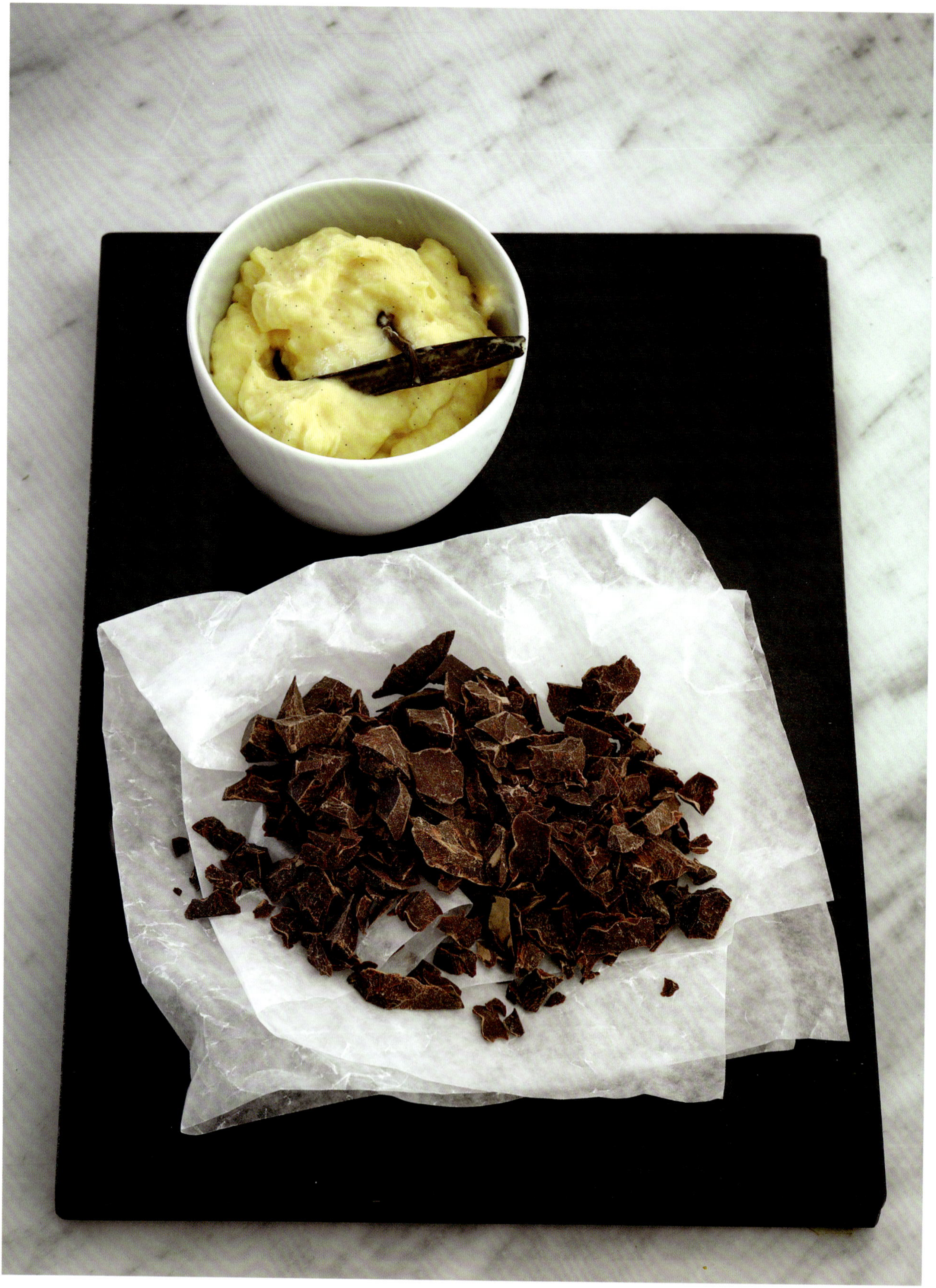

Creams

These are all the creams that we use throughout the recipes in this book and in our bakery. They are very versatile and some are actually a combination of two different creams, brought together to give different textures and flavours. They are also interchangeable, so if you like, you can substitute a simple cream for a more complex one and vice versa. Flavourings such as chocolate can be added (see overleaf).

Crème pâtissière

The all-purpose pastry cream is really a thickened custard, which can be used in any number of confections and desserts, from a filling for éclairs to a base for fruit tarts. You can use semi-skimmed milk if you prefer.

MAKES ABOUT 400G

250ml whole milk
1 vanilla pod
3 medium egg yolks
60g caster sugar
25g plain flour

Pour the milk into a heavy-bottomed pan. Lay the vanilla pod on a chopping board and slice along its length with a sharp knife. Open out and scrape the seeds into the milk, then put the halved pods in too.

Put the eggs and sugar into a bowl and whisk until pale and creamy. Add the flour and mix until smooth.

Put the pan of milk over a medium heat, bring to just under the boil, take off the heat and slowly pour half of it into the egg, sugar and flour mixture, whisking well as you do so. Add the remainder of the milk and whisk in well, then pour the mixture back into the pan.

(Continues overleaf)

Bring to the boil, whisking all the time, then keep boiling and whisking for 1 minute, take off the heat and pour into a clean bowl.

Scoop out the halves of the vanilla pod. You can wash and dry them and keep them in a jar of sugar, which will give you vanilla-flavoured sugar for use in all your baking. Cover the surface of the bowl with greaseproof paper straight away, as this will help to prevent a skin from forming. Cool and then keep in the fridge until ready to use.

FOR COFFEE CRÈME PÂTISSIÈRE: add 1 tablespoon of good ground coffee to the milk and then follow the recipe as usual.

FOR CHOCOLATE CRÈME PÂTISSIÈRE: add 3 teaspoons of cocoa powder to the milk and then follow the recipe as usual. Alternatively, you can use 75g of dark, milk or white chocolate chips.

Crème Chantilly

Probably the quickest, most simple and versatile cream of them all – it is nice and light for filling éclairs, or simply to serve with any tart or ice cream. You can perfume it with a few drops of rosewater or orange water instead of the vanilla extract if you prefer.

MAKES ABOUT 300G

250ml whipping or double cream
2 tablespoons caster sugar
a few drops of vanilla extract or paste

Whisk the ingredients together until thick, but don't over-whisk, or the cream will turn to butter!

Crème au beurre

This is simply crème pâtissière with butter added – the advantage of this is that the butter sets the cream quite firmly, so it is good in recipes where you need the cream to hold its shape.

MAKES ABOUT 300G

200g cold crème pâtissière (see page 41)
100g butter, cut into pieces and allowed to become very soft

Take your cold crème pâtissière from the fridge and whisk it until it has the consistency of a light mayonnaise, then whisk in the pieces of butter a little at a time until the cream is smooth and has turned quite white.

Crème légère

This is a beautiful cream and my favourite. It is lighter than crème au beurre, but more substantial than Chantilly, and I always think it has the flavour of a great vanilla ice cream, but without being frozen. You could use it as an alternative to crème au beurre for the Fraisier on page 93, for filling éclairs, or simply to fill a sweet pastry tart case and then top it with fresh fruit.

MAKES ABOUT 300G

200g cold crème pâtissière (see page 41)
100ml double cream

Take your cold crème pâtissière from the fridge and whisk it until it has the consistency of a light mayonnaise.

Whisk the double cream until thick and fluffy then fold into the crème pâtissière.

Crème anglaise

We use this for the Îles Flottantes on page 98 and the jelly on page 103, but you can serve it with any pudding or tart.

You could also substitute double cream for the milk, and churn it in an ice cream maker to make a great vanilla ice cream.

MAKES ABOUT 320G

3 medium egg yolks
40g caster sugar
250ml full fat milk
½ vanilla pod

Put the eggs and sugar into a bowl and whisk until pale and creamy.

Put the milk and vanilla pod and seeds into a heavy-bottomed pan and bring to just under the boil. Pour the milk slowly into the egg mixture, whisking well as you do so.

Return the mixture to the pan over a medium heat. Using a wooden spoon, stir continuously in a figure of 8 until the cream thickens enough to coat the back of a spoon. (To test, lift the spoon out of the cream and draw a line down the back of the spoon. If the line stays clean it is ready.)

Strain immediately into a clean bowl and continue stirring for a few minutes. Remove the vanilla pod. Either serve hot or leave to cool, covered with a sheet of greaseproof paper to prevent a skin forming. Once cool, store in the fridge until you are ready to use it.

Caramelised nuts

These are great to have on hand in the kitchen – you can make up batches of different varieties of nuts, and they will keep for about three months in airtight jars. You can then use them whenever you like, for example to make the Chocolate Lollipops on page 182.

MAKES ABOUT 300G

75g caster sugar
250g whole Brazil nuts, almonds, hazelnuts or pistachio nuts (shelled weight)

Heat the sugar in a pan until it dissolves and begins to bubble. Continue cooking until it is golden brown (if you have a sugar thermometer, the temperature will be 140°C). Take off the heat and stir in the nuts.

Have ready a non-stick baking tray or a silicone mat.

Lift the nuts out of the pan with a slotted spoon and spread them over the tray or mat so that they stay separate and don't touch one another. Leave to become cold and solidified, then transfer the nuts to an airtight jar.

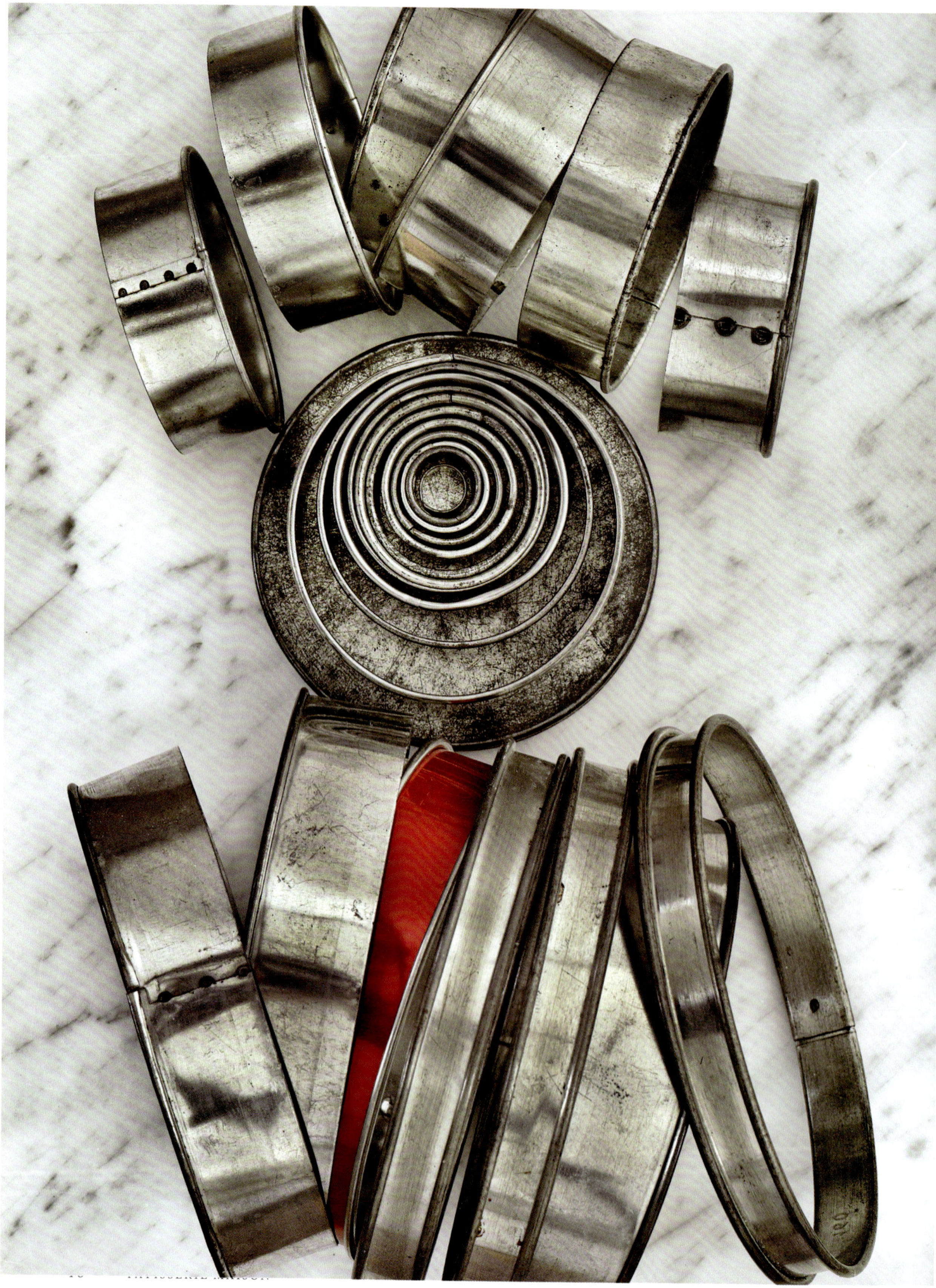

Raspberry jam

I always have home-made or high-quality jams on hand, for use in all kinds of assemblies and cakes. We serve this raspberry jam for breakfast before classes at the cooking school and everyone always asks for the recipe, so here it is. It is a very quick jam to make, cooked only briefly so that you retain all the vibrant colour and sharpness of the berries. Out of season you can still make it using frozen raspberries. You can use a thermometer to gauge when it is ready, or do the old-fashioned 'crinkle' test.

MAKES 2 SMALL (200G) KILNER JARS

½ teaspoon pectin powder
400g granulated sugar
500g raspberries
juice of 1 lemon
small pinch of salt

If you don't have a thermometer, put a plate into the fridge before you start so that it is well chilled.

Mix the pectin powder into the sugar.

Put all the ingredients in a large, heavy-based pan and bring to the boil. If you have a thermometer, bring the temperature up to 106°C – this will take about 10 minutes – then take off the heat.

Alternatively, after the jam has boiled for 10 minutes, take your saucer from the fridge and spoon a teaspoon of jam onto it. Put it back in the fridge for a minute, then with your finger, push the jam to see if it forms a crinkly skin. If so, it is ready. If not, let it boil for a further minute and then test again.

While the jam is still hot, pot it in sterilised jars (see page 51).

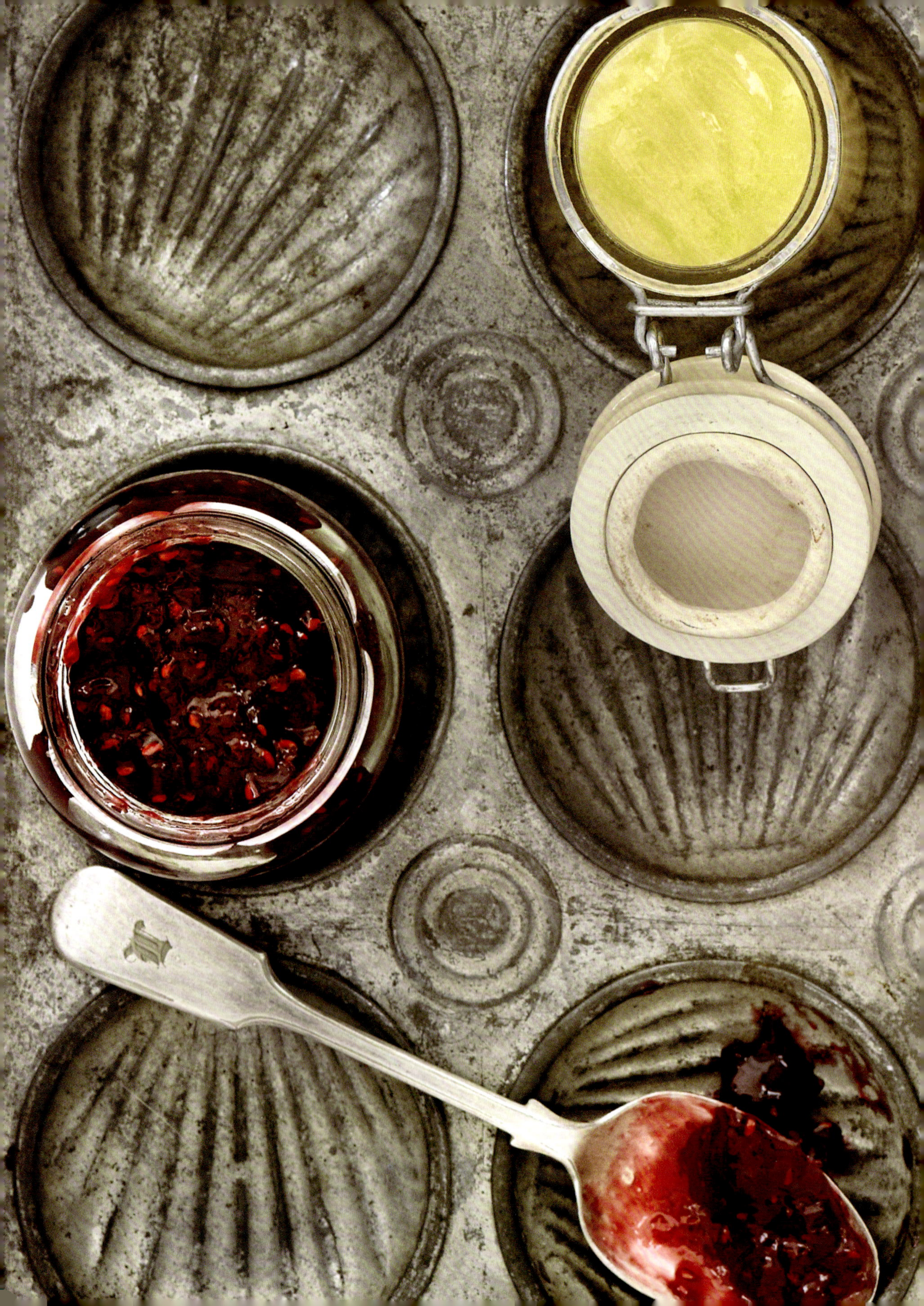

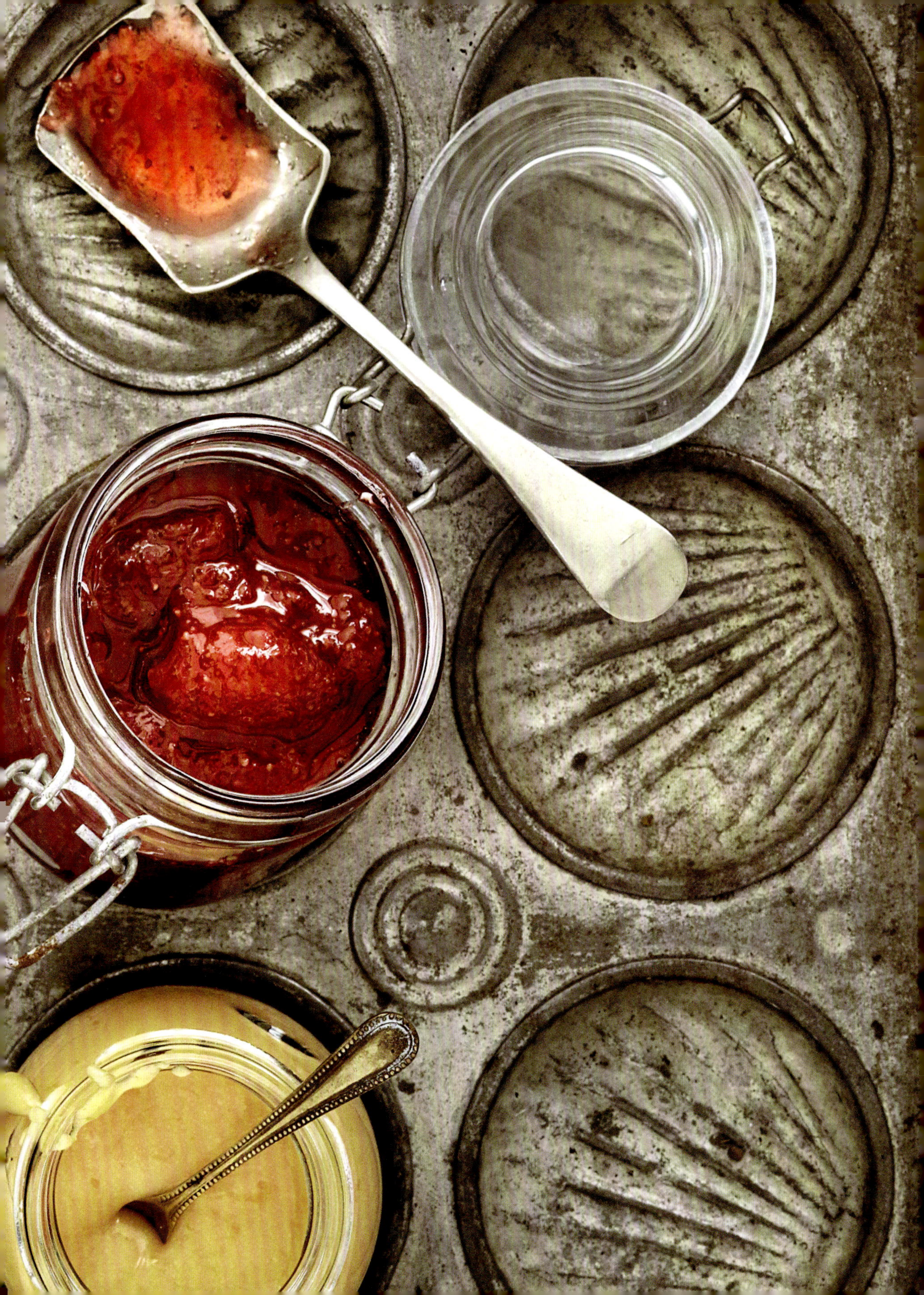

Strawberry jam

MAKES 2 SMALL (200G) KILNER JARS

1 teaspoon pectin powder
450g granulated sugar
500g strawberries, cleaned and hulled
juice of 2 lemons

If you don't have a thermometer, put a plate into the fridge before you start so that it is well chilled.

Mix the pectin powder into the sugar.

Put the strawberries in a pan and give them a squash with a potato masher to release a little of their juices. Add the sugar and lemon juice and bring to the boil. If you have a thermometer, bring the temperature up to 106°C – this will take about 10 minutes – then take off the heat.

Alternatively, after the jam has boiled for 10 minutes, take your saucer from the fridge and spoon a teaspoon of jam onto it. Put it back in the fridge for a minute, then with your finger, push the jam to see if it forms a crinkly skin. If so, it is ready. If not, let it boil for a further minute and then test again.

While the jam is still hot, pot it in sterilised jars (see page 51).

Lemon curd

We use this in the Lemon Trifles on page 103, or you could substitute it for the blood orange cream, made using the same technique, that is used in the tart on page 146. It also makes a good filling for choux buns, mixed in a ratio of one part curd to three parts crème pâtissière (see page 41) or Chantilly cream (see page 42).

Lemon curd is very simple to make: you just need to make sure that you let it thicken gently in a bowl over your pan of barely simmering water, watching and whisking all the time. If it goes too fast it can turn into scrambled egg, but if this starts to happen you can still rescue it by taking the pan off the heat and pushing the mixture through a fine sieve into a clean heatproof bowl. Put this over your pan as before, on a low heat, and carry on.

You can keep the curd in a bowl in the fridge (covered in clingfilm) for 3–4 days. Or pot it while it is still hot, in sterilised jars, in which case it will keep for up to two months. I sterilise my jars by putting them through a dishwasher cycle, then into a preheated oven at 100°C/gas ¼ for 15 minutes to dry out completely.

MAKES 2 SMALL (200G) KILNER JARS

zest and juice of 3 medium unwaxed lemons
2 large eggs
200g caster sugar
125g unsalted butter
1 teaspoon cornflour

In a heatproof bowl, whisk all the ingredients together, then put the bowl over a pan of barely simmering water, making sure the base doesn't actually touch the water. Whisk constantly over a low heat, moving the mixture around the bowl so that none sticks to the sides. Once it starts to become a little thicker than double cream, continue to whisk for one more minute then take off the heat.

To test that the mixture is ready, scoop a little of it with a teaspoon and push it against the inside of the bowl near the top. It should stay put without dripping. If it doesn't, put it back over the heat and whisk very briefly for another minute at a time, until it passes the test. Either pot into sterilised jars while still hot, or leave to cool, then put in the fridge until ready to use.

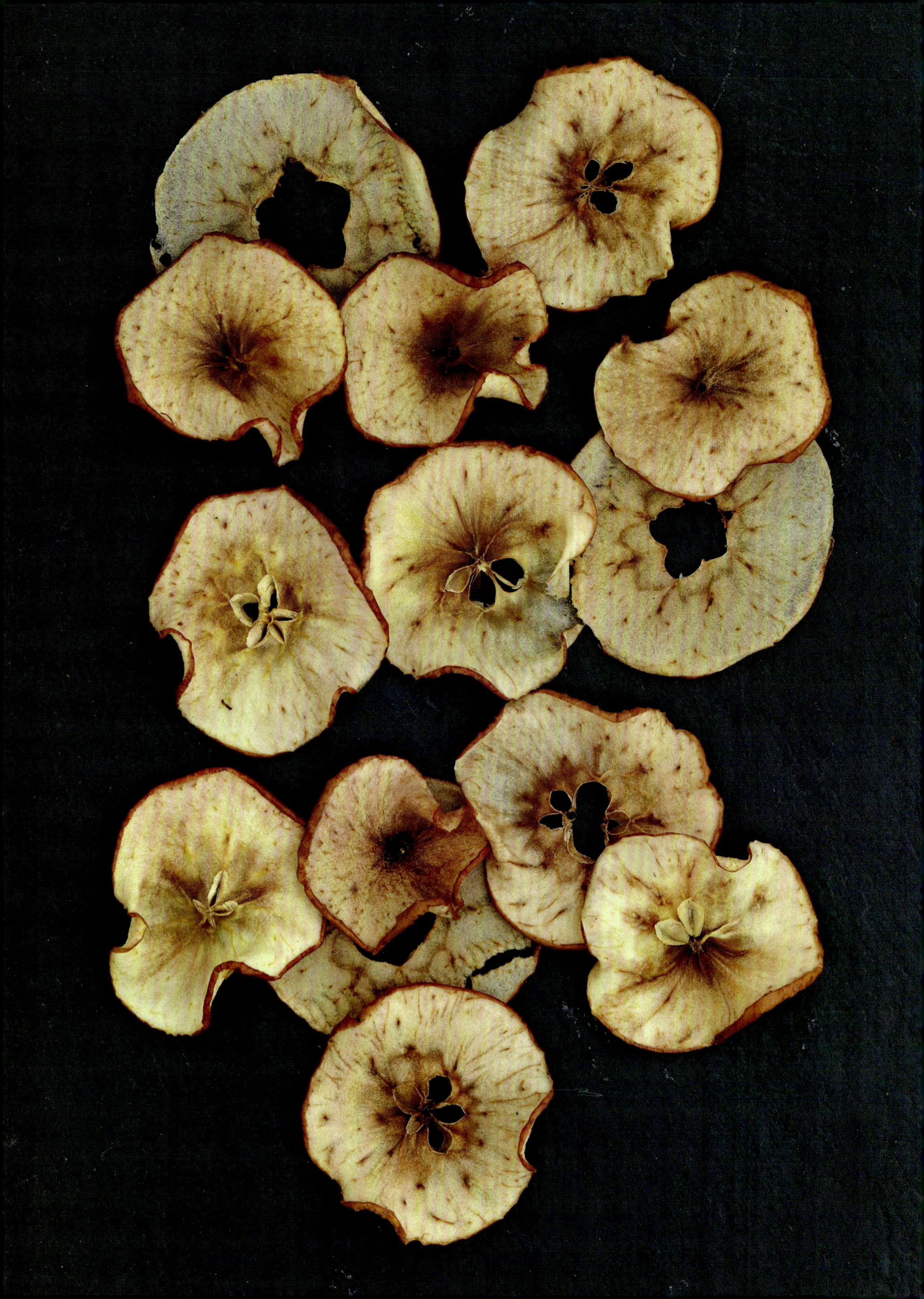

Drying fruit

You can buy special dehydrators for drying fruit, or a plate-warming drawer is fantastic for the job. Alternatively, dry your fruit after you have been using your oven and have switched it off. Slice the fruit and arrange on a non-stick baking tray or, better still, a silicone mat, then wait until the temperature has gone down to around 80–90°C before putting it in the oven. Leave overnight, and by morning the fruit should be ready: dry, but not brittle. If it still has too much moisure in it, turn your oven back on to the lowest temperature possible and leave in for a while longer.

The fruits that I mainly dry in this way are apples, bananas and pineapple, but you can also experiment with slices of mango, papaya, strawberry – whatever you like.

APPLE:
Don't peel them, just slice horizontally, about 2mm thick. Ignore the core, just cut through it. The pips will fall out after drying, and the slices look more attractive with little holes in the middle where the pips have been.

BANANA:
Use firm ones with their skins verging on green, rather than very yellow ones, which will be too soft. Peel them and slice them on the diagonal, 3–4mm thick (if you slice them too thinly, they will lose their shape and be difficult to use). Rub a little lemon juice over the top of each slice before drying, as bananas turn dark very quickly.

PINEAPPLE:
Cut the skin off and then slice crossways – about 5mm thick. Take a small pastry cutter and use it to stamp out the hard centre, then you can dry the rings whole, or cut them into wedges.

Decorating with cocoa powder and chocolate

Don't underestimate the power of a little dusting of cocoa powder over cakes or puddings. Where you have chocolate icing, try dusting half of it, using a small, very fine sieve (you can even dust through one of the many stencils you can buy at baking shops). If you want a sharp edge, lay a sheet of baking paper over one area of the icing, then dust the remaining area and lift off the paper – you will be surprised how the contrast of shiny and matt creates a smart effect.

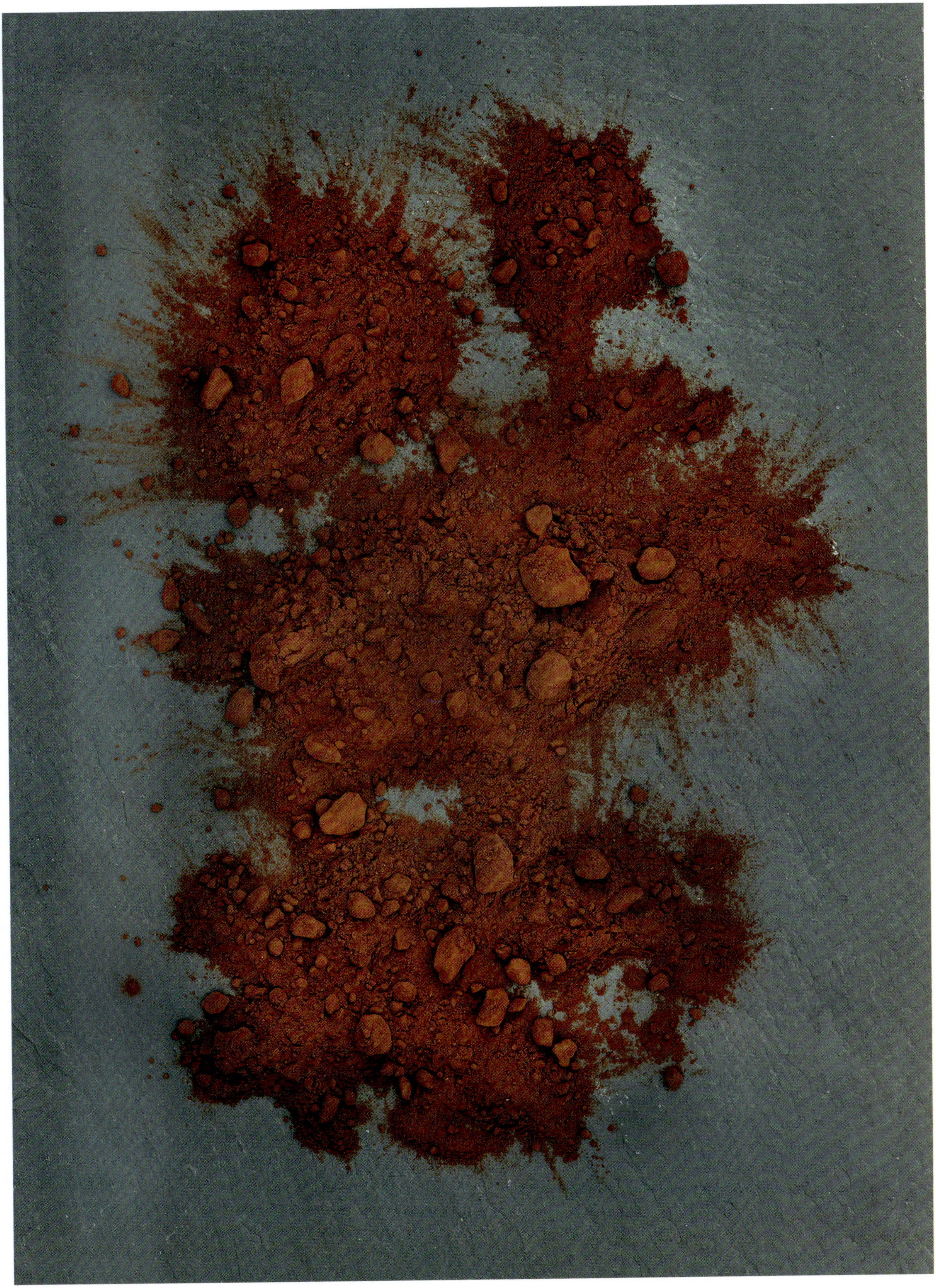

Chocolate shavings and 'pencils'

In France, chocolate shavings and curls are known as *copeaux*, and they are a very effective way of adding some drama to a cake or tart.

Have ready a piece of clean marble, or a heavy non-stick baking tray – the idea is that warm chocolate goes straight onto something cold to set it.

Break some good chocolate of your choice (it can be dark, milk or white) into chunks, put them in a heatproof bowl over a pan of barely simmering water – make sure the water comes close to the bottom of the bowl but doesn't actually touch it. Keep the heat very low so that you don't get steam into the bowl, as this can make the chocolate become dull-looking and stiff. Keep stirring all the time and let the chocolate melt slowly, then remove the bowl from the heat and pour it onto your marble or baking tray, spreading it out with a palette knife to about 2mm thick (no thinner, or it won't roll).

Leave at room temperature until set, but not completely hard, then take a wide spatula or metal scraper and push it through the chocolate. The further you do so the more the chocolate will roll up into curls and 'pencils'.

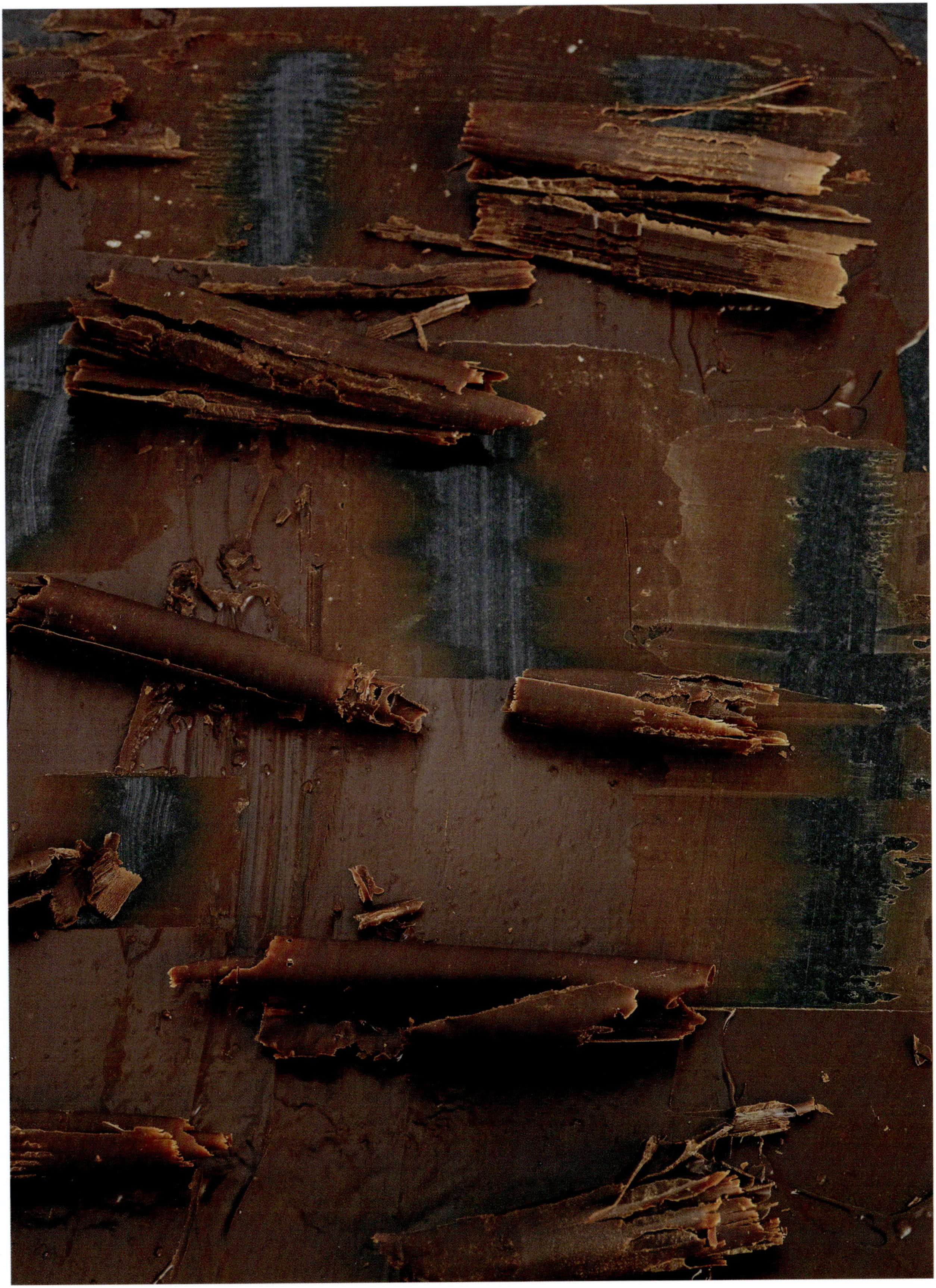

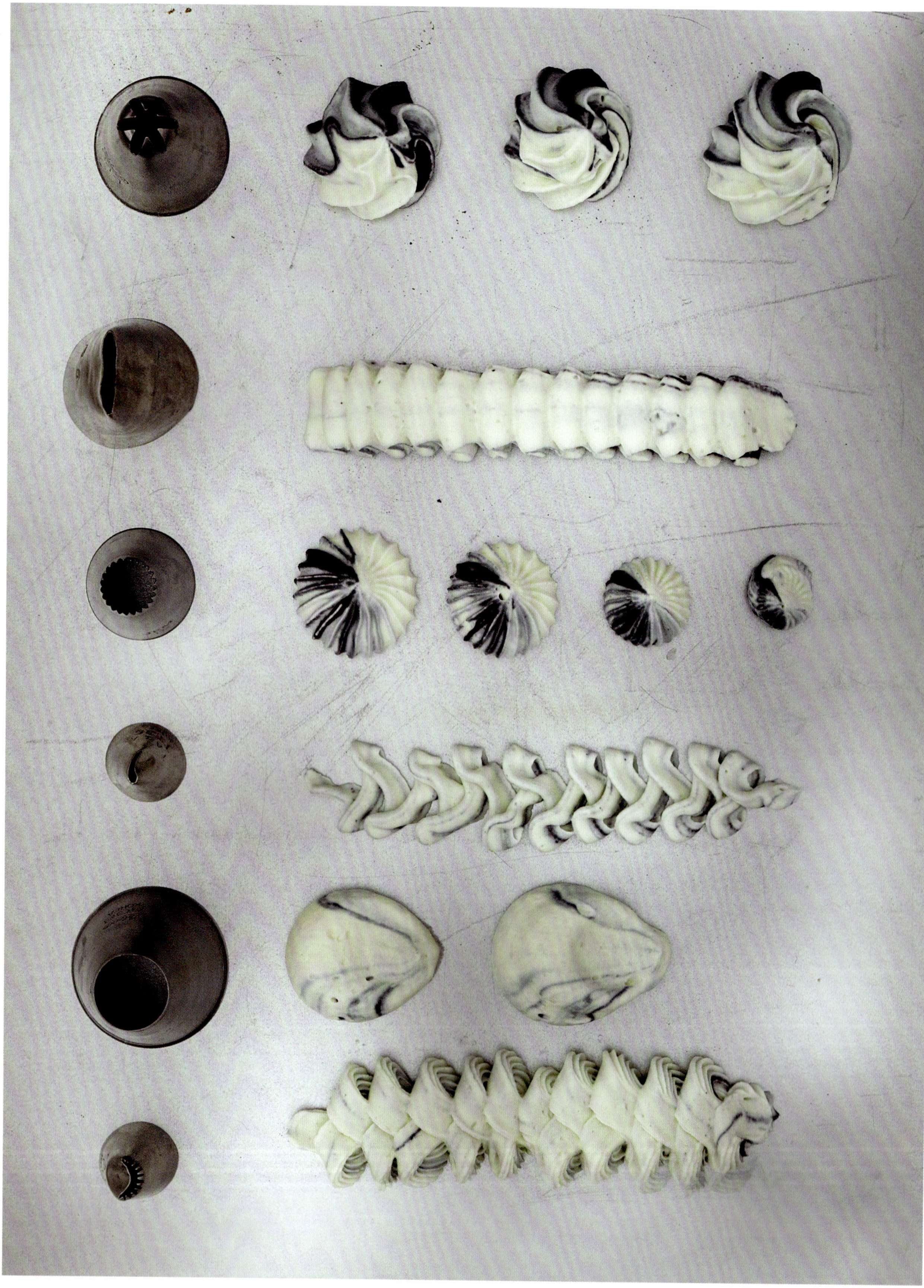

Piping creams

You can achieve easy, eye-catching patterns on tops of cakes and mousses, or fillings for éclairs, just by piping one of the creams on pages 41–44 using different shapes and sizes of nozzle. The tiniest dot of coloured food paste added to your icing, but just streaked through rather than mixed in thoroughly, will give a two-tone effect.

As with choux pastry, the first thing to do is be comfortable with filling a piping bag (see page 24). Then experiment with different nozzles. I have a collection of metal ones, because when I first started baking these were the only ones available, and there is something quite pleasing and permanent about metal. However, metal nozzles can get squashed out of shape if you are not careful with them, whereas plastic ones tend to hold their form better. Both do a good job, though, so it is up to you which you go for. The more you try out different ones you will discover that just by moving your wrist differently, you can make all kinds of new shapes. It is difficult to give specific names to the nozzles I have used for the examples in the picture opposite, as each manufacturer tends to have their own, but below is a rough guide:

1. This shape, known as *rosace,* is made with a large star nozzle. You need to squeeze and turn the wrist quickly in an anti-clockwise direction.

2. This is a wide ribbon nozzle. The skill here is to start at the top and work downwards, moving the nozzle forwards and backwards, forwards and backwards, in a wave-like motion.

3. This shape is made using a small star nozzle with tiny 'teeth'. Squeeze and lift up again straight away. The more pressure you use the bigger the shape.

4. A small petal nozzle can be used to create a single tear, or a woven effect. Start at the top and then move the nozzle repeatedly from right to left in a figure of 8.

5. A large plain nozzle can be used to make these shell-like shapes by squeezing and pressing downwards then dragging the nozzle slightly towards you.

6. A small shell nozzle can be piped in the same way as number 4 above.

Small

A COLLECTION OF SWEET THINGS
MADE IN INDIVIDUAL PORTIONS

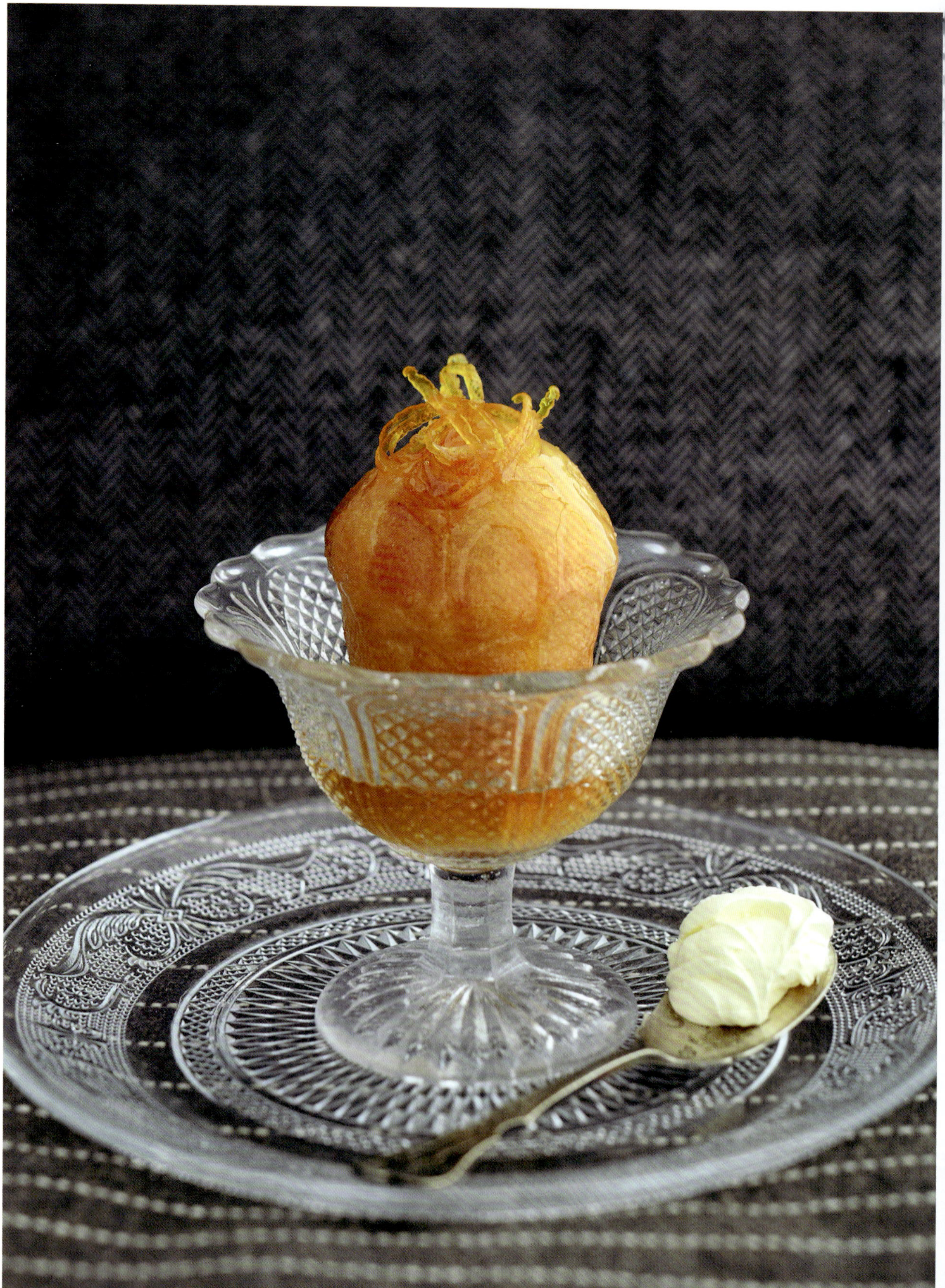

Rum baba

Babas are a classic Sunday lunch dessert in France. Often they are made in ring moulds, but in the bakery where I served my apprenticeship we used to bake them in dariole moulds, and this is the way I have continued to do them, as I like the shape. You also frequently see them decorated elaborately with cream and glacé cherries or other fruits, but I prefer to go for minimal decoration and maximum flavour. So I serve the babas with some of the good strong rum syrup in which they have soaked and just a little poached orange peel on top.

This recipe makes quite a lot of babas – around eighteen – as it is easier to make the batter using a food mixer than by hand, but you need a certain volume to work with. However, you can bake the babas and then freeze any that you don't want to serve immediately. You can also make the syrup and keep it in a plastic box in the fridge for up to three months, ready to soak the defrosted babas in it.

MAKES ABOUT 18 TALL MOULDS

FOR THE FERMENT:
150g strong bread flour
15g fresh yeast
150ml warm milk

FOR THE BATTER:
4 medium eggs
150g butter at room temperature, plus a little
　　extra for greasing the moulds
50g caster sugar
½ teaspoon salt
125ml warm milk
400g strong bread flour
grated zest of 1 orange

FOR THE SYRUP:
1 orange
1 lemon
800g sugar
500ml water
200ml rum

(Continues overleaf)

SMALL

First make the ferment. Place the flour in a bowl. Crumble the yeast into it by rubbing it between your fingertips. Whisk in the milk until the ferment is thick.

Leave for at least 2 hours at room temperature and out of draughts, by which time it will become bubbly (as shown in the right of the picture).

Using a mixer with a dough hook, beat the ferment with all the batter ingredients until the mixture is strong, elastic and stretchy.

Grease the moulds heavily with butter.

I find it easiest to pipe the mixture into the moulds, but if you don't want to do this, you can just moisten your hands with water then scoop out small pieces of the batter with your fingers and drop them into the moulds. Either way, fill the moulds two thirds full.

(Continues overleaf)

Leave the moulds in a warm place for about 40–50 minutes until the mixture has risen about 1cm above the rims of the moulds.

Preheat the oven to 190°C/gas 5.

For the syrup, first take off the orange and lemon peel in long, thin strips (ideally use a julienne peeler; or use a vegetable peeler and then cut the strips into thinner lengths) then put into a pan. Squeeze the juice and add to the pan along with the sugar and the water. Bring to the boil then turn down the heat and simmer for about 5–10 minutes until it thickens slightly into a syrup. Take off the heat, add the rum and allow to cool until just warm, then pour into a dish wide enough to hold the babas.

Meanwhile bake the babas in the preheated oven for about 15–20 minutes until they are golden and have risen up like champagne corks. Carefully turn each one out of its mould and cool on a wire rack. (At this point you can freeze any that you don't want to use immediately.)

Put the babas into the syrup, turning them to coat really well, and leave for 2–3 hours at room temperature so that they soak up as much syrup as possible. Very gently prod them every so often, and when they feel soft, they are ready.

Place each baba into a glass bowl or small dish. Scoop out some of the strips of peel from the syrup – a pair of kitchen tweezers is ideal for this – and curl on top of each baba. Spoon a little of the syrup around and serve.

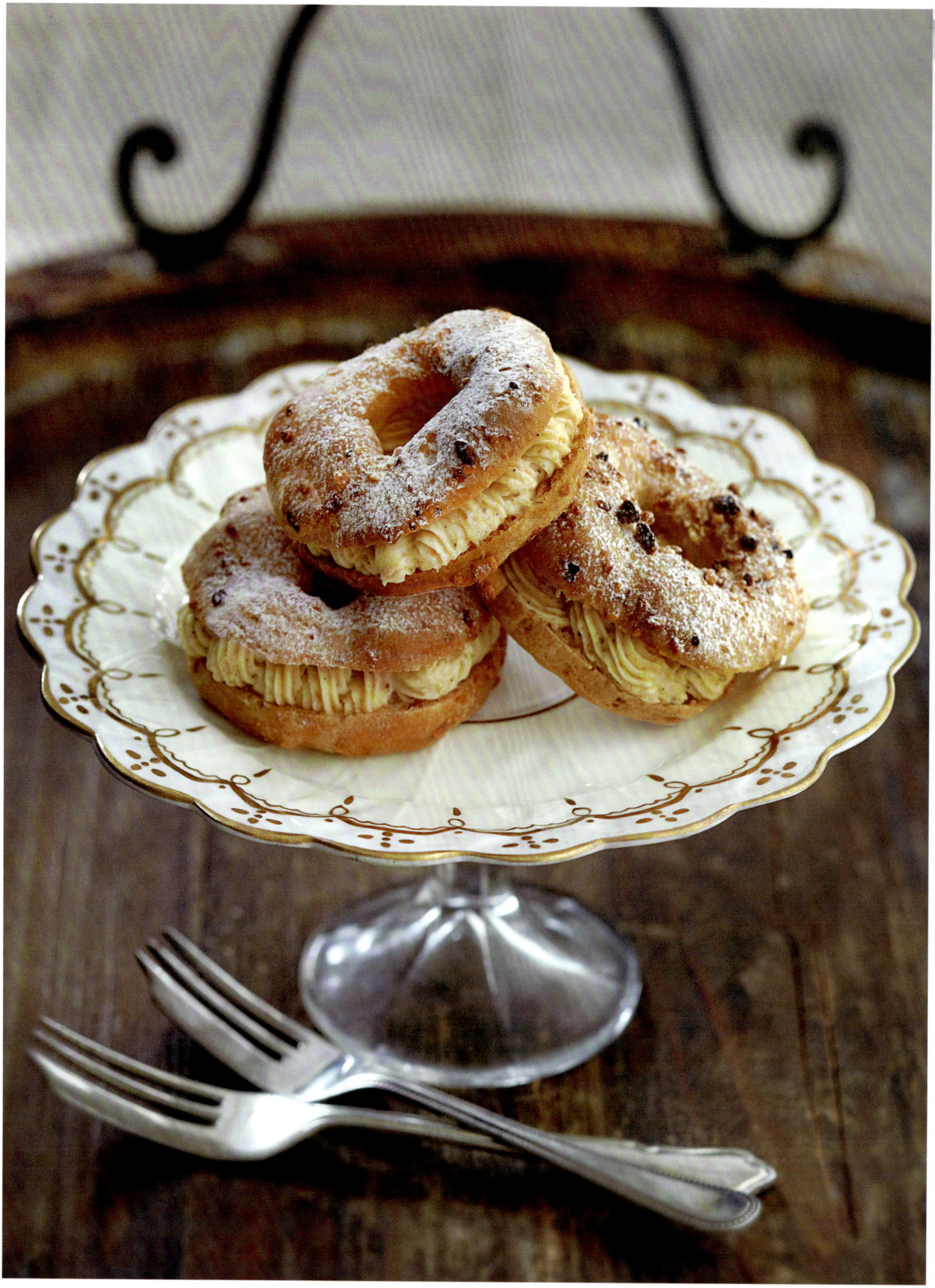

Paris Brest

These were created in 1891 to celebrate the first 1200km Paris-to-Brest bike race, one of cycling's oldest events. It is said that a pastry chef who was working along the route came up with the idea of the choux pastry rings to represent the puffy pneumatic tyres that were taking over from the old solid rubber ones.

Leave the skin on the nuts as this gives flavour and colour.

MAKES 10–12

100g hazelnuts in their skins
1 quantity crème au beurre (see page 43)
1 quantity choux pastry mixture (see page 20)
1 medium egg, beaten with a pinch of salt
icing sugar, for dusting

Preheat the oven to 200°C/gas 6.

Spread the hazelnuts out over a baking tray and put into the oven for about 10 minutes, shaking the tray occasionally so that they toast evenly. Take out of the oven, leave to cool, then crush half of them with a rolling pin and keep to one side. Put the rest into a coffee grinder, or use a pestle and mortar to grind them into a paste. Mix this into the crème au beurre, and keep to one side.

Snip the corner of a piping bag, if using a disposable one, insert a large star nozzle, fill with the choux pastry mixture, and then pipe 10–12 circles of around 8–10cm onto a silicone mat or non-stick baking tray (see picture on page 25). Brush lightly with the beaten egg. Scatter your reserved crushed nuts on top and put into the preheated oven.

(Continues overleaf)

Turn the oven down to 190°C/gas 5 and leave for about 15 minutes, until light golden and puffed up, turning the tray around halfway through. For the last few minutes of baking, prop the oven door slightly ajar with a wooden spoon to allow the steam to escape, and help the choux to dry out properly. Remove the tray from the oven and leave to cool.

Cut in half horizontally, pipe the base of each with the reserved hazelnut cream, replace the top and dust with icing sugar.

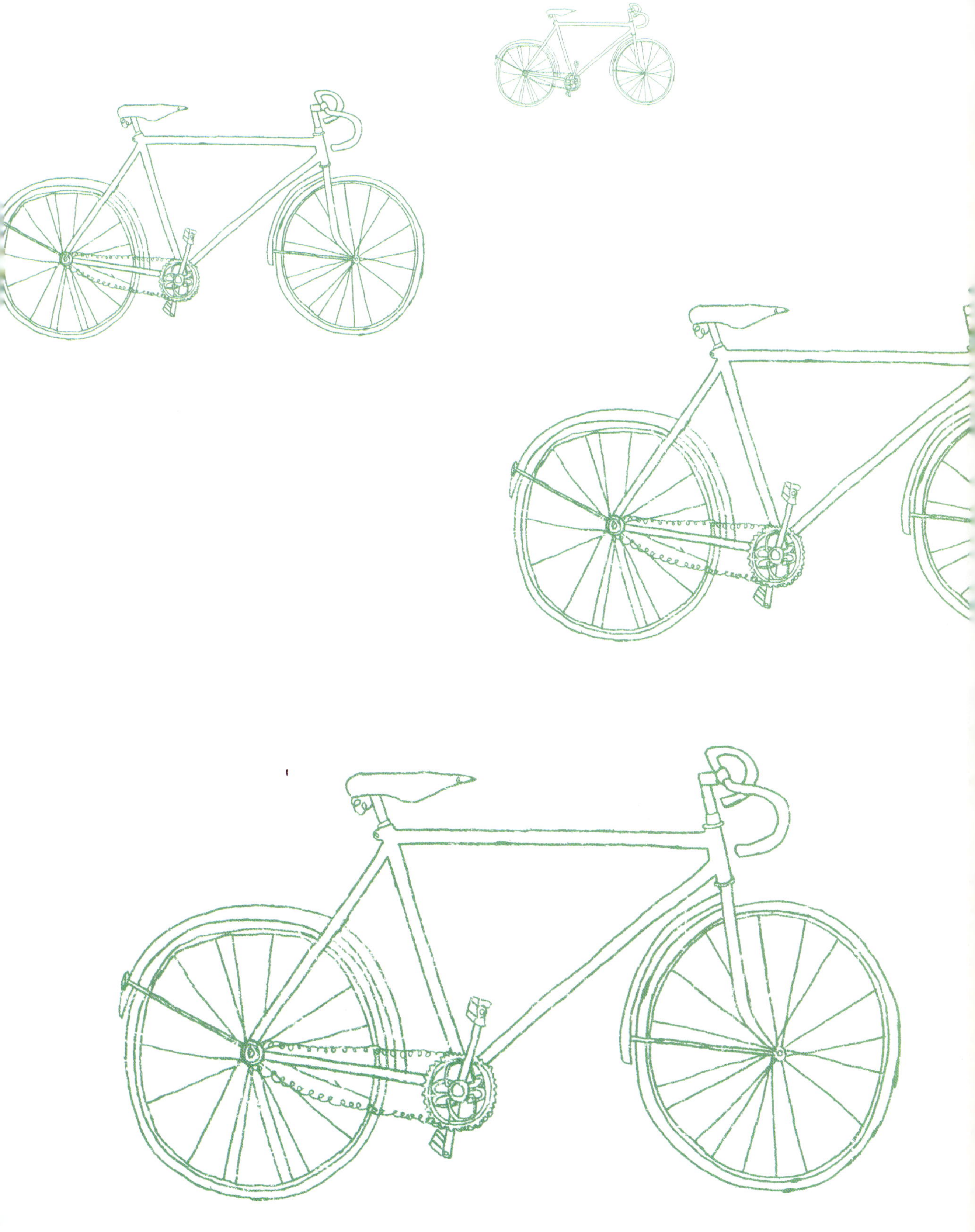

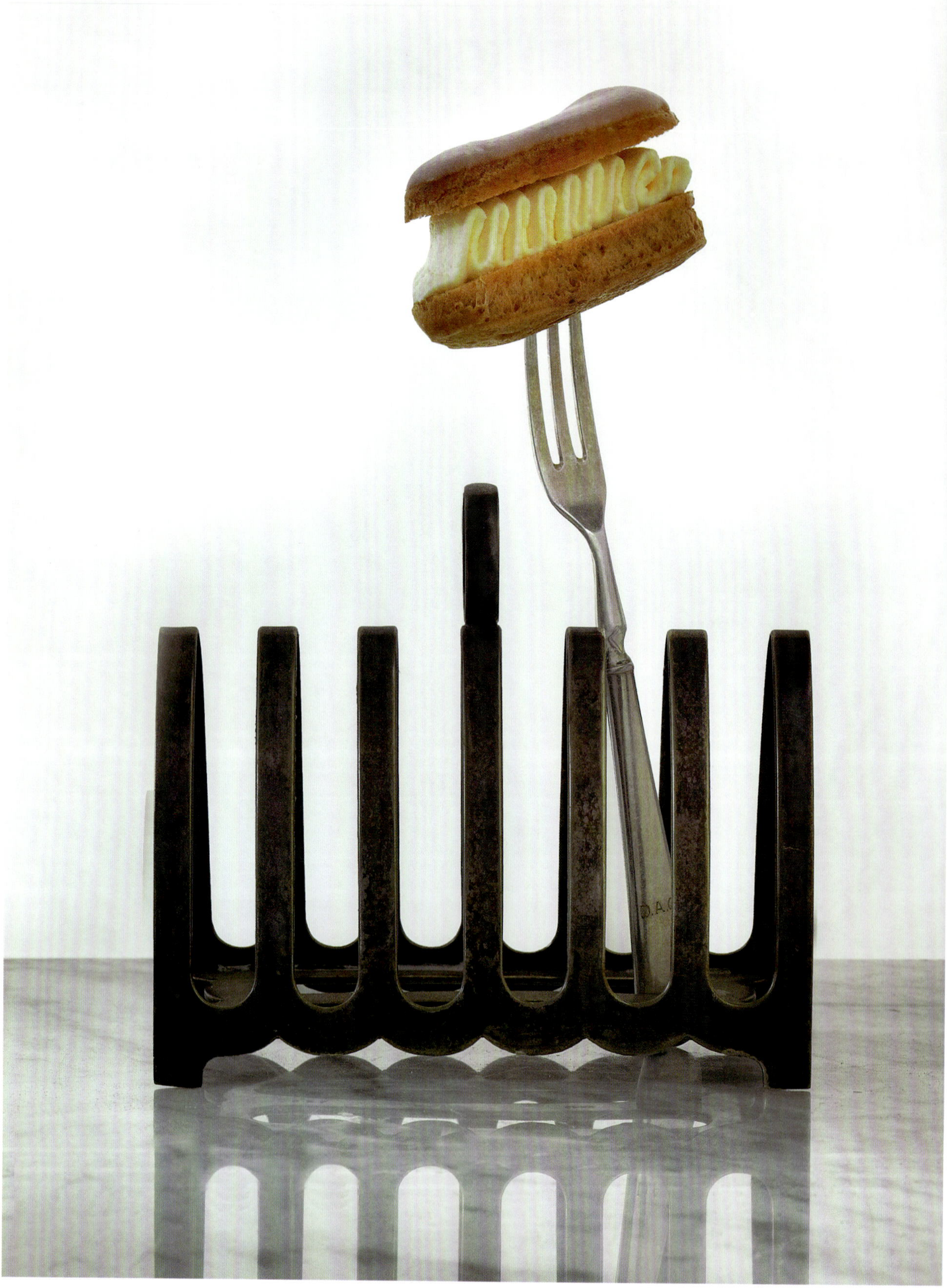

Mini coffee, chocolate, rosewater and almond éclairs

There are two different ways to fill éclairs. You can make a small hole in the base (or at one end) of the éclair, and using a piping bag with a straight nozzle (about 5mm), squeeze the cream into the hollow. This way you don't actually see the cream from the outside. Alternatively, you can halve the éclairs all the way along their length – or almost all the way – and then pipe in the cream, using an interesting nozzle (see page 59), which can make them look quite special. In the following recipes I have suggested one or the other technique, but it is really up to you.

You can use Chantilly cream for the filling, which is nice and light, or crème pâtissière, which is more substantial.

If you are glazing the éclairs with chocolate you don't need a very high percentage of cocoa solids or the glaze will be quite bitter. A good 53% dark or milk chocolate is fine. Dusting half of the glaze with some cocoa powder is an easy way of making the éclairs look smart.

MAKES 24 SMALL ÉCLAIRS

1 quantity choux pastry mixture
   (see page 20)
a little butter for greasing the baking tray

FOR CHOCOLATE ÉCLAIRS:

1 quantity crème Chantilly (see page 42)
400g good milk or dark chocolate
   (53% cocoa solids), broken into chunks
cocoa powder, for dusting

FOR COFFEE ÉCLAIRS:

1 quantity coffee crème pâtissière
   (see page 42)
300g white fondant icing
about 2 tablespoons water
a few drops of coffee essence
24 coffee beans, for decoration (optional)

FOR ROSEWATER ÉCLAIRS:

1 quantity crème Chantilly made with a few drops of rosewater instead of vanilla
   (see page 42)
300g white fondant icing
about 2 tablespoons water
a few drops of red food colouring

(Continues overleaf)

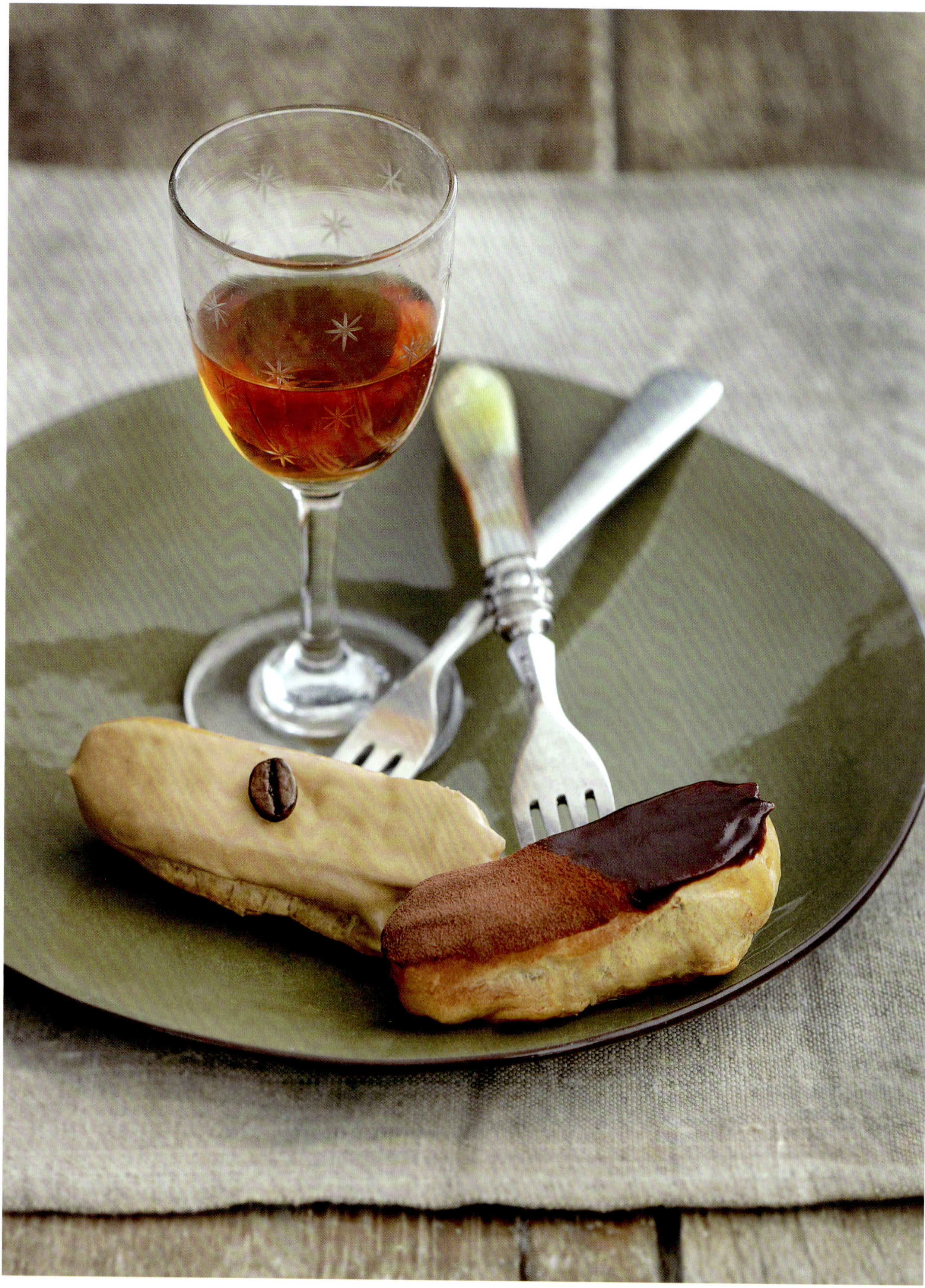

Preheat the oven to 190°C/gas 5. Lightly grease a non-stick baking tray or have ready a silicone mat.

Snip off the corner of a piping bag, if using a disposable one, insert a plain nozzle about 1cm in diameter, then fill with the choux pastry mixture and pipe 24 lines of around 8cm onto your baking tray or mat (see picture on page 25).

Bake in the preheated oven for 12–15 minutes until golden and puffed up. For the last 4 minutes of baking, leave the oven door slightly ajar to allow the steam to escape, and help the drying process. Remove the tray from the oven and leave to cool.

For chocolate éclairs:

Take each éclair, and use a skewer to make a hole large enough to insert your piping nozzle (5mm) in the centre of the underside. Fill a medium piping bag with Chantilly cream and squeeze gently until you can feel the cream filling the inside of the éclair.

Put the chocolate into a heatproof bowl over a pan of barely simmering water – make sure the water comes close to the bottom of the bowl but doesn't actually touch it. Keep the heat very low so that you don't get steam into the bowl, as this can make the chocolate become dull-looking and stiff. Keep stirring all the time and let the chocolate melt slowly, then remove the bowl from the heat.

One by one, dip the tops of the eclairs into the chocolate. Let the excess drain off into the bowl and then place on a rack until the chocolate has set. If you want to dust half of each top with cocoa powder, use a small piece of baking paper as a guide. Lay it across the first glazed top at an angle, and dust the other half finely with cocoa powder, using a small, fine sieve.

For coffee éclairs:

Fill with coffee crème pâtissière as for the chocolate éclairs on the previous page.

For the icing, put the fondant and water in a pan over a very low heat and beat with a wooden spoon until it melts. Stir in the coffee essence. Take off the heat.

Take the éclairs and dip the tops into the icing as for the chocolate éclairs on the previous page, then decorate each one, if you like, with a coffee bean.

For rosewater éclairs:

This time, to fill the éclairs, cut them carefully in half lengthways. Keep the top halves to one side, then using a piping bag fitted with a flat nozzle (or similar, see page 59), pipe the cream along the length of the lower halves, lifting the nozzle up and down as you go, to create a wave effect.

For the icing, put the fondant and water in a pan over a very low heat and beat with a wooden spoon until it melts. Stir in the red colouring. Take off the heat.

Dip each top half into the icing as for the coffee éclairs above, and then assemble.

Almond éclairs

The addition of toasted, flaked almonds on top gives a little crunchiness and an unusual look to these little éclairs.

MAKES 24 SMALL ÉCLAIRS

a little butter for greasing the baking tray
4 tablespoons flaked almonds
1 quantity choux pastry mixture (see page 20)
2 tablespoons ground almonds
2 tablespoons caster sugar
1 quantity crème Chantilly (see page 42)

FOR THE CARAMEL:
200g caster sugar
2 tablespoons water

Preheat the oven to 190°C/gas 5. Lightly grease a non-stick baking tray or have ready a silicone mat.

Toast the flaked almonds lightly in a dry frying pan until pale golden. Take off the heat and transfer to a plate. Keep to one side.

Snip off the corner of a piping bag, if using a disposable one, insert a plain nozzle about 1cm in diameter and fill with the choux pastry mixture.

Pipe 24 lines of around 8cm onto your baking tray or mat.

Mix the ground almonds with the sugar and sprinkle a little on top of each éclair.

Bake in the preheated oven for 12–15 minutes until golden and puffed up. For the last 4 minutes of baking, leave the oven door slightly ajar to allow the steam to escape, and help the drying process. Remove the tray from the oven and leave to cool.

(Continues overleaf)

Make a caramel by putting the sugar in a pan with the water, bring to the boil and continue to boil until golden brown (if you have a sugar thermometer, the temperature will be 140°C). It will be really hot, so be careful.

Spear each éclair with a fork and dip the top just into the surface of the caramel, and then straight onto the reserved plate of toasted almonds so that a cluster of them clings to the surface. Leave to set on a wire rack.

When the caramel has set, cut each éclair horizontally almost to the end, but not quite. Snip off the corner of a piping bag, if using a disposable one, insert a plain nozzle, and fill with Chantilly cream. One at a time, hold an éclair in your hand, prise the 'lid' up a little and pipe in the cream, squeezing and lifting as you go in a 'wave' fashion.

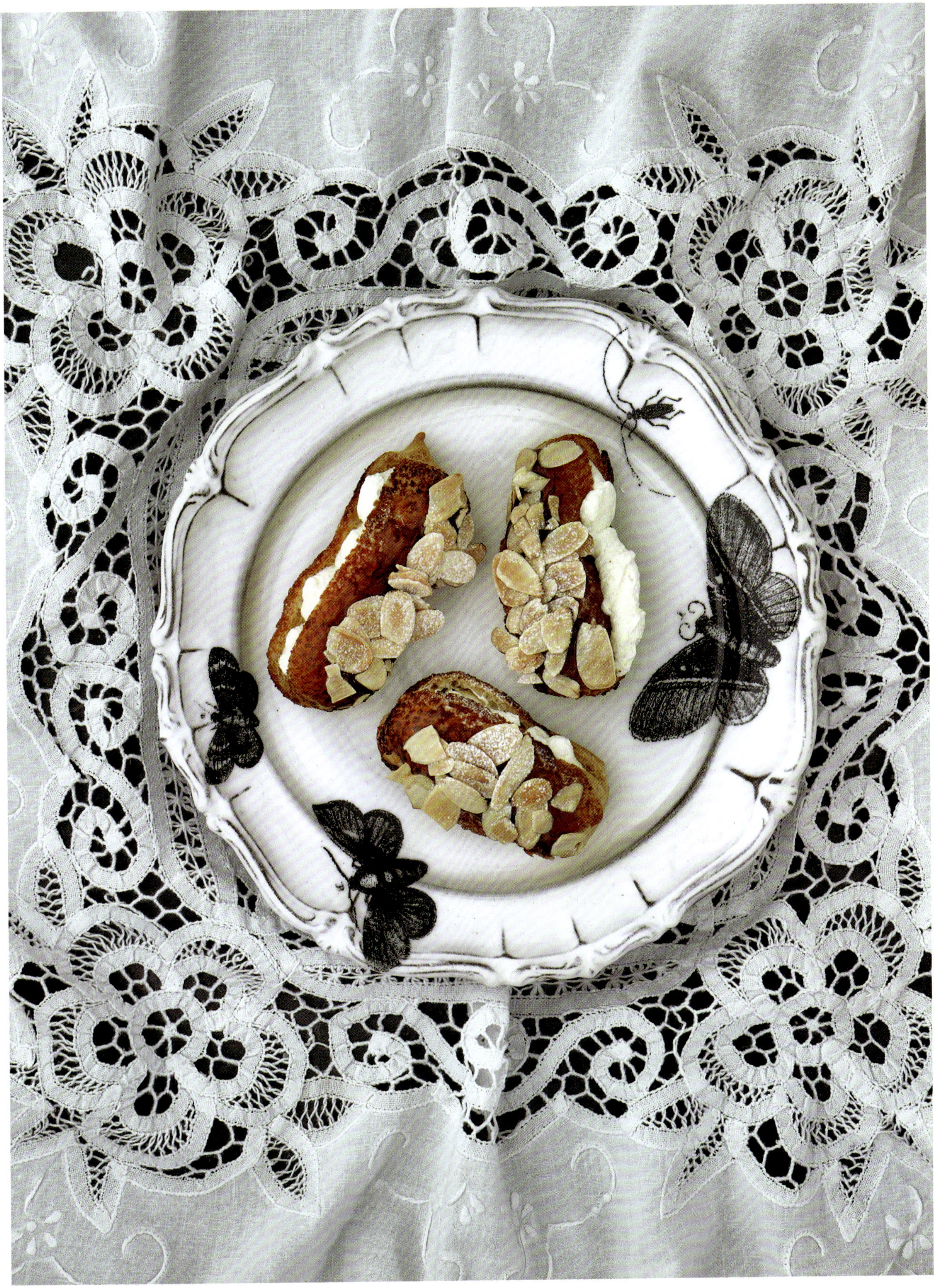

Meringues

We sell these big craggy meringues every day in our shop in Bath. I prefer to use Italian meringue (see page 37), but if you don't feel comfortable with using sugar syrup you can try the recipe for French meringue on page 38 instead; however, the meringue will be a little more dry and brittle inside, whereas the Italian meringue is soft and a little chewy. I like to run chocolate or coffee through them for flavour and colour, but you can also keep them plain, or decorate them with a little grated lemon zest or ground pistachio nuts before they go into the oven.

MAKES 6

1 quantity Italian meringue (see page 37)
1 good tablespoon cocoa powder or ground coffee (optional)

Preheat the oven to 90°C/gas ¼. Have ready a large baking tray lined with baking paper.

If using cocoa powder or ground coffee, sieve it over the top of your meringue mixture and fold in with a big spoon. You don't want to mix it in uniformly, just streak it through.

Using two spoons, scoop out the meringue, swapping the mixture from one spoon to the other to shape it into mounds, but don't entirely smooth it – leave some good peaks and crags.

Drop each mound onto your lined tray and put into the oven for about 4 hours. The meringues should dry out and feel hard to the touch, but should not colour, and if you lift one up and tap the base it should feel solid.

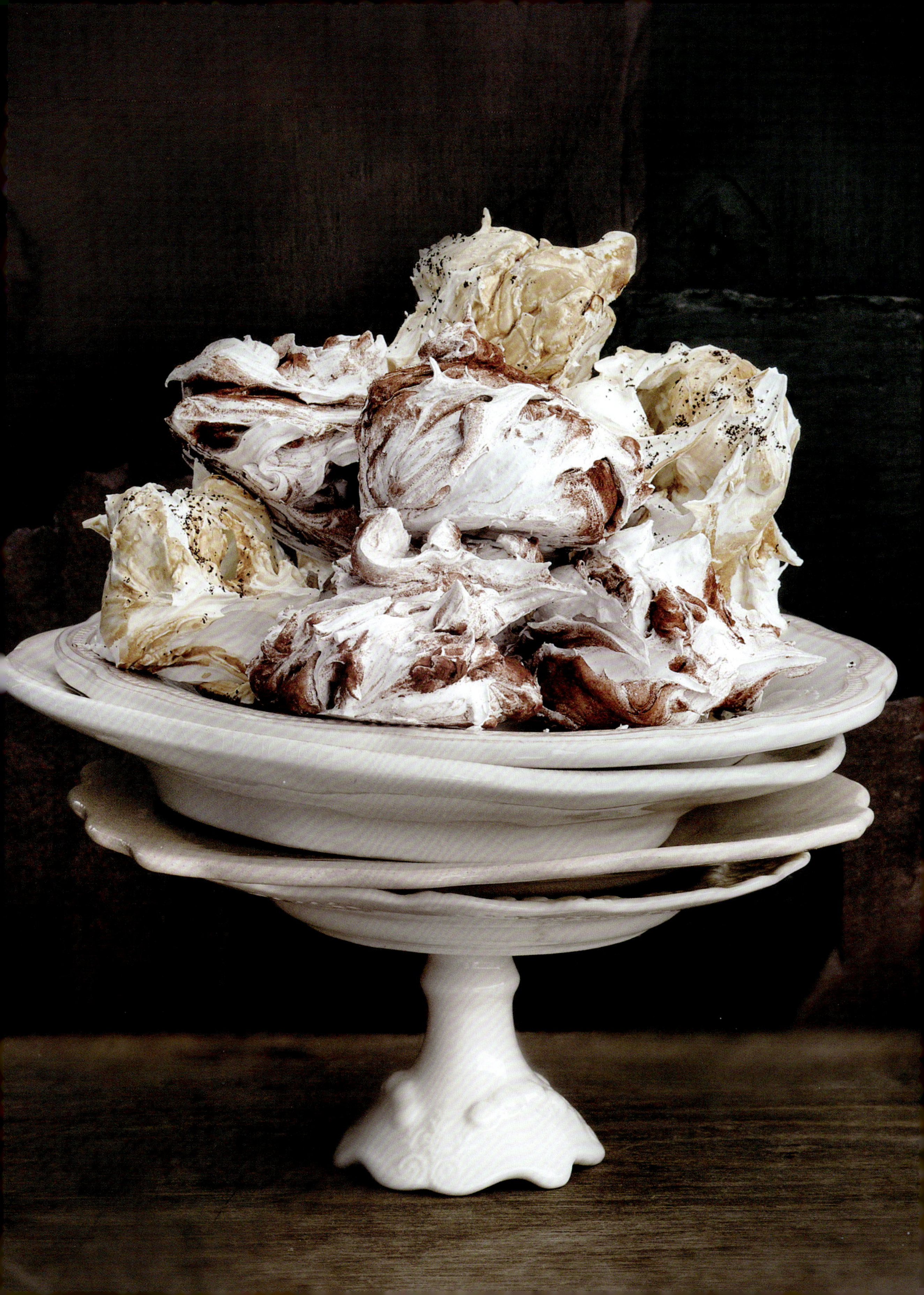

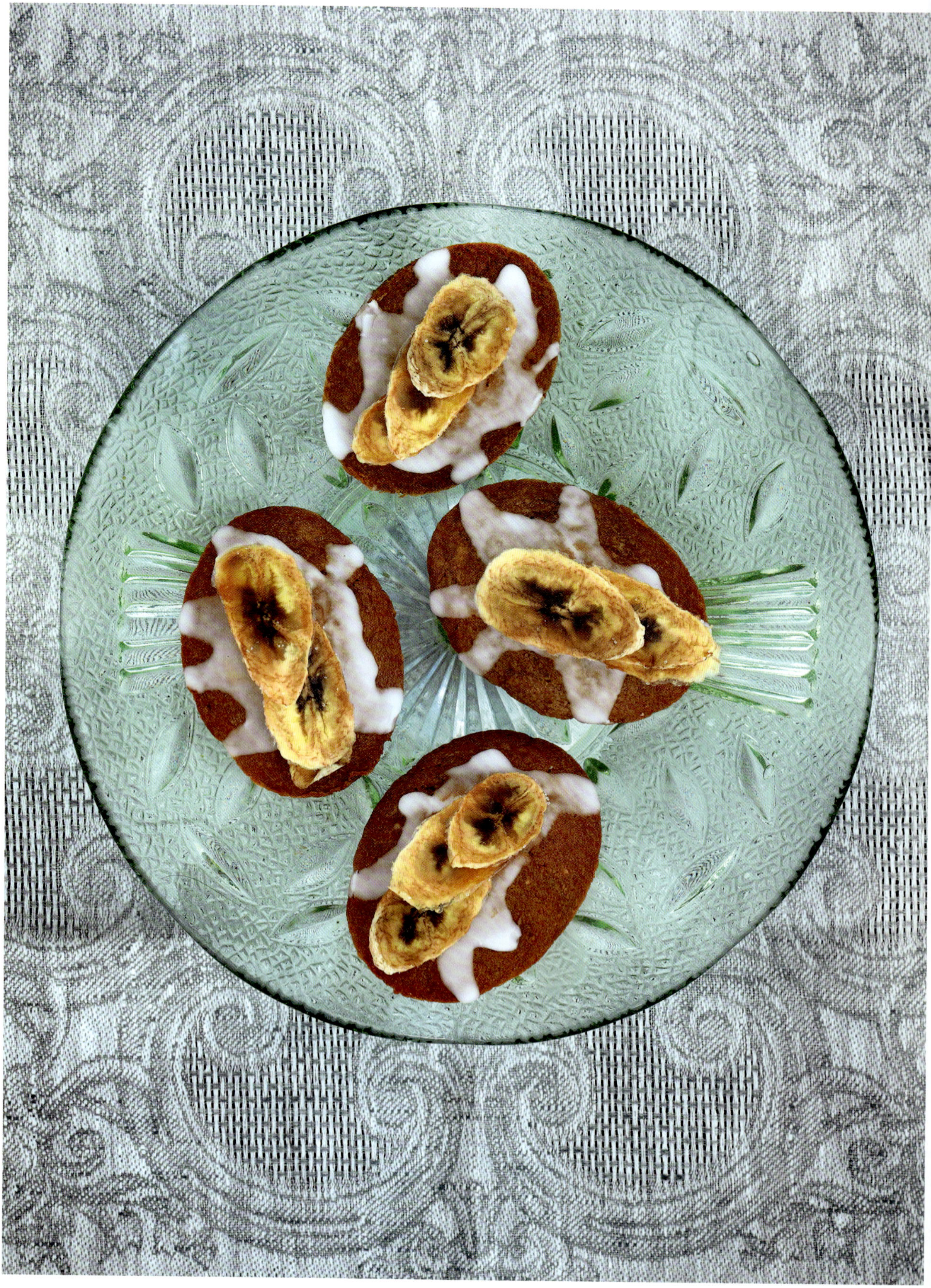

Mini banana cakes

These are individual versions of the more traditional loaf. Simple, but elegant for serving with afternoon tea.

MAKES 6–8

120g butter
220g dark brown sugar
2 medium eggs, beaten
3 ripe bananas, crushed
230g plain flour
1 teaspoon baking powder
pinch of salt
2 tablespoons hot milk

TO DECORATE:
100g icing sugar, sieved
3 tablespoons water
1 banana, dried (see page 53)

Preheat the oven to 190°C/gas 5.

In a bowl, cream the butter and sugar until fluffy. Beat in the eggs a little at a time.

Mix in the crushed bananas.

Sieve the flour, baking powder and salt together and fold into the mixture. Stir in the milk.

Spoon into individual oval or round tins or muffin trays, filling them three quarters full.

Bake in the preheated oven for 25–30 minutes until golden, the tops feel springy and a skewer inserted into the middle comes out clean. Take out of the oven, leave until cool enough to handle and then turn out and cool on a wire tray.

To decorate, mix the icing sugar with the water and with a small spoon drizzle over the top of each cake.

Top with two or three slices of dried banana.

Tiramisu

I like to make the tiramisu in a large slab, then cut it into rounds to serve it, but you could simply cut it into squares if you prefer.

MAKES 8 PORTIONS

3 gelatine leaves
100g caster sugar
3 tablespoons water
4 medium eggs, separated
250g mascarpone
250ml double cream
200ml Marsala wine
½ quantity genoise sponge (see page 14)
300ml strong coffee, cooled

TO DECORATE:
cocoa powder, for dusting

TO DECORATE WITH CARAMEL HAZELNUTS (OPTIONAL):
8 hazelnuts, shelled
100g caster sugar
1 tablespoon water

If you are decorating the tiramisu with caramel hazelnuts, make these first. Put the sugar in a pan with the water, bring to the boil and continue to boil until golden brown (if you have a sugar thermometer, the temperature will be 140°C). It will be really hot, so be careful. Using a pair of kitchen tweezers dip each hazelnut into the caramel and pull out slowly to create a little 'tail'. Lay on a sheet of baking paper to cool and harden up.

Soak the gelatine in cold water to soften, then squeeze out the excess water.

Put the sugar in a pan with the water and heat gently for about 5–8 minutes until the sugar has dissolved and formed a colourless syrup and small bubbles are breaking the surface. If you have a sugar thermometer, the syrup is ready when the temperature reaches 121/122°C. Remove from the heat.

In a bowl, whisk the egg whites until they form soft peaks, then slowly whisk in the sugar syrup.

(Continues overleaf)

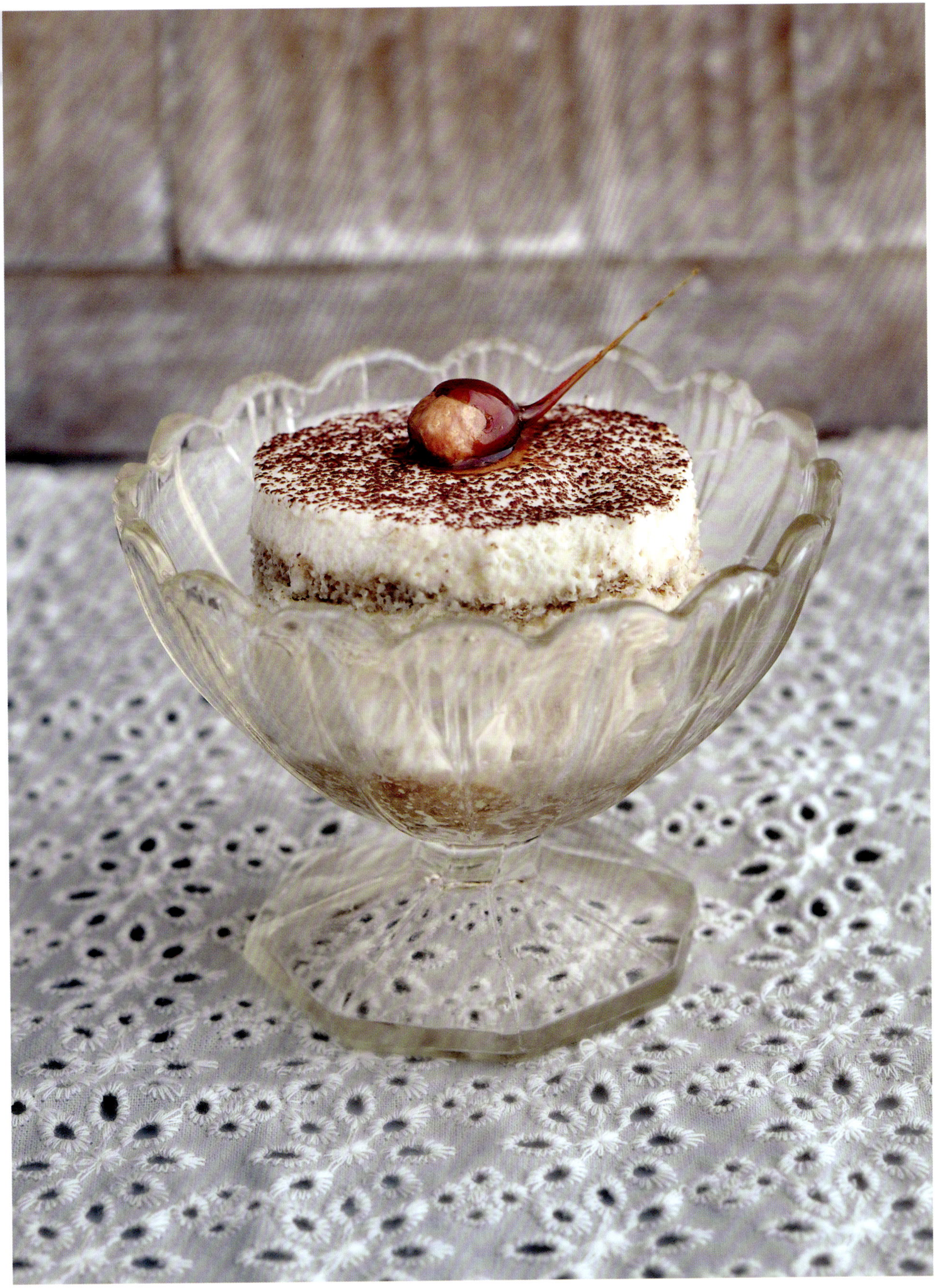

In a separate bowl, whisk the egg yolks with the mascarpone. In yet another bowl, whisk the cream until thick.

In a small pan, warm half of the Marsala, add the gelatine, stir until it has dissolved and then take off the heat and stir in the rest of the Marsala. Now stir this into the egg and mascarpone mixture.

Fold in the double cream and finally the egg white.

To assemble, cut the genoise sponge in half. Lay one half in the base of a deep serving dish. Brush liberally with half of the coffee, so that the sponge is well soaked.

Spread half of the Marsala mixture evenly over the top and dust with a little cocoa powder. Lay the other half of the sponge on top and press down a little. Soak with the rest of the coffee as before.

Spread the rest of the Marsala mixture over the top, smoothing it so that it is flat.

Put into the fridge for about 2–3 hours or preferably overnight.

To serve, take a pastry cutter (about 10cm in diameter) and stamp out eight circles. Use a wide palette knife or fish slice to lift out into serving bowls, dust with cocoa, and top each one with a caramel hazelnut, if using.

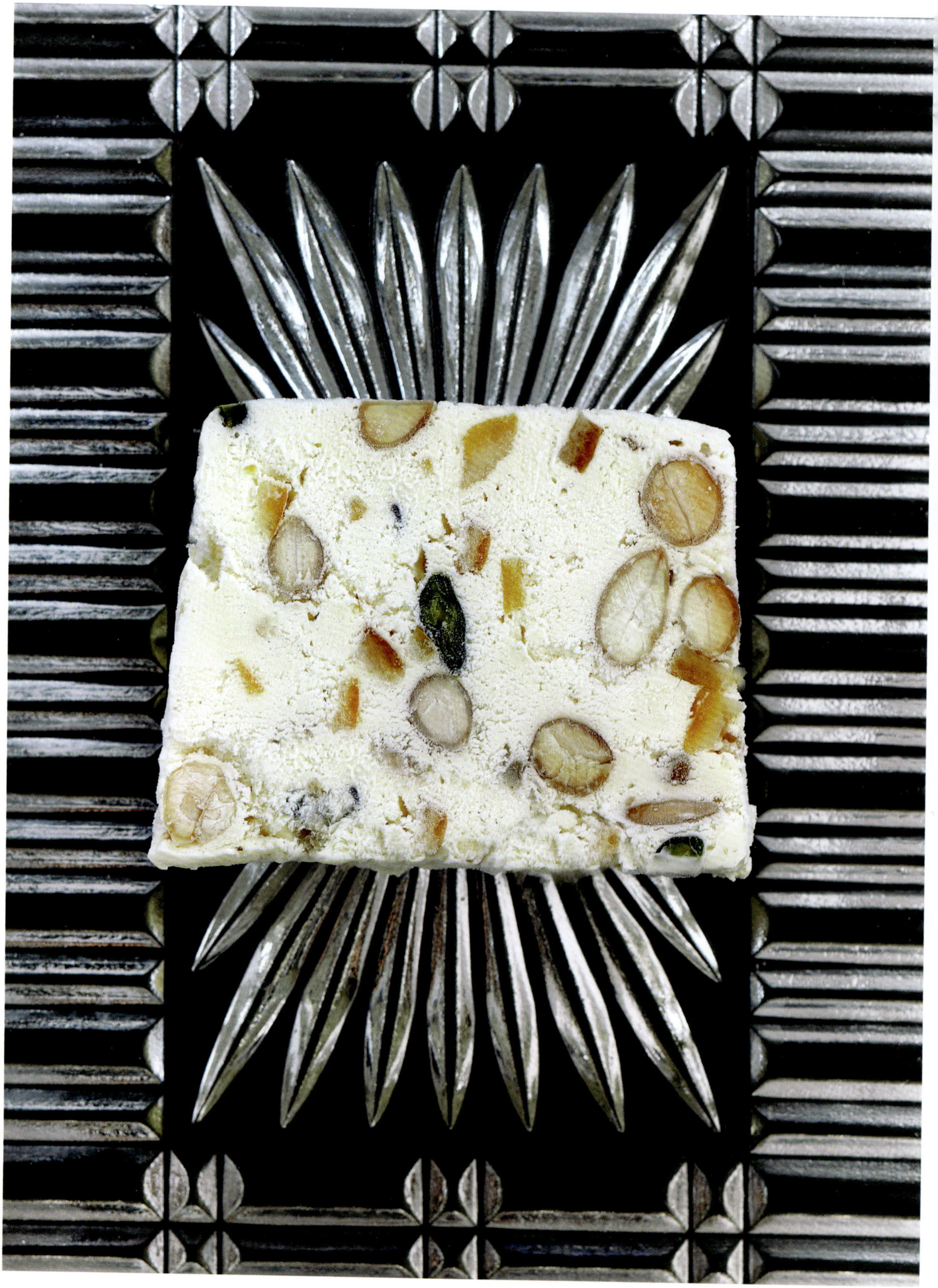

Nougat glace

This is a very easy recipe – and you can make two at a time and put one in the freezer, where it will keep for three months, so you always have a dessert ready to go. If you prefer a nut-free version, use some fresh fruit instead: raspberries, blueberries, blackberries, apricots or pineapple work especially well.

MAKES 1 X 30CM TERRINE

100g whole blanched almonds
100g hazelnuts, shelled weight
50g broken walnuts
25g pistachio nuts, shelled weight
1 heaped tablespoon caster sugar
150g mixed candied fruit
65g honey, preferably lavender
500ml double cream
4 medium egg whites

Preheat the oven to 180°C/gas 4.

Spread the nuts over a baking tray, sprinkle with the sugar, and put into the oven for 15–20 minutes, turning them halfway through, until caramelised and light golden. Take out and let them cool down. Then, with the back of a rolling pin, crush them lightly.

Mix the caramelised nuts with the candied fruit.

Put the honey in a pan and bring to the boil, then take off the heat.

In a bowl whisk the cream until firm.

(Continues overleaf)

SMALL

In a separate bowl, whisk the egg whites to soft peaks, then slowly add the honey and continue to whisk to firm peaks. Add the fruit and nuts.

Gently fold the fruit and nuts into the cream.

Line a 30cm long terrine (that will go into the freezer) with clingfilm, leaving an overhang all around. Spoon in the mixture and smooth the top, then fold the clingfilm over to enclose it. Put into the freezer for at least 4 hours.
To serve, take out and leave for 15–20 minutes to soften slightly, then unwrap the clingfilm. To turn out, place a flat plate or cake board on top of the terrine and, using both hands, firmly grip both and turn over together. Remove the clingfilm and slice.

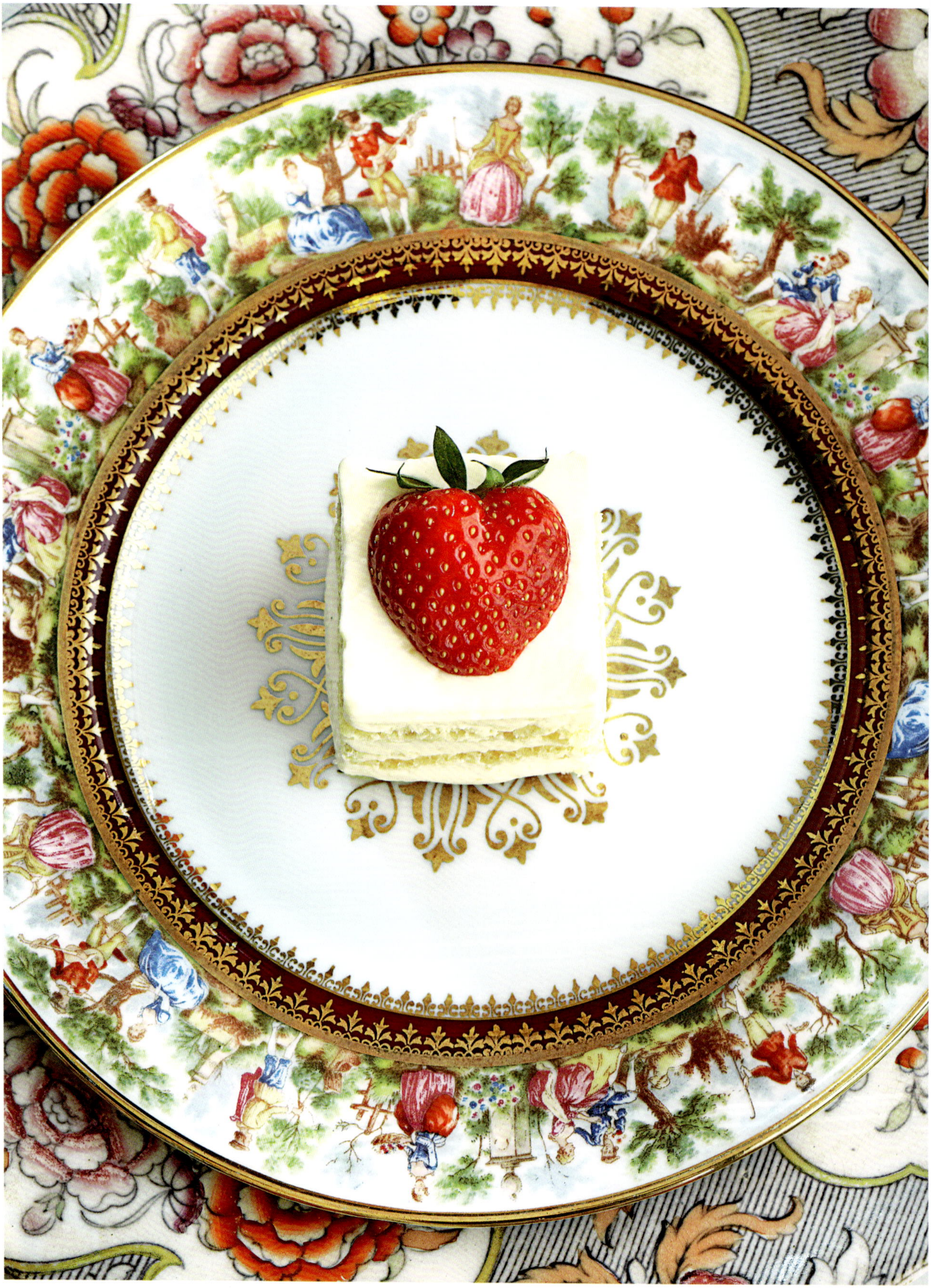

Fraisier

This is the lovely light layering of genoise sponge, strawberries and kirsch-flavoured cream that you see in every patisserie in France. When I was serving my apprenticeship, it was one of the first things we made when the strawberry season began: fraisier and strawberry tarts. Be patient and wait for the strawberries to be at their sweet, fruitiest best and don't be tempted to use out-of-season or unripe and hard berries, which won't match up in terms of flavour.

The classic way of presenting a fraisier is to layer everything inside a big ring or individual rings, starting with a layer of sponge for the base, and then arranging the strawberries in a circle around the edge, with their rounded ends sitting on the sponge and their pointed ends upwards. The cream is spooned inside and a second layer of sponge is placed on top, sometimes finished with strawberry glaze. When the ring slides off, you have a crown of strawberries all around the outside of the cake.

On one occasion, however, we wanted to make a fraisier for a big party so we experimented with these smaller square versions that people could just pick up and eat easily in a couple of mouthfuls. They are easier to make at home, while still delivering all the essential flavours of strawberries, kirsch and cream. If you want a more simple cream, you can use crème Chantilly instead of the crème au beurre.

MAKES 8 PORTIONS

½ quantity genoise sponge (see page 14)
double quantity crème au beurre (see page 43)
4 large ripe strawberries

FOR THE SYRUP:
100g sugar
100ml water
2 tablespoons kirsch

To make the syrup, put the sugar in a pan with the water and bring to the boil. Reduce the heat and simmer until the sugar has dissolved and you have a colourless syrup. Take off the heat and stir in the kirsch.

To assemble, cut the genoise sponge in half. Lay one half in the base of a deep serving dish. Brush liberally with half of the syrup, so that the sponge is well soaked.

(Continues overleaf)

Spread half of the crème au beurre evenly over the top. Lay the other half of the sponge on top and press down a little. Soak with more syrup as before (you may not need all of it). Spread the rest of the crème au beurre over the top, smoothing it so that it is flat. Put into the fridge for about 2–3 hours or preferably overnight.

To serve, dip a sharp knife into hot water and cut the fraisier neatly into eight squares or rectangles. Cut your strawberries in half and place a half, cut side down, on top of each.

Quatre-quart Breton

My mother used to make these little cakes for me for when I came home from school, and they are still fashionable in Brittany. The name, which means 'four quarters', comes from the fact that they are made with only four ingredients: you break the eggs and weigh them, and then add the same weight of butter, sugar and flour (with a little baking powder). The key to the flavour is the salted Breton butter.

MAKES 8

For 4 shelled medium eggs, you need the same weight of:
 caster sugar
 plain flour (plus 1 teaspoon baking powder)
 salted butter, melted (plus a little extra for greasing the tins)
2 eating apples (something with a little sharpness, like a Cox or Braeburn)

Preheat the oven to 200°C/gas 6.

In a bowl, beat the eggs and sugar until pale and fluffy.

Fold in the flour and baking powder.

Stir in the melted butter.

Grease eight small tart tins (about 10–12cm in diameter and 2.5cm deep) very well with butter, and divide the batter between them.

Peel the apples, cut in half, take out the core, and then slice each horizontally. Put around four slices on top of each tin of batter.

Put into the preheated oven and bake for 25–30 minutes until golden and slightly puffed up. Leave until cool enough to handle, then turn out and cool on a rack.

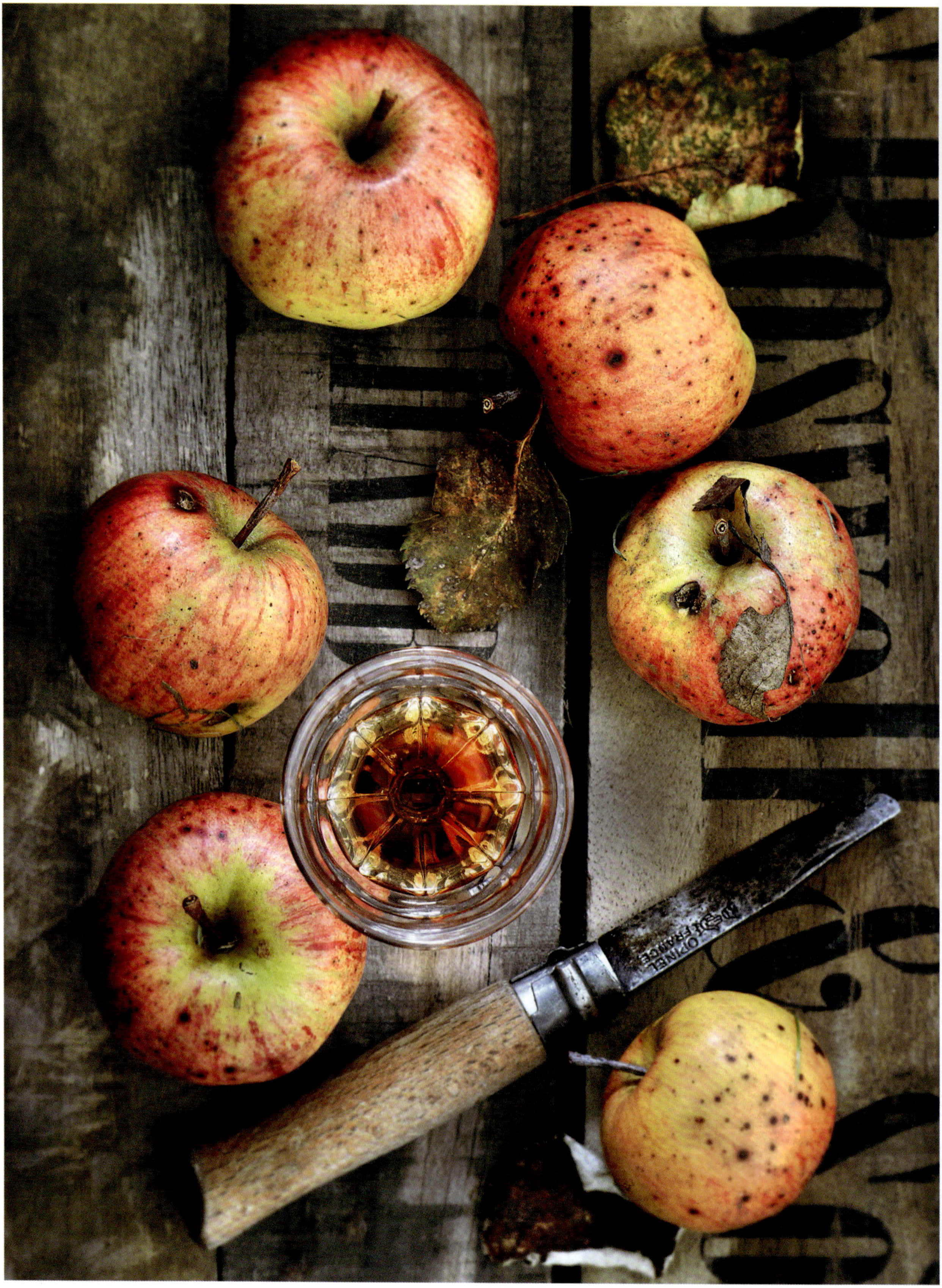
OPINEL
FRANCE

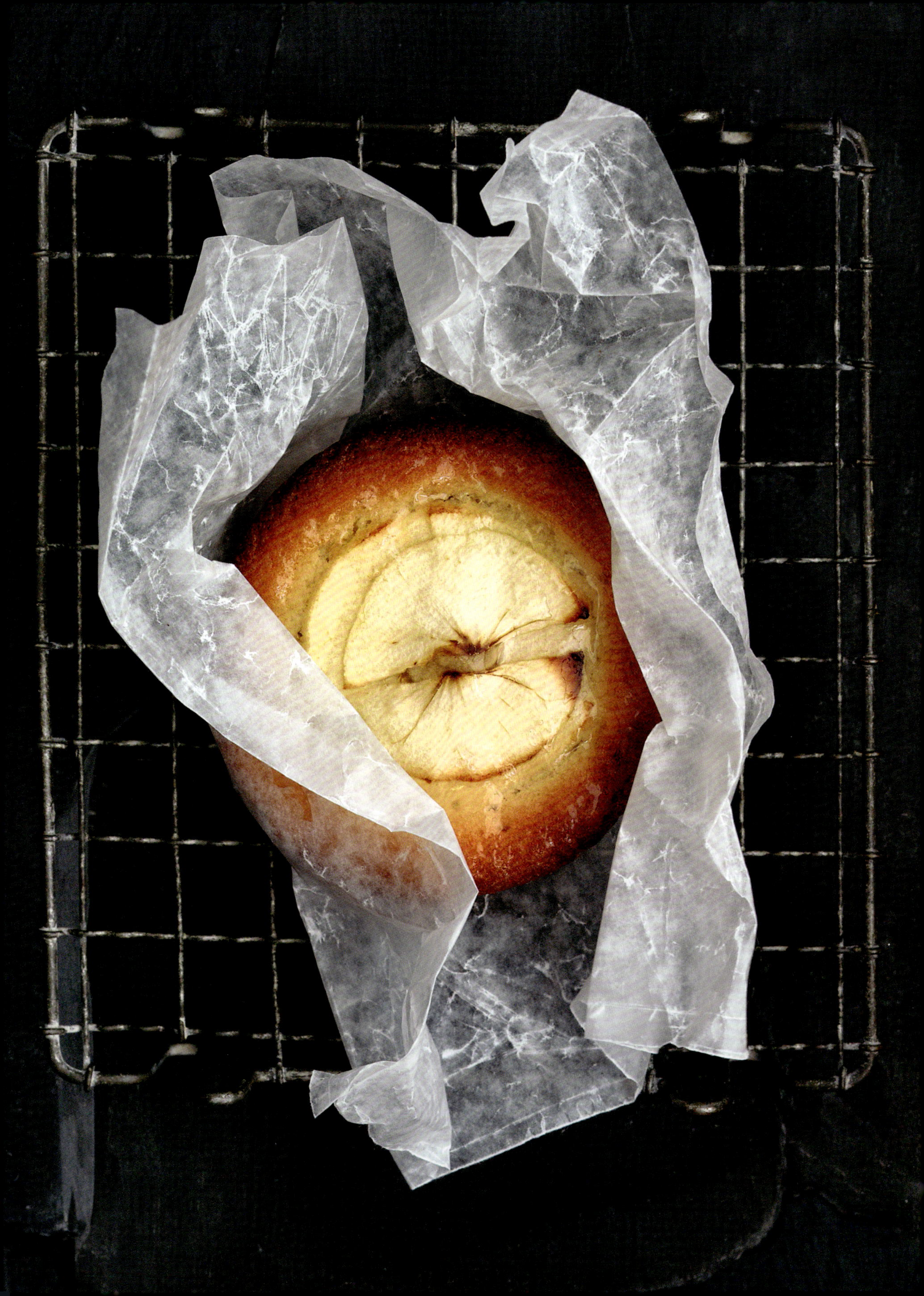

Îles flottantes

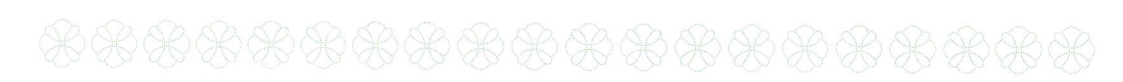

This is the classic pudding I remember from restaurants in France in the seventies, and you still find it across the country in local bistros. It is all about the contrasting softness of the poached meringue, the cold cream, and the crunchiness of the caramel.

MAKES 6

1 litre milk, for poaching
½ quantity Italian meringue (see page 37)
double quantity crème anglaise (see page 44)
80g flaked almonds

FOR THE CARAMEL:
200g caster sugar
4 tablespoons water

Put the milk in a wide pan and bring to a simmer.

Using two tablespoons, scoop up the meringue, swapping the mixture from one spoon to the other to shape it into six egg shapes – as smoothly as you can – and lower each one into the milk (you will probably have to do this in two batches). Keep the milk under a simmer and let the meringues poach for 8–9 minutes, turning them over halfway through, until they are firm to the touch. Lift out with a slotted spoon and place onto kitchen paper to drain. When they are dry, transfer them to a sheet of baking paper or a silicone mat.

Make a caramel by putting the sugar in a pan with the water, bring to the boil and continue to boil until golden brown (if you have a sugar thermometer, the temperature will be 140°C). It will be really hot, so be careful. Pour a little over each meringue and sprinkle a few flaked almonds on top of each one.

To serve, pour some crème anglaise into each of six bowls, put a meringue on top and sprinkle with any remaining almonds.

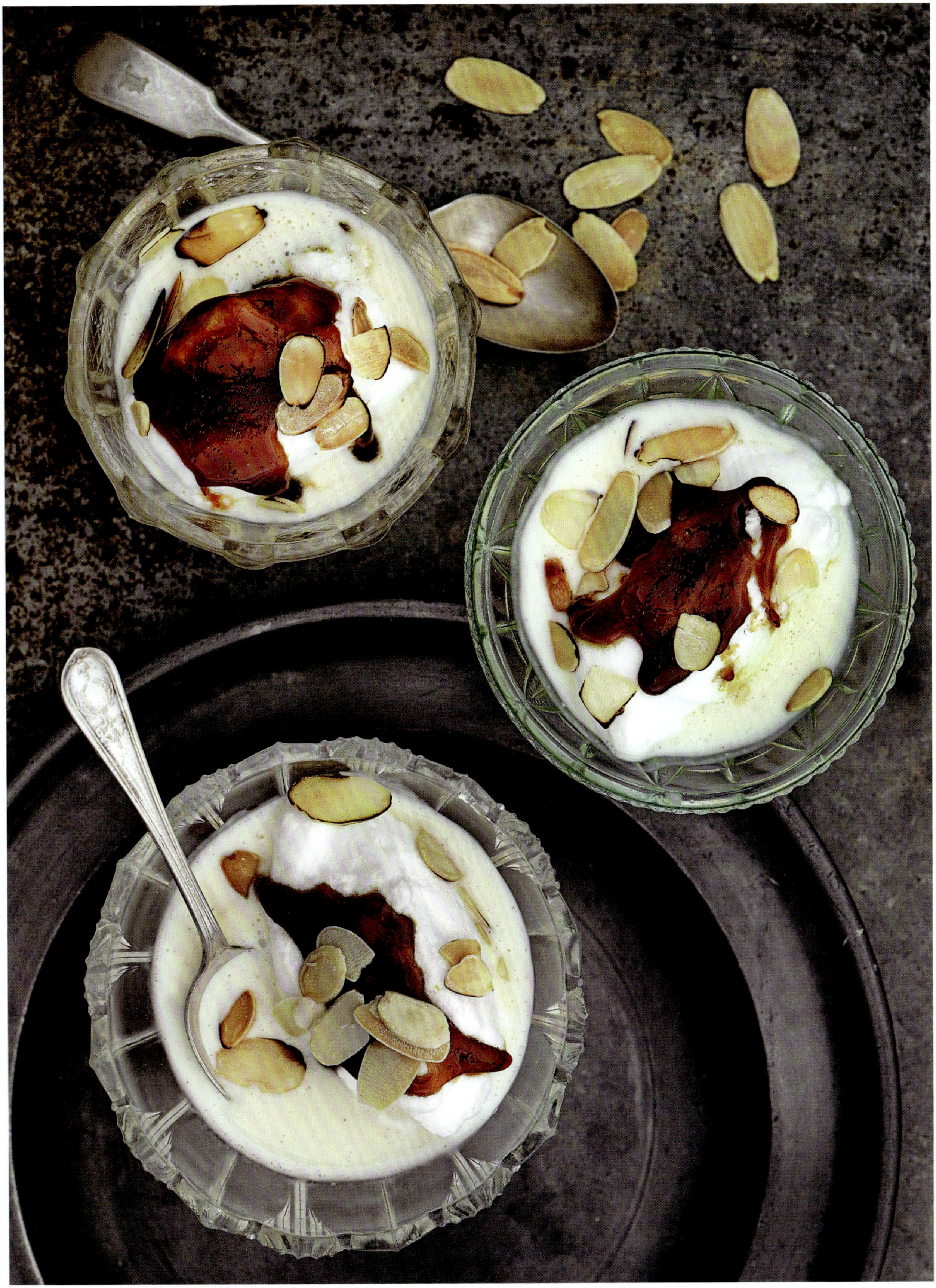

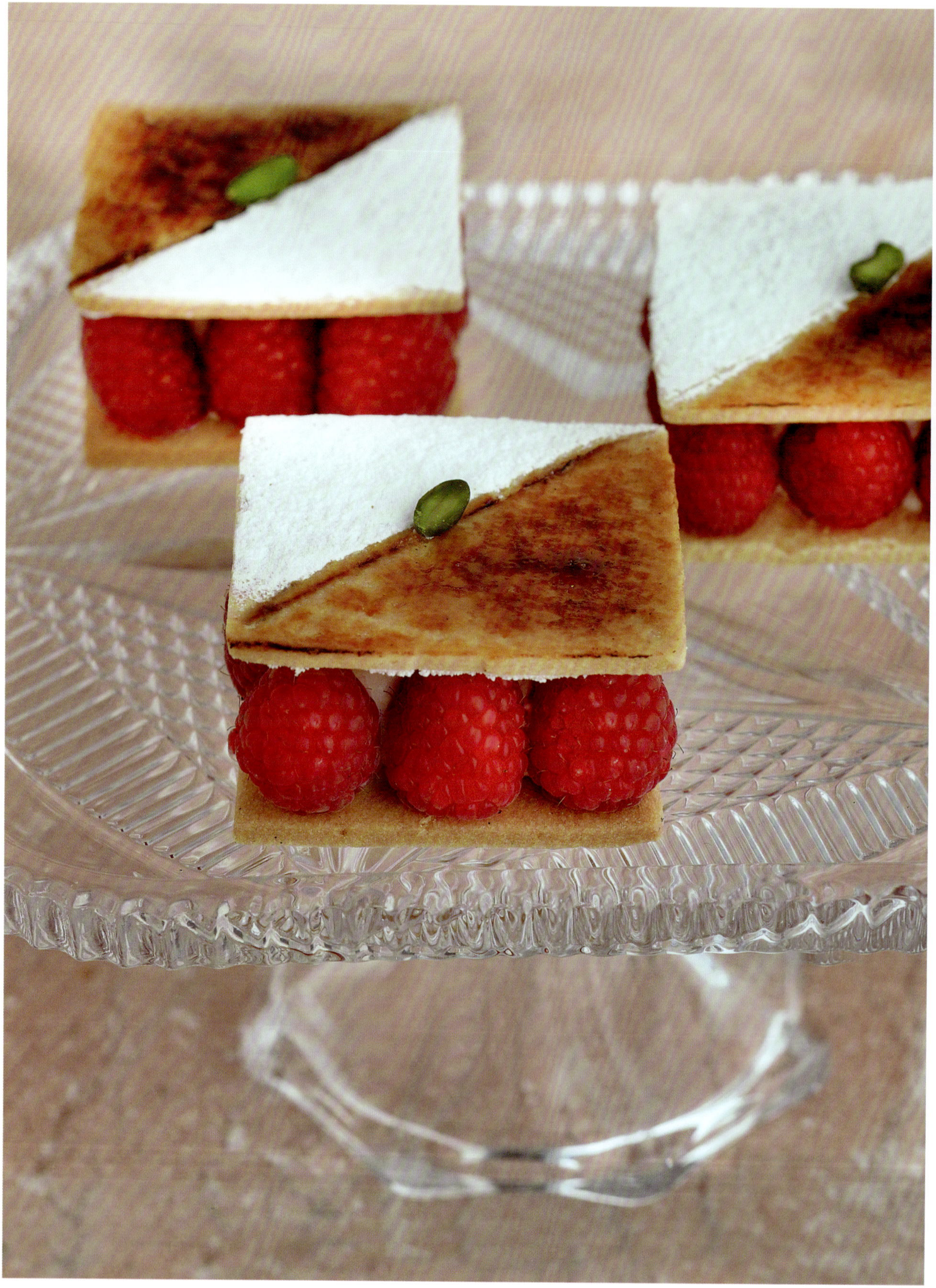

Raspberry biscuits

MAKES 6

1 quantity sweet pastry (see page 26), made with seeds scraped from a vanilla pod, added with the sugar
a little flour, for rolling

TO ASSEMBLE:
1 quantity crème légère (see page 43)
around 250g raspberries
icing sugar, for dusting
6 pistachio nuts or small leaves of mint, to decorate

Preheat the oven to 180°C/gas 4.

Lightly flour your work surface, roll out the sweet pastry dough thinly (about 2mm) and cut into twelve squares of about 8cm.

Lay the squares on a baking tray or trays and bake in the preheated oven for about 10 minutes until golden. Remove and leave to cool.

To assemble, take six of the biscuits and lay them rough side upwards, spoon some crème légère neatly in the middle of each one, then arrange your raspberries around the outside. Top with the rest of the biscuits, smooth side upwards. Sprinkle with icing sugar, then, if you like, place a metal scraper diagonally across one half to create a neat line and, using a blow torch, caramelise the visible area of sugar. Decorate with a pistachio or mint leaf in the centre.

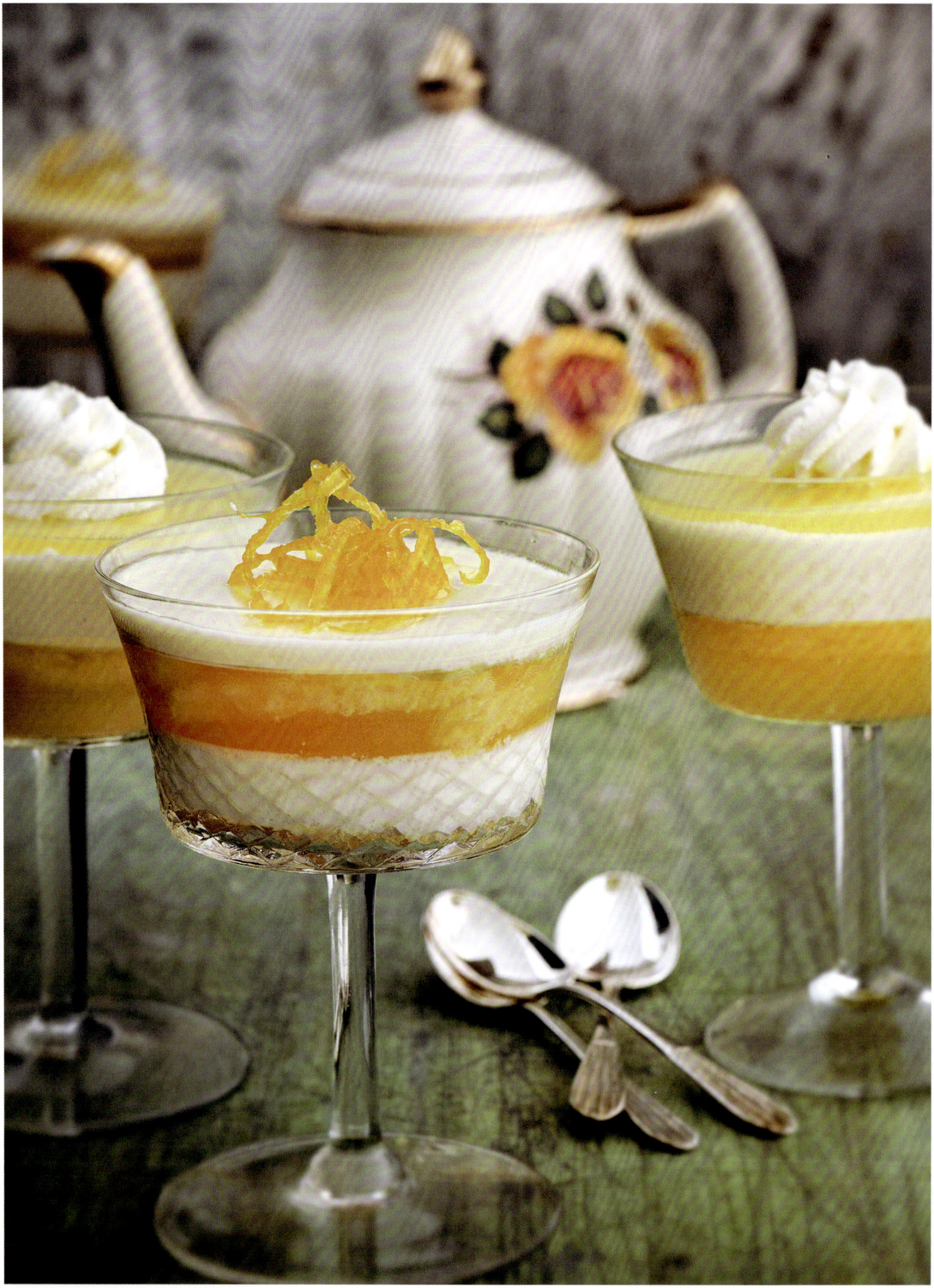

Lemon trifles

How many trifles you make really depends on the size of your glasses (or you can make one big one in a glass bowl).

If you keep any trimmings of genoise sponge left over from another recipe in the freezer (wrap them in greaseproof paper inside a freezer bag), you can use them here, rather than baking the sponge specially.

MAKES AROUND 6

½ quantity genoise sponge (see page 14)
    (or equivalent trimmings, see above)
100ml limoncello
½ quantity lemon curd (see page 51)

FOR THE LEMON JELLY:
3 gelatine leaves
100g caster sugar
100ml water
zest and juice of 3 unwaxed lemons

FOR THE CUSTARD JELLY:
3 gelatine leaves
1 quantity crème anglaise ingredients
    (see page 44)

TO DECORATE:
Chantilly cream, or whipped double cream, or
    some strips of lemon zest, poached in syrup
    (see page 63)

Soak the gelatine leaves for the lemon jelly and custard jelly briefly in cold water to soften, then squeeze out the excess water.

For the custard jelly, make the crème anglaise as on page 44, but while it is still warm, stir in the three leaves of gelatine.

For the lemon jelly, put the sugar and water in a pan with the lemon zest and juice and warm until the sugar has melted. Take off the heat, add the gelatine and stir until dissolved.

Cut your genoise sponge to fit each of six glasses (or use trimmings) and brush with limoncello, then put in the fridge for about 15 minutes until set. Now you can layer up the lemon curd, lemon jelly and custard jelly – if you have any sponge trimmings left over, you can add these to a jelly layer. I quite like to make each trifle a little different. The important thing is to put the glasses in the fridge to set each layer before adding the next one.

When all the layers are chilled, decorate with cream or poached lemon zest and serve.

Jelly party

These are fun, multi-coloured jellies with custard that I made for a children's party, and everyone loved them, adults included. You can use blackcurrant or orange squash instead of grenadine. If you like you can bake the biscuits on page 101 to serve with them.

MAKES 10–12

1 quantity lemon jelly (see previous page)
1 quantity custard jelly (see previous page)

FOR THE GRENADINE JELLY:
4 gelatine leaves
100g caster sugar
250ml grenadine
200ml water

sweet biscuits, to serve (optional)

For the grenadine jelly, soak the gelatine briefly in cold water to soften, then squeeze out the excess water.

Put the sugar, grenadine and water in a pan and warm until the sugar has dissolved. Take off the heat, add the gelatine and stir until dissolved.

Play around with layers of each jelly in glasses, or moulds that can be turned out. As in the trifle recipe on page 103, put your mould or glass in the fridge to allow each layer to set before adding the next one. When completely set, if you are using moulds, dip each one into a bowl of hot water for a second, turn it over, shake gently and the jellies should slither out easily onto a plate.

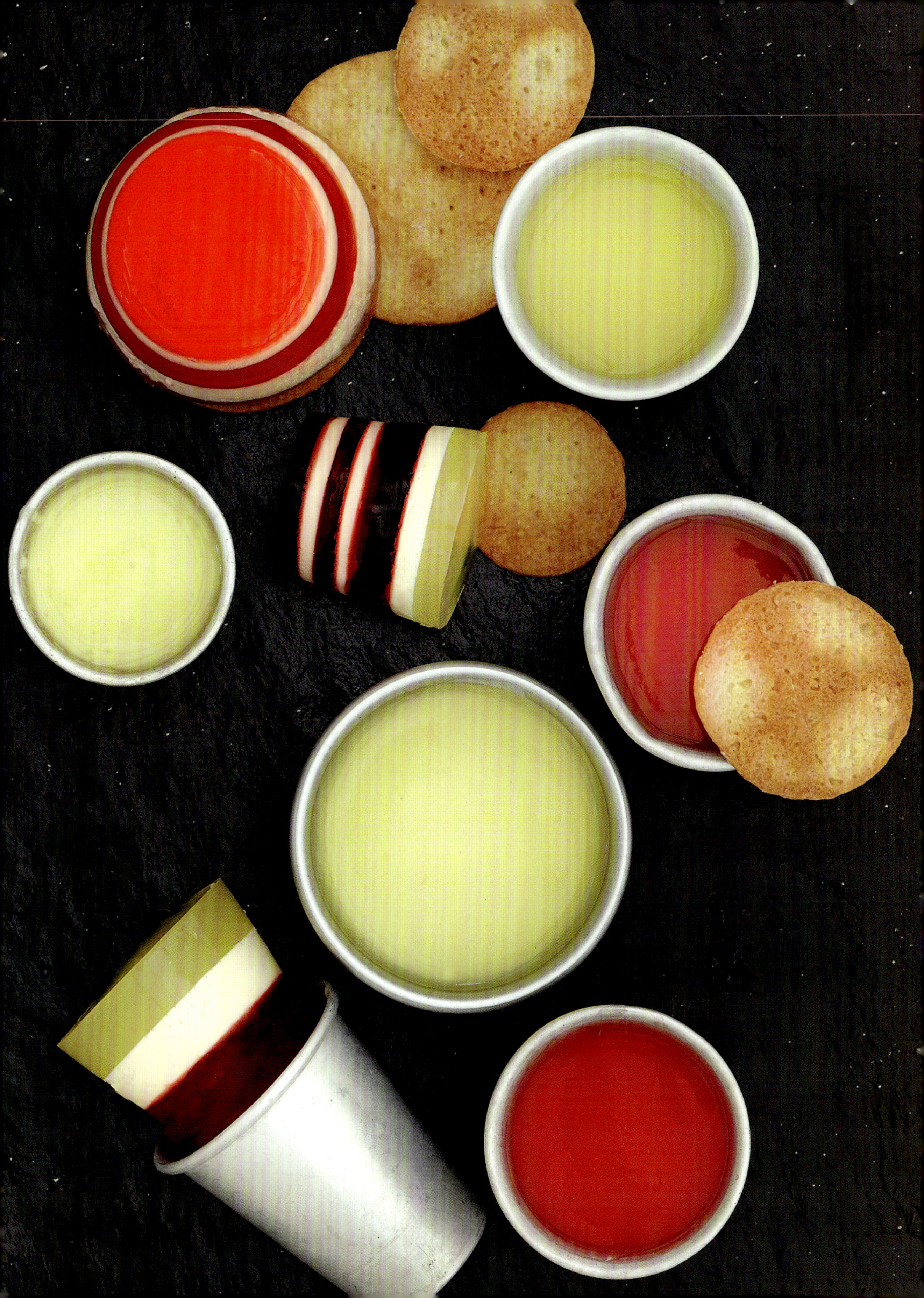

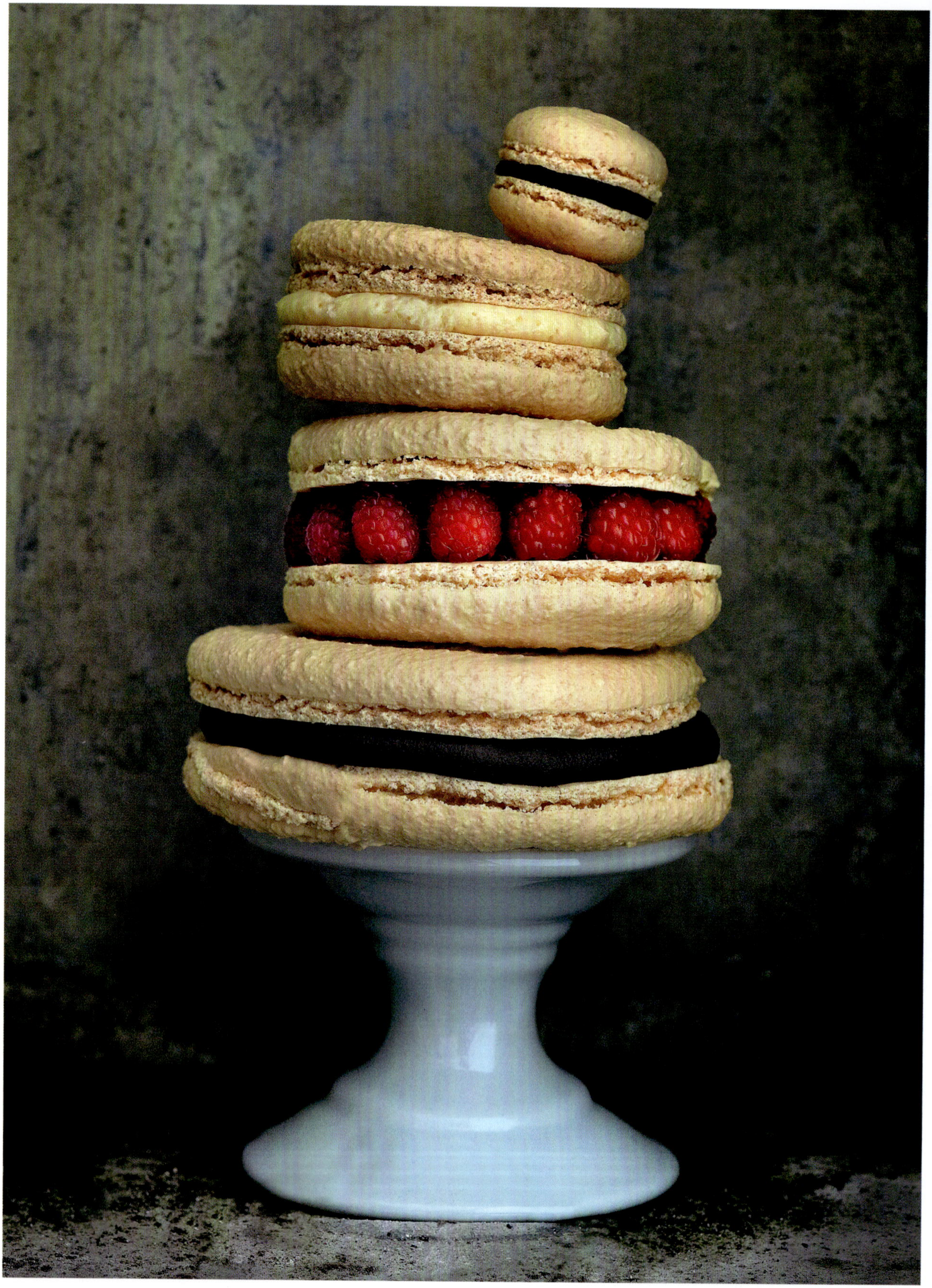

Macaron party

Mini macarons have become incredibly popular in every colour and flavour, but my favourite macaron is a big one that you can share – or for fun I like to pile up lots of them in a tower of diminishing sizes. The method for making them is essentially the same as for an Italian meringue, and like a good meringue, a macaron should be a little crispy on the outside and slightly chewy in the centre.

The recipe makes enough for four big macarons about 15cm in diameter, and the quantities given for each of the fillings will be enough for these, or you can mix and match with whatever you have. And of course you can make the macarons in any size you like.

MAKES 4 LARGE MACARONS

FOR THE MACARON MIX:
300g icing sugar
45ml water
220g egg white (from about 6 medium eggs)
300g ground almonds
300g granulated sugar

FOR THE FILLINGS:
choose from:
½ quantity chocolate ganache (see page 119)
½ quantity lemon curd (see page 51)
½ quantity of crème Chantilly (see page 42), plus a punnet of fresh raspberries

Preheat the oven to 130°C/gas 1.

Put the sugar in a pan with the water and heat gently for about 5–8 minutes until the sugar has dissolved and formed a colourless syrup and small bubbles are breaking the surface. If you have a sugar thermometer, the temperature should be 121/122°C.

Now you are ready to whisk your egg whites. You can do this using a food mixer with a whisk attachment, or use a hand-held whisk, but whichever you use, make sure your bowl is absolutely clean and dry, as water or grease can prevent the egg white from stiffening. Whisk the egg whites until soft, foamy peaks form then stop as soon as you reach this point, as if you over-whisk, the air bubbles that you have created will burst and the egg whites will collapse back into liquid.

(Continues overleaf)

Next you are going to pour the hot syrup onto the egg whites. Since you need both hands – one to whisk, one to pour – if you are whisking by hand, then before you start, wrap a tea towel around your bowl and wedge it inside an empty saucepan to hold it steady.

Whisk in the syrup, then mix the ground almonds and sugar together and tap through a sieve into the meringue, folding in with a big spoon.

Snip the corner from a piping bag, if using a disposable one, insert a 1cm plain nozzle and fill with the mixture (see page 24).

Pipe onto a silicone mat or baking tray lined with baking paper, in spirals starting in the centre – you can make them any size you like. Remember you need two spirals per macaron.

Put into the preheated oven for about 25–30 minutes for a large macaron of about 15cm in diameter, and allow less time, down to about 12–14 minutes, for small ones of about 3–4cm. Keep an eye on them: they are ready when they are firm to the touch on top.

Sandwich the rounds with the fillings of your choice.

Shared

MOUSSES, CAKES AND TARTS TO SLICE AND SHARE

Blackcurrant mousse

One of my fondest memories of working as an apprentice is the intense smell of the blackcurrants and passion fruit when the mousses were being made. The aromas and flavours were incredible. While the mousses were setting in their rings, I couldn't help running my fingertips around the mixing bowls and licking my fingers.

MAKES 1 X 23CM MOUSSE

1 quantity genoise sponge (see page 14)
50ml crème de cassis

FOR THE MOUSSE:
6 gelatine leaves
400g blackcurrants (fresh or frozen) plus a few extra for decoration
1 quantity Italian meringue (see page 37)
150ml double cream

FOR THE GLAZE:
2 gelatine leaves
50g caster sugar
150ml crème de cassis

For the mousse, soak the gelatine leaves briefly in cold water to soften, then squeeze out the excess water.

In a blender, purée the blackcurrants and push through a fine sieve to remove the skin and any stems.

Heat a quarter of the purée in a pan (don't let it boil) then take off the heat and stir in the gelatine, then stir in the rest of the purée. Leave until completely cold then fold into the Italian meringue.

Whip the cream until it forms soft peaks (just enough to hold), and then fold this into the meringue mixture.

You need a pastry ring (about 23cm in diameter and 6cm deep). Use this as a guide to cut out a circle of genoise sponge.

(Continues overleaf)

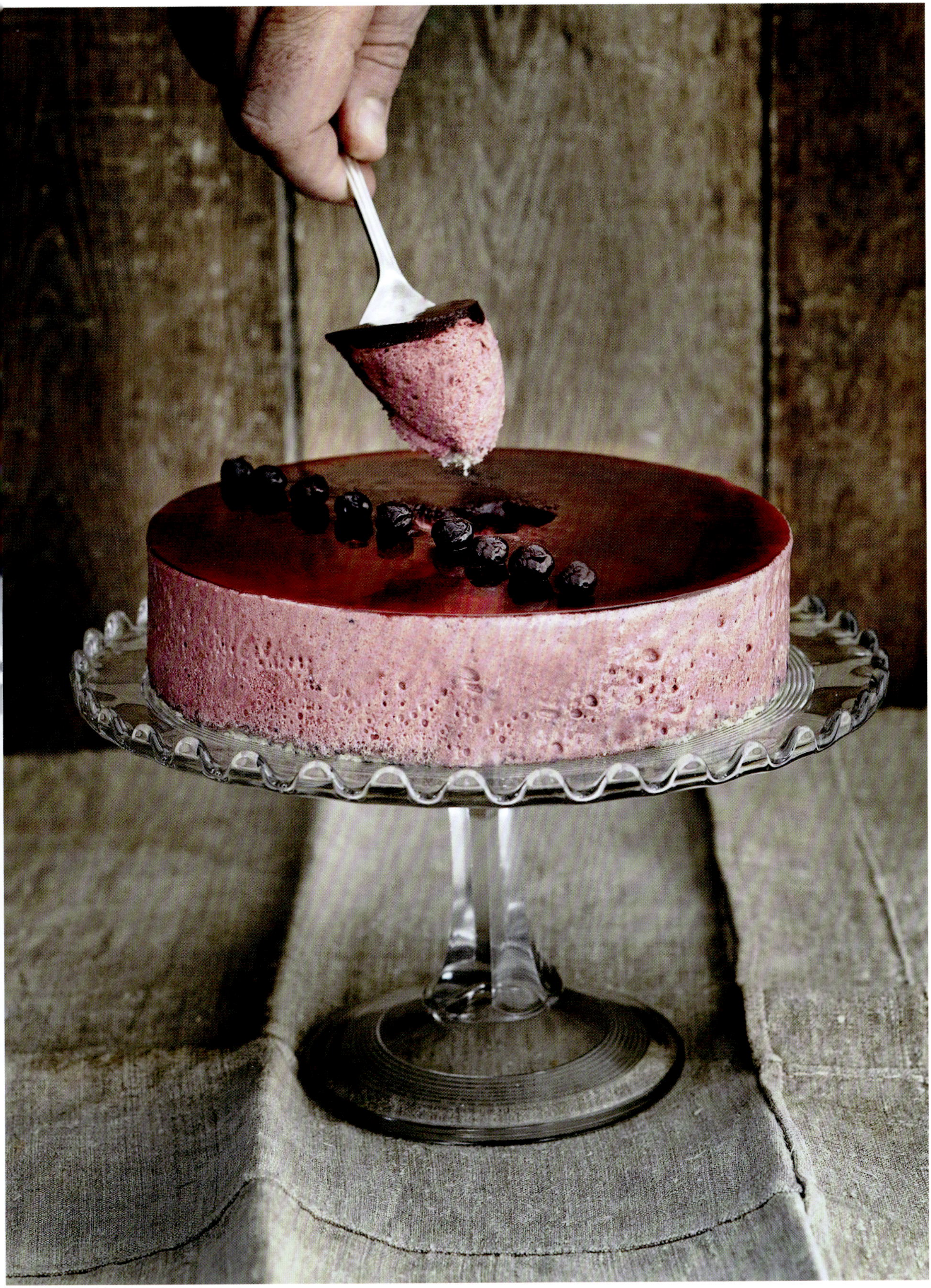

Place the ring on a round cake board and put the sponge into the base. Brush with the crème de cassis. Pour the mousse mixture on top and spread out gently so that it is level. You need to stop about 1mm below the rim of the ring, to allow space for a layer of glaze on top. Lift one corner of the cake board very slightly with a palette knife, and tap it very gently up and down just to remove any large pockets of air from the mousse. Put in the fridge for at least an hour until set and cold.

To make the glaze, soak the gelatine in cold water to soften, then squeeze out the excess water. Put the sugar and crème de cassis in a pan and warm until the sugar has dissolved.

Take off the heat, add the gelatine and stir until dissolved. Leave until cool but not set.

Dip the currants for decoration into the glaze to coat them, and keep to one side.

Take the mousse from the fridge, pour a thin layer of glaze over the top. Decorate the top with reserved blackcurrants and put back into the fridge for a minimum of 4 hours, or preferably overnight, to set.

To remove the ring, loosen it first around the edge of the mousse with a very slim bendy blade, or warm the ring with a blow torch very briefly from a distance, then slide off.

Passion fruit mousse

I first made this in the eighties when passion fruit were all the rage in France, and it is still one of my favourite fruit mousses. Ideally use fresh passion fruit – but be aware that you need around twenty! Alternatively, there are some good ready-made frozen purées out there (see page 210 for stockists).

MAKES 1 × 23CM MOUSSE

6 gelatine leaves
50g caster sugar
8 medium egg yolks
around 20 ripe passion fruit (enough to give 250g pulp) or 250g ready-made frozen purée, defrosted
550ml double cream
80ml milk
1 vanilla pod
½ quantity Italian meringue (see page 37)
1 quantity genoise sponge (see page 14)

FOR THE SUGAR SYRUP:

100g sugar
100ml water
2 tablespoons rum or Malibu

FOR THE GLAZE:

2 gelatine leaves
50g caster sugar
250ml apple juice
seeds from three or four of the passion fruit

Soak the gelatine in cold water to soften, then squeeze out the excess water.

To make the syrup, put the sugar in a pan with the water and bring to the boil. Reduce the heat and simmer until the sugar has dissolved and you have a colourless syrup. Take off the heat and stir in the rum or Malibu and allow to cool.

Whisk the sugar and egg yolks in a bowl until the mixture has become pale.

If using fresh passion fruit, cut them in half, scoop out the seeds and scrape the pulp into a pan (keep the seeds from three or four of the fruit to one side to use for the glaze later), or use purée. Add 50ml of the cream and all of the milk to the pan, with the vanilla pod (cut in half and seeds scraped in), and bring to a simmer. Take off the heat and slowly pour onto the sugar and egg mixture, whisking all the time.

(Continues overleaf)

Return the mixture to the pan and simmer gently, stirring, until you have a custard thick enough to coat the back of a wooden spoon.

Take off the heat and leave to cool slightly. Remove the vanilla pod, then stir in the gelatine until it dissolves. Leave to cool completely. Fold in the Italian meringue.

In a separate bowl, whisk the rest of the double cream until thick enough for the whisk to leave a ribbon trail when you lift it up, then fold this into the custard and meringue mixture.

You need a pastry ring (about 23cm in diameter and 6cm deep). Use this as a guide to cut out a circle of genoise sponge.

Place the ring on a round cake board and put the sponge into the base. Brush liberally with the syrup. Pour the mousse mixture on top and spread out gently so that it is level. You need to stop about 1mm below the rim of the ring, to allow space for a layer of glaze on top. Lift one corner of the cake board very slightly with a palette knife, and tap it very gently up and down just to remove any large pockets of air from the mousse. Put in the fridge for at least an hour until set and cold.

Meanwhile, make the glaze. Soak the gelatine in cold water to soften, then squeeze out the excess water. Put the sugar, fruit juice and passion fruit seeds, if you have them, in a pan and warm through. Take off the heat and stir in the gelatine. Leave until cool but not set.

Take the mousse from the fridge, pour a thin layer of glaze over the top and put back into the fridge for a minimum of 4 hours, or preferably overnight, to set.

To remove the ring, loosen it first around the edge of the mousse with a very slim bendy blade, or warm the ring with a blow torch very briefly from a distance, then slide off.

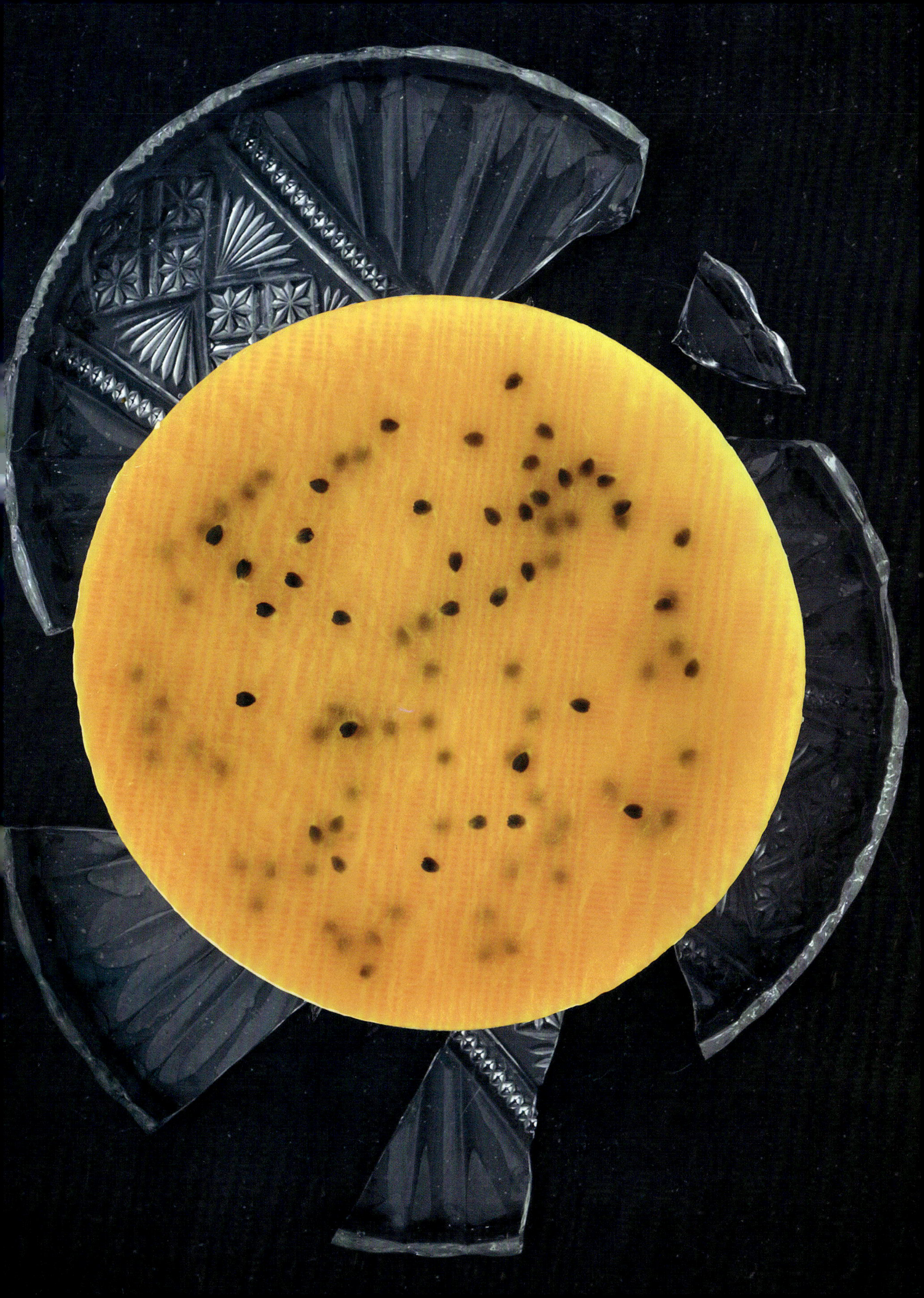

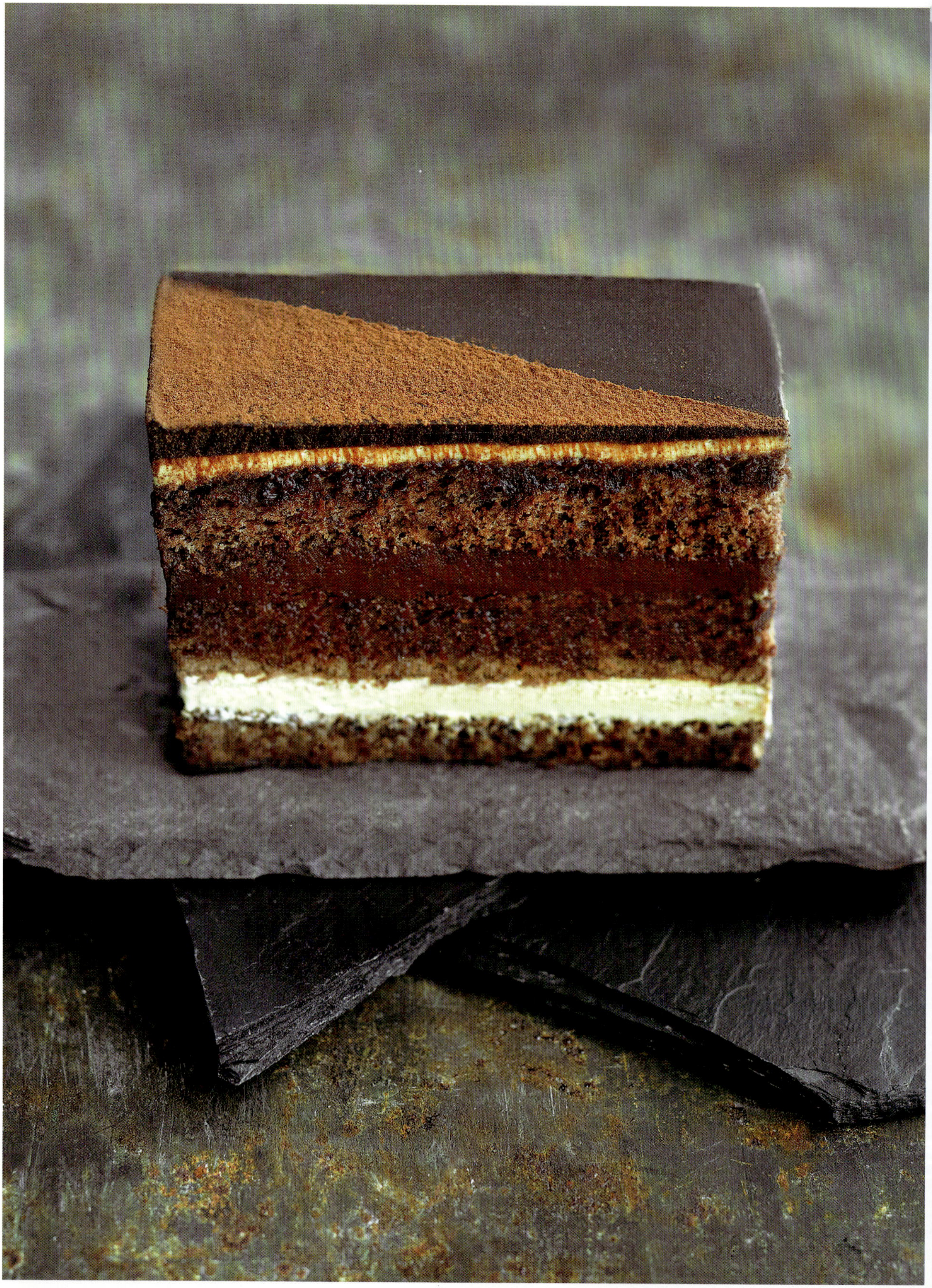

Chocolat liegeois

This is a take on the classic café liegeois, which is made with coffee ice cream and cream. We use chocolate sponge and Chantilly cream – and no ice cream.

MAKES AROUND 8 SLICES

1 quantity chocolate genoise sponge (see page 19)
1 quantity crème Chantilly (see page 42)
cocoa powder, for dusting

FOR THE CHOCOLATE GANACHE:
400ml double cream
50ml liquid glucose
500g good quality dark chocolate (at least 70% cocoa solids)
100g butter

FOR THE SYRUP:
100g sugar
100ml water
2 tablespoons strong coffee

FOR THE GLAZE:
200g good quality dark chocolate (at least 70% cocoa solids)
50ml vegetable oil

Cut the sponge into three strips lengthways.

To make the ganache, heat the cream and glucose in a pan until just below the boil, pour onto the dark chocolate and whisk or use a hand blender to emulsify everything together. Allow to cool for 5–10 minutes then whisk in the butter.

To make the syrup, put the sugar in a pan with the water and bring to the boil. Reduce the heat and simmer until the sugar has dissolved and you have a colourless syrup. Take off the heat and stir in the coffee.

To assemble, beat the chocolate ganache just before using, as this helps to lighten it. Lay the first layer of sponge on a rectangular cake board and brush liberally with the syrup until well soaked, then spread with three quarters of the Chantilly cream. Add the next layer of sponge and brush with syrup as before. Spread with the ganache.

(Continues overleaf)

Top with the final layer of sponge and brush with syrup again. Spread with the remaining Chantilly cream and put into the fridge for at least 30 minutes to firm up. Meanwhile, to make the glaze, break the chocolate into chunks and put into a heatproof bowl over a pan of gently simmering water, making sure the base doesn't touch the water – you don't want to get any heat or steam in the bowl, which would make the chocolate stiffen and become dull.

Let the chocolate melt gently, stirring, then stir in the oil with a whisk and allow to cool to a spreading consistency.

Take the cake out of the fridge and pour the glaze over the top. Don't worry if it drizzles over the side a little. Put back into the fridge for another 2 hours, then if you want to neaten it up you can trim the sides where the glaze has drizzled, with a knife dipped first into hot water. Then slice crossways into around eight slices, depending on how wide you like them.

Dust each slice with cocoa through a fine sieve. If you like you can cover half of the top with baking paper diagonally as you do this. When you lift it off you will have a sharp line between matt and shiny chocolate.

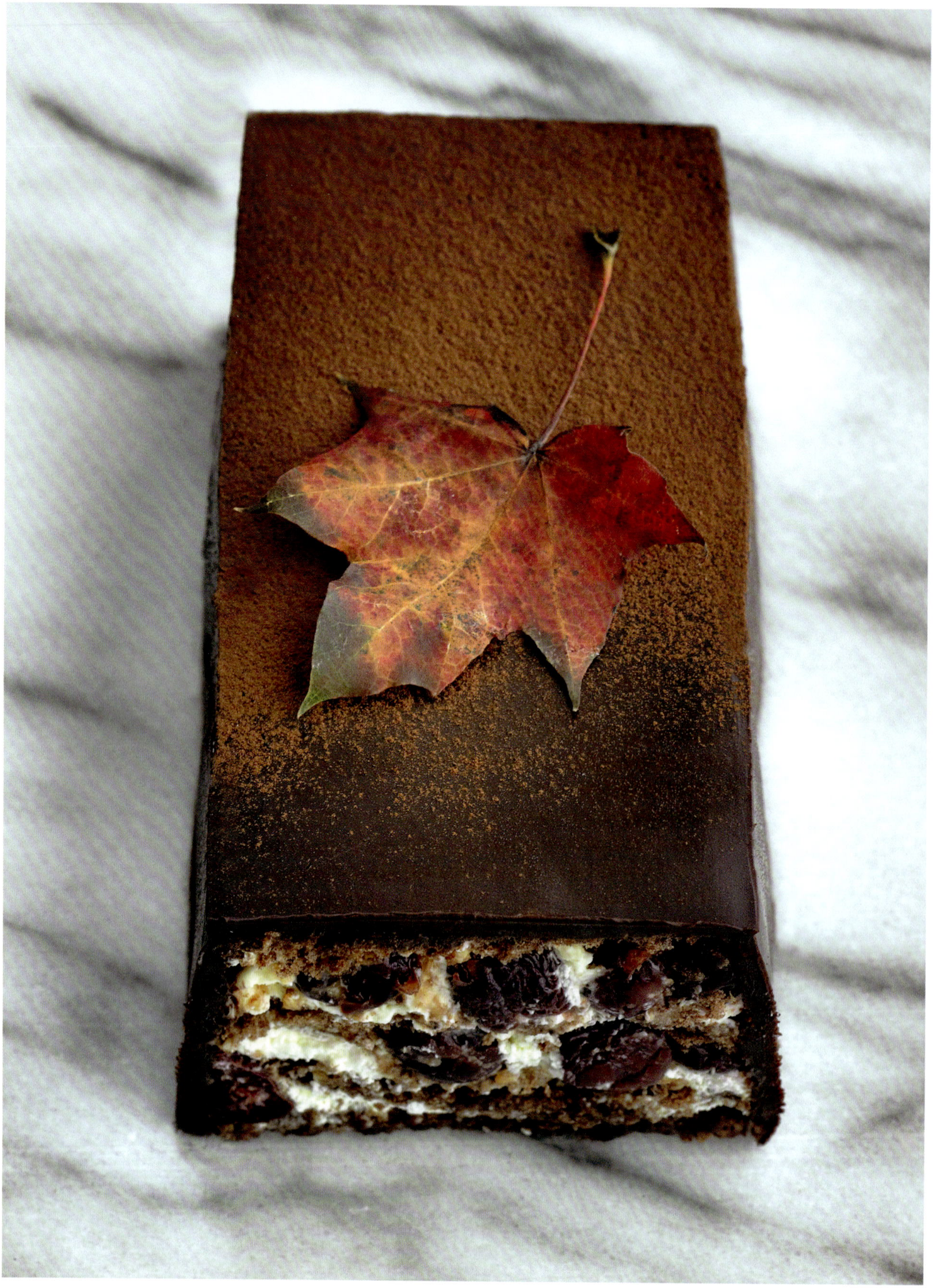

Black Forest gâteau

This famous cake is actually very similar to the Chocolat Liegeois on page 119, in that it is constructed with layers of chocolate sponge and cream, but of course it has cherries added – preferably use the big syrupy Italian Amarena ones, if you can find them.

MAKES 1 X 30CM CAKE

200g cherries in syrup
about 4 tablespoons kirsch
1 quantity chocolate genoise sponge (see page 19)
1 quantity crème Chantilly (see page 42)
cocoa powder, for dusting (optional)

FOR THE CHOCOLATE GANACHE:
400ml double cream
50ml liquid glucose
500g good quality dark chocolate (at least 70% cocoa solids)
100g butter

Drain the cherries, reserving the syrup, and mix this with the kirsch.

Cut the cherries in half if they are large.

Line a 30cm-long terrine or bread tin with clingfilm to overhang the edges.

Cut the sponge into three strips that will fit inside the mould. Lay the first strip in place and brush liberally with the kirsch syrup so that it is well soaked.

Spread with half of the Chantilly cream. Push in half of the cherries as evenly as you can. Lay the next layer of sponge on top and brush with syrup as before.

Spread with the rest of the Chantilly cream and push in the rest of the cherries. Finish with the remaining layer of sponge and press down gently. Fold the clingfilm over the top.

Put in the fridge for at least 2 hours to set.

(Continues overleaf)

Meanwhile, to make the ganache, heat the cream and glucose in a pan until just below the boil, pour onto the dark chocolate and whisk or use a hand blender to emulsify all together. Allow to cool for 5–10 minutes then whisk in the butter.

Take the gâteau from the fridge and open the clingfilm. To turn out, place a cake board on top of the terrine or bread tin and, using both hands, firmly grip both and turn over together. Remove the clingfilm.

Pour half of the ganache over the top and sides of the gâteau and smooth it a little with a palette knife. Put into the fridge to set for at least half an hour, then take out and pour over the rest of the ganache, smoothing it well with a palette knife so that it is even. Put back into the fridge and chill for a further 2 hours at least before serving. Dust with cocoa powder, if desired.

Vin d'orange

This cool drink recipe comes courtesy of La Fontaine d'Ampus, a lovely restaurant in a courtyard in the pretty little hillside village of Ampus, France, near my wife Jo's family holiday home in Provence. It is brilliant on a summer's evening with a wedge of Tarte Tropezienne. In France you can buy 'l'alcool pour fruit' in the supermarket, but I suggest you use vodka. You do need space for a big tupperware box in the bottom of the fridge (or you could halve the quantity) – and you need patience, as you have to wait 40 days for it to be ready!

Quarter 8 oranges and 2 lemons, leaving the skin on. Put in a large tupperware box (that has a lid) along with 5 litres of rosé wine, 1 litre vodka, 850g sugar, a bayleaf, 3 cloves and a stick of cinnamon. Put on the lid and leave in the bottom of the fridge for 40 days, then filter, bottle and keep chilled.

Tarte Tropezienne

This is a traditional tarte in and around St Tropez. My friend Thierry Pezzuli, who runs a bakery in nearby Les Arcs sur Argens, makes great big tartes, and when we are there on holiday, he always brings one when he comes around for an aperitif. This recipe is inspired by his version.

It isn't a classic tart as we think of them in the UK; it is more like a Victoria sponge, but made with a light, sweet dough. Although it will keep for a couple of days in the fridge, it is best eaten fresh at room temperature with a glass of rosé or, even better, vin d'orange, the local tipple.

The dough is difficult to make in small quantities, so I suggest you either freeze half of the dough for another time, or use it to make tiny doughnuts (see page 167). The easiest way to make it is using a food mixer, otherwise you need to follow my special stretch-and-fold technique for dough (see website link on page 221).

MAKES 2 X 23CM TARTES

a little butter for greasing and flour for dusting,
   if using a baking ring

FOR THE FERMENT:
125ml full-fat milk
½ teaspoon fresh yeast
125g strong bread flour

FOR THE DOUGH:
375g strong bread flour
10g fresh yeast
35g caster sugar
10g salt
1 medium egg
60g butter
125ml full-fat milk

Warm the milk for the ferment until just tepid then pour into the bowl of a food mixer. Crumble the yeast into the flour, add to the milk and whisk until you have a mixture like a thick porridge. Cover the bowl with clingfilm and leave for a minimum of 2 hours at room temperature.

Add all the dough ingredients to the ferment and mix for 3–4 minutes on a slow speed, then about 10 minutes at medium speed until the dough comes away cleanly from the sides of the bowl.

Lightly flour your work surface and turn out the dough. Fold it over on itself a few times then form it into a tight ball. Cover with a clean tea towel and leave to rest for at least an hour in a draught-free place.

(Continues overleaf)

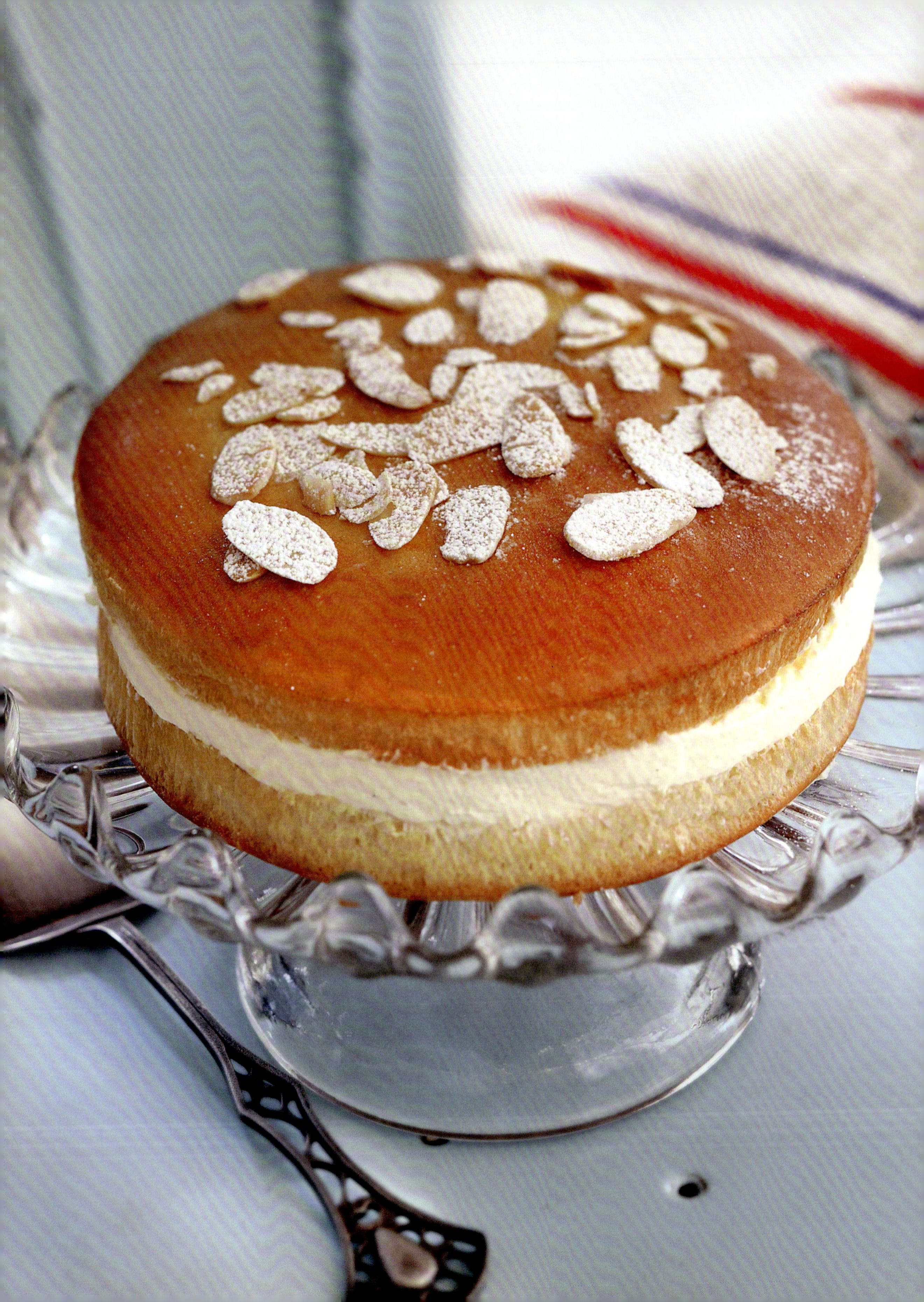

FOR THE FILLING
   (FOR 1 TARTE):
a few drops of orange flower essence
1 quantity crème légère
   (see page 43)

TO DECORATE:
1 medium egg, beaten with a pinch of salt
2 tablespoons flaked almonds
a little icing sugar, for dusting

Divide into two balls. Freeze one at this point, or use it for doughnuts (see page 167). Roll the remaining ball into a circle, roughly 23cm in diameter and about 5mm thick.

You can either lay the dough straight onto a non-stick baking tray, or if you want a neater edge, place a ring, about 23cm and lightly buttered and floured, on top of the tray, and lift the circle of dough into it. Cover again with a clean tea towel and leave to prove for 1 hour.

Preheat the oven to 190°C/gas 5, and ideally put a baking stone or upturned baking tray on the middle shelf to heat up – when you place your tray of dough on it, this will help to direct the heat quickly to the base of the tart.

Brush the top of the dough with the beaten egg. Scatter with flaked almonds. Place the baking tray on top of your baking stone or upturned tray in the oven for about 20–25 minutes until dark golden brown on the top. If you lift an edge of the base with a palette knife, it should be light brown and firm underneath.

Take out of the oven, lift off the ring if using, and leave the tarte to cool on a rack.

Mix the orange flower essence into the crème légère and when the tarte is cool, slice in half horizontally and sandwich with the cream. Dust the almonds with icing sugar.

Gâteau St Honoré

St Honoré is the patron saint of the boulanger, and this construction of choux pastry, cream and caramel was created as a kind of tribute to him. Honoré was also the name of my first boss, which I found very amusing at the time.

MAKES 2 SMALL GÂTEAUX

1 quantity choux pastry mixture
    (see page 20)
double quantity crème Chantilly
    (see page 42)
4 tablespoons flaked almonds (optional)

FOR THE CARAMEL:
200g caster sugar
2 tablespoons water

Preheat the oven to 190°C/gas 5. Lightly grease a non-stick baking tray or have ready a silicone mat.

If decorating with almonds, toast these lightly in a dry frying pan until pale golden. Take off the heat and keep to one side.

Snip off the corner of a piping bag, if using a disposable one, insert a plain nozzle about 1cm in diameter and fill with the choux pastry mixture.

Pipe two spiral bases about 15–18cm in diameter onto the baking tray or mat (start piping from the centre and work outwards in circles). Then pipe twelve dots (about the size of a £1 coin in diameter) – make sure they are spaced well apart.

Bake in the preheated oven for 12–15 minutes until golden and puffed up. For the last 4 minutes of baking, leave the oven door slightly ajar to allow the steam to escape and help the drying process. Remove the tray from the oven and leave to cool.

(Continues overleaf)

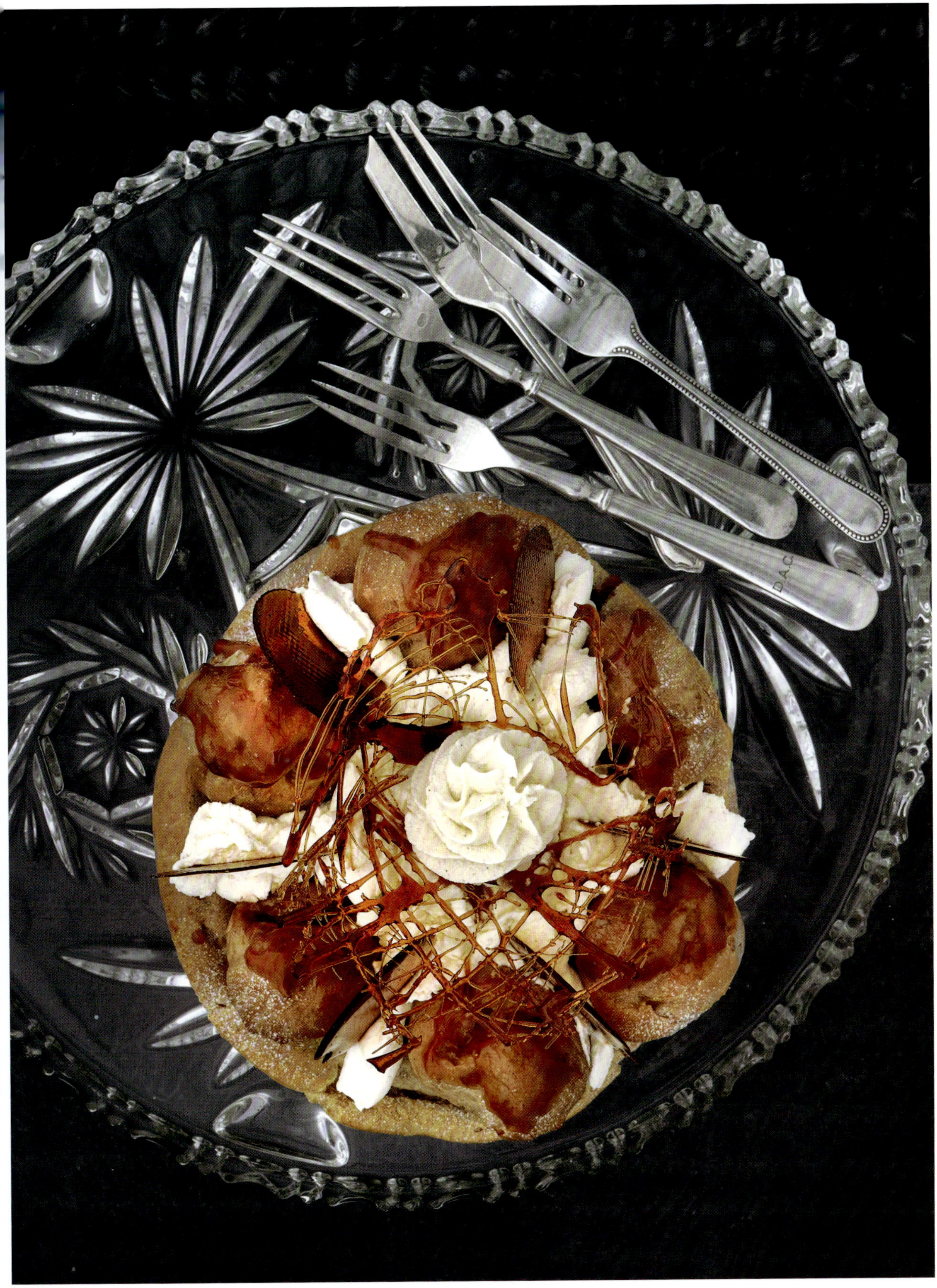

Make a hole in the base of each bun. Fill a new piping bag fitted with a small plain nozzle with the Chantilly cream and pipe a little into each bun – keep about half of the cream back for decorating the gâteaux.

Make the caramel by putting the sugar in a pan with the water, bring to the boil and continue to boil until golden brown (if you have a sugar thermometer, the temperature will be 140°C). It will be really hot, so be careful.

To assemble, carefully dip the base of each bun into the caramel and stick six of them around the edge of each spiral.

Pipe the rest of the Chantilly cream in the centre and in the gaps around the buns.

Take a spoon or fork, dip it into the caramel and swirl it around the top of the gâteaux in thin strands to decorate. Finish, if you like, with toasted almonds scattered over.

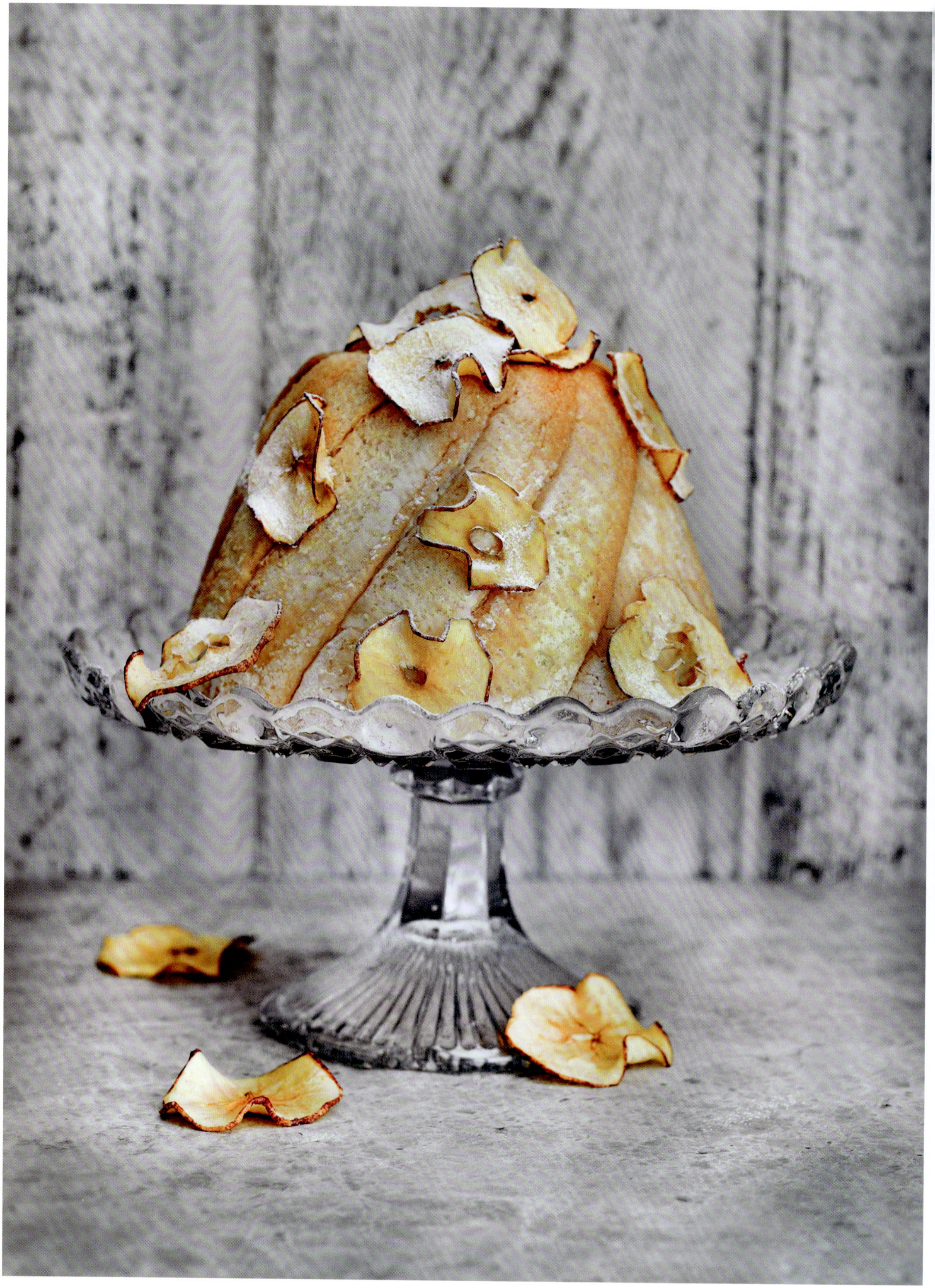

Charlotte aux pommes

This always looks impressive, and so people think it must be difficult to make, but it isn't. It just takes a bit of time and planning … and it is well worth the effort.

It is made with a *bavarois* – a light cream, made with custard and meringue – mixed with caramelised apples, encased in slim, light, puffy *biscuits à la cuillère* (the long, thin biscuits that go around the side of a cake are often called 'ladyfingers'). You want some apples with a bit of character and sharpness for this, such as Cox or Braeburn or a good local variety. You could also use pears.

I like to decorate the charlotte with wafer-thin slices of dried apple scattered over the top, which gives it an autumnal look.

MAKES AROUND 8 SLICES

FOR THE APPLE BAVAROIS:
50g butter
2 tablespoons sugar
4 eating apples, peeled, cored and diced
2 tablespoons Calvados or Somerset Cider Brandy
4 gelatine leaves
80g caster sugar
3 medium egg yolks
150ml apple juice
1 vanilla pod
250ml double cream
1 quantity Italian meringue (see page 37)

FOR THE BISCUITS À LA CUILLÈRE:
3 medium eggs, separated
90g caster sugar
90g plain flour, sifted

TO DUST THE BISCUITS:
60g icing sugar

FOR THE SUGAR SYRUP:
100g sugar
1 tablespoon Calvados or Somerset Cider Brandy
100ml water

TO DECORATE:
Dried apples (see page 53)

(Continues overleaf)

You need a number 3 (2-pint) pudding bowl. Preheat the oven to 170°C/gas 3.

To caramelise the apples for the bavarois, melt the butter and sugar in a pan until light golden, put in the apples and stir well. Add the Calvados and toss the apples around, until tender and lightly caramelised, then take off the heat and keep to one side.

To make the sugar syrup, put the sugar in a pan with the Calvados and water and bring to the boil. Reduce the heat and simmer until the sugar has dissolved and you have a colourless syrup. Take off the heat and allow to cool.

To make the *biscuits à la cuillère*, whisk the egg whites to soft peaks, then add 60g of the sugar and continue to whisk until you have a meringue that is thick enough to hold onto the whisk.

In a separate bowl, whisk the rest of the sugar with the egg yolks until pale and creamy.

Mix the meringue into the egg yolk mix with a wooden spoon, then fold in the flour – the mixture will now be very thick and creamy.

(Continues overleaf)

Have ready a non-stick baking tray, or preferably a silicone mat. Snip off the corner of a piping bag, if using a disposable one, insert a 1cm plain nozzle, fill with the *biscuits* mixture and pipe fourteen fingers, each around 11cm long. Next you need to pipe three spirals (start piping from the centre and work outwards in circles). The first, for the base of the bowl, should be around 8cm; the second, which will go in the middle of the bowl, should be around 10cm; and the largest, which will be for the top, needs to be around 12cm.

Sprinkle the icing sugar over the top using a small sieve.

Put the tray or mat into the preheated oven and bake for 10 minutes until the *biscuits* colour very lightly, expand and are spongy to the touch. Take out of the oven and leave to cool.

(Continues overleaf)

For the bavarois, soak the gelatine in cold water to soften, then squeeze out the excess water.

Whisk the sugar and egg yolks in a bowl until pale.

Put the apple juice in a pan with the vanilla pod (halved and seeds scraped in) and bring to a simmer. Take off the heat and slowly pour onto the sugar and egg mixture, whisking all the time.

Return this apple custard to the pan and simmer gently, stirring, until thickened slightly.

Take off the heat, remove the vanilla pod, then leave to cool slightly and stir in the gelatine until it dissolves. Leave to cool completely.

In a large bowl whisk the double cream until thick enough for the whisk to leave a ribbon trail when you lift it up. Now fold in the Italian meringue, caramelised apple, and apple custard.

To assemble the charlotte, line your pudding basin with clingfilm and put the smallest spiral of *biscuit* into the base, with the sugary side facing downwards. Arrange the fingers of *biscuit* vertically around the basin, with the sugary side facing outwards, and overlapping slightly – make sure there are no gaps – then brush the insides of all the biscuits liberally with the reserved sugar syrup – they will soak it up well, so be generous.

(Continues overleaf)

Spoon in the apple bavarois mixture to come halfway up the basin.

Place the medium-sized spiral of *biscuit* on top – again this should go in sugared side downwards – and brush with syrup.

Spoon in the rest of the bavarois mixture. You are going to put the final *biscuit* on top, with the sugared side upwards this time, so before you do so, brush the smooth underside with the rest of the syrup.

Place the *biscuit* gently on top. Don't worry about the fingers sticking up beyond the final spiral of *biscuit* at this point, as once the charlotte is set you will trim them. If you have any mixture left over, put it into a freezer box and let it set – apple ice cream!

Put the bowl into the fridge for 4–5 hours, ideally overnight, to set. When ready to serve, trim the tops of the sponge fingers so that they are level with the top spiral.

To turn out, place a serving plate on top of the basin and, using both hands, firmly grip the plate and basin and turn both over together. The charlotte should slide easily onto the plate. Decorate with slices of dried apple – they will stick wherever you put them.

Chocolate meringue tart

This is a play on the classic fondant pudding – soft and melting inside – combined with Italian meringue. Sometimes I embed nuggets of chocolate salted caramel into the chocolate filling before baking – if you want to do this the recipe for the caramels is on page 177. With or without them it is a serious hit of rich sweetness: you have been warned!

MAKES 1 X 30CM TART

1 quantity Italian meringue (see page 37)

FOR THE CHOCOLATE FILLING:
50g caster sugar
2 large eggs, plus 3 medium yolks
200g good quality dark chocolate
    (at least 70% cocoa solids)
150g unsalted butter
80g plain flour

TO DECORATE:
Long, thin chocolate pencils
    (see page 56), optional

Preheat the oven to 90°C/gas ¼.

To pipe the meringue for the tart case, cut the corner of a piping bag, if using a disposable one, and insert a 1cm star nozzle. Fill with half of the meringue and, beginning in the centre, pipe it round and round in a spiral until you have a circle of about 24–25cm in diameter, which will be the base of your tart case. Next pipe an edge about 2cm high – you can either do this by going around twice, or just once, lifting the nozzle up and down as you go, in a wave motion (see picture page 144).

Put into the preheated oven for about 4 hours until dried out and solid to the touch but not coloured. Remove and keep to one side.

Turn up the oven to 160°C/gas 3.

For the chocolate filling, whisk the sugar and the whole eggs and yolks until they turn a pale straw colour and creamy.

(Continues overleaf)

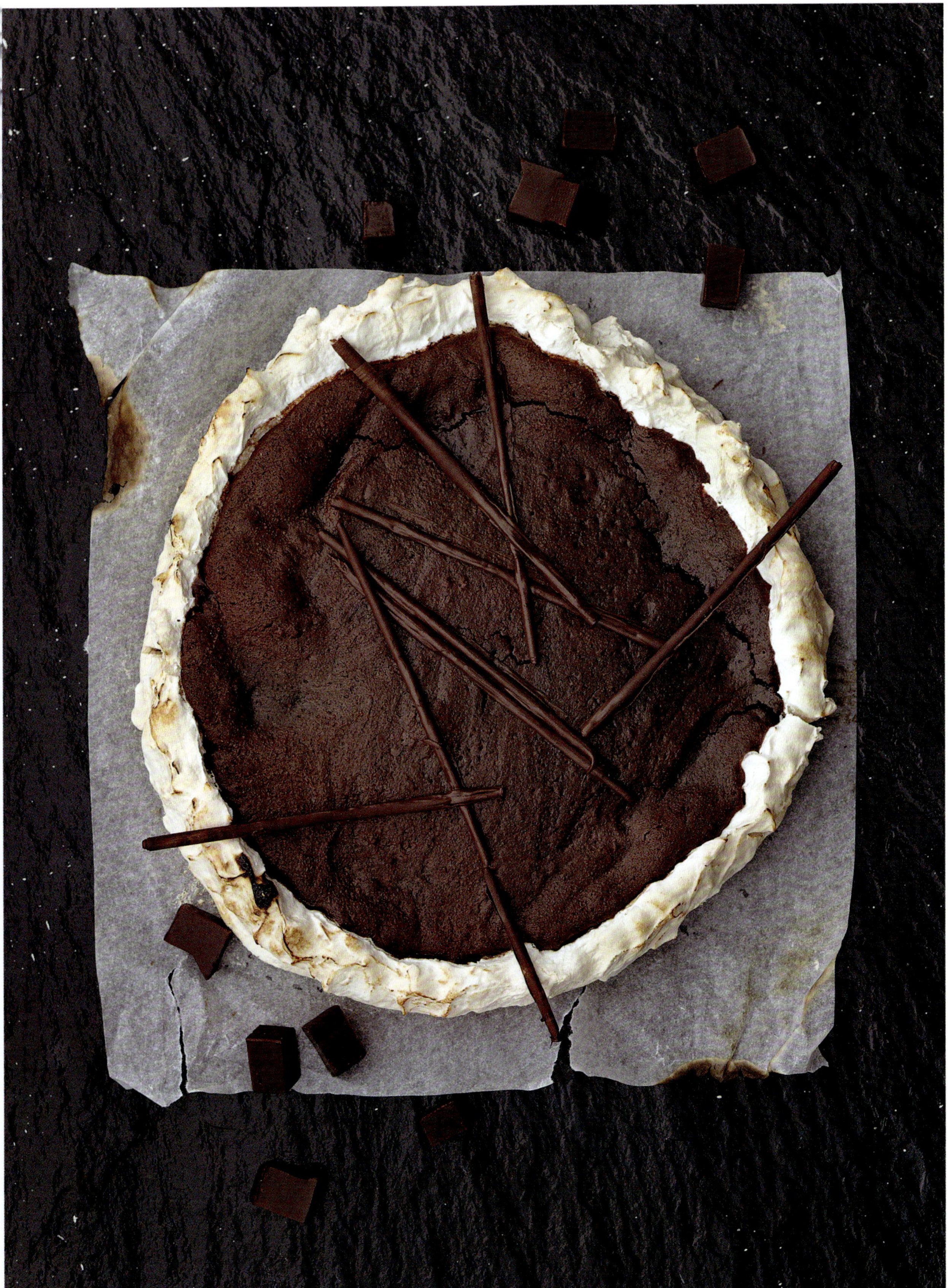

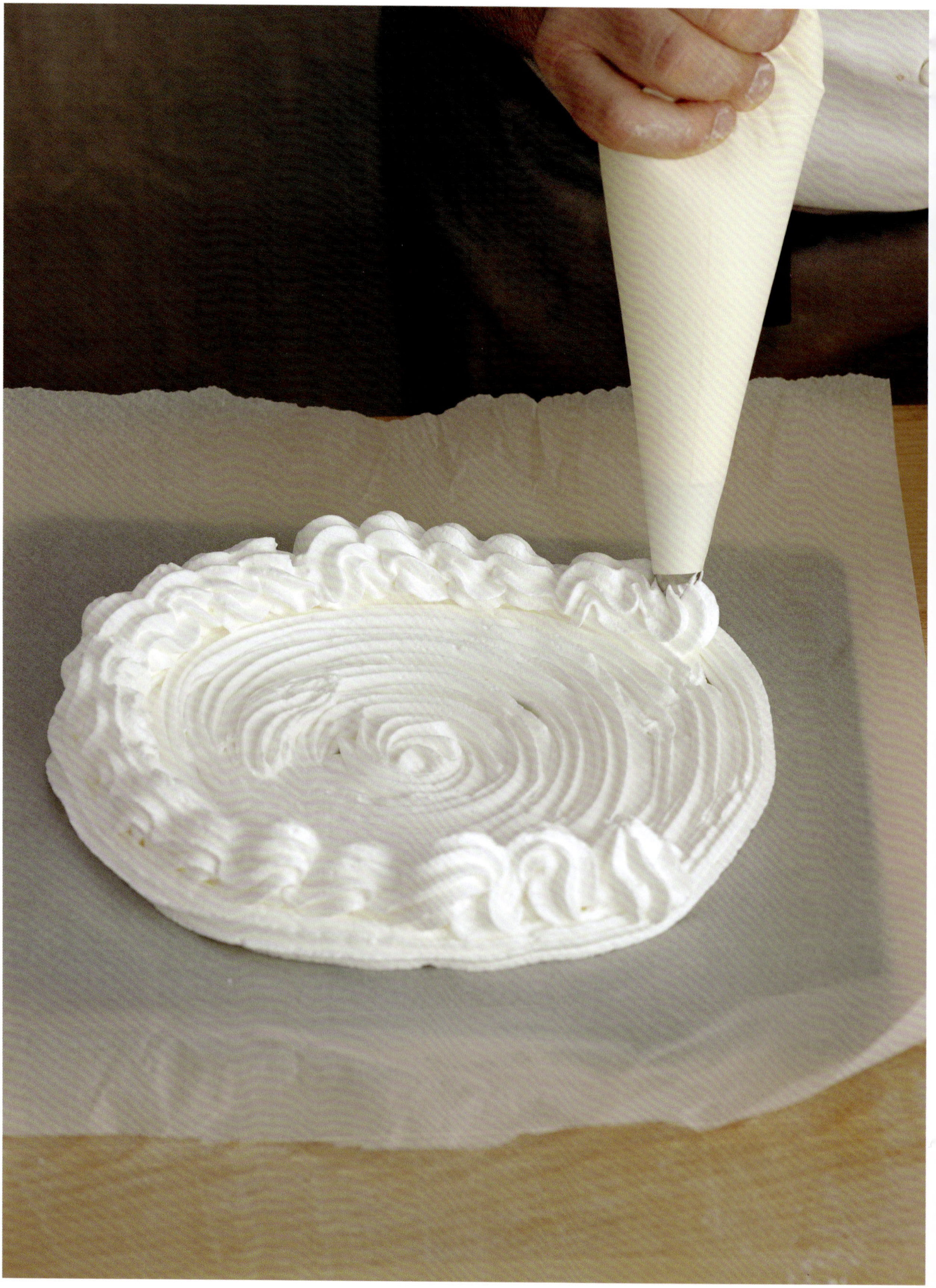

Break the chocolate into chunks and put into a bowl over a pan of gently simmering water, making sure the base doesn't touch the water – you don't want to get any heat or steam in the bowl, which would make the chocolate stiffen and become dull.

Let the chocolate melt gently, stirring, then add the butter and continue to stir until this too has melted.

Take off the heat and stir into the sugar and egg mixture, until it is all incorporated. Gently fold in the flour.

Spoon into the meringue case and smooth the top, then put into the preheated oven and bake for 15 minutes until the mixture is springy to the touch. Don't be tempted to leave it in any longer as the centre should be soft and gooey when you cut into the tart.

Leave to cool and then decorate, if you like, with the chocolate pencils.

Blood orange tart

Blood oranges have an almost grapefruity flavour, but when they are not in season, you can use bought blood orange juice, plus the zest of three ordinary oranges.

You could dust the top of the tart with icing sugar after baking, and caramelise it with a blow torch, however it looks quite special if you decorate it with slices of caramelised oranges. If you like, you can make more than you need and pot them while still hot into sterilised jars (see page 51), where they will keep for several months.

MAKES 1 X 20CM TART

1 quantity sweet pastry (see page 26)
butter or baking spray, for greasing the tart tin
a little flour, for rolling
6 medium eggs, plus 1 medium egg beaten with a pinch of salt
zest and juice from around 3 blood oranges (you need 250ml of juice)
400g caster sugar
250g unsalted butter
1 tablespoon cornflour

FOR THE CARAMELISED ORANGE DECORATION:

100g sugar
200 ml water
1 blood orange or ordinary orange, cut crossways into thin rounds (about 5mm)

(Continues overleaf)

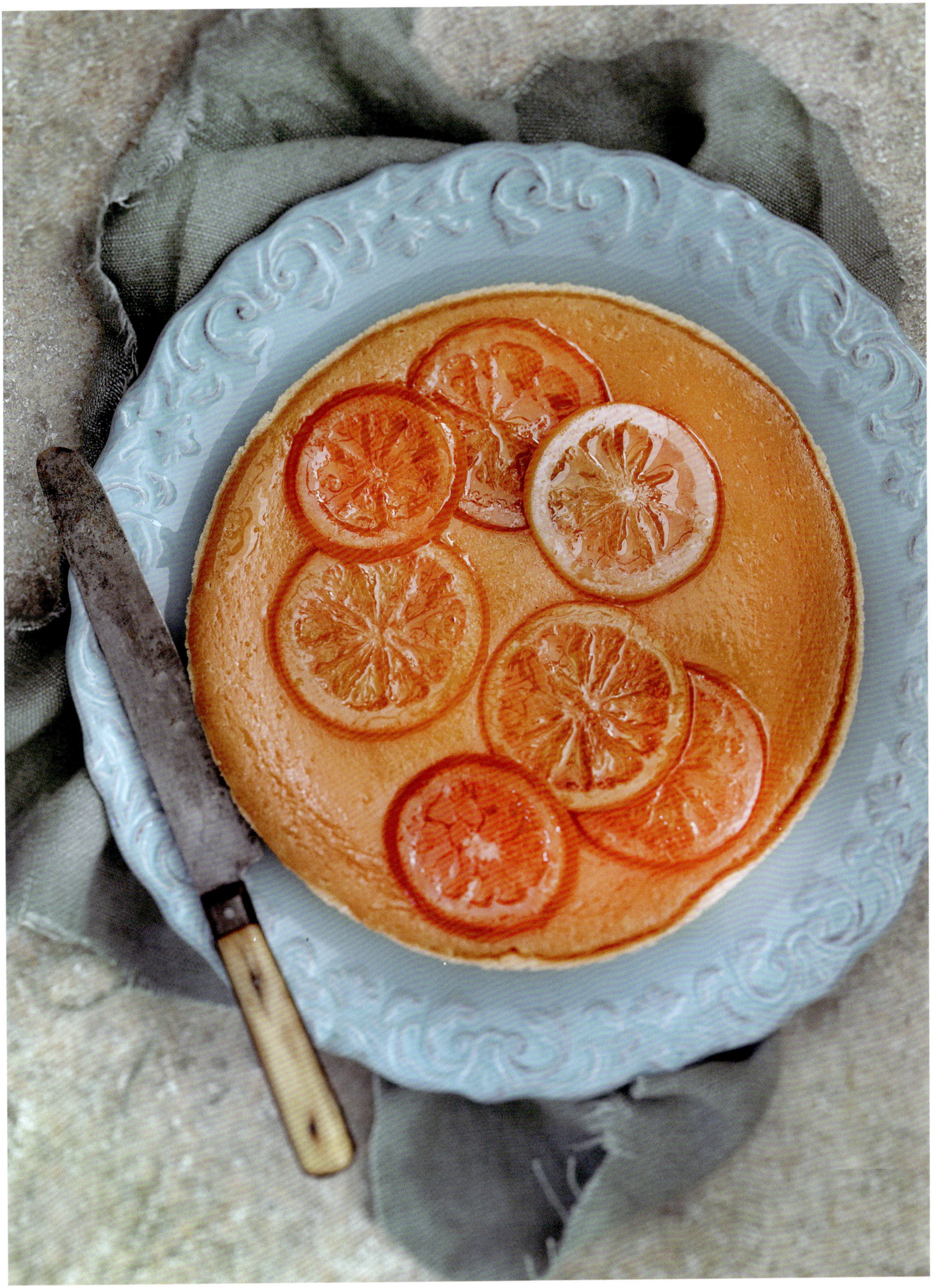

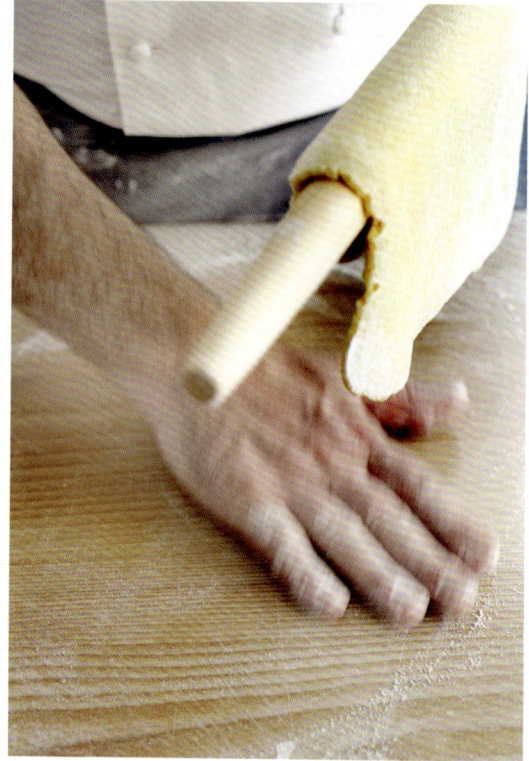

Lightly grease a 20cm loose-bottomed tart tin with butter or baking spray.

Lightly dust your work surface with flour, then roll out the pastry into a circle 5mm thick and large enough to fit into the tin, leaving an overhang of about 2.5cm.

Roll the pastry around your rolling pin so that you can lift it up without stretching it, then drape it over the tin and let it fall inside.

Ease the pastry carefully into the base and sides of the tin without stretching it, and leave it overhanging the edges. Tap the tin lightly against your work surface to settle it in. Prick the base of the pastry all over with a fork to stop it from trying to rise up when in the oven (even though it will be held down by baking beans, it can sometimes lift a little).

You can use a large sheet of baking paper for lining your tart case, however I prefer to use clingfilm (the kind that is safe for use in the oven or microwave) as it is softer than paper and won't leave indents in the pastry.

Place three sheets of clingfilm (or one sheet of baking paper) over the top of the pastry case, then tip in your baking beans and spread them out so that they completely cover the base. Don't trim the pastry yet. Put the case into the fridge for at least an hour (or the freezer for 15 minutes) to relax it.

Preheat the oven to 190°C/gas 5.

Remove the pastry case from the fridge and put into the preheated oven for about 20 minutes until the base has dried out and is very lightly coloured, like parchment.

(Continues overleaf)

Remove from the oven and lift out the clingfilm (or baking paper) and beans. Don't worry if the overhanging edges are quite brown, as you will be trimming these away after you have finished baking your tart.

Brush the inside of the pastry case with the beaten egg and put it back into the oven for another 10 minutes. The inside of the pastry, and particularly the base, will now be quite golden brown and shiny from the egg glaze, which will act as a barrier so that the pastry will stay crisp when you put in the filling.

Let the pastry case cool down and then you can trim away the overhanging edges.

Turn down the oven heat to 120°C/gas ½.

To make the filling, whisk together the orange zest and juice, the eggs, sugar, butter and cornflour in a bowl, then place over a pan of barely simmering water, making sure the base of the bowl doesn't actually touch the water. Whisk constantly over a low heat, moving the mixture around the bowl well, so that none sticks to the sides.

Once it starts to become a little thicker than double cream, continue to whisk for one more minute then take off the heat. To test that it is ready, scoop a little bit of mixture with a teaspoon and push it against the inside of the bowl towards the top. It should stay where it is without dripping. If it doesn't, put it back over the heat and whisk briefly for another minute at a time, until it passes the test.

Pour into the pastry case and bake in the preheated oven for about 15 minutes or until the filling is set.

Leave to cool for a couple of hours to room temperature before eating.

Meanwhile, for the caramelised oranges, make a syrup by putting the sugar in a pan with the water and bringing it to the boil. Reduce the heat and simmer until the sugar has dissolved and you have a colourless syrup. Turn the heat as low as possible.

Put in the orange slices and let them poach very gently in the syrup for a good hour at least. Take off the heat, cool and drain off the syrup before arranging on the top of the tart.

Flan patissier

This is the tart that you see in patisseries all over France (the equivalent of a custard tart). It is often made in a long slab that can be sliced as a treat at any time of the day, but especially for children coming home from school.

MAKES 1 X 20CM FLAN

1 quantity sweet pastry (see page 26)
a little butter or baking spray, for greasing the tin
a little flour, for rolling

FOR THE FILLING:
200ml full-fat milk
200ml double cream
1 vanilla pod
1 medium egg, plus 1 medium yolk
100g caster sugar
40g cornflour
20g butter, melted

Preheat the oven to 190°C/gas 5.

Lightly grease a 20cm loose-bottomed tart tin with butter or baking spray.

Lightly dust your work surface with flour, then roll out the pastry into a circle 5mm thick and large enough to fit into the tin, leaving an overhang of about 2.5cm.

Roll the pastry around your rolling pin so that you can lift it up without stretching it, then drape it over the tin and let it fall inside. Bake blind according to the instructions on pages 149–150.

Turn down the oven to 180°C/gas 4.

To make the filling, put the milk, cream and vanilla pod (split and seeds scraped in) in a pan, bring to a simmer (be careful not to let the mixture boil), then take off the heat and leave to infuse for at least an hour. Remove the vanilla pod.

(Continues overleaf)

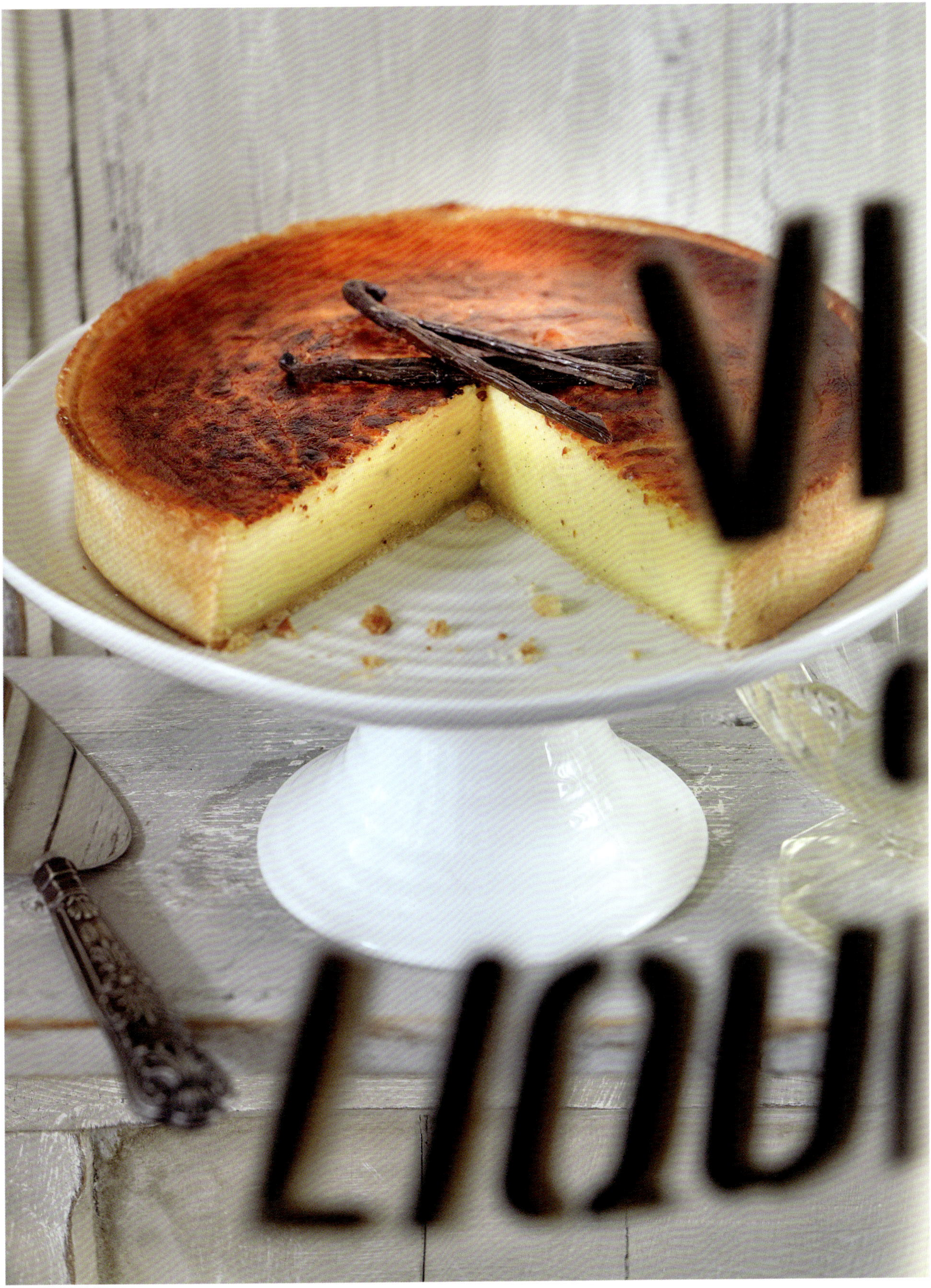

In a bowl, mix the egg, yolk and sugar until pale and creamy, and then whisk in the cornflour. Stir in the melted butter.

Put the pan containing the milk and cream mixture back on the heat and bring slowly to the boil, whisking all the time, then turn down to a simmer for 1 minute, still whisking all the time. Take off the heat and pour onto the egg and sugar mixture, stirring well.

Pour the mixture into the tart case and bake for around 45 minutes, until the filling is firm to the touch and a deep, dark golden on top – like the top of a crème brûlée. Take out of the oven, slide off the tin, and cool completely on a wire rack before serving.

BOULANGERIE
23
PATISSERIE
CONFISERIE
PAINS RUSTIQUE
PATISSERIE FINE
SPECIALITE DE
CROISSANTS

Treats

MOUTHFULS, MORSELS AND MUNCHIES

Rice pudding tartlets

A really moreish, comforting combination of creamy rice pudding, jam and sweet pastry. You could bake these in a 12-hole tart tin or use individual tins, such as the leaf-shaped tins shown here.

MAKES AROUND 12

1 quantity sweet pastry (see page 26)
a little flour, for rolling
a little butter, for greasing the tins
1 egg, beaten with a pinch of salt
around 100g raspberry jam (see page 47 for home-made)
icing sugar, to serve

FOR THE RICE PUDDING:

350ml full-fat milk
150ml double cream
1 vanilla pod
1 cardamom pod, lightly crushed
zest of 1 lemon
60g sugar
100g arborio rice

Preheat the oven to 190°C/gas 5.

To make the rice pudding, put the milk, cream and vanilla pod (split and seeds scraped in) in a pan with the cardamom pod and lemon zest and bring to a simmer. Stir in the sugar and the rice and continue to simmer very gently for around 30 minutes until the milk and cream have been absorbed and the rice is tender. Take off the heat.

Skim a fine film of flour over your work surface and roll out the pastry to around 2–3mm thick. Lightly grease a 12-hole tart tin or individual tins. Cut out the pastry into twelve rounds or shapes, depending on what tins you decide to use. If using a 12-hole tin, stamp out your circles of pastry with a cutter that is about 2.5cm bigger than the holes. If using individual tins these tend to be a little deeper, so allow an extra 3cm all round. If the tins are an unusual shape, turn one of them upside down on top of your pastry as a guide and then cut around it, making your shape

(Continues overleaf)

PATISSERIE MAISON

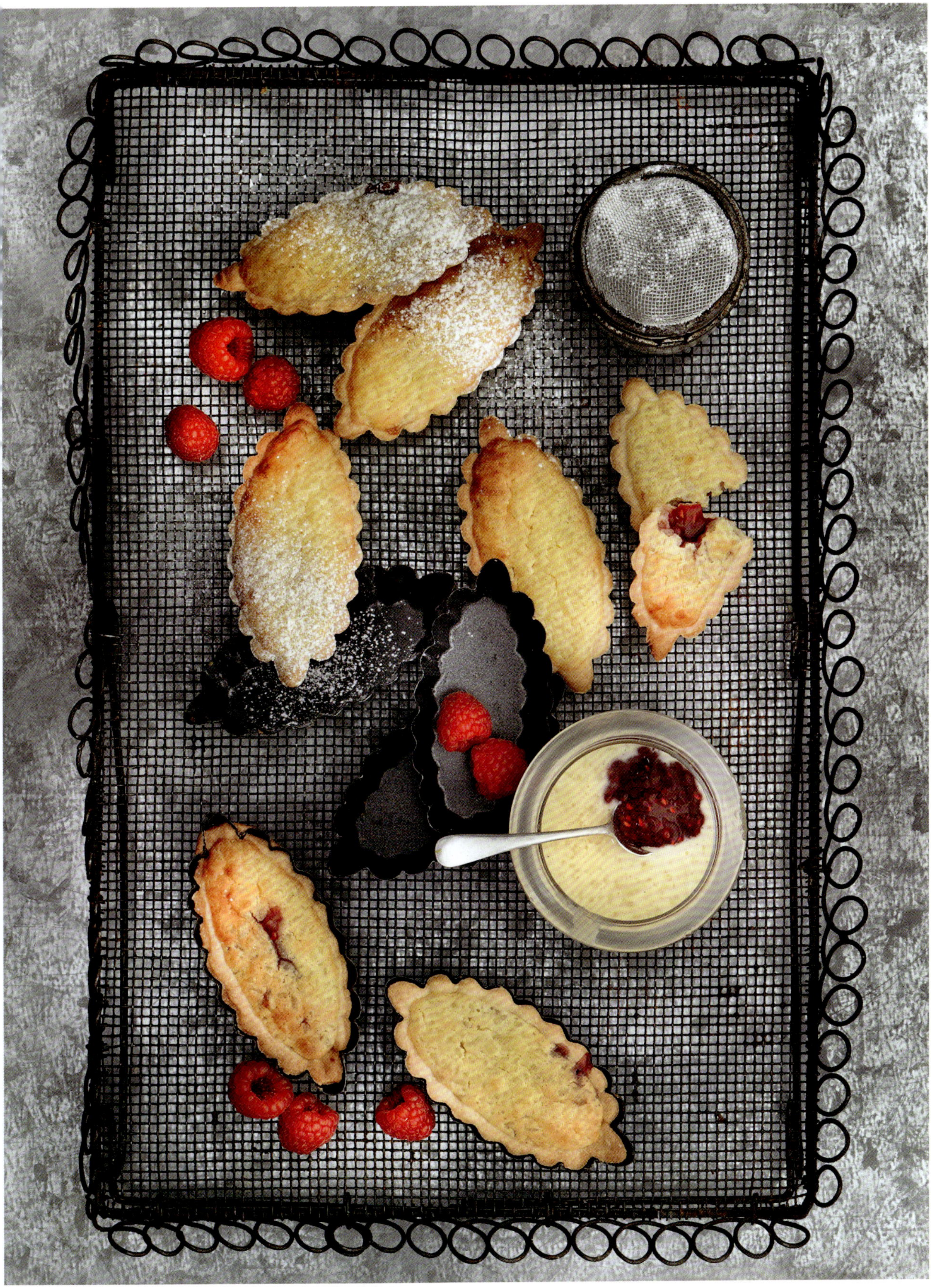

3cm bigger all round. Press the pastry into the tins and run a rolling pin over the top, which will trim the edges neatly. Then line each case with a small piece of clingfilm and some baking beans and bake blind (see pages 149–150) in the preheated oven for 15 minutes, then remove and brush the insides with beaten egg. Put back into the oven for another 8 minutes until golden brown and shiny.

Remove from the oven and turn down the heat to 180°C/gas 4.

Spread about a teaspoonful of jam into the base of each tartlet case, and then fill with rice pudding (remove the vanilla pod first). Put back into the oven for about 15–20 minutes until a little crust forms on top of the rice.

Serve either warm or cold, dusted with a little icing sugar.

Madeleines

You can buy madeleines – cakes with a little dome on top – in big packets in supermarkets all over France, but if you make your own, it is very rewarding. You can buy metal or silicone madeleine trays big enough to make up to 24 at a time.

In the bakery where I worked in France we would add toppings of chocolate and nuts – it is up to you, but I have suggested dipping some of the madeleines into melted chocolate and then hazelnuts, and the rest in chocolate followed by a little dusting of cocoa powder.

MAKES AROUND 24

4 eggs
180g caster sugar
50g honey
275g plain flour
25g baking powder
250g butter, plus a little extra for greasing the moulds (unless using silicone)
zest of ½ lemon

TO DECORATE (OPTIONAL):

about 200g good quality dark chocolate (70% cocoa solids), broken into pieces
a little cocoa powder, for dusting
about 2 tablespoons crushed roasted hazelnuts

In a bowl, whisk together the eggs, sugar, honey, flour and baking powder and leave for a minimum of four hours in the fridge, ideally overnight.

Preheat the oven to 190°C/gas 5.

Put the butter into a food mixer with the lemon zest and beat it to soften (or use a hand-held mixer). Take the egg and honey mixture from the fridge and add to the butter. Mix until it is well incorporated. Lightly grease your madeleine trays, then spoon the mixture into the trays and put into the preheated oven.

Turn down the heat to 170°C/gas 3 and bake for 7–8 minutes until risen and golden. Take out of the oven, turn out and cool on a wire rack.

(Continues overleaf)

TREATS

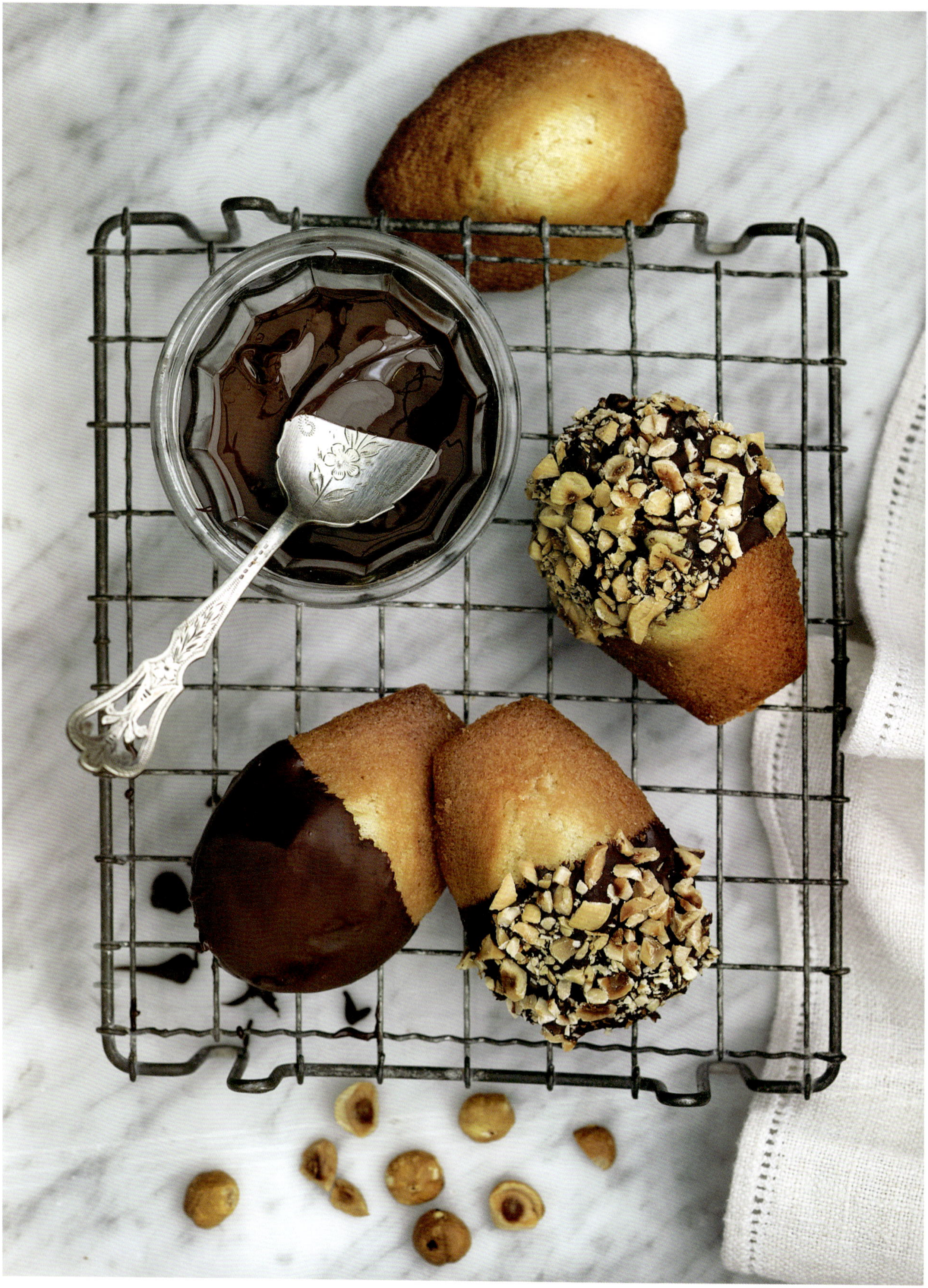

If you want to make chocolate madeleines, put the chocolate into a heatproof bowl over a pan of barely simmering water – make sure the water comes close to the bottom of the bowl but doesn't actually touch it. Keep the heat very low so that you don't get steam into the bowl, as this can make the chocolate become dull-looking and stiff. Keep stirring all the time and let the chocolate melt slowly, then remove the bowl from the heat.

Have the hazelnuts ready in a shallow bowl. Dip the rounded ends of the madeleines into the chocolate and then dip half of them into the bowl of crushed nuts so that the nuts coat the chocolate. Return to the wire rack to set.

For the rest, dust part of the chocolate-dipped area with cocoa powder using a small, fine sieve and place on the rack.

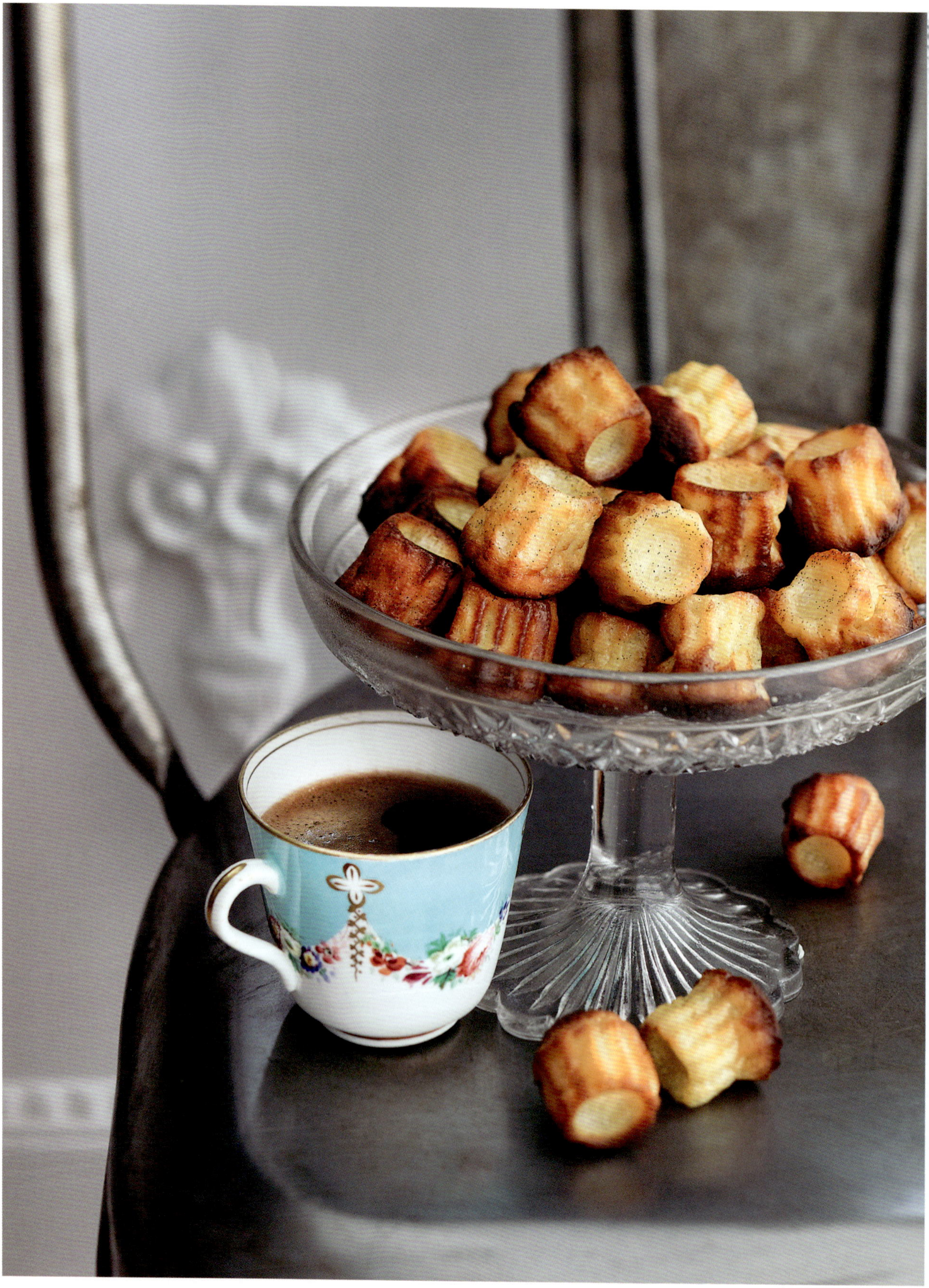

Cannelés

A speciality from the Bordeaux region, cannelés are these days fashionable all over France. They are chewy and caramelised, and it is impossible to eat just one! The old-fashioned cannelé moulds were individual and made of copper, however these days you can buy silicone trays of them that allow you to bake up to around 18 at a time.

MAKES 18–20

200ml full-fat milk
50ml double cream
25g butter
pinch of sea salt
2 tablespoons dark rum
100g caster or granulated sugar
1 vanilla pod
1 medium egg, plus 1 medium yolk
70g plain flour

Put the milk in a saucepan and add the cream, butter, salt, rum, half the sugar and the vanilla pod (split and seeds scraped in). Bring to a simmer, taking care not to let the mixture boil, then take off the heat straight away.

In a bowl, whisk the egg and yolk with the rest of the sugar until pale, then whisk in the flour.

Slowly add the hot milk and cream mixture, stirring constantly with the whisk.

Leave to cool and then put in the fridge for at least 4 hours, ideally overnight. Remove the vanilla pod.

Preheat the oven to 240°C/gas 9.

Half fill each mould with the mixture and bake for around 15 minutes until puffed up and caramelised.

Remove from the oven and allow to cool before turning out.

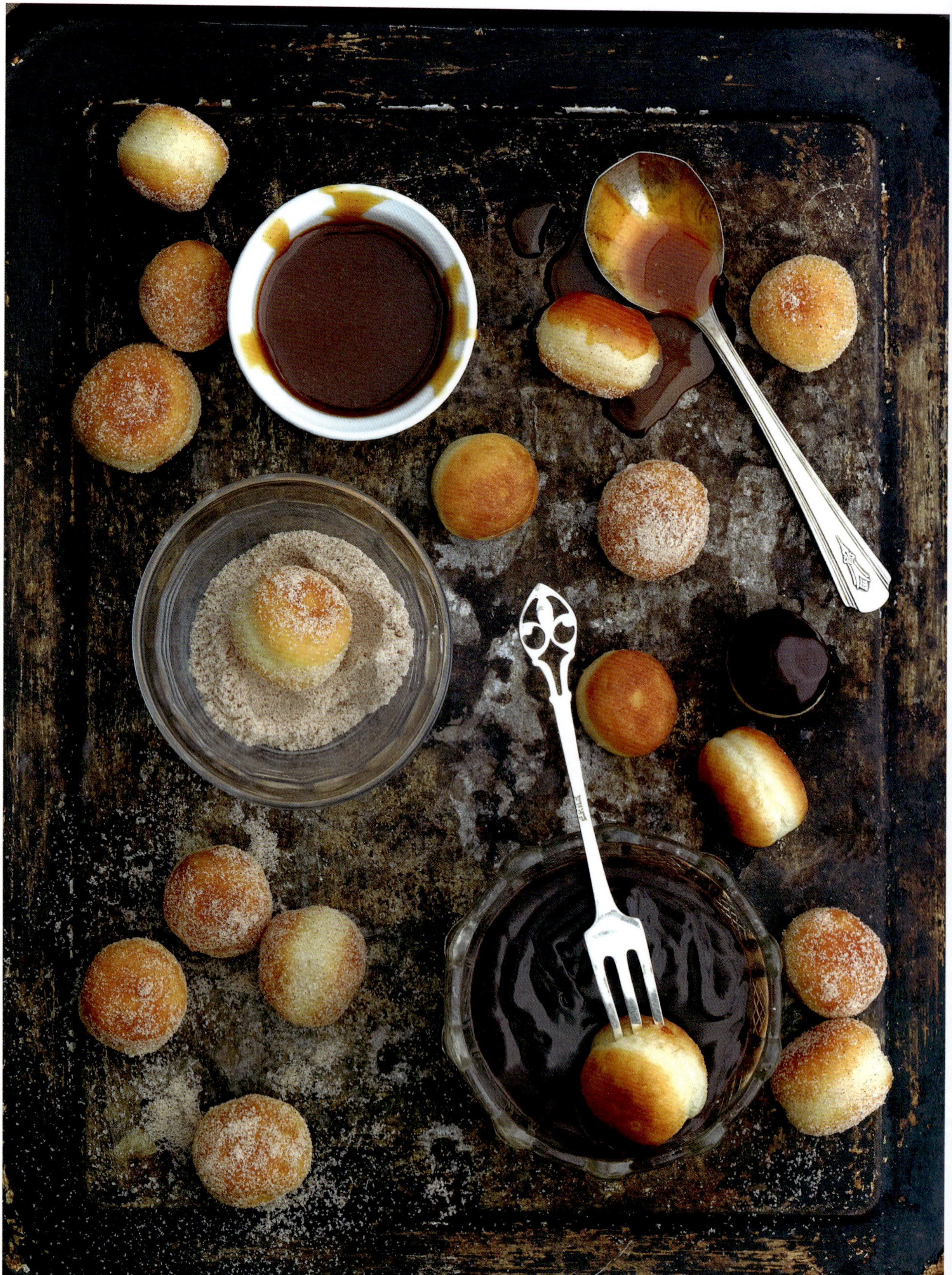

Mini doughnuts

These are bite-sized doughnuts that you can make with the unused dough from the Tarte Tropezienne recipe (see page 125). They are too small to fill, so I put out some little bowls of raspberry jam (see page 47) and a few small forks and let people spear the doughnuts and dip them into the jam as they like.

Roll out the dough to about 5mm, then take a tiny cutter – about 2cm in diameter – and stamp out as many rounds as you can. Place a clean tea towel on a large baking tray, lay the rounds of dough on top, not too close together, and cover with another clean tea towel. Leave to rest and swell for about 30 minutes.

To deep fry the doughnuts, pour some vegetable oil into a pan, making sure it comes no higher than a third of the way up. Heat until it reaches 180°C (if you don't have a thermometer use a doughnut as a tester: it should sizzle gently). Fry the doughnuts in small batches (or you will overcrowd the pan and bring the temperature down) for 30 seconds maximum until they begin to turn golden, then turn them over and fry for the same amount of time, until golden all over.

Lift out with a slotted spoon and drain on several layers of kitchen paper.

Have a bowl of granulated sugar ready and when the doughnuts are drained but still warm, roll them in it and serve with raspberry jam. You could also serve them with chocolate sauce (made with 100g melted chocolate and 100ml double cream, mixed together) or crème pâtissière (see page 41).

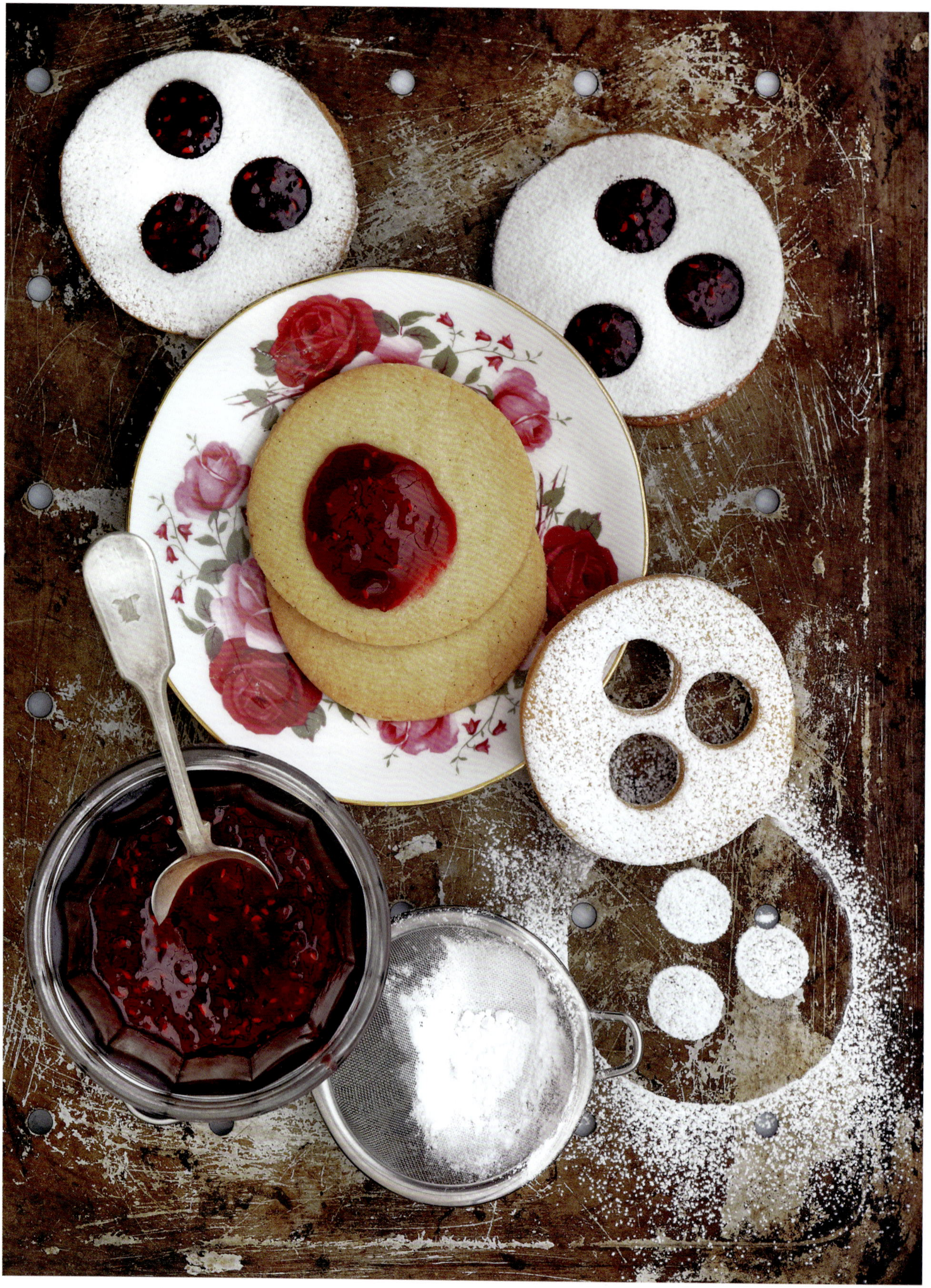

Framboisiers

These are the French equivalent of Jammy Dodgers! Biscuit and jam: what is not to like? They always seem to disappear as soon as I make them. You can use any flavour of jam.

MAKES 8

1 quantity sweet pastry
   (see page 26)
a little flour, for rolling
jar of raspberry jam
   (see page 47 for home-made)
icing sugar, for dusting

Preheat the oven to 180°C/gas 4.

Lightly dust your work surface, and roll out the pastry to around 2mm thick. Using a 6cm diameter cutter, cut out sixteen rounds.

Take half of the rounds and with a small (2cm) cutter, stamp out three holes in each round.

Have ready a baking tray lined with baking paper. Lay the rounds on top and bake in the preheated oven for about 12–14 minutes until light golden brown.

Take out and leave to cool, then spread the eight bases (the rounds without holes) with raspberry jam. Dust the rest with icing sugar using a fine sieve, and then place on top.

Strawberry and lavender marshmallows

Marshmallows are not just for kids – these are easy to make and are a great gift.

MAKES A BIG TRAYFUL

12 gelatine leaves
double quantity Italian meringue ingredients (see page 37)
a few buds of lavender
100g good strawberry jam

TO COAT:
100g icing sugar
50g cornflour

Soak the gelatine in cold water until soft, then squeeze out the excess water.

Make the meringue according to the method on page 37, but dissolve the gelatine in the syrup before pouring it onto the egg whites.

Have ready a deep baking tray (about 4cm) lined with baking paper.

Mix the lavender into the strawberry jam in a small bowl then fold this into the meringue very lightly with a wooden spoon – you don't want to turn it a uniform pink, but just streak it with swirls and dots of red.

Tip into the prepared tray, level with a spoon and leave for a minimum of 4 hours, preferably overnight, in a cool place to set.

Cut the marshmallow into squares. Mix the icing sugar and cornflour in a shallow bowl, and dip each square of marshmallow into it to dust lightly.

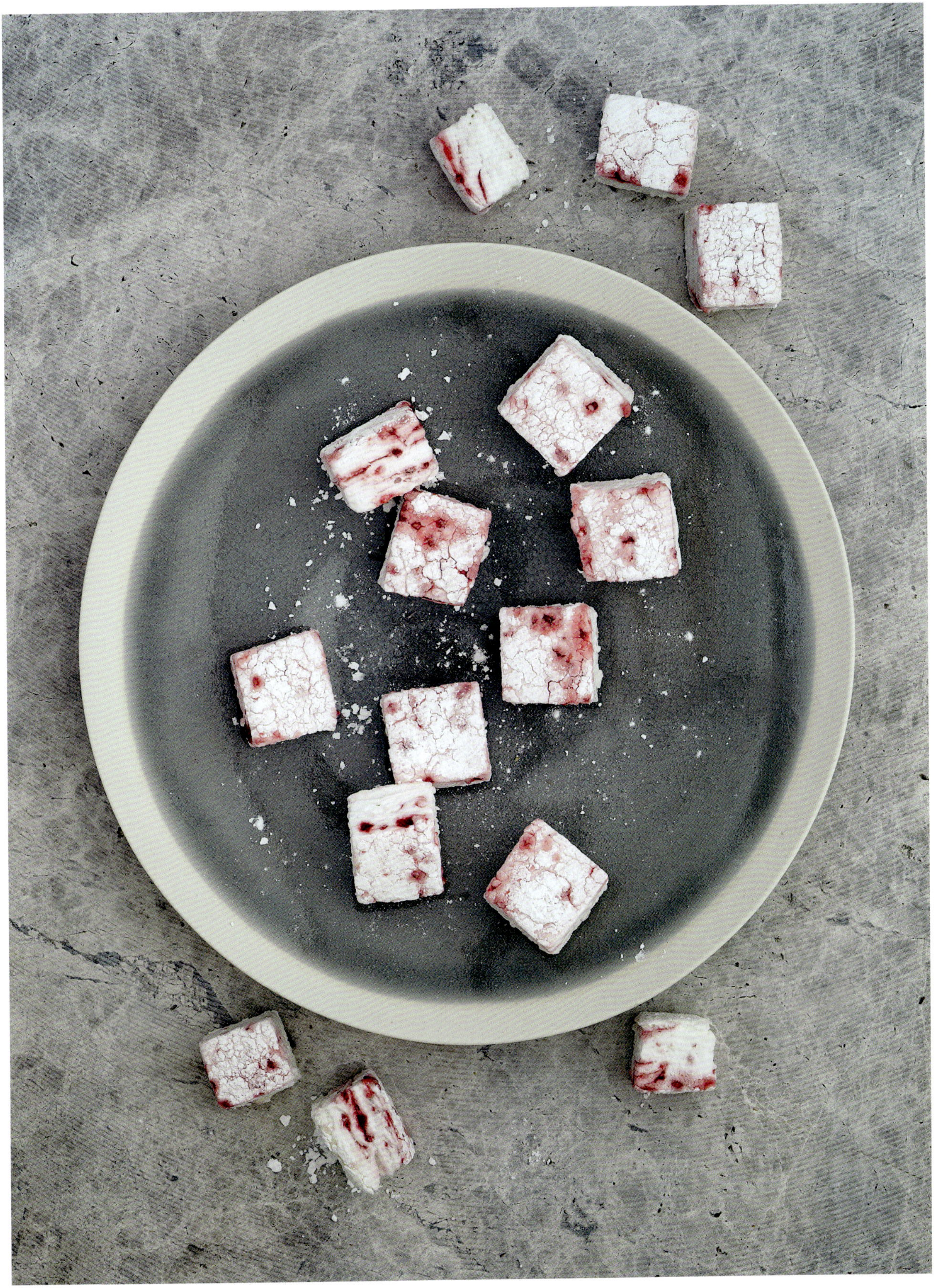

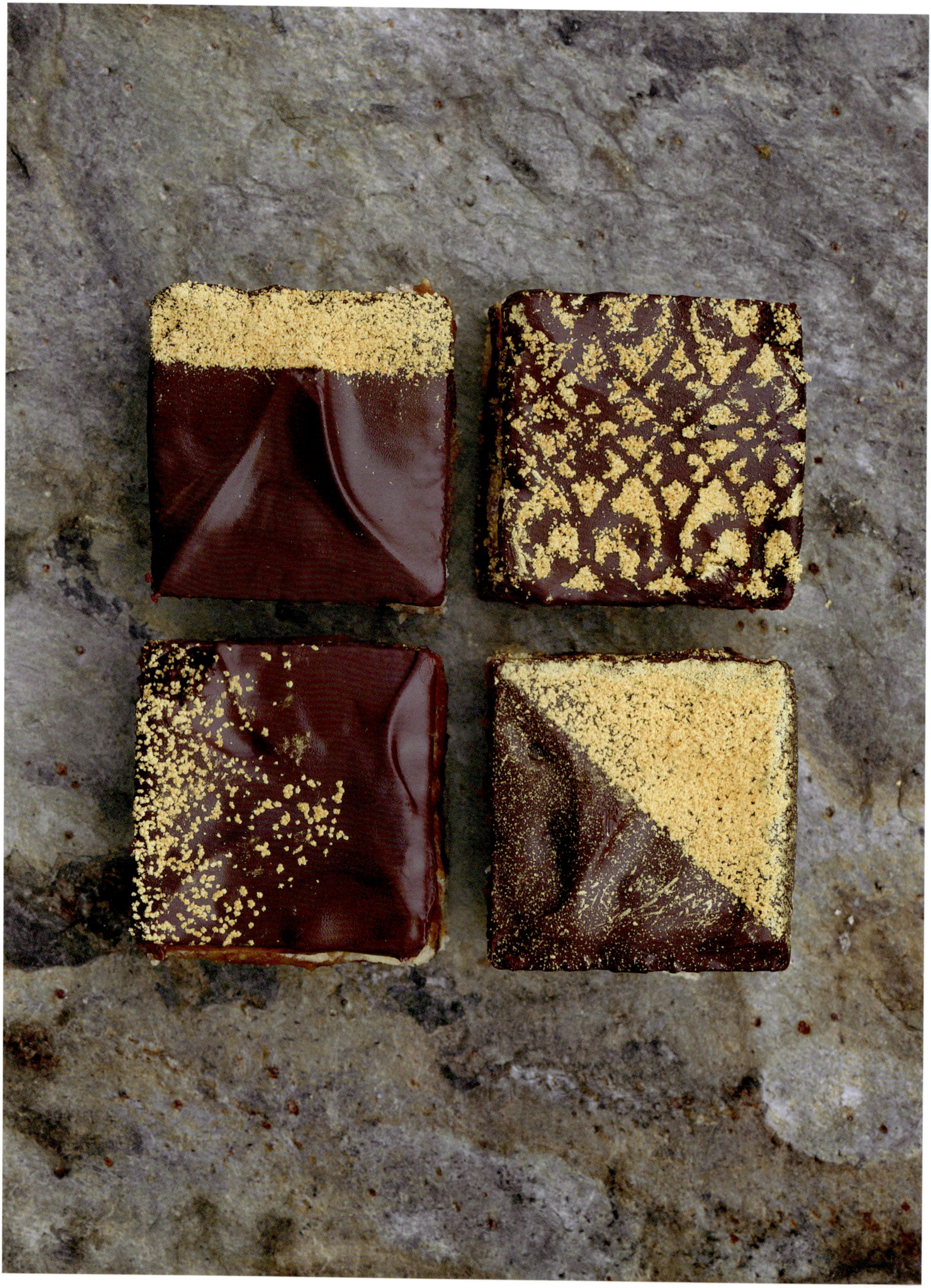

Billionaire biscuits

There are biscuits, there are millionaire biscuits, and now I give you billionaire biscuits! Rich, glamorous and glitzy with a gold-dust finish.

MAKES 10–12

1 quantity ingredients for Chocolate Salted Caramels (see page 177)
1 quantity sweet pastry (see page 26)
a little flour, for rolling

FOR THE CHOCOLATE SPONGE:
50g caster sugar
2 large eggs, plus 3 medium yolks
200g good quality dark chocolate (at least 70% cocoa solids)
150g unsalted butter
80g plain flour

FOR THE CHOCOLATE GANACHE:
160ml double cream
25ml liquid glucose
250g dark chocolate
25g butter, softened

TO DECORATE:
a little edible gold powder or gold leaf

Preheat the oven to 180°C/gas 4.

Follow the method for Chocolate Salted Caramels on page 177, but instead of pouring the mixture into a dish to set, just allow it to cool down until it is warm but still spreadable.

Lightly dust your work surface with flour and roll out the pastry into a square of about 30cm and around 2mm thick. Cut this into four strips, lay them on two non-stick baking trays or silicone mats and prick the surface of the pastry with a fork.

Bake in the preheated oven for about 12–14 minutes until light golden brown, then take out and allow to cool.

For the chocolate sponge, whisk together the sugar, eggs and yolks until they become creamy and turn a pale straw colour.

(Continues overleaf)

TREATS

Break the chocolate into chunks and put into a bowl over a pan of gently simmering water, making sure the base doesn't touch the water – you don't want to get any heat or steam in the bowl, which would make the chocolate stiffen and become dull-looking.

Let the chocolate melt gently, stirring, then add the butter and continue to stir until this too has melted.

Take off the heat and stir into the sugar and egg mixture, until it is all incorporated. Gently fold in the flour.

Spread the mixture thinly over a non-stick baking tray or silicone mat – you need a rectangle a little more than 30cm x 15cm (as you will trim the edges to this size once it is baked).

Bake for 5–6 minutes until firm to the touch. Take out of the oven, then, with a sharp knife, trim into a neat rectangle of 30cm x 15cm, then cut in half lengthways.

To assemble, lay two of the strips of pastry on a large sheet of baking paper on your work surface and spread with half of the chocolate salted caramel.

Lay a strip of chocolate sponge on top of each. Spread with the rest of the caramel, then top with the remaining strips of pastry.

To make the ganache, heat the cream and glucose in a pan until just below the boil, pour onto the dark chocolate and whisk, or use a hand blender to emulsify. Allow to cool for 5–10 minutes then whisk in the butter.

Pour the ganache over each strip of layered pastry, caramel and sponge and leave to set. When firm, cut into squares or slices, using a very sharp knife – clean the blade as you go so that you get nice sharp edges.

Decorate with gold powder – either dust it on freely through a fine sieve, use a stencil, or place a small piece of baking paper over one area and dust the rest with gold, so that you have a sharp line between gold and non-gold.

Alternatively, you could just decorate each biscuit with a little edible gold leaf.

Chocolate rum prunes

MAKES AROUND 20

4 cardamom pods
200g prunes
4 tablespoons dark rum
250g good quality dark chocolate (at least 70% cocoa solids), broken into pieces
a little cocoa powder, for dusting

Crush the cardamom pods lightly, just enough to split the pods, and put in a clean jar with the prunes and rum. Put on the lid and leave to soak for 2–3 days at room temperature, shaking the jar regularly.

Put the chocolate into a heatproof bowl over a pan of barely simmering water – make sure the water comes close to the bottom of the bowl but doesn't actually touch it. Keep the heat very low so that you don't get steam into the bowl, as this can make the chocolate become dull-looking and stiff. Keep stirring all the time and let the chocolate melt slowly, then remove the bowl from the heat.

Drain the prunes of excess liquid, then put into the chocolate and make sure they are completely coated. Lift out with a fork, shaking the excess chocolate back into the bowl, and lay on a sheet of greaseproof paper to set at room temperature.

Have a bowl of cocoa powder ready, and when the chocolate has set, roll the prunes in it to dust them.

Chocolate salted caramels

These are little squares for serving with coffee after a meal, or for nibbling at any time of day. Always take care when working with caramel, as if you splash any on your skin, it can burn. You really need a sugar thermometer for this.

MAKES AROUND 36

125g good quality dark chocolate (70% cocoa solids), chopped
100ml double cream
100g crème fraîche
200g caster sugar
75ml water
150ml liquid glucose
25g salted Breton butter
cocoa powder, for dusting (optional)

Have ready a rectangular dish about 20cm x 12cm, lined with baking paper.

Put the chopped chocolate into a bowl.

Put the double cream and crème fraîche into a pan and bring to the boil, then take off the heat and keep to one side.

In a separate pan, bring the sugar and water to the boil, then turn down the heat, add the glucose syrup and simmer for about 10 minutes until the mixture is thick and syrupy.

Take off the heat and stir in the butter, then slowly stir in the reserved cream mixture. Put back on the hob and bring to 115°C, then take off the heat and carefully pour over the chocolate, stirring well.

Pour the mixture into the prepared dish and leave to cool for 8 hours at room temperature until firm. Cut into small squares, and dust in cocoa powder if you like.

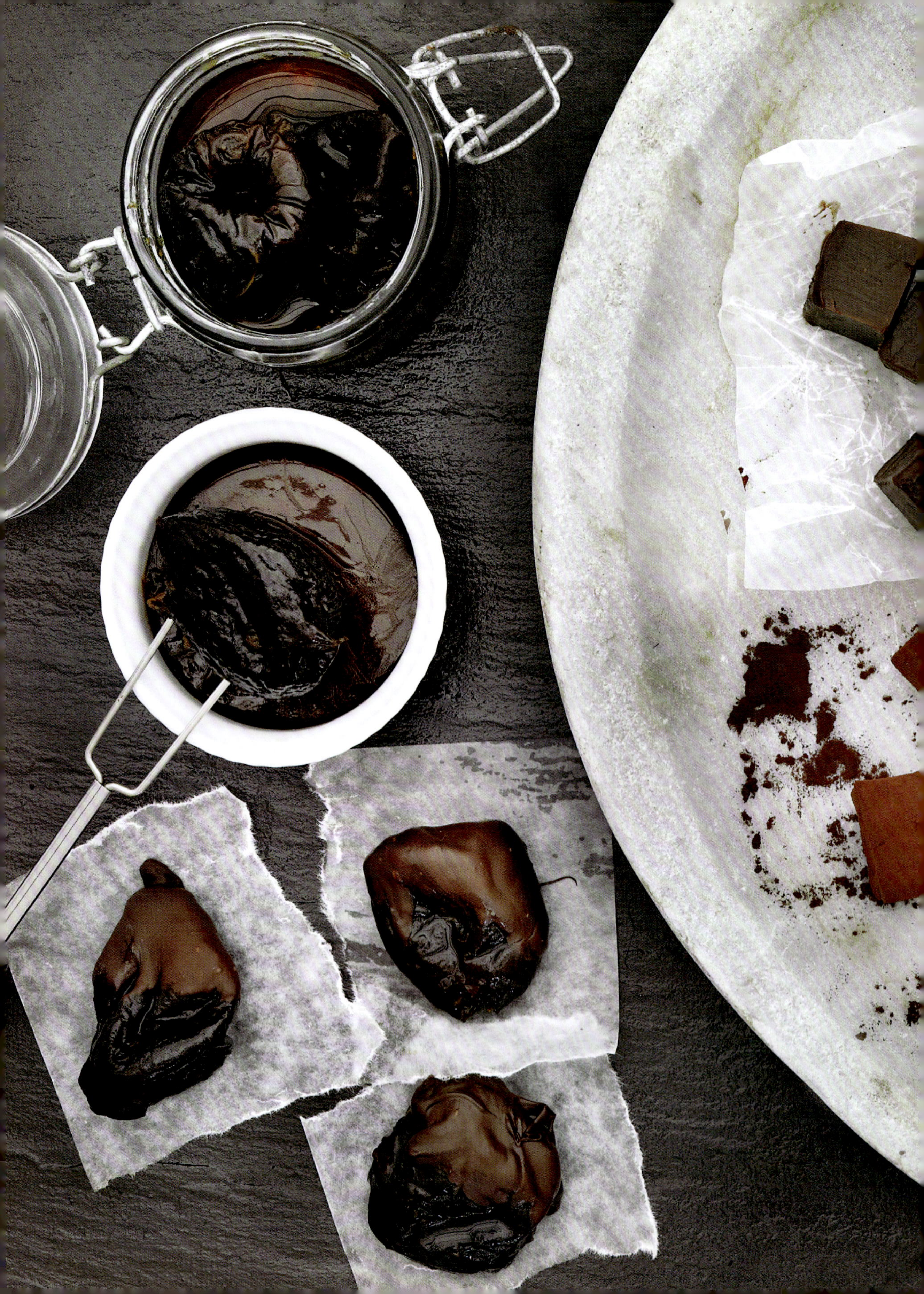

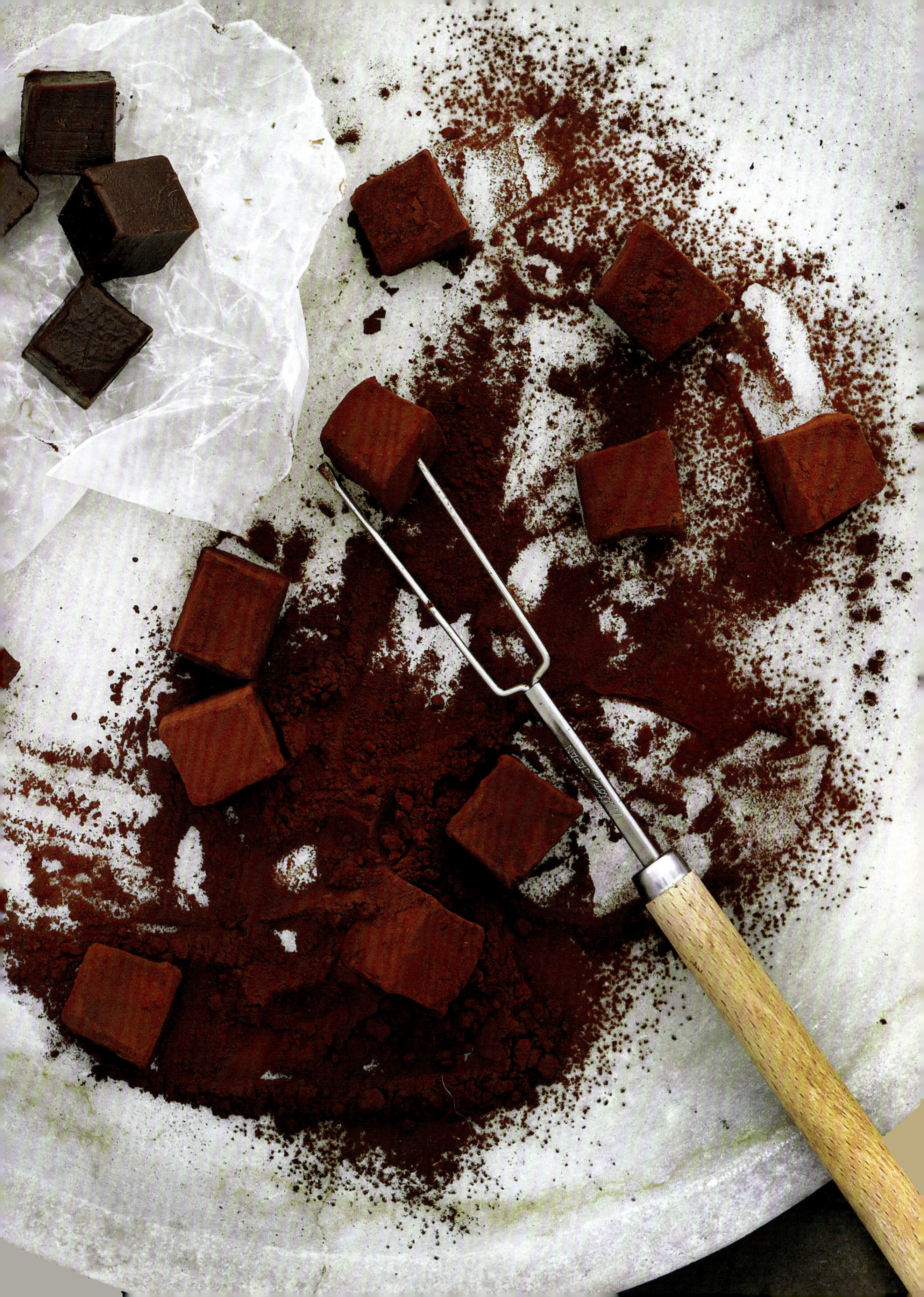

Coconut and pineapple bites

These are very retro, but as a kid I always loved Bounty bars – my first taste of coconut – and these are a grown-up version, made with the addition of Malibu and pineapple.

MAKES AROUND 12

150g desiccated coconut
4 tablespoons Malibu
50g diced semi-dried pineapple
250g milk chocolate, broken into pieces

Toast the coconut in a dry frying pan for a few minutes until it just colours, then take off the heat. Weigh 100g of it into a coffee grinder, or a mortar, add the Malibu and pineapple and grind into a rough paste that will hold together.

Form into small, tight balls and lay on a sheet of greaseproof paper. Put into the fridge for about an hour, or into the freezer for 10–15 minutes, to firm up.

Put the rest of the toasted coconut in a shallow bowl.

Put the chocolate into a heatproof bowl over a pan of barely simmering water – make sure the water comes close to the bottom of the bowl but doesn't actually touch it. Keep the heat very low so that you don't get steam into the bowl, as this can make the chocolate become dull-looking and stiff. Keep stirring all the time and let the chocolate melt slowly, then remove the bowl from the heat.

Take the balls from the fridge and, using a spoon, dip each one into the chocolate, letting the excess drain off, then roll in the bowl of coconut and lay on a sheet of greaseproof paper until set.

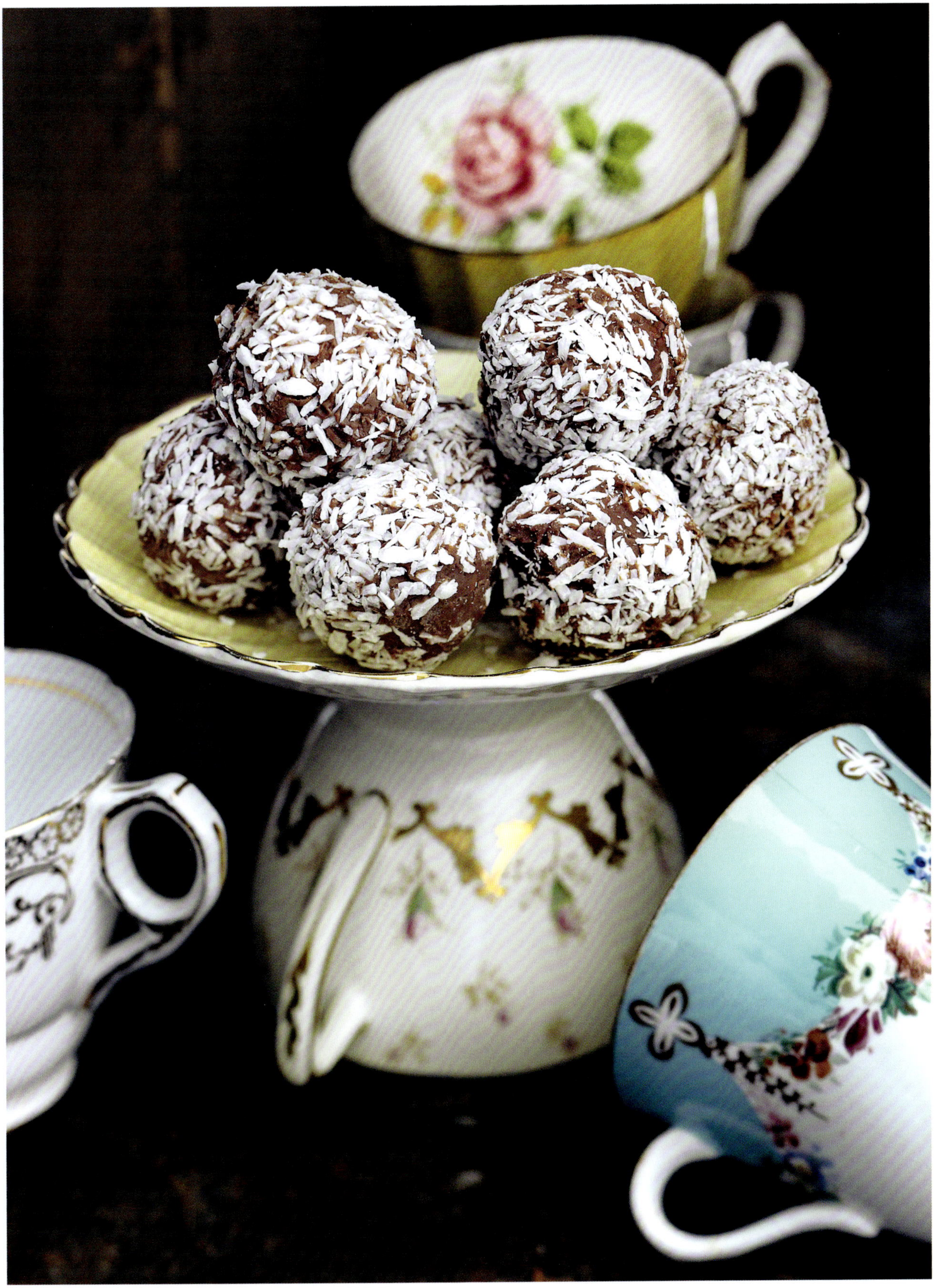

Chocolate lollipops

The way you decorate these is really up to you. You will need 10–12 lollipop sticks.

MAKES 10–12

200g good quality dark chocolate (70% cocoa solids), broken into pieces
200g white chocolate
mixture of some or all of:
frozen raspberries, broken up; crushed hazelnuts; pieces of dried apricot; raisins; caramelised pistachio nuts (see page 45)

Lay a large sheet of baking paper on your work surface.

Put the dark chocolate into a heatproof bowl over a pan of barely simmering water – make sure the water comes close to the bottom of the bowl but doesn't actually touch it. Keep the heat very low so that you don't get steam into the bowl, as this can make the chocolate become dull-looking and stiff. Keep stirring all the time and let the chocolate melt slowly, then remove the bowl from the heat.

Snip off the corner of a small piping bag, if using a disposable one, and insert a fine nozzle. Fill with the melted chocolate and pipe about 10–12 lacy, petal-like patterns onto the baking paper – be as creative as you like.

Melt the white chocolate in the same way as above, then use a teaspoon to blob small amounts in the centre of each of your petal shapes. Flatten out into discs big enough to decorate with fruit and nuts.

Lay a lollipop stick on each round of white chocolate, press lightly and then spoon some more white chocolate on top. Again flatten this out into a disc, to hold the stick in place. Decorate with a mixture of fruit and nuts, leave to set, then peel carefully from the paper.

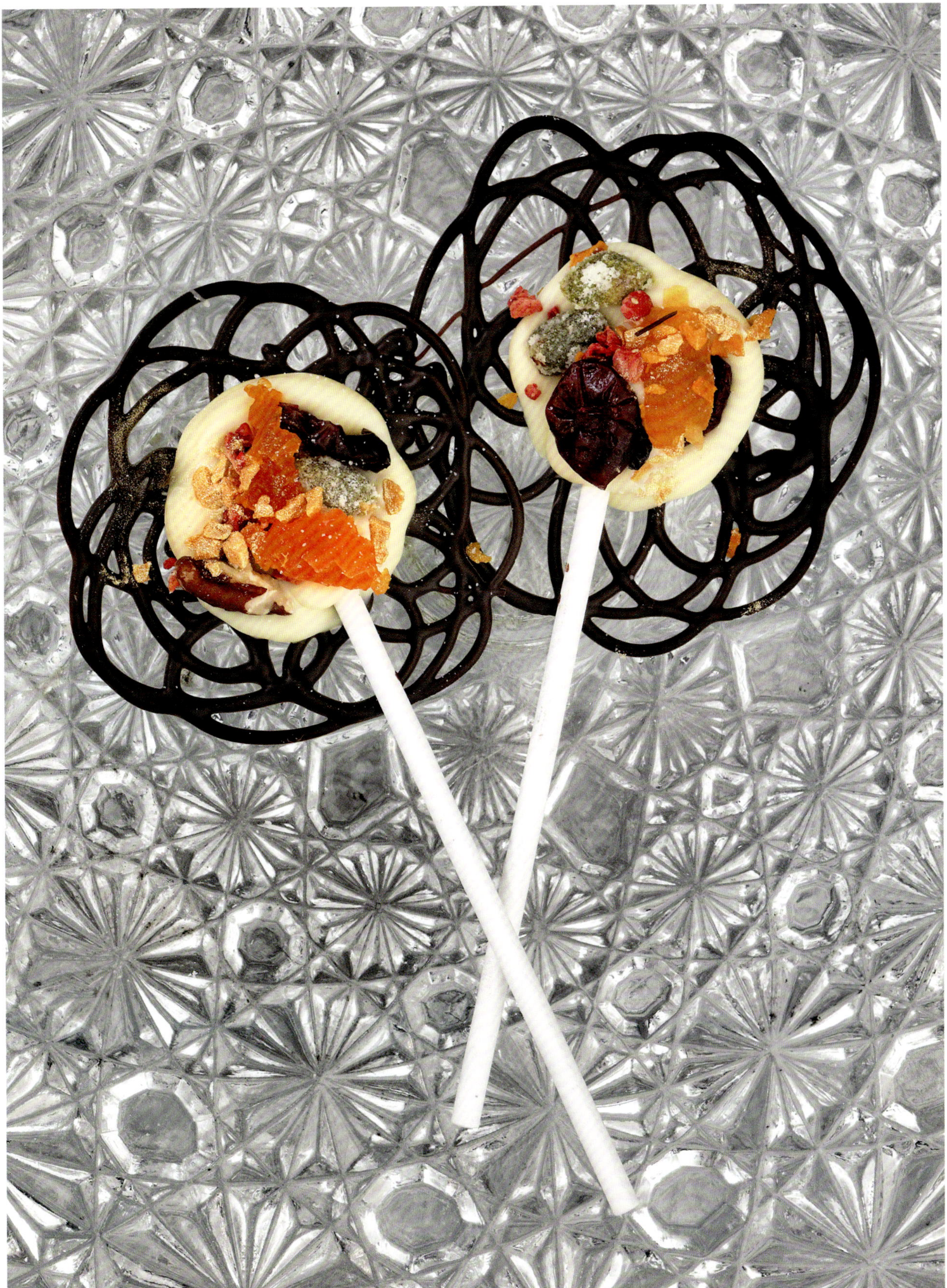

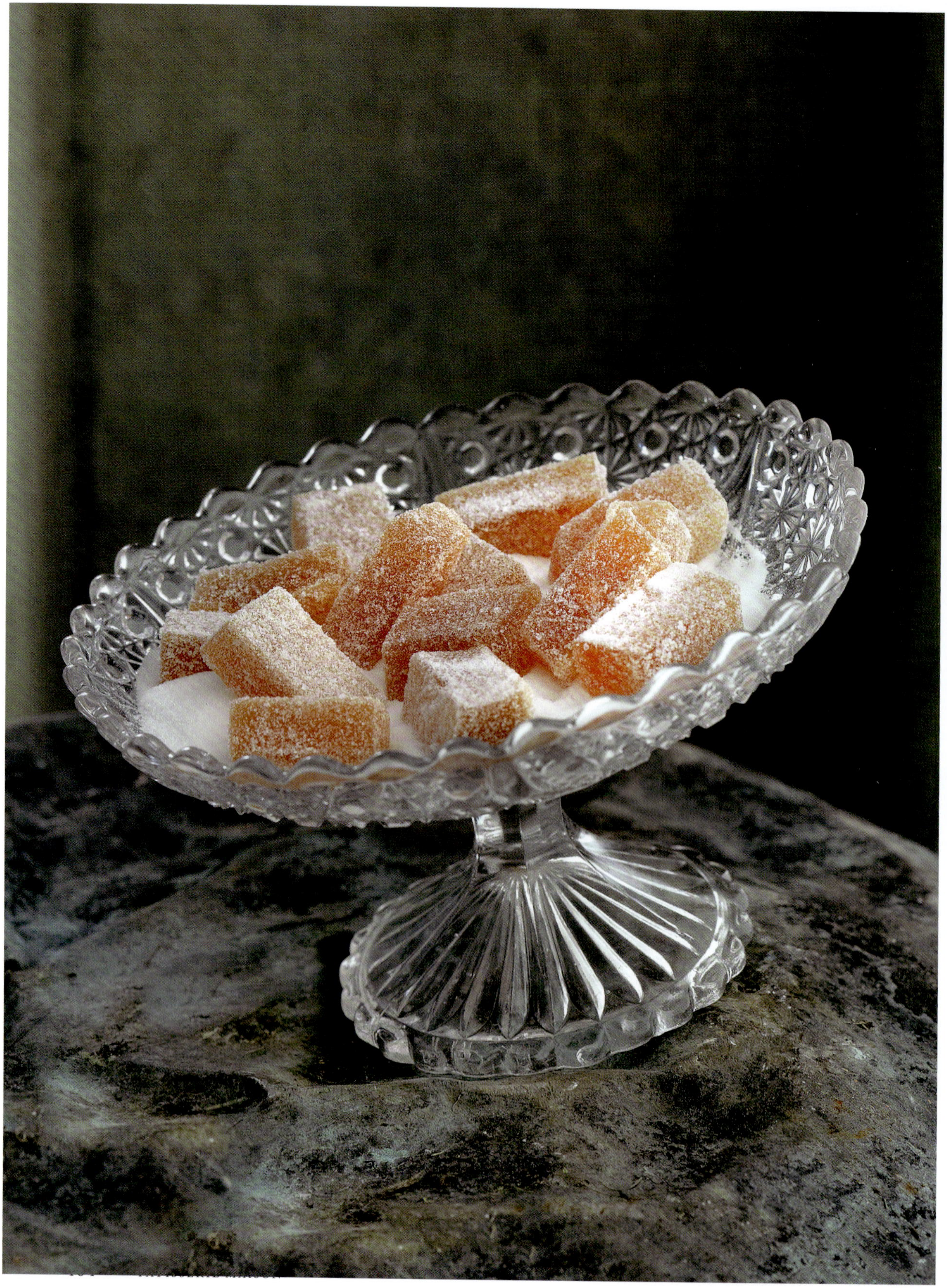

Pâte de fruits

This is a recipe from pastry chef Yolande Stanley, who is one of only seven people in the UK to hold the title of Master of the Culinary Arts for Pastry, and who teaches masterclasses in sugar and chocolate at our cookery school.

You will need a sugar thermometer to make sure you bring the mixture to just the right temperature.

MAKES A BOWLFUL

10g pectin powder
555g caster sugar, plus a little extra for dusting
500ml apricot purée
100ml liquid glucose
1 teaspoon lemon juice
1 teaspoon vodka, rum or Pernod

Mix together the pectin and 55g sugar then put in a pan with the apricot purée.

Bring to the boil, stirring all the time, then add the rest of the sugar a little at a time, stirring all the time and making sure each addition has completely dissolved before adding more.

Add the glucose and bring to 107°C, then take off the heat and add the lemon juice and alcohol.

Pour into a deep-sided dish and leave somewhere cool until set (not in the fridge, as this is too cold), then turn out and cut into rectangles of about 2 cm.

Have some more caster sugar in a shallow bowl and dip each cube into it before serving.

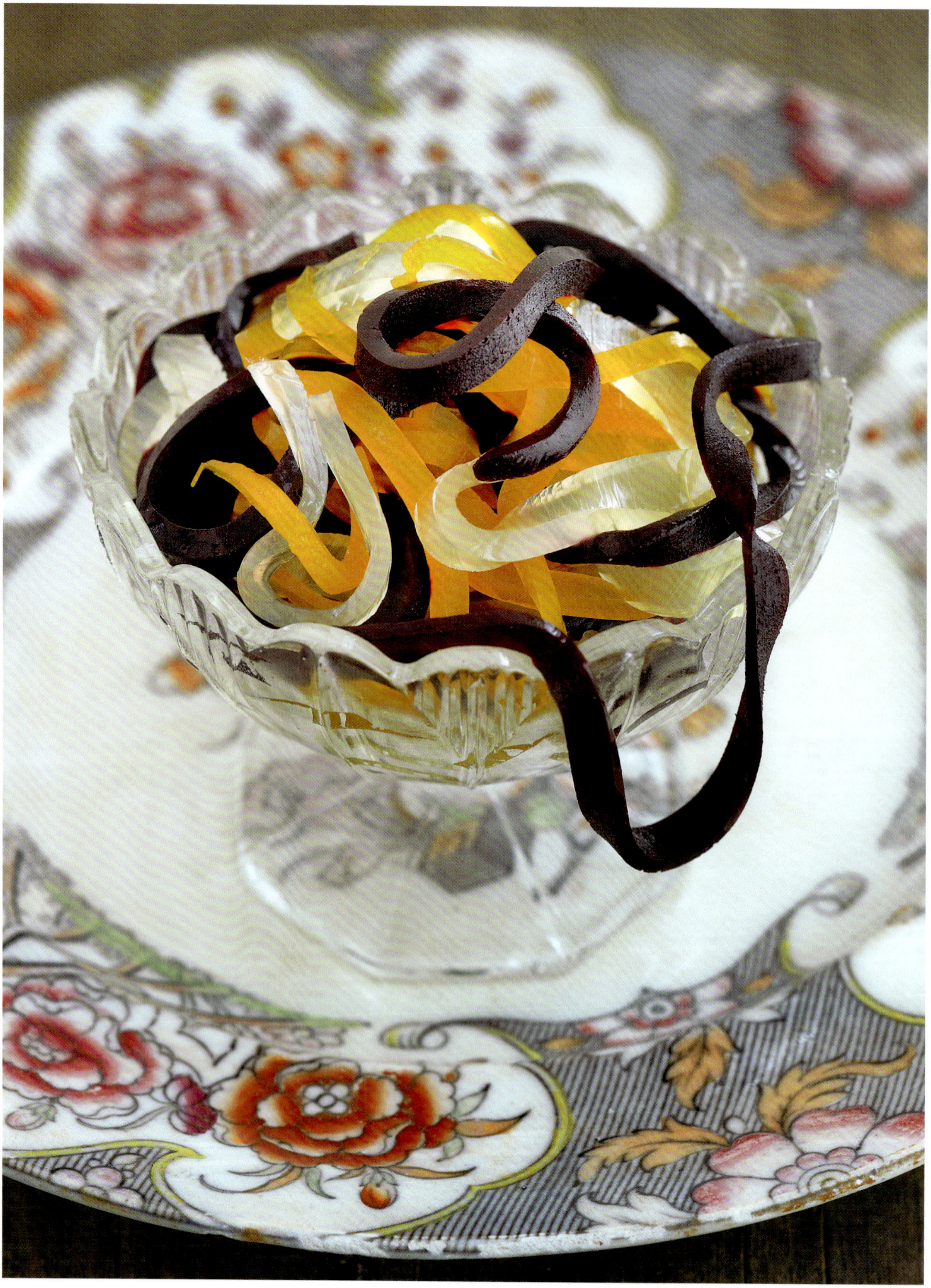

Fruitworms

One day after making fruit jellies, I had some jelly mixture left over so I set it thinly in a tray and cut it into strips for the kids. They rolled them in caster sugar to resemble the ones they buy from the sweet shop. They loved them.

MAKES A BOWLFUL

6 gelatine leaves
60g sugar
either 100ml fruit cordial, such as blackcurrant or elderflower, mixed with 200ml water; or 300ml of good fruit juice, such as mango, apricot or peach
a little caster sugar, for dusting (optional)

Soak the gelatine in cold water to soften, then squeeze out the excess water.

Have ready a flat baking tray, about 38cm x 28cm, lined with clingfilm.

Put the sugar and cordial or juice in a pan and heat enough to allow the sugar to dissolve (don't let it boil). Whisk in the gelatine until it has dissolved.

Pour into the tray and put into the fridge to set for about 30 minutes–1 hour.

Lift out using the clingfilm, and turn out onto a chopping board. Take off the clingfilm and, with a sharp knife or a pizza wheel, cut the jelly into long strips about 5mm wide. Dust them in caster sugar if you like.

Dodos

When I first made these and took them home my wife, Jo, loved them. I didn't have a name for them, so for a joke we christened them dodos – since Dodo was her nickname when she was a little girl – and it has stuck!

I use a silicone tray with oval-shaped moulds, about 5cm long by 2cm deep.

MAKES 12–18

100g unsalted butter, softened
100g caster sugar
pinch of salt
100g ground almonds or hazelnuts
2 medium eggs
40g plain flour
12–18 small raspberries
   (or 6–9 large ones, halved),
   blackcurrants or chocolate chips
some small mint leaves, to decorate
   (optional)

Preheat the oven to 180°C/gas 4.

Beat the butter, sugar and salt together until pale and creamy. Stir in the ground nuts and beat in the eggs one at a time.

Stir in the flour.

Use a teaspoon to fill your moulds to three quarters full, push in a raspberry, blackcurrant or chocolate chip and bake in the preheated oven for 15–18 minutes until golden on top and springy to the touch.

Remove from the oven and leave to cool down in the moulds before turning out.

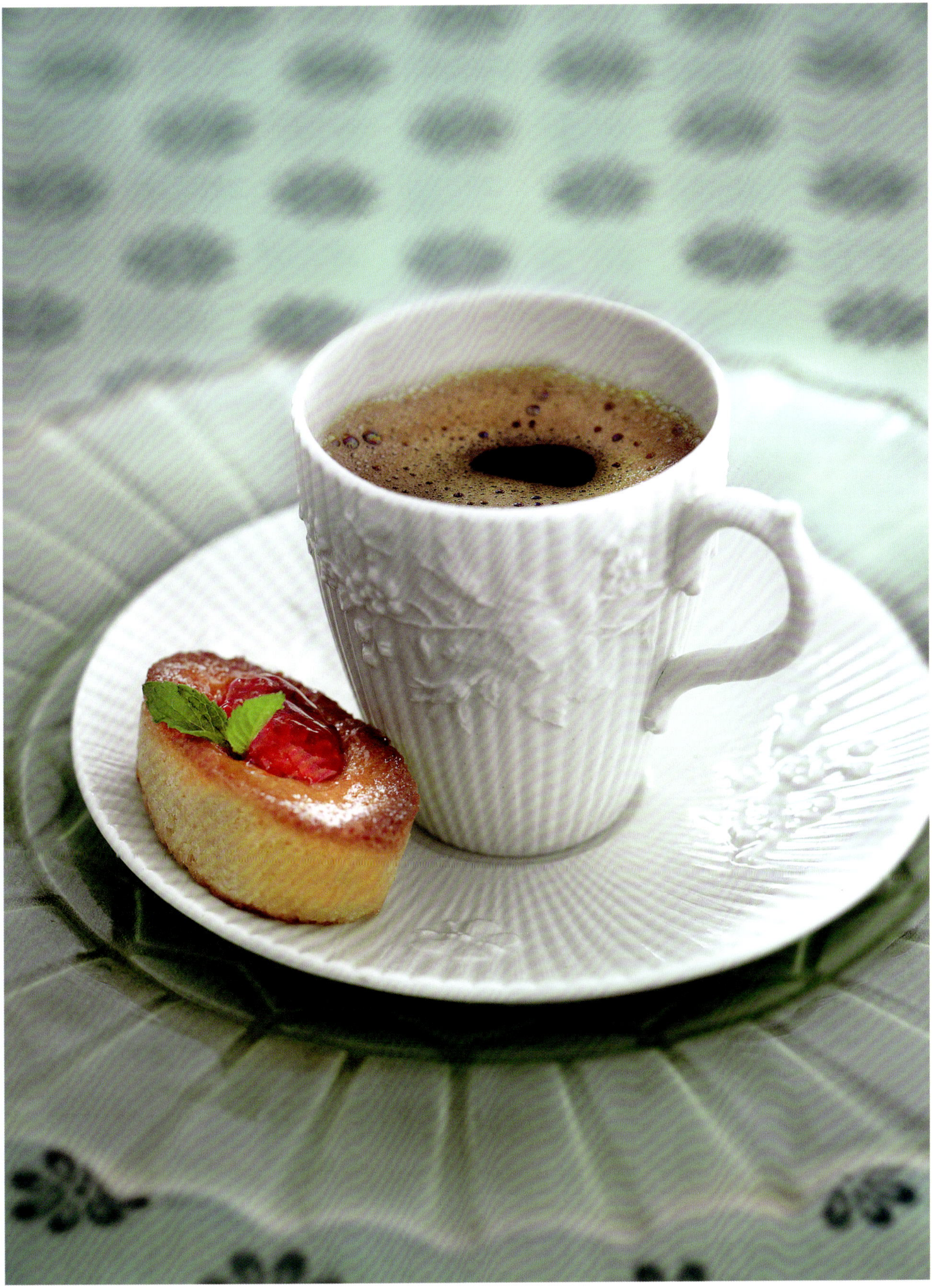

Festive

EVERY YEAR I AM ASKED FOR MY
CHRISTMAS RECIPES – SO HERE THEY ARE

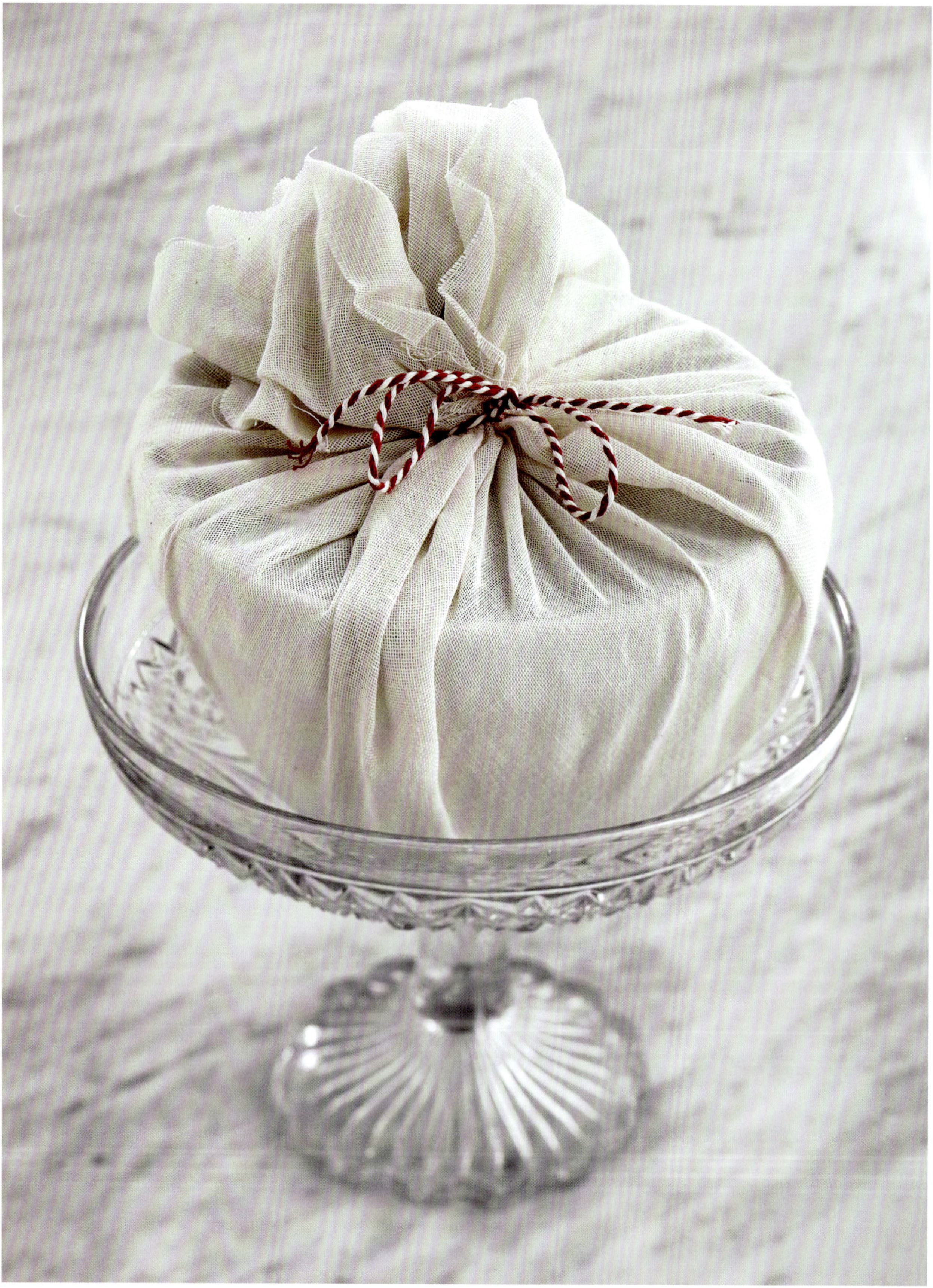

Christmas pudding

I always send a Christmas pudding to my family in France each year and they love it, as it is something completely different for them. The French still don't understand the concept of mincemeat!

My recipe is a little different to the traditional one, as I don't soak the fruit first. Instead I rest the whole pudding mixture before steaming, during which time the fruit can plump up and infuse with the rest of the flavours.

Although rum or brandy butter is the traditional accompaniment, most of my family like it with cream, but I make crème anglaise for myself!

The pudding should be made at least three weeks in advance, but can be stored for up to a year.

MAKES 1 X 2-PINT PUDDING (SIZE 3)

100g currants
200g seedless raisins
200g sultanas
60g mixed chopped candied peel
60g glacé cherries
90g blanched almonds, sliced into slivers
½ medium cooking apple, peeled, cored and coarsely chopped
½ small carrot, peeled and grated
zest and juice of ½ an orange
zest and juice of ½ a lemon
115g finely chopped suet
115g plain flour

60g white bread or brioche crumbs
115g soft brown sugar
½ teaspoon mixed spice
½ teaspoon ground cinnamon
¼ nutmeg, grated
½ teaspoon salt
3 medium eggs
½ can of Guinness
2 tablespoons brandy

(Continues overleaf)

Put all of the ingredients apart from the orange and lemon juices, eggs, Guinness and brandy in a large bowl and mix together well.

In a separate bowl, beat the eggs until frothy, then add the Guinness, brandy and orange and lemon juices. Add to the bowl containing the rest of the ingredients and mix well until all incorporated.

Fill your basin with the mixture, press a circle of greaseproof paper firmly over the top and put into the fridge for at least 12 hours, but up to 48 hours.

Wipe the outside of the basin clean of any mixture, if necessary, and cover with clingfilm.

Place the pudding on a trivet in a large pan on the hob and pour in enough boiling water to come about three quarters of the way up the side of the basin. Bring the water back to the boil, cover the pan tightly with a lid, and then turn down the heat and steam for 3 hours. Check the water level regularly, and top up with boiling water from the kettle as necessary.

Take the pan off the heat and, when cool enough to touch, carefully lift out the pudding. Leave to cool and store, still covered in the clingfilm, until you are ready to re-steam for another 3 hours.

To turn out, take off the clingfilm, and carefully slide a table knife around the edge of the basin to loosen the pudding. Place a serving plate on top of the basin and using both hands firmly grip the plate and basin and turn both over together. The pudding should slide easily onto the plate.

To serve, warm a glass of brandy in a small pan over a low heat, ignite it with a match and pour it while it is flaming over the pudding. Serve immediately.

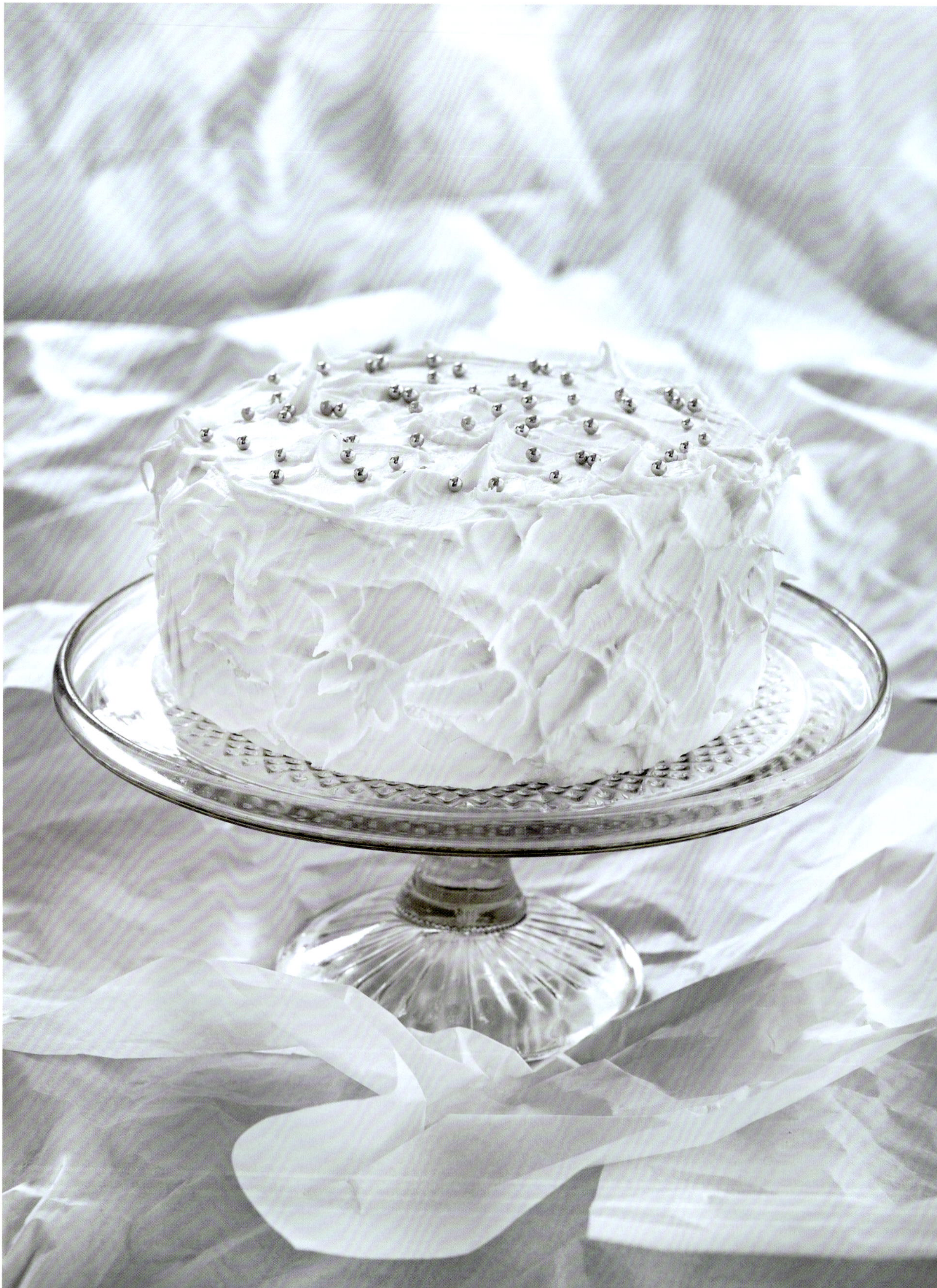

Christmas cake

Sometimes fruit cakes can be really dry, but this is a recipe that is very moist, full of fruit and nuts. It can double up as a wedding cake, or you can eat it un-iced at any tea time.

When I line my tin, so that the cake cooks evenly and doesn't have any burnt or crunchy bits around the edge or the base, as well as lining it inside with baking paper I tie a folded strip of brown paper around the outside.

Of course you can decorate your cake as you like. Some people like to simply brush the top with melted apricot jam and cover it with assorted nuts and dried fruit, then glaze these with a little more jam. You can then just tie a ribbon around the cake. However, if you want to cover it with marzipan and icing, ideally start doing this around 10 days before Christmas.

As with my Christmas pudding, I don't soak my fruit in advance, but instead leave the cake mixture to rest as a whole before baking.

MAKES 1 X 23CM CAKE

245g flour
1 teaspoon baking powder
¼ level teaspoon salt
2 teaspoons mixed spice
½ level teaspoon ground nutmeg
½ level teaspoon ground cinnamon
¼ level teaspoon ground cloves
85g ground almonds
320g currants
320g raisins
320g sultanas
150g glacé cherries
150g whole mixed peel
85g blanched almonds

210g soft dark brown sugar
250g unsalted butter
grated zest and juice of 1 medium lemon
6 large eggs
8 tablespoons brandy
a little butter, for greasing the tin

TO ICE THE CAKE:

2 tablespoons clear apricot jam
500g good natural marzipan
4 medium egg whites
750g icing sugar, sifted, plus extra for dusting
4 teaspoons lemon juice
2 teaspoons glycerine
small edible silver balls, to decorate

(Continues overleaf)

Butter a 23cm round (or equivalent square) tin (about 9cm deep), and line with a double layer of baking paper.

With string, tie a double layer of brown paper around the outside of the tin – the paper needs to be tall enough to rise well above the edge of the tin (about 8–9cm).

Mix the flour, baking powder, salt, spices and ground almonds in a large bowl, then stir in the fruits, mixed peel and almonds.

In a separate bowl, cream together the sugar, butter and grated lemon zest until pale and fluffy, then beat in the eggs one at a time. Stir this mixture into the flour and fruit, followed by the lemon juice and half of the brandy. The mixture should be soft and moist.

Spoon the mixture into your prepared tin, level the top and leave to settle at room temperature for 2–3 hours before baking. Preheat the oven to 150°C/gas 2 and adjust the shelf to just below the centre.

Bake the cake in the preheated oven for an hour then turn down the heat to 130°C/gas 1 and bake for a further 2½–3 hours, covering the top with a sheet of baking paper for the last two hours to prevent it from burning. The cake is ready when it begins to shrink from the sides and the top is no longer spongy if you press it with a fingertip.

Take the cake from the oven and leave it to cool a little in the tin before turning it out onto a wire rack. When completely cold, wrap it tightly in foil. Once a week make some holes in the cake using a skewer, then drizzle a little brandy over it and allow it to soak in. Re-wrap and repeat the following week.

To decorate with marzipan and icing:

Heat the apricot jam until liquid and brush it all over the surface of the cake.

Dust your work surface lightly with icing sugar and then roll out the marzipan into a circle big enough to cover the entire cake.

Roll the marzipan around your rolling pin, then lift and drape it over the cake, and with your hands gently smooth and press it against the top and sides of the cake. Trim it around the base.

Wrap the cake in foil again and leave for three days.

To make the royal icing, beat the egg whites until frothy then fold in the icing sugar a spoonful at a time, stir in the lemon juice and glycerine, and then beat until the mixture is stiff enough to form strong peaks.

With a palette knife, spread the icing all over the cake, lifting the knife up and down as you go to form little peaks that look like snow. Decorate the top with the silver balls.

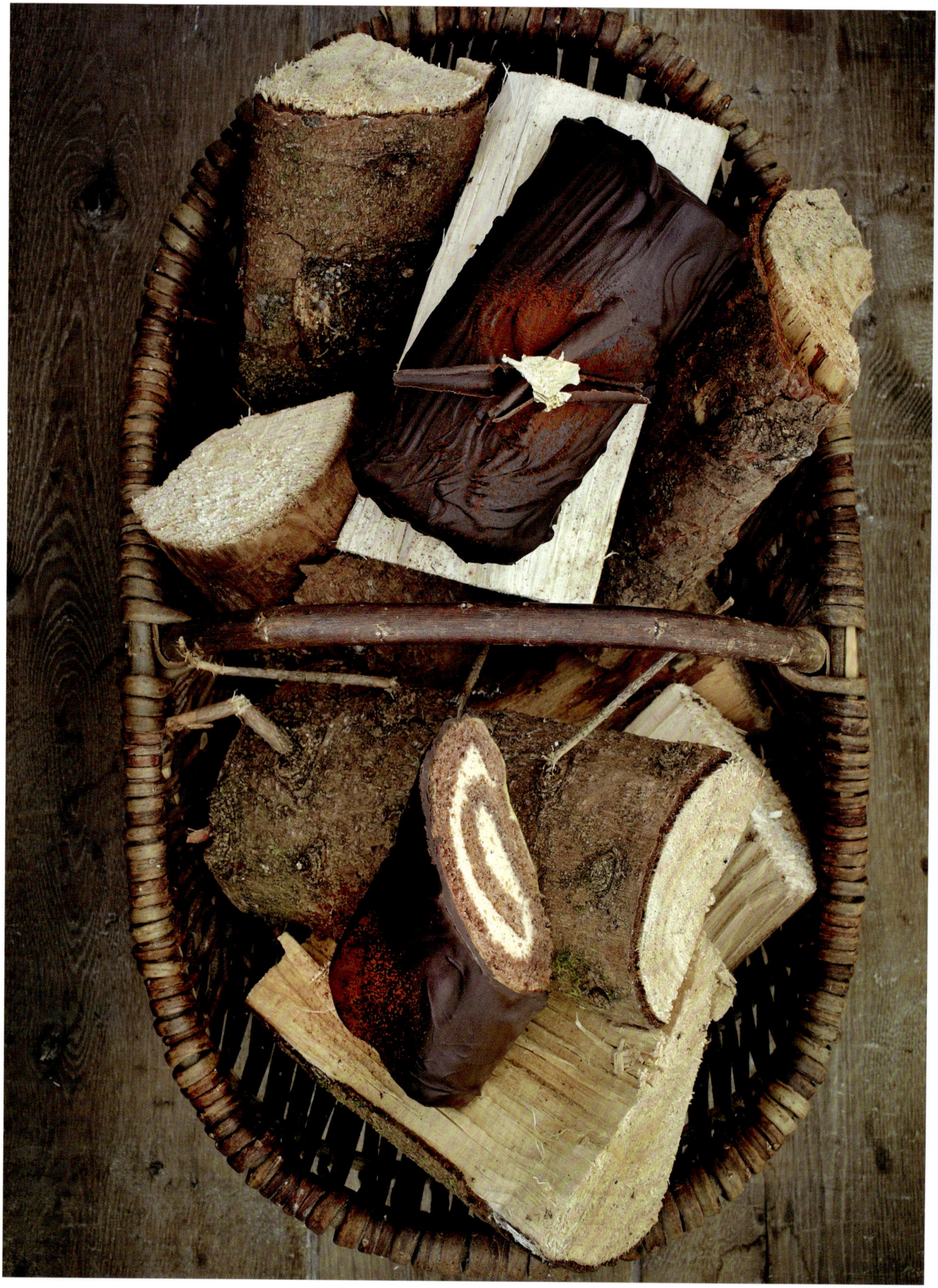

Bûche de Noël

There are Yule log traditions all over northern Europe, and some say its history goes back to Celtic times when people would burn a huge log at the end of December to see in the Winter solstice, then they would keep the ashes for good luck throughout the following year. Others say it was fashionable in rich houses to burn such a log each Christmas Eve, but keep a piece of it back with which to light the next one. When coal began to be burned instead of logs, these cakes were made as a reminder of the old custom.

As a variation on the hazelnuts in the cream filling you could mix in some chestnut purée instead. You can buy this in small tins, and you will need about 150g. Mash it a little with a fork to loosen it before mixing into the crème au beurre.

Of course you can decorate your log as much as you like, but I think it looks most elegant with just a dusting of cocoa powder, a touch of edible gold leaf, and a little rolled or shaved chocolate.

MAKES 1 LOG

50g hazelnuts in their skins
1 quantity crème au beurre (see page 43)
1 quantity chocolate genoise sponge (see page 19)
a little icing sugar, for dusting
500g good natural marzipan
400g good quality dark chocolate (70% cocoa solids), broken into pieces

FOR THE KIRSCH SYRUP:

100g sugar
200ml water
2 tablespoons kirsch

FOR THE DECORATION:

dark chocolate curls or 'pencils' (see page 56)
cocoa powder, for dusting
1 small sheet edible gold leaf (optional)

(Continues overleaf)

Preheat the oven to 180°C/gas 4. Spread the hazelnuts out over a baking tray and put into the oven for 15–20 minutes, shaking the tray occasionally so that they toast evenly. Take out of the oven, leave to cool, and then grind to a paste using a coffee grinder or pestle and mortar. Mix this into the crème au beurre, and keep to one side.

To make the syrup, put the sugar in a pan with the water and bring to the boil. Reduce the heat and simmer until the sugar has dissolved and you have a colourless syrup. Take off the heat, stir in the kirsch, and leave to cool.

Have ready a large sheet of baking paper. Turn the genoise sponge onto it so that the top is downwards. Brush with two thirds of the syrup, then spread the hazelnut crème au beurre on top.

Now roll up like a swiss roll. Lift up the baking paper and as the sponge starts to roll, help it to tuck in with your fingertips, then continue to lift the paper and it will continue to roll.

Lightly dust your work surface with icing sugar and roll out the marzipan – I like it quite thin, about 2mm, but you can make it a little thicker if you prefer. Cut out a rectangle just large enough to wrap the log in and keep the trimmings to one side.

Brush the log with the remaining syrup, then lay the log on top of the rectangle of marzipan, off centre, with the seam side upwards.

(Continues overleaf)

FESTIVE   203

Bring the marzipan over the top and press down lightly, so that it fits snugly.

Tuck in under the log and fold in the ends.

Take pieces of the marzipan trimmings and soften into balls between your fingers. Roll out into long sausages, then snake them over the top of the log, pressing them down lightly so they stick. This will give a bark-like texture once the log is covered in melted chocolate.

Have ready a rack over a tray or sheet of baking paper. Using a palette knife or fish slice under each end of the log, lift it onto the rack. Leave these in position so you can easily lift the log up again.

Put the chocolate into a heatproof bowl over a pan of barely simmering water – make sure the water comes close to the bottom of the bowl but doesn't actually touch it. Keep the heat very low so that you don't get steam into the bowl, as this can make the chocolate become dull-looking and stiff. Keep stirring all the time and let the chocolate melt slowly, then remove the bowl from the heat.

Take off the heat and, a little at a time and with the help of a spoon, pour the chocolate over the top of the log until it is all covered.

As it begins to cool and set a little, use the tip of the spoon or a fork to make rough bark-like marks in the chocolate. When it is set enough to stay in position, lift it off the rack and onto a board or plate.

Decorate with a dusting of cocoa powder, chocolate curls or 'pencils' and some gold leaf, if you like.

Leave for 3–4 hours at room temperature, then put in the fridge, if necessary, in a plastic or cardboard box, and it will keep its shine.

Croque en bouche

The famous French celebratory tower of choux buns 'cemented' together with caramel is easier to make than you might think. The key is to be organised and have two pans of caramel on the go at the same time, so that when you take the first one off the heat to begin dipping your buns into, you have a second keeping warm, ready to swap over when the first cools down and the caramel starts to solidify.

As long as you keep the finished Croque en Bouche somewhere cool and dry, it will hold together for 2–3 hours, but beware that any humidity will soften the caramel.

MAKES A CELEBRATORY TOWER FOR 12 PEOPLE

triple quantity choux pastry mixture (see page 20)
a little butter, for greasing the baking sheet
4 tablespoons kirsch
double quantity crème pâtissière (see page 41)
800g sugar
8 tablespoons water

FOR THE NOUGATINE BASE:
200g flaked almonds
500g caster sugar
225ml glucose syrup

Preheat the oven to 190°C/gas 5.

Lightly grease a non-stick baking sheet or have ready a silicone mat.

Snip off the corner of a piping bag, if using a disposable one, insert a plain nozzle about 1cm in diameter, then fill with the choux pastry mixture and pipe as many dots (about the size of a £1 coin in diameter) as you can onto baking trays or silicone mats – make sure they are spaced well apart.

Bake in batches in the preheated oven for 12–15 minutes until golden and puffed up. For the last 4 minutes of baking, leave the oven door slightly ajar to allow the steam to escape, and help the drying process. Remove the tray from the oven and leave to cool.

Turn down the oven to 160°C/gas 3.

(Continues overleaf)

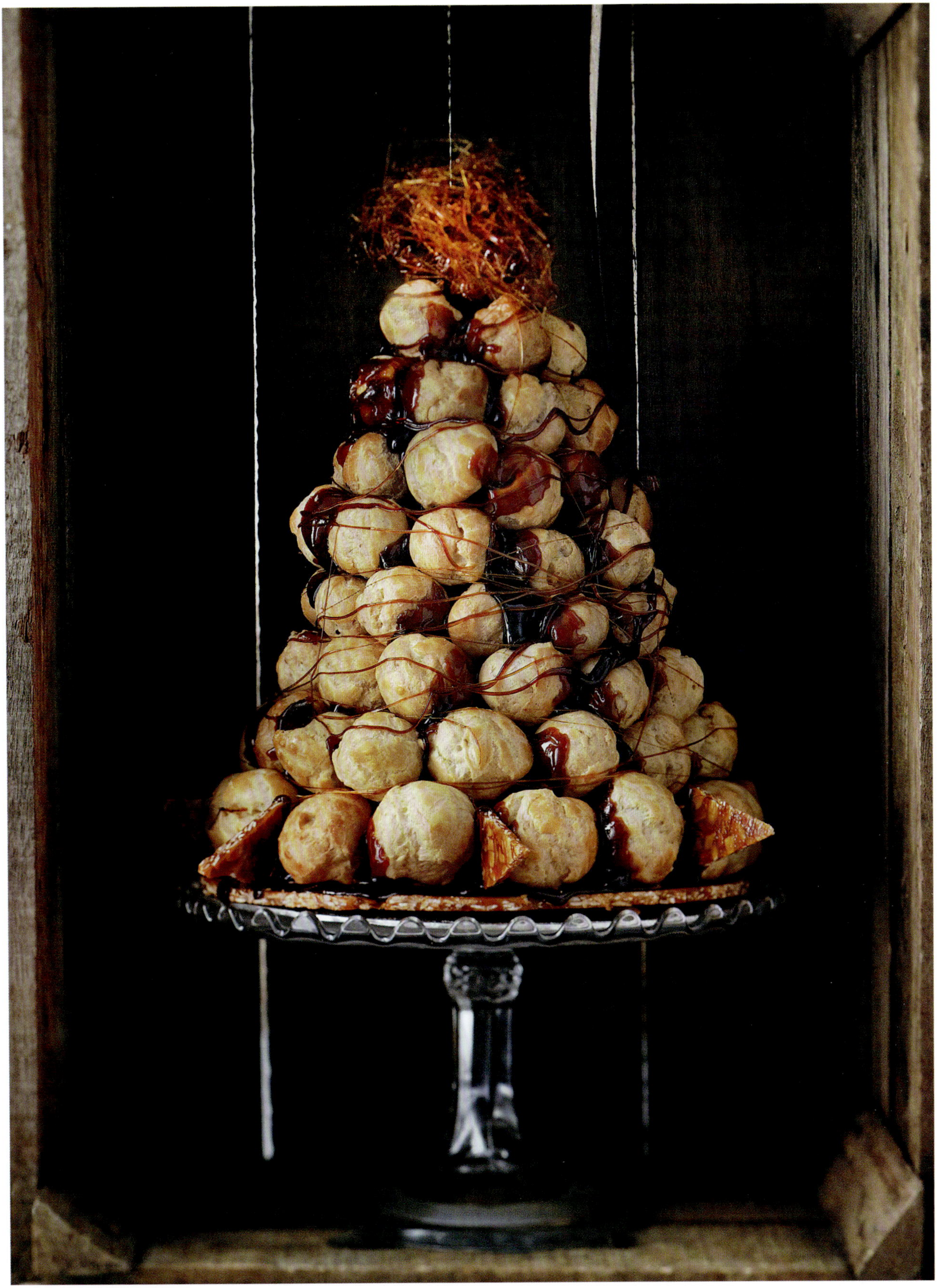

Lay the flaked almonds on a baking tray and put them into the oven for about 5–6 minutes until golden, turning them halfway through. Remove and keep to one side.

Put the 500g of sugar and the glucose in a pan over a medium heat and bring to the boil, then continue to boil until golden brown (if you have a sugar thermometer, the temperature will be 140°C). Add the toasted almonds and mix thoroughly, then take off the heat and spread over a silicone mat.

Let it set a little, then using a tart ring (about 22cm) as a guide, cut around it. Cut the trimmings into little triangles to use for decorating the croque en bouche later. Leave to set fully.

Mix the kirsch into the crème pâtissière. Make a hole in the base of each choux bun. Fill a new piping bag fitted with a small plain nozzle with the crème pâtissière and pipe a little into each bun. Keep to one side.

Have ready a bowl of cold water. Divide the 800g of sugar between two pans and add 4 tablespoons of water to each. Put both on the hob at the same time, and bring to the boil, then continue to boil until golden brown (if you have a sugar thermometer, the temperature will be 140°C). The caramel will be really hot, so be careful.

Turn off the heat beneath both pans. Take the first one off the heat and lower the base into a bowl of cold water, to cool it down enough to work with safely. Leave the other pan on the hob, but with the heat turned off.

Now you are ready to start building your tower. Have ready your nougatine base. Take your first bun and carefully dip the top (the opposite side to the one you pierced to fill with cream) into the caramel, then place it on the outside of your nougatine base, with the caramel facing to the left.

Working as quickly as you can, dip the next bun into the caramel in the same way, and butt it up against the first one (facing in the same direction) and press very gently, so that the caramel sticks the two together. Repeat, inserting your reserved little triangles of nougatine in between the buns at equal intervals as you go, until you have a complete circle of buns.

Now you are going to start tapering the tower up to a single bun. So, for the next layer, as if you were laying bricks, stick each bun over the join in the previous layer, but in a slightly smaller circle.

As soon as the first pan of caramel starts to set, put it back on the hob, turn the heat to very low (but keep an eye on it) and move on to the second pan.

Keep layering in ever smaller circles, pressing the buns gently so that they stick to each other, and swapping pans, until finally you can finish with just one bun. Keep the remaining caramel warm on the hob.

As soon as the tower of buns has set firmly lift the whole thing up very gently and transfer to a serving plate.

Now, bring the pan of caramel that you are keeping warm close to the croque en bouche, take a spoon or fork and dip it in, then pull and swirl the caramel in thin strands round and round the tower, finishing it in a ball at the top – you can be as crazy as you like with it! Again leave to set firmly.

To serve, let people just break off buns as they like – preferably working from the top downwards!

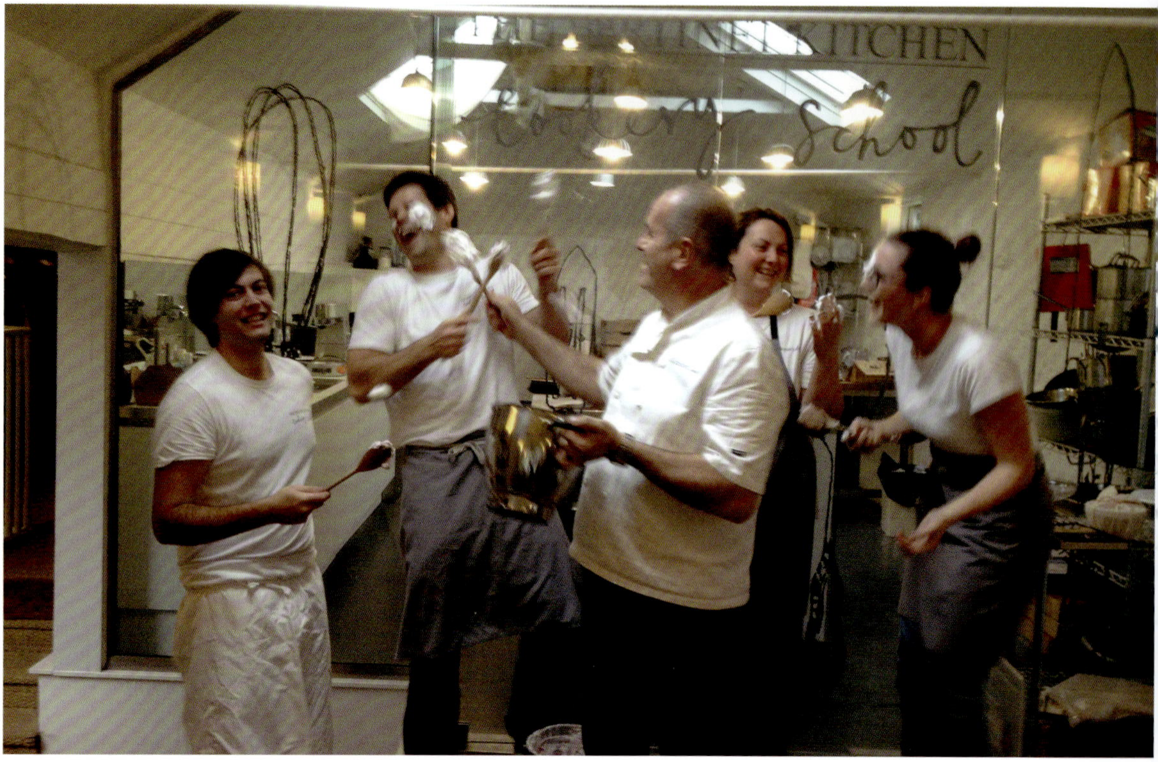
KITCHEN
cookery school

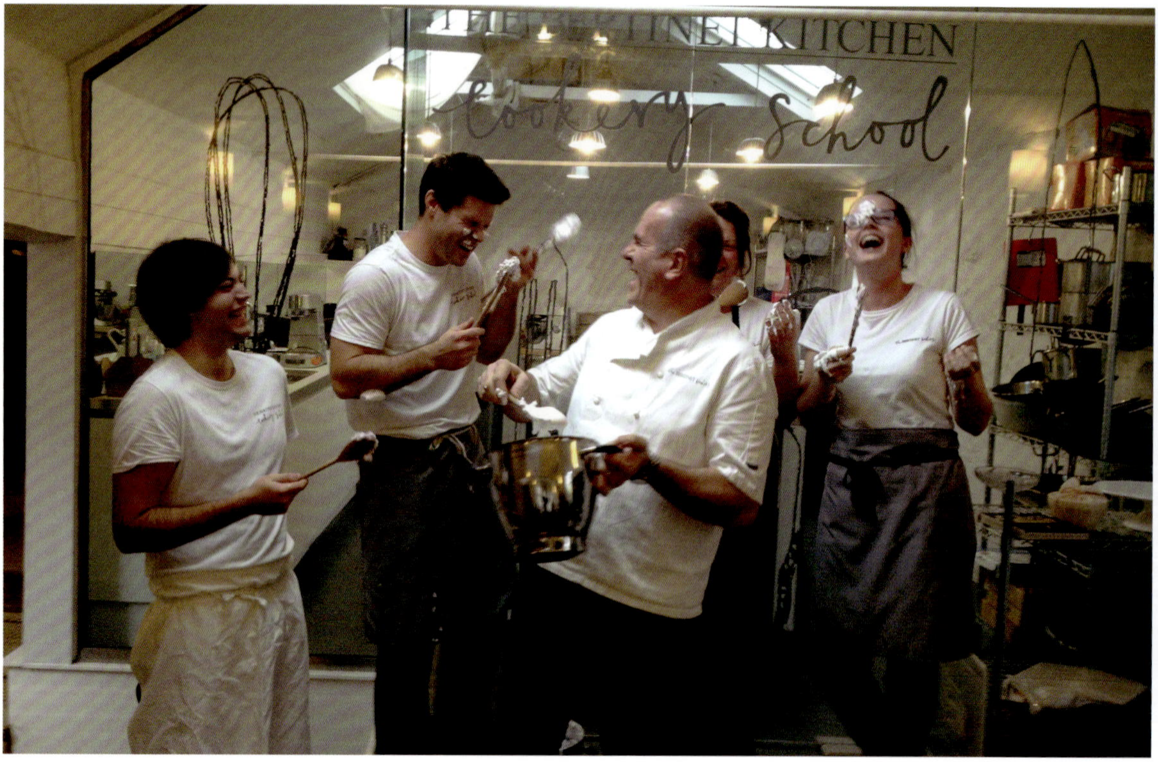
KITCHEN
cookery school

THE BERTINET KITCHEN
Cookery School

THE BERTINET KITCHEN
Cookery School

Index

A

almond
    caramelised 45
    Christmas cake 196–8
    Christmas pudding 193–4
    gâteau St Honoré 128–30
    îles flottantes 98–9
    macaron party 106–8
    mini éclairs 77–9
    nougantine 206–8
    nougat glace 88–90
    tarte Tropezienne 126–8

apple
    bavarois 133–5, 138–40
    charlotte aux pommes 132–41
    dried 52–3, 132–3, 141
    quatre-quart Breton 95–7

apricot
    fruitworms 186–7
    pâte de fruit 184–5

B

banana
    dried 52–3
    mini cakes 82–3

bavarois, apple 133–5, 138–40
Bertinent Bakery 7
Bertinent Kitchen cookery school 7
biscuits
    à la cuillère 133, 135–7, 140–1
    billionaire 172–4
    raspberry 100–1

Black Forest gâteau 122–4
blackcurrant
    fruitworms 186–7
    mousse 112–14

blood orange tart 146–51
Brazil nut, caramelised 45
bûche de noël 200–5

C

cakes
    Black Forest gâteau 122–4
    bûche de noël 200–5
    chocolat liegeois 118–20
    Christmas 196–9
    dodos 188–9
    fruit 196–9
    madeleines 161–3
    mini banana 82–3
    quatre-quart Breton 95–7

Calvados sugar syrup 133–4, 140
candied fruit, nougat glace 88–90
candied peel, Christmas pudding 193–4
cannelés 164–5
caramel 35
    for almond éclairs 77–9
    chocolate salted 172–4, 177–9
    for croque en bouche 206–9
    for gâteau St Honoré 128–30
    hazelnuts 84–6
    for îles flottantes 98–9

caramelised nuts 45
caramelised oranges 146–7, 151
charlotte aux pommes 132–41
cherry, Black Forest gâteau 122–4
chocolate
    billionaire biscuits 172–4
    Black Forest gâteau 122–4
    bûche de noël 201–5
    chocolat liegeois 118–20

coconut and pineapple bites 180–1
decorating with 54–7
ganache 106–8, 118–20, 122–4, 172–4
genoise sponge 19, 118–20, 122–4, 201–5
glaze 73, 74–5, 118–20
lollipops 182–3
madeleines 161–3
meringue 80–1
meringue tart 142–5
mini éclairs 73, 74–5
pencils 56–7, 142–5, 200–1, 205
rum prunes 176, 178
salted caramels 172–4, 177–9
sauce 166–7
shavings 56–7
sponge 172–4

choux pastry
baking 25
for croque en bouche 206–9
for gâteau St Honoré 128–30
for mini almond éclairs 77–9
for mini chocolate éclairs 73, 74–5
for mini coffee éclairs 73, 74, 76
for mini rosewater éclairs 73, 76
for Paris Brest 68–70
piping 24
recipe 20–3

Christmas
bûche de noël 200–5
cake 196–9
pudding 192–4

cocoa powder, decorating with 54–5
coconut and pineapple bites 180–1
coffee
genoise sponge 19
meringue 80–1
mini éclairs 73, 74, 76

syrup 119–20
tiramisu 84–6

creams 40–4
colouring 58–9
piping 58–9
see also crème anglaise; crème au beurre, crème Chantilly; crème légère; crème pâtissière

crème anglaise 44
for custard jelly 102–3
for îles flottantes 98–9

crème au beurre 43
for bûche de noël 200–2
for fraisier 92–4
hazelnut 200–2
for Paris Brest 68–70

crème Chantilly 42
for Black Forest gâteau 122–4
for chocolat liegeois 118–20
for éclairs 73, 75, 77–8
for gâteau St Honoré 128–30
for macaron party 106–8

crème de cassis, blackcurrant mousse 112–14

crème légère 43
for raspberry biscuits 100–1
for tarte Tropezienne 126–8

crème pâtissière 41–2
coffee 73, 76
for croque en bouche 206
for éclairs 73
kirsch 206, 208
for mini doughnuts 167
see also crème au beurre

croque en bouche 206–9
curd, lemon 51, 102–3, 106–8
custard jelly 102–3, 104–5

D

dodos 188–9
doughnuts, mini 166–7
dried fruit 52–3
    apple 52–3, 132–3, 141
    banana 52–3
    chocolate lollipops 182–3
    Christmas cake 196–8
    Christmas pudding 193–4
    pineapple 52–3

E

éclairs
    chocolate glaze for 73, 74–5
    filling 73, 75, 78
    mini almond 77–9
    mini chocolate 73, 74–5
    mini coffee 73, 74, 76
    mini rosewater 73, 76
elderflower, fruitworms 186–7

F

flan patissier 152–4
food processors 31
fraisier 92–4
framboisiers 168–9
French meringue 34–5, 38–9, 80
fruit cake, Christmas 196–9
fruitworms 186–7

G

ganache 118–20, 122–4, 172–4
gâteau
    Black Forest 122–4
    St Honoré 128–30

genoise sponge 14–18
    for Black Forest gâteau 122–4
    for blackcurrant mousse 112–14
    for bûche de noël 201–5
    for chocolat liegeois 118–20
    chocolate 19, 118–20, 122–4, 201–5
    coffee 19
    for fraisier 92–4
    lemon 19
    for lemon trifle 102–3
    orange 19
    for passion fruit mousse 115–17
    sugar syrups for 35
    for tiramisu 84–6
    vanilla 19
glaze 115–17
    chocolate 73, 74–5, 118–20
grenadine jelly 104–5

H

hazelnut
    bûche de noël 201–2
    caramel 84–6
    caramelised 45
    chocolate lollipops 182–3
    crème au beurre 200–2
    madeleines 161–3
    nougat glace 88–90
    Paris Brest 68–70
honey
    madeleines 161–3
    nougat glace 88–90

I

icing
    for Christmas cake 196–7, 199
    white fondant 73, 76
îles flottantes 98–9
Italian meringue 34–7, 80–1
    for apple bavarois 133, 135, 139
    for blackcurrant mousse 112–14
    for chocolate meringue tart 142–5
    for îles flottantes 98–9
    for passion fruit mousse 115–17
    for strawberry and lavender marshmallows 180–1

J

jam
    raspberry 47–8, 158–60, 166–7
    strawberry 49, 50, 180–1
jelly
    custard 102–3, 104–5
    fruitworms 186–7
    grenadine 104–5
    lemon 102–3, 104–5
    party 104–5

K

kirsch
    Black Forest gâteau 122–4
    crème pâtissière 206, 208
    syrup 93–4, 201–3

L

lavender and strawberry marshmallows 180–1
lemon
    curd 51, 102–3, 106–8
    genoise sponge 19
    jelly 102–3, 104–5
    madeleines 161–3
    trifle 102–3
    vin d'orange 124
lollipops, chocolate 182–3

M

macaron party 106–8
madeleines 161–3
Malibu
    coconut and pineapple bites 180–1
    sugar syrup 115–16
mango, fruitworms 186–7
Marsala wine, tiramisu 84–6
marshmallows, strawberry and lavender 180–1
marzipan
    for bûche de noël 201, 203–4
    for Christmas cake 196–7, 199
meringue *see* French Meringue; Italian Meringue
mixers 31
mousse
    blackcurrant 112–14
    passion fruit 115–17

N

nougantine 206–8
nougat glace 88–90
nozzle types 58–9
nuts
    caramelised 45
    see also Brazil nut; hazelnut; pistachio; walnut

O

orange
- blood orange tart 146–51
- caramelised 146–7, 151
- genoise sponge 19
- vin d'orange 124

P

Paris Brest 68–70
passion fruit mousse 115–17
pastry *see* choux pastry; sweet pastry
pâte de fruit 184–5
peach, fruitworms 186–7
Pernod, pâte de fruit 184–5
pineapple
- and coconut bites 180–1
- dried 52–3

piping
- choux pastry 24
- creams 58–9

pistachio
- caramelised 45
- chocolate lollipops 182–3
- nougat glace 88–90
- raspberry biscuits 100–1

prune, chocolate rum 176, 178

Q

quatre-quart Breton 95–7

R

raspberry
- biscuits 100–1
- chocolate lollipops 182–3
- dodos 188–9
- jam 47–8, 158–60, 166–7
- macaron party 106–8

rice pudding tartlets 158–60
rosé wine, vin d'orange 124
rosewater, mini éclairs 73, 76
rum
- baba 62–7
- cannelés 164–5
- chocolate prunes 176, 178
- pâte de fruit 184–5
- sugar syrup 62–7, 115–16

S

St Honoré, gâteau 128–30
salted chocolate caramels 177–9
- for billionaire biscuits 172–4

sponge
- chocolate 172–4
- *see also* genoise sponge

strawberry
- fraisier 92–4
- jam 49, 50, 180–1
- and lavender marshmallows 180–1

sugar syrup 35
- Calvados 133–4, 140
- coffee 119–20
- kirsch 93–4, 201–3
- Malibu 115–16
- rum 62–7, 115–16

sugar thermometers 35–6
sugar work 35
sweet pastry 26–33
- for billionaire biscuits 172–4
- for blood orange tart 146–51
- for flan patissier 152–4
- for framboisiers 168–9
- making by machine 31
- for raspberry biscuits 100–1
- recipe 26–30

resting 32–3
for rice pudding tartlets 158–60

syrup *see* sugar syrup

T

tartlets, rice pudding 158–60

tarts
blood orange 146–51
chocolate meringue 142–5
tarte Tropezienne 125–7

tiramisu 84–6

trifle, lemon 102–3

Tropezienne, tarte 125–7

V

vanilla
crème Chantilly 42
crème légère 43
crème pâtissière 41–2
genoise sponge 19

vin d'orange 124

vodka
pâte de fruit 184–5
vin d'orange 124

W

walnut, nougat glace 88–90

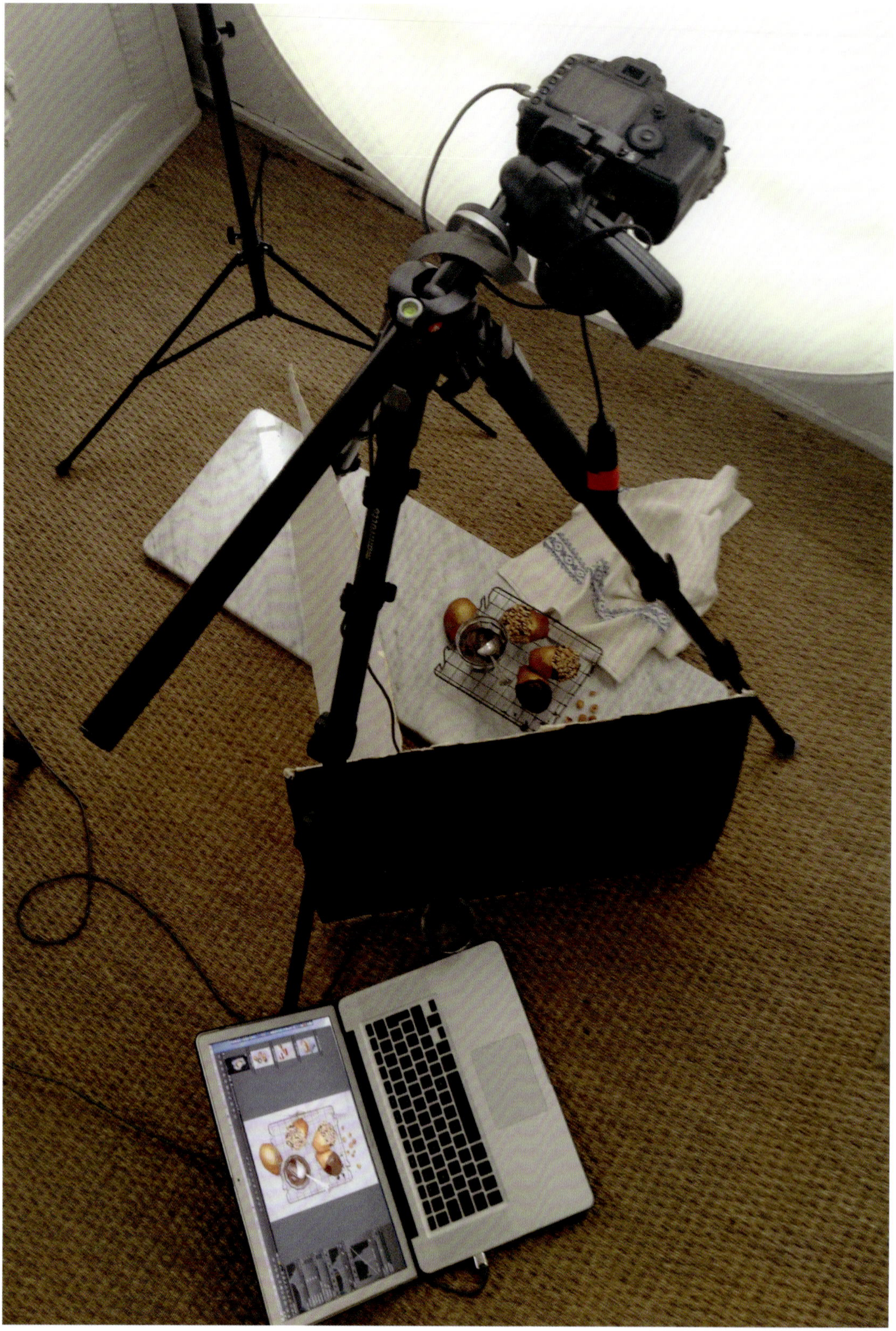

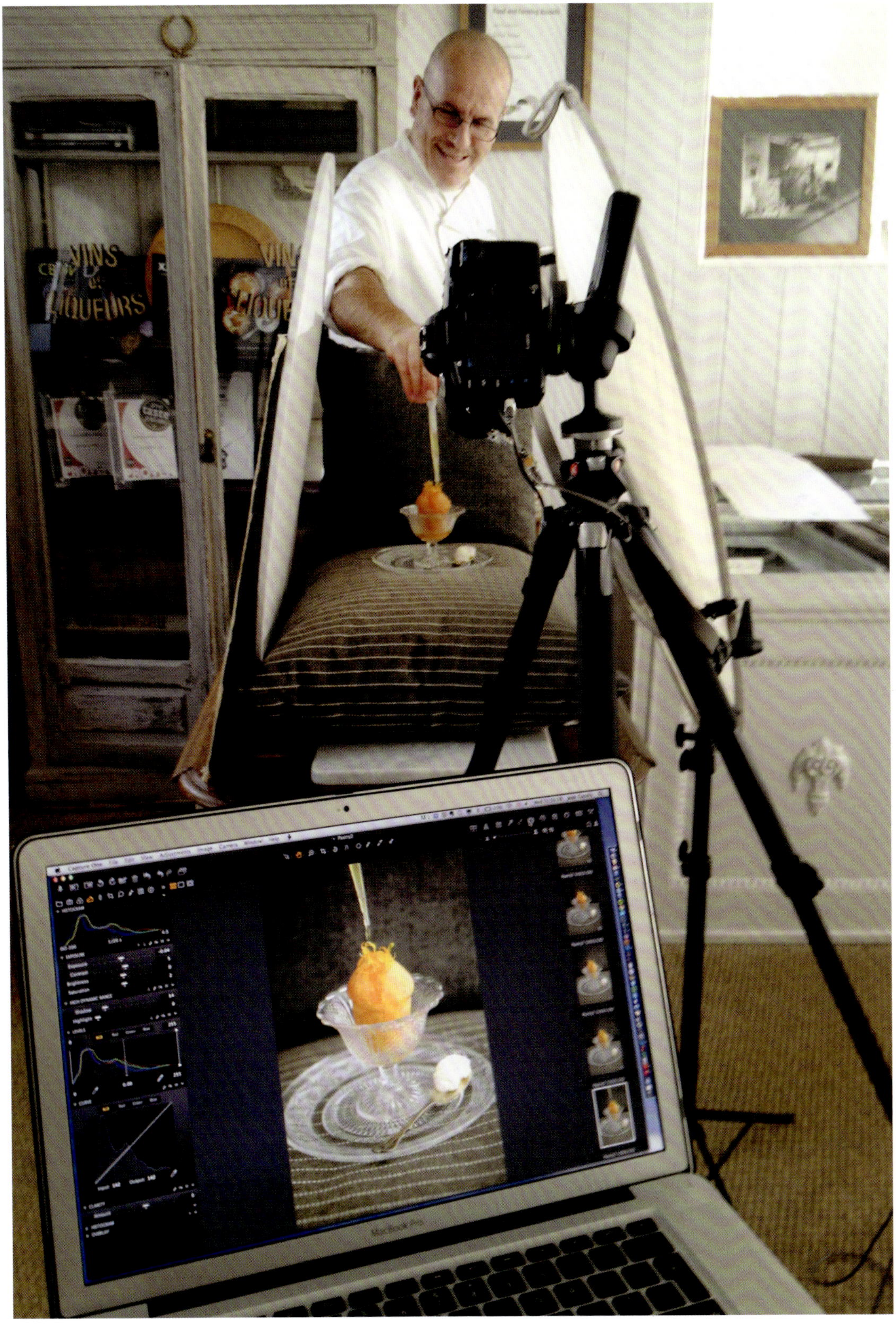
VINS

Suppliers

All of the equipment in this book should be easily available from your local kitchen shop. There are a host of different brands available for your tart moulds and tins. Many of mine I have had for years but when I need something new I find Tala are excellent.

As far as ingredients are concerned, the rule of thumb is to read the label carefully and buy the best you can afford. Chocolate is a case in point: quality chocolate will give you a much better result than a cheap chocolate. I use Barry Callebaut which is widely available professionally and is starting to become available to retail customers.

Online resources

For videos of Richard demonstrating basic pastry methods, please go to:
http://www.thebertinetkitchen.com/customer/videos

Acknowledgements

In memory of my dear friend Richard Barson

Perhaps more than ever before, this book has needed the support of my brilliant teams at the cookery school and bakery. Thank you to Yolande Stanley for your support and incredible depth of knowledge – surely one day you will write your own book and I will be first in line to buy it. Thanks to Brett, my head pastry chef at the bakery for your assistance both with recipes and during the shoot for the book; to Ghalid Assyb for your assistance during the shoots; and to Fionn, Dan, Alex and Angus at the kitchen for all the support, prep and tireless clearing up! A huge thank you to Sheila Keating who continues to translate my garbled notes and scratchings to the most beautiful and instructive text. I simply could not do it without you. Thank you to Jean Cazals for the amazing photographs – it is always fun and the results are fabulous; to Will Webb for the brilliant design; Charlotte Farmer for your lovely illustrations; as well as all of the fabulous team at Ebury: Sarah, Helen, Claire, Rae and all of the other people who work tirelessly to get the book right.

Thank you also to the rest of the team in the office who keep me sane and make it all possible but especially Carrie at the kitchen and Debbie at the bakery.

Finally thank you to my family: Jo and my children and chief tasters, Jack, Tom & Lola. I love you all.

1 3 5 7 9 10 8 6 4 2

Published in 2014 by Ebury Press, an imprint of Ebury Publishing

A Random House Group Company

Text © Richard Bertinet 2014
Photography © Jean Cazals 2014

Richard Bertinet has asserted his right to be identified as the author of this Work in accordance with the Copyright, Designs and Patents Act 1988

All rights reserved. No part of this publication may be reproduced, stored in a retrieval system, or transmitted in any form or by any means, electronic, mechanical, photocopying, recording or otherwise, without the prior permission of the copyright owner.

The Random House Group Limited Reg. No. 954009

Addresses for companies within the Random House Group can be found at www.randomhouse.co.uk

A CIP catalogue record for this book is available from the British Library

The Random House Group Limited supports the Forest Stewardship Council® (FSC®), the leading international forest-certification organisation. Our books carrying the FSC label are printed on FSC®-certified paper. FSC is the only forest-certification scheme supported by the leading environmental organisations, including Greenpeace. Our paper procurement policy can be found at www.randomhouse.co.uk/environment

To buy books by your favourite authors and register for offers visit www.randomhouse.co.uk

Design: Will Webb
Photography: Jean Cazals
Styling: Richard Bertinet and Jean Cazals,
Props: Lucy Comparelli, Lucy Elworthy and Jaine Bevan

Thanks to The Loft, Barlett Street, Bath for kindly supplying props used in the photography.

Colour origination by Altaimage, London
Printed and bound in China by C&C Offset Printing Co., Ltd

ISBN 9780091957612